W9-CQT-217

When Dreams Came True

When Dreams Came True

Classical Fairy Tales and Their Tradition

SECOND EDITION

JACK ZIPES

 Routledge
Taylor & Francis Group
New York   London

Routledge
Taylor & Francis Group
270 Madison Ave,
New York NY 10016

Routledge
Taylor & Francis Group
2 Park Square,
Milton Park, Abingdon,
Oxon, OX14 4RN

Routledge is an imprint of Taylor & Francis Group, an Informa business

Transferred to Digital Printing 2008

International Standard Book Number-10: 0-415-98007-0 (Softcover) 0-415-98006-2 (Hardcover)
International Standard Book Number-13: 978-0-415-98007-4 (Softcover) 978-0-415-98006-7 (Hardcover)

Library of Congress Cataloging-in-Publication Data

Zipes, Jack David.
    When dreams came true : classical fairy tales and their tradition - 2nd ed. / Jack Zipes.
        p. cm.
    ISBN 0-415-98006-2 (alk. paper) -- ISBN 0-415-98007-0 (alk. paper)
    1. Fairy tales--History and criticism. I. Title.

PN3437.Z57 2007
398.209--dc22   2006101179

Visit the Taylor & Francis Web site at
http://www.taylorandfrancis.com

and the Routledge Web site at
http://www.routledge.com

For Catherine Mauger and Charlie Williams, wonderful friends, who helped many of my dreams come true in Paris

Preface to the 2007 Edition

In the first edition of *When Dreams Came True* I remarked that the scholarship on fairy tales, as well as the genre itself, had flourished during the past twenty years, and in the time that has passed since the initial publication of this book, the situation has not changed. More and more studies about the significance of the fairy tale have appeared, and more and more innovative experiments with the genre in the fields of painting, film, advertisement, literature, the internet, theater, opera, toys, and clothing have been produced almost daily—and not just in the West. It is almost as if there were a fierce drive to keep the utopian spirit of the fairy tales alive, even when this spirit may be commodified in our age of consumerism.

Though the fairy tale is frequently emptied of its substantial utopian longings through commodification, it still denotes a loss or a lack. The postmodern giants, ogres, and witches that haunt us may twist meanings and deplete the quality of our lives by destroying our hope and maiming our lives, but they will never be able to eliminate the essence of dreams for a better life.

In revising and expanding *When Dreams Came True*, I have corrected some minor factual and stylistic errors that appeared in the first edition. The major changes involve the addition of four new essays, which, I believe, will make my book more comprehensive and more substantial. Chapter 5, "The "Merry" Dance of the Nutcracker: Discovering the World through Fairy Tales," deals with the brilliant writer E. T. A. Hoffmann, a German romantic, whose presence is much more with us than we realize. Chapter 6 contains two new essays, "The Hans Christian Andersen We Never Knew" and "Critical Reflections about Hans Christian Andersen, the Failed Revolutionary," which replace "Hans Christian Andersen and the Discourse of the Dominated." I have eliminated this latter essay because I have republished it in my book, *Hans Christian Andersen: The Misunderstood Storyteller*, which appeared in

2005. These new essays elaborate my critical views on Andersen that I presented in my book study and make clear why Andersen is such a troubling writer of fairy tales. Chapter 12, "Revisiting J. M. Barrie's *Peter and Wendy* and Neverland," explores another "troublesome" writer of a fairy tale whose major protagonist has become iconic for many different reasons. As icon, Peter Pan seems to represent what is still missing in our lives and may also be missing in our dreams.

In revising *When Dreams Came True*, I want to express my gratitude to Caroline White and Michael Millman, who encouraged me to write introductions to new editions of classical fairy tales at Viking Press and gave me great counsel and support. Special thanks goes to Marte Hult, with whom I collaborated on a new edition of Hans Christian Andersen's fairy tales, and to Joachim Neugroschel, whose new translations of Hoffmann and Dumas's "The Nutcracker and the Mouseking" are splendid. As usual I have benefited from Matt Byrnie's sage editorial advice and from Christine Andreasen's thorough and careful supervision of the final production of the book. Finally, I would like to thank Mary Bearden for her meticulous copyediting and Bev Weiler for preparing a useful index.

Jack Zipes
January 1, 2007

Preface to the 1999 Edition

During the past twenty years the scholarship dealing with fairy tales has exploded, and we now have numerous enlightening studies about those mysterious tales that delight and haunt our lives from the cradle to death. We now have every conceivable approach, I think, that reflects how seriously we interpret and value fairy tales. Most recently Marina Warner has incisively explored the role women play as tellers and heroines of the tales in *From the Beast to the Blonde: On Fairytales and Their Tellers* (1994) to recuperate the significance of their contribution to the oral and literary tradition. Lewis Seifert has examined how fairy tales use the marvelous to mediate between conflicting cultural desires in *Fairy Tales, Sexuality, and Gender in France 1690–1715: Nostalgic Utopias* (1996). Philip Lewis has situated Charles Perrault in the literary and philosophical debates of the late seventeenth century in *Seeing Through the Mother Goose Tales: Visual Turns in the Writings of Charles Perrault* (1996) and demonstrated how Perrault reappropriated what was vital to institutionalizing culture in his fairy tales. Cristina Bacchilega has dealt with the question of gender and highly complex contemporary tales from a feminist viewpoint in *Postmodern Fairy Tales: Gender and Narrative Strategies* (1997). Nancy Canepa has edited a superb collection of essays in *Out of the Woods: The Origins of the Literary Fairy Tale in Italy and France* that lays the groundwork for a comprehensive history of the genre. U. C. Knoepflmacher has undertaken a psychological exploration of the constructions of childhood in Victorian fairy tales in *Ventures into Childland: Victorians, Fairy Tales, and Femininity* (1998) that were shaped by a common longing for a lost feminine complement. All six of these exceptional studies advance our knowledge of literary fairy tales, yet they leave many questions unanswered because we do not have a social history of the fairy tale within which to frame their findings.

My present study is a move in that direction. During the last fifteen years I have written approximately twelve introductions and afterwords to collections of fairy tales with an eye toward writing a social history of the literary fairy tale. My focus has been on the role that the literary fairy tale has assumed in the civilizing process by imparting values, norms, and aesthetic taste to children and adults. If the fairy tale is a literary genre, I have insisted that we try to grasp the sociogeneric and historical roots of the tales and investigate the manner in which particular authors used the genre of the fairy tale to articulate their personal desires, political views, and aesthetic preferences. The fairy tale has been historically determined and is overdetermined by writers with unusual talents and tantalizing views about their search for happiness, which is coincidentally ours as well. The dramatic quality of the best fairy tales lies in the tension between the author's utopian longings and society's regulation of drives and desires.

It is my hope that in bringing together the diverse introductions and afterwords that I have written, I can provide a sociohistorical framework for the study of the classical tradition of the literary fairy tale in Western society. I make no claims for complete coverage of the classical fairy tales, but I do try to deal with the most significant writers and their works in Europe and North America from the sixteenth century to the beginning of the twentieth century. And I do try to raise questions and provide partial answers to the sociocultural web woven by fairy-tale writers and the ramifications of this web for our use and abuse of fairy tales today. Most of the scholarship that I have used in writing this book will be apparent in my text. Therefore, I have decided to forgo footnotes in this work. Readers may consult the bibliography for further study. I have listed the sources of my own essays at the end of the bibliography. All of the essays have been revised and brought up to date with respect to details important for drafting a social and literary history.

As usual, I should like to thank Bill Germano, who prods me with magical ideas and has been most supportive in all my endeavors at Routledge. Lai Moy has done a great job in managing the production of my book, and I am very grateful to Alexandria Giardino for the careful and thorough copyediting of this volume.

Jack Zipes
June 1998

Contents

one

SPELLS OF ENCHANTMENT:
AN OVERVIEW OF THE HISTORY
OF FAIRY TALES

I

two

THE RISE OF THE FRENCH FAIRY TALE
AND THE DECLINE OF FRANCE

33

three

THE SPLENDOR OF THE ARABIAN NIGHTS

53

four

ONCE THERE WERE TWO BROTHERS
NAMED GRIMM

65

five

The "Merry" Dance of the Nutcracker: Discovering the World through Fairy Tales

85

six

I'm Hans Christian Andersen

109

seven

The Flowering of the Fairy Tale in Victorian England

143

eight

Oscar Wilde's Tales of Illumination

167

nine

Carlo Collodi's *Pinocchio* as Tragic-Comic Fairy Tale

175

ten

Frank Stockton, American Pioneer of Fairy Tales

187

eleven

L. FRANK BAUM AND THE UTOPIAN SPIRIT OF OZ

195

twelve

REVISITING J. M. BARRIE'S *PETER AND WENDY* AND NEVERLAND

219

thirteen

HERMANN HESSE'S FAIRY TALES AND THE PURSUIT OF HOME

239

BIBLIOGRAPHY

255

INDEX

285

one

Spells of Enchantment

An Overview of the History of Fairy Tales

I t has generally been assumed that fairy tales were first created for children and are largely the domain of children. Nothing could be further from the truth.

From the very beginning, thousands of years ago, when all types of tales were told to create communal bonds in the face of inexplicable forces of nature, to the present, when fairy tales are written and told to provide hope in a world seemingly on the brink of catastrophe, mature men and women have been the creators and cultivators of the fairy-tale tradition. When introduced to fairy tales, children welcome them mainly because the stories nurture their great desire for change and independence. On the whole, the literary fairy tale has become an established genre within a process of Western civilization that cuts across all ages. Even though numerous critics and psychologists such as C. G. Jung and Bruno Bettelheim have mystified and misinterpreted the fairy tale because of their own spiritual quest for universal archetypes or need to save the world through therapy, both the oral and literary forms of the fairy tale have resisted the imposition of theory and manifested their enduring power by articulating relevant cultural information necessary for the formation of civilization and adaptation to the environment. Oral and literary fairy tales are grounded in history. They emanate from specific struggles to humanize bestial and barbaric forces that have terrorized our minds and communities in concrete ways, threatening to destroy free will and human compassion. The fairy tale sets out, using various forms and information, to conquer this concrete terror through metaphors that are accessible to readers and listeners and provide hope that social and political conditions can be changed.

Though it is impossible to determine when the first *literary* fairy tale was conceived and extremely difficult to define exactly what a fairy tale is, we do know that oral folk tales, which contain wondrous and marvelous elements, have existed for thousands of years and were told largely by adults for adults. Motifs from these tales, which were memorized and passed on by word of mouth, made their way in the Western world into the Bible and the Greek classics such as *The Iliad* and *The Odyssey* and the Greek and Roman myths. The recent important studies, *Fairytale in the Ancient World* (2000) by Graham Anderson and *Fairy Tales from Before Fairy Tales* (2006) by Jan Ziolkowski, shed light on this evolution. The early oral tales that served as the basis for the development of literary fairy tales were closely tied to the rituals, customs, and beliefs of tribes, communities, and trades. They fostered a sense of belonging and hope that miracles involving some kind of magical transformation were possible to bring about a better world. They instructed, amused, warned, initiated, and enlightened. They opened windows to imaginative worlds inside that needed concrete expression outside in reality. They were to be shared and exchanged, used and modified according to the needs of the tellers and the listeners.

Tales are marks that leave traces of the human struggle for immortality. Tales are human marks invested with desire. They are formed like musical notes of compositions, except that the letters constitute words and are chosen individually to enunciate the speaker/writer's position in the world, including his or her dreams, needs, wishes, and experiences. The speaker/writer posits the self against language to establish identity and to test the self with and against language. Each word marks a way toward a future different from what may have been decreed, certainly different from what is being experienced in the present: The words that are selected in the process of creating a tale allow the speaker/writer freedom to play with options that no one has ever glimpsed. The marks are magical.

The fairy tale celebrates this magic: marks as letters, words, sentences, signs, and discourses. More than any other literary genre, the fairy tale has persisted in emphasizing transformation of the marks with spells, enchantments, disenchantments, resurrections, and re-creations. During its inception, the fairy tale distinguished itself as genre both by appropriating the oral folk tale and expanding it, for it became gradually necessary in the modern world to adapt the oral tale to standards of literacy and to make it acceptable for diffusion in the public sphere. The fairy tale is only one type of appropriation of a particular oral storytelling tradition: the wonder folk tale, often called the *Zaubermärchen* or the *conte merveilleux*. As more and more wonder tales were written down in the fifteenth, sixteenth, and seventeenth centuries, they constituted the genre of the literary fairy tale that began establishing its own conventions, motifs, topoi, characters, and plots, based to a large extent on those developed in the oral tradition, but altered to address a reading public formed by the aristocracy and the middle classes. Though the peasants were excluded in the formation of this literary tradition, it was their material, tone, style, and beliefs that were incorporated into the new genre during this time.

What exactly is the oral wonder tale? In Vladimir Propp's now famous study, *Morphology of the Folk Tale* (1968), he outlined thirty-one basic functions that constitute the formation of the paradigm, which was and still is common in Europe and North America. By functions, Propp meant the fundamental and constant components of a tale that are the acts of a character and necessary for driving the action forward. To summarize the functions with a different emphasis:

1. The protagonist is confronted with an interdiction or prohibition that he or she violates in some way. Often the protagonist commits an error or seeks to improve his or her social status by embarking on a journey. One way or another the protagonist is commissioned — sent on a mission.

2. Departure or banishment of the protagonist, who is either given a task or assumes a task related to the interdiction and prohibition, or to the desire for improvement and self-transformation. The protagonist is *assigned* a task, and the task is a *sign*. That is, his or her character will be marked by the task that is his or her sign.

3. The protagonist then encounters: (a) the villain; (b) a mysterious individual or creature, who gives the protagonist gifts; (c) three different animals or creatures who are helped by the protagonist and promise to repay him or her; or (d) three different animals or creatures who offer gifts to help the protagonist, who is in trouble. The gifts are often magical agents, which bring about miraculous change.

4. The endowed protagonist is tested and moves on to battle and conquer the villain or inimical forces.

5. The peripety or sudden fall in the protagonist's fortunes is generally only a temporary setback. A wonder or miracle is needed to reverse the wheel of fortune. Sometimes a fairy, hermit, wise man or woman, or magically endowed human or animal will intervene to benefit the protagonist.

6. The protagonist makes use of gifts (and this includes the magical agents and cunning) to achieve his or her goal. The result is (a) three battles with the villain; (b) three impossible tasks that are nevertheless made possible; and/or (c) the breaking of a magic spell.

7. The villain is punished or the inimical forces are vanquished.

8. The success of the protagonist usually leads to (a) marriage; (b) the acquisition of money; (c) survival and wisdom; or (d) any combination of the first three.

Rarely do wonder tales end unhappily. They triumph over death. The tale begins with "once upon a time" or "once there was" and never really ends when it ends. The ending is actually the true beginning. The once upon a time is not a past designation but futuristic: The timelessness of the tale and lack of geographic specificity endow it with utopian connotations — utopia in its original meaning designated "no place," a place that no one had ever envisaged. We form and keep the utopian kernel of the tale safe in our imaginations with hope.

The significance of the paradigmatic functions of the wonder tale is that they facilitate recall for teller and listeners. They enable us to store, remember, and reproduce the utopian spirit of the tale and to change it to fit our experiences and desires due to the easily identifiable characters who are associated with particular assignments and settings. For instance, we have the simpleton who turns out to be remarkably cunning; the third and youngest son who is oppressed by his brothers and/or father; the beautiful but maltreated youngest daughter; the discharged soldier who has been exploited by his superiors; the shrew who needs taming; the evil witch; the kind elves; the cannibalistic ogre; the clumsy stupid giant; terrifying beasts like dragons, lions, and wild boars; kind animals like ants, birds, deer, bees, ducks, and fish; the clever tailor; the evil and jealous stepmother; the clever peasant; the power-hungry and unjust king; treacherous nixies; and the beast-bridegroom. There are haunted castles; enchanted forests; mysterious huts in woods; glass mountains; dark, dangerous caves; and underground kingdoms. There are seven-league boots that enable the protagonist to move faster than jet planes; capes that make a person invisible; magic wands that can perform extraordinary feats of transformation; animals that produce gold; tables that provide all the delicious and sumptuous food you can eat; musical instruments with enormous captivating powers; swords and clubs capable of conquering anyone or anything; and lakes, ponds, and seas that are difficult to cross and serve as the home for supernatural creatures.

The characters, settings, and motifs are combined and varied according to specific functions to induce *wonder*. It is this sense of wonder that distinguished the wonder tales from other oral tales such as the myth, the legend, the fable, the anecdote, and the exemplum. It is clearly the sense of wonder that distinguishes the *literary* fairy tale from the moral story, novella, sentimental tale, and other modern short literary genres. Wonder engenders astonishment. As marvelous object or phenomenon, it is often regarded as a supernatural occurrence and can be an omen or portent. It gives rise to admiration, fear, awe, and reverence. The *Oxford Universal Dictionary* states that wonder is "the emotion excited by the perception of something novel and unexpected, or inexplicable; astonishment mingled with perplexity or bewildered curiosity." In the oral wonder tale, we are to wonder about the workings of the universe where anything can happen at any time, and these happy or fortuitous events are never to be explained. Nor do the characters demand an explanation — they are opportunistic. They are encouraged to be so, and if they do not take advantage of the opportunity that will benefit them in their relations with others, they are either dumb or mean-spirited. The tales seek to awaken our regard for the miraculous condition of life and to evoke in a religious sense profound feelings of awe and respect for life as a miraculous process, which can be altered and changed to compensate for the lack of power, wealth, and pleasure that most people experience. Lack, deprivation, prohibition, and interdiction motivate people to look for signs of fulfillment and emancipation. In the wonder tales, those who are naive and simple are able to succeed because they are untainted and can recognize the wondrous signs. They have retained their belief in the miraculous condition of nature, revere nature in all its aspects. They have not been spoiled by conventionalism, power, or rationalism. In contrast to the humble characters, the villains are those who use words intentionally to exploit, control, transfix, incarcerate, and destroy for their benefit. They have no respect or consideration for nature and other human beings, and they actually seek to abuse magic by preventing change and causing everything to be transfixed according to their interests. Enchantment equals petrification. Breaking the spell equals emancipation. The wondrous protagonist wants to keep the process of natural change flowing and indicates possibilities for overcoming the obstacles that prevent other characters or creatures from living in a peaceful and pleasurable way.

The focus on wonder in the oral folk tale does not mean that all wonder tales, and later the literary fairy tales, served and serve an emancipatory purpose. The nature and meaning of folk tales have depended on the stage of development of a tribe, community, or society. Oral tales have served to stabilize, conserve, or challenge the common beliefs, laws, values, and norms of a group. The ideology expressed in wonder tales always stemmed from the position that the narrator assumed with regard to the developments in his or her community, and the narrative plot and changes made in it depended on the sense of wonder or awe that the narrator wanted to evoke. In other words, the sense of wonder in the tale and the intended emotion sought by the narrator are ideological.

Since these wonder tales have been with us for thousands of years and have undergone so many different changes in the oral tradition, it is difficult to determine the ideological intention of the narrator. When we disregard the narrator's intention, it is often difficult to reconstruct (and/or deconstruct) the ideological meaning of a tale. In the last analysis, however, even if we cannot establish whether a wonder tale is ideologically conservative, sexist, progressive, emancipatory, and so forth, it is the celebration of wonder that accounts for its major appeal. No matter what the plot may be, this type of tale calls forth our capacity as readers and potential transmitters of its signs and meanings to wonder. We do not want to know the exact resolution, the "happily ever after," of a tale; that is, what it is actually like. We do not want to name God, gods, goddesses, wise people, sorcerers, or fairies who will forever remain mysterious and omnipotent. We do not want to form craven images. We do not want Utopia designated for us. We want to remain curious, startled, provoked, mystified, and uplifted. We want to glare, gaze, gawk, behold, and stare. We want to be given opportunities to change. Ultimately we want to be told that we can become kings and queens, or lords of our own destinies. We remember wonder tales and fairy tales to keep our sense of wonderment alive and to nurture our hope that we can seize possibilities and opportunities to transform ourselves and our worlds.

Ultimately, the definition of both the wonder tale and the fairy tale, which derives from it, depends on the manner in which a narrator/ author arranges *known* functions of a tale aesthetically and ideologically to induce wonder and then transmits the tale as a whole according to customary usage of a society in a given historical period. The first stage for the literary fairy tale involved a kind of class and perhaps even gender appropriation. The voices of the nonliterate tellers were submerged, and since women in most cases were not allowed to be scribes, the tales were scripted according to male dictates or fantasies, even though they may have been told by women. Put crudely, one could say that the literary appropriation of the oral wonder tales served the hegemonic interests of males within the upper classes of particular communities and societies, and to a great extent, this is true. However, such a crude statement must be qualified, for the writing down of the tales also preserved a great deal of the value system of those deprived of power. The more the literary fairy tale was cultivated and developed, the more it became individualized and varied by intellectuals and artists, who often sympathized with the marginalized in society or were marginalized themselves. The literary fairy tale allowed for new possibilities of subversion in the written word and in print; therefore, it was always looked upon with misgivings by the governing authorities in the civilization process.

During early Christianity there were few indications that oral folk tales would develop and flourish as a major *literary* genre in the West, and there were obvious reasons for this lack: Most people were nonliterate and shared strong oral cultural traditions; the tales had not been changed sufficiently to serve the taste and interests of the ruling classes; Latin was the dominant intellectual and literary language until the late Middle Ages when the vernacular languages gradually formed general standards of grammar and orthography for communication; and the technology of printing did not make much progress until the fifteenth century so that the distribution of literary works was not very widespread. Consequently, it is not surprising that the first appearance of a major literary fairy tale, Apuleius's "Cupid and Psyche," was written in Latin in the second century. Moreover, it was included in a book, *The Golden Ass*, which dealt with metamorphoses, perhaps the key theme of the fairy tale up to the present. However, whereas many oral wonder tales had been concerned with the humanization of natural forces, the literary fairy tale, beginning with "Cupid and Psyche," shifted the emphasis more toward the civilization of the protagonist who must learn to respect particular codes and laws to become accepted in society and/ or united to reproduce and continue the progress of the world toward perfect happiness.

At first, this new literary fairy tale could not stand by itself, that is, it did not have a receptive audience and had to be included within a frame story or in a collection of instructive and amusing stories and anecdotes. Therefore, up to the fifteenth century, the evidence we have of complete fairy tales are within such manuscripts as the *Gesta Romanorum* (c. 1300), medieval romances, sermons delivered by priests, and short Latin poems and narratives. Nevertheless, there are many signs in medieval literature that a kind of fairy tale circulated in oral forms, as Jan Ziolkowski has recently demonstrated in his book *Fairy Tales from Before Fairy Tales: The Medieval Latin Past of Wonderful Lies* (2006). Literary tales like "Of Feminine Subtlety" in the *Gesta Romanorum* were generally used to provide instruction for the education of young Christian boys and had a strong moralistic strain to them. In addition, like "Cupid and Psyche," the early Latin fairy tales were largely focused toward males and on their acquisition of the proper moral values and ethics that would serve them in their positions of power in society.

It was not until the publication of Giovan Francesco Straparola's *Le piacevoli notti* (*The Pleasant Nights*, 1550–53) in two volumes that a sizable number of fairy tales were first published in the vernacular and for a mixed audience of upper-class men and women (fig. 1). Straparola brings together a group of aristocrats who flee Milan for political reasons and decide to tell tales to one another to amuse themselves during their exile. The frame narrative is set up to include erotic anecdotes, fables, and fairy tales like "The Pig Prince" and "Constantino," forerunners of "Hans My Hedgehog" and "Puss in Boots," and it is modeled after Giovanni Boccaccio's *The Decameron* (1353). However, Boccaccio did not include fairy tales in his collection, so Straparola can be considered the first writer in Europe to have published numerous fairy tales in the vernacular for an educated audience. Though his tales did not achieve the popularity of Boccaccio's collection, they were reprinted several times in Italian during the next few centuries and were translated into French in the eighteenth century and German and English in the nineteenth century.

There is no direct evidence, however, one way or another that Straparola influenced Giambattista Basile, whose *Lo Cunto de li cunti*, also known as *The Pentameron*, was published posthumously in 1634. Written in Neapolitan dialect, Basile was the first writer to use an old folktale motif about laughter to frame an entire collection of fifty fairy tales. His book begins with a tale about a princess named Zoza who cannot laugh, no matter what her father, the King of Vallepelosa, does to try to assuage her melancholy. Finally, her father orders that a fountain of oil be erected before the palace gate so that people would skip and jump to avoid being soiled. Thereby, the king hoped that his daughter would laugh at the stumbling people and overcome her melancholy. Indeed, the princess does laugh but at the wrong person, an old witch of a woman, who places a curse on her and declares that if Zoza is ever to marry it must be to Taddeo, a bewitched sleeping prince, whom only she can wake and save with her tears. With the help and advice from three fairies, Zoza succeeds in weeping a sufficient amount of tears, but she then falls asleep before she can achieve the honor of rescuing

Figure 1. "The Pig Prince." From Giovan Francesco Straparola's The Facetious Nights. *Trans. William G. Waters. Illustr. E. R. Hughes. London: Lawrence & Bullen, 1894.*

Taddeo. In the meantime, a malicious slave steals her vessel of tears and claims the honor of liberating Taddeo, who marries her. Yet, this does not deter Zoza, who rents a fine house opposite Taddeo's palace and manages through her beauty to attract his attention. Once the slave, who is pregnant, learns about this, she threatens to kill her unborn child if Taddeo does not obey her every whim. Zoza responds by enticing the slave with three gifts that she had received from the fairies. The third one is a doll that makes the slave become addicted to fairy tales, and she forces Taddeo to gather storytellers who will amuse her during the final ten days of her pregnancy. So, Taddeo gathers a group of ten motley women, who tell five fairy tales a day until Zoza concludes the sessions with her own tale that exposes the slave's theft and brings the frame story to its conclusion. As a result, Taddeo has the pregnant slave put to death and takes Zoza for his new wife.

Basile was very familiar with the customs and behavior of the Neapolitans and had also traveled widely in Italy and served at different courts, where his tales were often read or performed. Therefore, he was able to include a wealth of folklore, anecdotes, and events in his fairy tales that celebrate miraculous changes and communion. A good example is "The Merchant's Two Sons," which has many different folk and literary versions. As in the frame narrative, the humane ties between people based on compassion and love can only be solidified if the protagonists recognize what and where evil is. The fairy tale involves arousing the protagonists and sharpening their perception of what is really occurring so that they can change or bring about changes to master their own destinies. In this respect, the narrative structure of the fairy tale is conceived so that the listener will learn to distinguish between destructive and beneficial forces, for the art of seeing and intuiting is nurtured by the fairy tale.

It is not by chance that the literary fairy tale began flourishing in Italy before other European countries. During the fifteenth and sixteenth centuries, the Italian cities and duchies had prospered by developing great commercial centers, and the literacy rate had grown immensely. Cultural activity at the courts and in the city-states was high, and there was a great deal of foreign influence on storytelling as well as strong native oral traditions among the people. Although it cannot be fully documented, it is highly likely that the Italian literary fairy tales were gradually spread in print and by word of mouth throughout Europe. Interestingly, England, another powerful maritime country, was the other nation that began cultivating a literary fairy-tale tradition. There are fairy-tale elements in Chaucer's *The Canterbury Tales* (c. 1386–1400), in Spenser's *The Faerie Queen* (1590–96), and, of course, in many of Shakespeare's plays such as *King Lear*, *A Midsummer Night's Eve*, *The Taming of the Shrew*, and *The Tempest*, all written between 1590 and 1611. However, due to the Puritan hostility toward amusement during the seventeenth century, the fairy tale as a genre was not able to flourish in England. Instead, the genre had more propitious conditions in France and virtually bloomed in full force toward the end of the ancien régime from 1690 to 1714.

There were many contributing factors that account for the rise and spread of the fairy tale in France at this time. First, France had become the most powerful country in Europe and the French language, considered to be the most cultivated, was used at most courts throughout all of Europe. Second, the evolution of printing favored more experimentation with different kinds of literature. Third, there was great cultural creativity and innovation in France. Finally, about the middle of the seventeenth century, the fairy tale gradually became more accepted at literary salons and at the court, particularly in theatrical form as pageant. Fairy-tale recitations and games were devised, generally by women in their salons, and they eventually led to the publication of the fairy tales during the 1690s. Perhaps the most prodigious (and also most prolific) of the French fairy-tale writers was Mme Marie-Catherine d'Aulnoy, whose first tale, "The Island of Happiness," was embedded in her novel *Histoire d'Hippolyte, comte de Duglas* (1690). However, it was not until she had established a popular literary salon, in which fairy tales were regularly presented, that she herself published four volumes of fairy tales between 1696 and 1698. Though Charles Perrault is generally considered to be the most significant French writer of fairy tales of this period, Mme d'Aulnoy was undoubtedly more typical and more of a catalyst for other writers. Her narratives are long and rambling and focus on the question of *tendresse*, that is, true and natural feelings between a man and a woman, whose nobility will depend on their manners and the ways they uphold standards of civility in defending their love. "Green Serpent" is a good example of Mme d'Aulnoy's concerns and shows how she was influenced by Apuleius's "Cupid and Psyche" and was familiar with the Italian tradition of fairy tales, not to mention French folklore. In turn her fairy tales set the stage for the works of Mlle Lhéritier, whose "Ricdin-Ricdon" (1696) is a remarkable courtly interpretation of "Rumpelstiltskin," and Mlle de la Force, whose "Parslinette" (1697) is a fascinating version of "Rapunzel." Of course, the writer, whose name has become practically synonymous with the term *conte de fée* (fairy tale) is Charles Perrault, who wrote two verse tales, "The Foolish Wishes" (1693) and "Donkey Skin" (1694), and then published the famous prose renditions of "Cinderella," "Little Red Riding Hood," "Sleeping Beauty," (fig. 2) "Blue Beard," "Tom Thumb," "Ricky with the Tuft," and "The Fairies" in *Histoires ou contes du temps passé* (1697). Perrault, who frequented the literary salons in Paris, purposely sought to establish the literary fairy tale as an innovative genre that exemplified a modern sensibility that was coming into its own and was to be equated with the greatness of French *civilité*. Not all the French writers of this period intended to celebrate the splendor of the ancien régime, but they all were concerned with questions of manners, norms, and mores in their tales and sought to illustrate proper behavior and what constituted noble feelings in their narratives. Almost all the writers lived in Paris, where their tales were published. Therefore, the "mode" of writing fairy tales was concentrated within a feudal sphere and led to what could be called the institutionalization of the genre. After the appearance of *The Thousand and One Nights* (1704–17) in ten volumes translated and adapted into French by Antoine Galland, the literary fairy tale became an acceptable, social-symbolic form through which conventionalized motifs, characters, and plots were selected, composed, arranged, and rearranged to comment on the civilizing process and to keep alive the possibility of miraculous change and a sense of wonderment.

The very name of the genre itself — *fairy tale* — originated during this time, for the French writers coined the term *conte de fée* during the seventeenth century, and it has stuck to the genre in Europe and North America ever since. This "imprint" is important because it reveals something crucial about the fairy tale that has remained part of its nature to

Figure 2. "Sleeping Beauty." From Household Stories Collected by the Brothers Grimm. *Illustr. E. H. Wehnert. London: Routledge, c. 1900.*

the present. The early writers of fairy tales placed the power of meta-
morphosis in the hands of women — the redoubtable fairies. In addition, this miraculous power was not associated with a particular religion
or mythology through which the world was to be explained. It was a secular mysterious power of compassion that could not be explained, and it
derived from the creative imagination of the writer. Anyone could call
upon the fairies for help. It is clear that the gifted French women writers
at the end of the seventeenth century preferred to address themselves to
a fairy and to have a fairy resolve the conflicts in their fairy tales, rather
than the Church with its male-dominated hierarchy. After all, it was the
Church that had eliminated hundreds of thousands of so-called female
witches during the previous two centuries in an effort to curb heretical
and nonconformist beliefs. However, those "pagan" notions survived in
the tradition of the oral wonder tale and surfaced again in published
form in France when it became safer to introduce in a symbolical code
other supernatural powers and creatures than those officially sanctioned
by the Christian code. In short, there was something subversive about
the institutionalization of the fairy tale in France during the 1790s, for
it enabled writers to create a dialogue about norms, manners, and power
that evaded court censorship and freed the fantasy of the writers and
readers, while at the same time paying tribute to the French code of
civilité and the majesty of the aristocracy. Once certain discursive para-
digms and conventions were established, a writer could demonstrate his
or her "genius" by rearranging, expanding, deepening, and playing with
the known functions of a genre, which, by 1715, had already formed a
type of canon that consisted not only of the great classical tales such as
"Cinderella," "Sleeping Beauty," "Rapunzel," "Rumpelstiltskin," "Puss in
Boots," "Little Red Riding Hood," "Beauty and the Beast," "Bluebeard,"
"The Yellow Dwarf," "The Blue Bird," and "The White Cat," but also
the mammoth collection of *The Arabian Nights.*

Galland's project of translating the Arabic tales from original manuscripts, which stemmed from the fourteenth century and were based
on an oral tradition, was important for various reasons: His translation
was not literal, and he introduced many changes influenced by French
culture into his adaptations; eight of the tales, one of which was "Prince
Ahmed and the Fairy Pari-Banou," were obtained from a Maronite

Christian scholar named Youhenna Diab, living at that time in Paris, and were in part Galland's literary re-creations. The exotic setting and nature of these Oriental tales attracted not only French but numerous European readers, so that Galland's translation stimulated the translation of other Arabic works such as *The Adventures of Abdalah, Son of Anif* (1712–14) by the abbot Jean-Paul Bignon, as well as hundreds of his own translations into English, Italian, German, Spanish, and so on.

The infusion of the Oriental tales into the French literary tradition enriched and broadened the paradigmatic options for Western writers during the course of the eighteenth century. It became a favorite device (and still is) to deploy the action of a tale to the Orient while discussing sensitive issues of norms and power close to home. Aside from the great impact of the Arabic and Persian tales on Western writers through translations, there was another development that was crucial for the institutionalization of the fairy tale in the eighteenth century. Soon after the publication of the tales by d'Aulnoy, Perrault, Lhéritier, Galland, and others, they were reprinted in a series of chapbooks called the *Bibliothèque Bleue*, inexpensive volumes distributed by peddlers called *colporteurs* throughout France and central Europe to the lower classes. The fairy tales were often abridged; the language was changed and simplified; and there were multiple versions, which were read to children and nonliterates. Many of these tales were then appropriated by oral storytellers so that the literary tradition became a source for the oral tradition. As a result of the increased popularity of the literary fairy tale as chapbook, which had first been prepared by the acceptance of the genre at court, the literary fairy tale for children began to be cultivated. Already during the 1690s, Fénelon, the important theologian and Archbishop of Cambrai who had been in charge of the Dauphin's education, had written several didactic fairy tales as an experiment to make the Dauphin's lessons more enjoyable. However, they were not considered proper and useful enough for the grooming of children from the upper classes to be published. They were first printed after Fénelon's death in 1730. From that point on it became more acceptable to write and publish fairy tales for children, just as long as they indoctrinated children according to gender-specific roles and class codes in the civilizing process. The most notable example here, aside from Fénelon's tales, is the voluminous work of Madame Leprince de Beaumont, who published *Magasin des Enfants* (1756), which included "Beauty and the Beast," "Prince Chéri," and other overtly moralistic tales for children. Mme Leprince de Beaumont used a frame story to transmit different kinds of didactic tales in which a governess engaged several young girls between six and ten in discussions about morals, manners, ethics, and gender roles that lead her to tell stories to illustrate her points. Her utilization of such a frame was actually based on her work as a governess in England, and the frame was set up to be copied by other adults to institutionalize a type of storytelling in homes of the upper classes. It was only as part of the civilizing process that storytelling developed within the aristocratic and bourgeois homes in the seventeenth and eighteenth centuries, first through governesses and nannies, and later in the eighteenth and nineteenth centuries through mothers who told good-night stories. Incidentally, Mme Leprince de Beaumont's work was based on Sarah Fielding's *The Governess, or Little Female Academy* (1749), which included two moralistic fairy tales for young girls and began paving the way for the reception of the fairy tale in England.

As the literary fairy tale now spread in France to every age group and to every social class, it began to serve different functions, depending on the writer's interests: (1) representation of the glory and ideology of the French aristocracy; (2) symbolical critique of the aristocratic hierarchy with utopian connotations, largely within the aristocracy from the female viewpoint; (3) introduction of the norms and values of the bourgeois civilizing process as more reasonable and egalitarian than the feudal code; (4) amusement for the aristocracy and bourgeoisie, whereby the fairy tale was a *divertissement*; it diverted the attention of listeners/readers from the serious sociopolitical problems of the times, and it compensated for the deprivation that the upper classes perceived themselves to be suffering; (5) self-parody to reveal the ridiculous notions in previous fairy tales and to represent another aspect of court society to itself — such parodies can be seen in Jean-Jacques Cazotte's "A Thousand and One Follies" (1742), Jean-Jacques Rousseau's "The Queen Fantasque" (1758), and Voltaire's "The White Bull" (1774); and (6) careful cultivation of the literary genre for children. Fairy tales with clear didactic and moral lessons were finally approved as reading matter to serve as a subtle, more pleasurable means of initiating children into the class rituals and customs that reinforced the status quo.

The climax of the French institutionalization of the fairy tale was the publication of Charles Mayer's forty-one-volume *Le Cabinet des Fées* between 1785 and 1789, a collection that included most of the important French tales written during the previous hundred years. From this point on, most writers, whether they wrote for adults or children, consciously held a dialogue with a fairy-tale discourse that had become firmly established in the Western intellectual tradition. For instance, the French fairy tale, which, we must remember, now included *The Arabian Nights*, had a profound influence on the German classicists and the romantics, and the development of the literary fairy tale in Germany provided the continuity for the institution of the genre in the West as a whole. Like the French authors, the German middle-class writers like Johann Karl Musäus, in his collection *Volksmärchen der Deutschen* (1782–86), which included "Libussa," began employing the fairy tale to celebrate German customs. Musäus combined elements of German folklore and the French fairy tale in his work in a language clearly addressed to educated Germans. At the same time, Christoph Martin Wieland translated and adapted numerous tales from the *Cabinet des Fées* in *Dschinnistan* (1786–87). "The Philosopher's Stone" is his own creation but reveals how he, too, consciously used the fairy tale to portray the decadence of German feudal society and introduced Oriental motifs to enhance its exoticism and to conceal the critique of his own society. Aside from these two collections for upper-class readers, numerous French fairy tales became known in Germany by the turn of the century through the popular series of the *Blaue Bibliothek* and other translations from the French. In fact, some like "Sleeping Beauty," "Cinderella," and "Little Red Riding Hood" even worked their way into the Brothers Grimm collection of the *Kinder- und Hausmärchen* (*Children's and Household Tales*, 1812–15), which were considered to be genuinely German. Romantic writers such as Wilhelm Heinrich Wackenroder, Ludwig Tieck, Novalis, Joseph von Eichendorff, Clemens Brentano, Adelbert von Chamisso, Friedrich de la Motte Fouqué, and E. T. A. Hoffmann wrote extraordinary tales that revealed a major shift in the function of the genre: The fairy tale no longer represented the dominant aristocratic ideology. Rather, it was written as a critique of the worst aspects of the Enlightenment and absolutism. This viewpoint was clearly expressed in Johann Wolfgang von Goethe's classical narrative simply titled "The Fairy Tale" (1795) as though it were to be the fairy tale to end all fairy tales. Goethe optimistically envisioned a successful rebirth of a rejuvenated monarchy that enjoyed the support of all social classes in his answer to the chaos and destruction of the French Revolution. In contrast, the romantics were generally more skeptical about the prospects for individual autonomy, the reform of decadent institutions, and a democratic public sphere in a Germany divided by the selfish interests of petty tyrants and the Napoleonic Wars. Very few of the German romantic tales end on a happy note. The protagonists either go insane or die. The evil forces assume a social hue, for the witches and villains are no longer allegorical representations of evil in the Christian tradition, but are symbolically associated with the philistine bourgeois society or the decadent aristocracy. Nor was the purpose of the romantic fairy tale to amuse in the traditional sense of divertissement. Instead, it sought to engage the reader in a serious discourse about art, philosophy, education, and love. It is not by chance that the German term for the literary fairy tale is *Kunstmärchen* (art tale), for the utopian impulse for a better future was often carried on by an artist or a creative protagonist in the romantic narratives, and his fate indicated to what extent the civilizing process in Germany inhibited or nurtured the creative and independent development of the citizens.

Although the function of the fairy tale for adults underwent a major shift — and this was clear in other countries as well — that made it an appropriate means to maintain a dialogue about social and political issues within the bourgeois public sphere, the fairy tale for children remained suspect until the 1820s. Although there were various collections published for children in the latter part of the eighteenth century and at the turn of the nineteenth, along with individual chapbooks containing "Cinderella," "Jack the Giant Killer," "Beauty and the Beast," "Little Red Riding Hood," and "Sleeping Beauty" (fig. 2), they were not regarded as the prime reading material for children. Nor were they considered to be "healthy" for the development of children's minds and bodies. In Germany, for instance, there was a debate about *Lesesucht* (reading addiction) that could lead children to have crazy ideas and to masturbate. The stories considered most detrimental to the well-being of children were fantasy works. For the most part, Church leaders and educators favored other genres of stories — more realistic, sentimental, didactic — which were intended to demonstrate what good manners and morals were. Even the Brothers Grimm, in particular Wilhelm, began in 1819 to revise their collected tales, targeting them more toward children than they had done in the beginning, and cleansing their narratives of erotic, cruel, or bawdy passages. However, the fantastic and wondrous elements were kept so that they were not at first fully accepted by the bourgeois reading public, which only began changing its attitude toward the fairy tale for children during the course of the 1820s and 1830s throughout Europe. It was signaled in Germany by the publication of Wilhelm Hauff's *Märchen Almanach* (1826), which contained "The Story of Little Muck," and in England by Edgar Taylor's translation of the Grimms' *Kinder- und Hausmärchen* under the title of *German Popular Stories* (1823) with illustrations by the famous George Cruikshank. The reason for the more tolerant acceptance of the literary fairy tale for children may be attributed to the realization on the part of educators and parents, probably due to their own reading experiences, that fantasy literature and amusement would not necessarily destroy or pervert children's minds. Whether the children were of the middle classes and attended school, or were of the lower classes and worked on the farm or in a factory, they needed a recreation period — the time and space to re-create themselves without having morals and ethics imposed on them, without having the feeling that their reading or listening had to involve indoctrination.

Significantly it was from 1830 to 1900, during the rise of the middle classes, that the fairy tale came into its own for children. It was exactly during this time, from 1835 onward, to be precise, that Hans Christian Andersen, greatly influenced by the German romantic writers and the Grimms, began publishing his tales that became extremely popular throughout Europe and America. Andersen combined humor, Christian sentiments, and fantastic plots to form tales that amused and instructed young and old readers at the same time. More than any writer of the nineteenth century, he fully developed what Perrault had begun: to write tales such as "The Ugly Duckling" and "The Red Shoes," which could be readily grasped by children and adults alike but with a different understanding. Some of his narratives like "The Shadow" were clearly intended for adults alone. This is a good example of Andersen's use of the doppelgänger motif, developed by E. T. A. Hoffmann, and his exploration of paranoia within the fairy-tale genre to express his individual and very peculiar fears of the diminished possibilities for autonomy in European society and the growing alienation of people from themselves.

In fact, the flowering of the fairy tale in Europe and America during the latter half of the nineteenth century had a great deal to do with alienation. As daily life became more structured, work more rationalized, and institutions more bureaucratic, there was little space left for daydreaming and the imagination. It was the fairy tale that provided room for amusement, nonsense, and recreation. This does not mean that it abandoned its more traditional role in the civilizing process as the agent of socialization. For instance, up until the 1860s the majority of fairy-tale writers for children, including Catherine Sinclair, George Cruikshank, and Alfred Crowquill in England; Carlo Collodi in Italy; Comtesse Sophie de Ségur in France; and Heinrich Hoffmann and Ludwig Bechstein in Germany, emphasized the lessons to be learned in keeping with the principles of the Protestant ethic — industriousness, honesty, cleanliness, diligence, virtuousness — and male supremacy. However, just as the "conventional" fairy tale for adults had become subverted at the end of the eighteenth century, there was a major movement to write parodies of fairy tales, which were intended both for children *and* adults. In other words, the classical tales were turned upside down and inside out to question the value system upheld by the dominant socialization process and to keep wonder, curiosity, and creativity alive. By the 1860s, it was clear that numerous writers were using the fairy tale to subvert the formal structure of the canonized tales, as well as the governing forces in their societies that restricted free expression of ideas. Such different authors as William Makepeace Thackeray ("Bluebeard's Ghost," 1843), Nathaniel Hawthorne ("Mosses from an Old Manse," 1846), Theodor Storm ("Hinzelmeier," 1857), Mor Jokai ("Barak and His Wives," c. 1858), Gottfried Keller ("Spiegel the Cat," 1861), Edouard-René Laboulaye ("Zerbin the Wood-Cutter," 1867), Richard Leander ("The Princess with the Three Glass Hearts," 1871),

George MacDonald ("The Day Boy and the Night Girl," 1879), Catulle Mendés ("The Sleeping Beauty," 1885), Mary De Morgan ("The Three Clever Kings," 1888), Oscar Wilde ("The Fisherman and His Soul," 1891), Robert Louis Stevenson ("The Bottle Imp," 1892), and Hugo von Hofmannsthal ("The Fairy Tale of the 672nd Night," 1895) were all concerned with exploring the potential of the fairy tale to reform both the prescripted way it had become cultivated, and the stereotypes and prejudices in regard to gender and social roles that it propagated. The best example of the type of subversion attempted during the latter part of the nineteenth century is Lewis Carroll's *Alice's Adventures in Wonderland* (1865), which has had a major influence on the fairy-tale genre up to the present.

Although many of the fairy tales were ironic or ended on a tragic note, they still subscribed to the utopian notion of the transformation of humans, that is, the redemption of the humane qualities and the overcoming of bestial drives. In America, for instance, Frank Stockton, who could be considered the "pioneer" writer of the fairy tale in America, and Howard Pyle, one of the finest writer-illustrators of fairy tales, touch upon the theme of redemption in their tales "The Griffin and the Minor Canon" (1885) and "Where to Lay the Blame" (1895). But the most notable American fairy tale of the nineteenth century was L. Frank Baum's *The Wonderful Wizard of Oz* (1900), which depicts Dorothy's great desire and need to break out of Kansas and determine her own destiny, a theme that Baum also explored in "The Queen of Quok" in *American Fairy Tales* (1901).

By the beginning of the twentieth century, the fairy tale had become fully institutionalized in Europe and America, and its functions had shifted and expanded. The institutionalization of a genre means that a specific process of production, distribution, and reception has become regularized within the public sphere of a society and plays a role in forming and maintaining the cultural heritage of that society. Without such institutionalization in advanced industrialized and technological countries, the genre would perish. Thus the genre itself becomes a kind of self-perpetuating institute involved in the socialization and acculturation of readers. It is the interaction of writer, publisher, and audience within a given society that makes for the definition of the genre in any given epoch. The aesthetics of each fairy tale will depend on how and why an individual writer wants to intervene in the discourse of the genre as institution.

By the beginning of the twentieth century, the fairy tale as institution had expanded to include drama, poetry, ballet, music, and opera. In fact, one could perhaps assert that the pageants at the various European courts in the sixteenth and seventeenth centuries, especially the court of Louis XIV, had actually influenced and helped further the development of the literary fairy tale. Certainly, after André-Ernest Modeste Grétry's *Zémire et Azore* (1771), based on "Beauty and the Beast," and Wolfgang Amadeus Mozart's *The Magic Flute* (1790), fairy-tale themes became abundant in the musical world of Europe in the nineteenth century, as can be seen in E. T. A. Hoffmann's own *Undine* (1814), Gioacchino Rossini's *La Cenerentola* (1817), Robert Schumann's *Kreisleriana* (1835–40), Léo Delibes's *Coppélia* (1870), Peter Ilyich Tschaikovsky's *Sleeping Beauty* (1889) and *Nutcracker Suite* (1892), Engelbert Humperdinck's *Hänsel and Gretel* (1890), and Jacques Offenbach's *The Tales of Hoffmann* (1890). Again, the manner in which the fairy tale incorporated other art forms into its own institution reveals the vital role that adults have played in maintaining the genre. Never has the fairy tale ever lost its appeal to adults, and the fairy tale for adults or mixed audiences underwent highly significant changes in the twentieth century.

During the first half of the century, the major shift in the function of the literary tale involved greater and more explicit politicization. In France, Apollinaire, who wrote "Cinderella Continued" (1918), joined a group of experimental writers who published their fairy tales in *La Baionette* to comment on the ravages of World War I. Hermann Hesse, who had written "The Forest Dweller" (1917–18) to criticize the conformity of his times, also published "Strange News from Another Planet" in 1919 to put forward his pacifist views. Thomas Mann also made a major contribution to the fairy-tale novel with *The Magic Mountain* (1924), which is filled with political debates about nationalism and democracy. Moreover, there was a wave of innovative and expressionist fairy tales in Germany written by Edwin Hoernle, Hermynia zur Mühlen, Mynona, Franz Hessel, Kurt Schwitters, Oskar Maria Graf, Bertolt Brecht, Alfred Döblin, and others who were politically tendentious. In England, the experimentation was not as great. Nevertheless, a volume titled *The Fairies Return, Or, New Tales for Old* appeared in 1934 and contained tales with unusual social commentaries by A. E. Coppard, Lord Dunsany, Eric Linklater, Helen Simpson, Edith Anna Œnone Somerville, Christina Stead, and G. B. Stern. Of course, after the Nazi rise to power and during the Spanish Civil War, the fairy tale became more and more the means to convey political sentiments. In Germany, the fairy tale was interpreted and produced according to Nazi ideology, and there are numerous examples of *völkisch* and fascist fairy-tale products, even in France. These, in turn, brought out a response of writers opposed to nazism such as American H. I. Phillips's "Little Red Riding Hood as a Dictator Would Tell It" (1940).

Germany offers an extreme case of how the fairy tale became politicized or used for political purposes. But this extreme case does illustrate a general trend in the political intonation of fairy tales that continued into the 1940s and 1950s. For example, a work like J. R. R. Tolkien's *The Hobbit* (1938) was written with World War I in mind and with the intention of warning against a second world war. James Thurber's "The Girl and the Wolf" (1939) focused on power and violation. Georg Kaiser's "The Fairy Tale of the King" (1943) reflected upon dictatorship. Erich Kästner's "The Fairy Tale about Reason" (1948) projected the possibility of world peace. Ingeborg Bachmann's "The Smile of the Sphinx" (1949) recalled the terror of the Holocaust.

Once again, following World War II, the fairy tale set out to combat terror, but this time the terror did not concern the inhibitions of the civilizing process, rationalization, and alienation, but rather the demented and perverse forms of civilization that had in part caused atrocities and threatened to bring the world to the brink of catastrophe. Confronted with such an aspect at the onset of the Cold War with other wars to follow, some writers like Henri Pourrat (*Le Trésor des Contes*, 1948–62) and Italo Calvino (*Fiabe Italiane*, 1956) sought to preserve spiritual and communal values of the oral wonder tales in revised versions, while numerous other writers drastically altered the fairy tale to question whether the utopian impulse could be kept alive and whether our sense of wonderment could be maintained. If so, then the fairy tale had to deal with perversity and what Hannah Arendt called the banality of evil. Writers like Philip K. Dick ("The King of the Elves," 1953), Naomi Mitchison

("Five Men and a Swan," 1957), Sylvia Townsend Warner ("Bluebeard's Daughter," 1960), Christoph Meckel ("The Crow," 1962), Stanislaw Lem ("Prince Ferix and the Princess Crystal," 1967), and Robert Coover ("The Dead Queen," 1973, and *Briar Rose*, 1996) provoke readers not by playing with their expectations, but by disturbing them. To a certain extent, they know that most of their readers have been "Disneyfied," that is, they have been subjected to the saccharine, sexist, and illusionary stereotypes of the Disney-culture industry. Therefore, these authors have felt free to explode the illusion that happy endings are possible in real worlds that are held together by the deceit of advertisements and government. Especially since the 1970s and up through the present, the fairy tale has become more aggressive, aesthetically more complex and sophisticated, and more insistent on *not* distracting readers but helping them focus on key social problems and issues in their respective societies. This standpoint is especially apparent in the works of Janosch, Günter Kunert, Günter Grass, and Michael Ende in Germany; Michel Tournier, Pierre Gripari, and Pierrette Fleutiaux in France; Donald Bartheleme, Robert Coover, Jane Yolen, Francesca Lia Block, Donna Jo Napoli, Gregory Maguire, and Aimee Bender in the United States; Margaret Atwood in Canada; Angela Carter, A. S. Byatt, Emma Donoghue, and Peter Redgrove in Great Britain; and Gianni Rodari in Italy. Perhaps the major social critique carried by the fairy tale can be seen in the restructuring and reformation of the fairy tale itself as genre on the part of feminists. The result has been a remarkable production of nonsexist fairy tales for children and adults, as well as theoretical works that explore the underlying implications of gender roles in fairy tales. Not only have individual writers such as Anne Sexton, Angela Carter, Olga Broumas, Margaret Atwood, A. S. Byatt, Tanith Lee, Rosemarie Künzler, Jane Yolen, and Robin McKinley created highly innovative tales that reverse and question traditional sex roles, but there also have been collective enterprises in Italy, England, Ireland, and the United States that have reacted critically to the standard canon representing catatonic females flat on their backs waiting to be brought to life by charming princes. A good example is the work of Attic Press in Ireland, which has published such books as *Rapunzel's Revenge* (1985), *Cinderella on the Ball* (1991), and *Ride on Rapunzel* (1992). In a similar vein but sorts of fairy-tale motifs and characters in a nonconventional Broadway-musical manner and explores some of the more profound implications of the canonical tales. The emphasis is more on the tragic aspects to demonstrate how we have been misguided by fairy tales and delude ourselves because we neglect social responsibility for our actions.

The nonconformist *Into the Woods* can be contrasted with the general run-of-the-mill Broadway productions of *Cinderella* and *Beauty and the Beast*, performed frequently in the past twenty years and based either on the Rodgers and Hammerstein or Disney model. If it is true that the fairy tale in the seventeenth century was bound by the rules and regulations of court society and that it largely served to represent court society to itself and to glorify the aristocracy; and if it is true that the social and political development in the nineteenth century set art free so that the fairy tale as genre became autonomous on the free market and in the public sphere; then it appears that there is a return, at least in theater, television, and cinema, to the representative function of the fairy tale. Of course, this time the society that is being represented to itself as glorious is the capitalist-consumer society with its "free" market system. In addition, the fairy tale implicitly and explicitly reflects the state's endeavors to reconcile divergent forces, to pacify discontents, and to *show* how there are basically good elements within the bourgeois elite groups vying for control of American society. These agents (often understood as heroes) are portrayed as seeking the happiness of *all* groups, especially the disenfranchised, who create the drama in real life and in the fairy-tale productions.

The 1987–89 television series of *Beauty and the Beast* is a good example of how the fairy tale as representation (and also legitimation) of elite bourgeois interests functions. No matter which thirty-minute sequel a viewer watches, the basic plot of this television adaptation of the classic tale follows the same lines: The young woman, Catherine, who is from the upper classes, devotes her talents to serving as a legal defender of the oppressed; and the Beast, Vincent, represents the homeless and the outcasts in America, forced to live underground. These two continually unite because of some elective affinity to oppose crime and corruption and clear the way for the moral forces to triumph in America. Though the different sequels do expose the crimes of the upper classes as well as the lower classes, the basic message is that there can be reconciliation between beauty and beast, and we can live in a welfare state without friction.

Messages of reconciliation and elitism are clear in almost all the Disney cinematic productions of fairy tales from *Snow White and the Seven Dwarfs* (1937) to *Beauty and the Beast* (1993). With the possible exception of the innovative fairy-tale films produced by Jim Henson and Tom Davenport, the dominant tendency of most popular fairy-tale films for the big screen and television tend to follow the conventional patterns of the anachronistic classical fairy tales of Perrault, the Grimms, and Andersen, especially when the productions cater to children as consumers.

Despite the tendency of the film and television industry to use the fairy tale to induce a sense of happy ending and ideological consent, and to mute its subversive potential for the benefit of those social groups controlling power in the public sphere, the fairy tale as institution cannot be defined one dimensionally or totally administered by its most visible producers in mass media and publishing. Writers, directors, and producers are constantly seeking to revise classical fairy tales with extraordinary films that address contemporary social issues. For instance, Neil Jordan in *The Company of Wolves* (1984), an adaptation of an Angela Carter story, and Matthew Bright in *Freeway* (1996) focus on the nature of violation and rape in their films that deal with female sexual desire and male sexual predatory drives. Implicit is a critique of *Little Red Riding Hood* as a tale that suggests little girls want and cause their own rape. Other filmmakers, such as Mike Newell (*Into the West*, 1990) and John Sayles (*The Secret of Roan Innish*, 1993), have created their own fairy-tale films based on Irish folklore that critically depict contemporary social predicaments while providing a means for viewers to contemplate the stories with hope and a critical view toward the future. Andy Tennant's *Ever After* (1998), a cinematic adaptation of Charles Perrault's famous fairy tale "Cinderella," uses a clever conceit to catch our attention. Jacob and Wilhelm Grimm arrive at the castle of a French aristocratic woman played by the majestic Jeanne Moreau, and after she shows them a glittering glass slipper, she invites them to spend a few hours with her while she regales them with the true story of Cinderella, who was ostensibly her grandmother. As she tells her story, the Grimms are dazzled, for at the end of it, they realize that Charles Perrault's version was based on historical fact and that they had perpetuated a lie through their own particular version. Indeed, they learn that Cinderella, played by the pugnacious Drew Barrymore, was a liberal feminist before her times. She read Thomas More's *Utopia*, defended the rights of bonded servants, advocated educational and social reforms, enchanted a prince as well as Michelangelo, and became the queen of France. When the Grimms leave the castle, we smile because we are part of an inside joke and, at the same time, we wish that Tenant's fraudulent version of "Cinderella" might really be true, just as we wish that utopian aspects of the fairy tale were less commodified than they are in the Disney tradition. The recent fairy tale films *Shrek* (2001) and *Shrek 2* (2003) produced by the American film company Dreamworks, and *Spirited Away* (2001) and *Howl's Moving Castle* (2004) created by the Japanese filmmaker Hayao Miyasaki, suggest that the fairy-tale film is now being used to question the degeneration of utopia. In particular, the two *Shrek* films make obvious reference to the Disney Corporation and ideological world in order to critique and question it. In the first film all the fairy-tale characters from the Grimms' tales up through the Disney films are banished to Shrek's swamp. There they are happy and find refuge from the brutal puritanical force of Lord Farquaad, who resembles Michael Eisner, the former head of the Disney Corporation, and who hates fantasy and strange characters that look like mutants. What is neat, clean, and beautiful at his court, which resembles the antiseptic Disneyland, masks the violence and ugliness of Farquaad's empire. Eventually, the Lord is exposed as a petty tyrant and made into a laughing stock while the ugly Shrek and ugly Fiona can retire to the messy swamp — but not to live happily ever after, for there is a sequel. In the second Shrek film, notions of beauty, consumerism, and celebrity are undercut by the behavior of Shrek, the princess Fiona, and a cunning Puss in Boots. In this hilarious film, the parents of Fiona live in a kingdom that resembles Hollywood, and Prince Charming is the son of a witch, who creates an artificial world that she controls until Shrek and his friends reveal her methods of blackmail and pretension. Once again, at the end, Fiona chooses to remain with Shrek and live in a swamp with marginalized creatures. No longer do handsome princes save helpless virgins in the Shrek fairy-tale films. The an older woman. In another story, a newlywed queen, who apparently is doted on by her husband, learns that his love is like a cage that she must flee. In all of Donoghue's tales, the protagonists come miraculously to a new awareness that will stamp their lives, and her fairy tales seek artfully to enter in and change the lives of her readers.

This is the ultimate paradox of the literary fairy tale: It wants to mark reality without leaving a trace of how it creates the wondrous effects. There is no doubt that the fairy tale has become totally institutionalized in Western society, part of the public sphere, with its own specific code and forms through which we communicate about social and psychic phenomena. We initiate children and expect them to learn the fairy-tale code as part of our responsibility in the civilizing process. This code has its key words and key marks, but it is not static. As in the oral tradition, its original impulse of hope for better living conditions has not vanished in the literary tradition, although many of the signs have been manipulated in the name of male authoritarian forces. As long as the fairy tale continues to awaken our wonderment and enable us to project counterworlds to our present society, it will serve a meaningful social and aesthetic function, not just for compensation but for revelation: The worlds portrayed by the best of our fairy tales are like magic spells of enchantment that actually free us. Instead of petrifying our minds, they arouse our imagination and compel us to realize how we can fight terror and cunningly insert ourselves into our daily struggles, turning the course of the world's events in our favor.

two

The Rise of the French Fairy Tale and the Decline of France

Your people ... whom you ought to love as your children, and who up to now have been passionately devoted to you, are dying of hunger. The culture of the soil is almost abandoned; the towns and the country are being depopulated; every trade is languishing and no longer supports the workers. All commerce is destroyed.... The whole of France is nothing but a huge hospital, desolated and without resources.

—Fénelon, Letter to King Louis XIV, 1694

U p until the 1690s, the oral folk tale in France had not been deemed worthy enough of being transcribed and transformed into literature, that is, written down and circulated among the literate people. In fact, with the exception of the significant collections of tales, *The Pleasant Nights* (1550–53) by Giovan Francesco Straparola and *The Pentameron* (1634–36) by Giambattista Basile, in Italy, most of the European aristocracy and intelligentsia considered the folk tale beneath them. It was part of the vulgar, common people's tradition, beneath the dignity of cultivated people and associated with pagan beliefs and superstitions that were no longer relevant in Christian Europe. If the literate members of the upper classes did acknowledge the folk tale, it was only as crude entertainment, divertissement, anecdote, or homily in its oral form, transmitted through such intermediaries as wet nurses, governesses, servants, peasants, merchants, priests, and court performers.

From the Middle Ages up through the Renaissance, folk tales were told by nonliterate peasants among themselves at the hearth, in spinning rooms, or in the fields. They were told by literate merchants and travelers to people of all classes in inns and taverns. They were told by priests in the vernacular as part of their sermons to reach out to the peasantry. They were told to children of the upper classes by nurses and governesses. They were remembered and passed on in different forms and versions by all members of society and told to suit particular occasions — *as talk.* Sometimes this talk was merely for amusement or provided communication; sometimes the talk contained vital information. Gradually, this talk was elevated, cultivated, and made acceptable so it could enter into the French salons by the middle of the seventeenth century. Only by 1690, in fact, was it regarded worthy of print in France, and by 1696, there was a veritable vogue of printed fairy tales. The literary fairy tale had come into its own, and French aristocratic writers for the most part established the conventions and motifs for a genre that is perhaps the most popular in the Western world — and not only among children.

How did all this come about? Why the change in attitude toward the lowly oral folk tale? What kinds of literary fairy tales were created? Though it is impossible to set a date for the rise of the literary fairy tale in France, such important studies as Roger Picard's *Les Salons Littéraires et la société française 1610–1789* (1946), Marie Gougy-Francois's *Les grands salons feménins* (1965), Renate Baader's *Dames de Lettres* (1986), and Verena von der Heyden-Rynsch's *Europäische Salons* (1992) have shown that its origin can be located in the conversation and games developed by highly educated aristocratic women in the salons that they formed in the 1630s in Paris and that continued to be popular up through the beginning of the eighteenth century. Deprived of access to schools and universities, French aristocratic women began organizing gatherings in their homes to which they invited other women and gradually men in order to discuss art, literature, and topics such as love, marriage, and freedom that were important to them. In particular, the women wanted to distinguish themselves as unique individuals, who were above the rest of society and deserved special attention. Generally speaking, these women were called *précieuses* and tried to develop a *précieux* manner of thinking, speaking, and writing to reveal and celebrate their innate talents that distinguished them from the vulgar and common elements of society. Most important here was the emphasis placed on wit and invention in conversation. The person who was a *précieux* (and numerous men were included in this movement) was capable of transforming the most banal thing into something brilliant and unique. Although there was a tendency among them to be effete and elitist, these women were by no means dilettantes. On the contrary, some of the most gifted writers of the time, such as Mlle de Scudéry, Mlle de Montpensier, Mme de Sévigné, and Mme de Lafayette, came out of this movement, and their goal was to gain more independence for women of their class and to be treated more seriously as intellectuals. In fact, one of the most important consequences of *préciosité* was its effect on women from the lower aristocracy and bourgeoisie, who were inspired to struggle for more rights and combat the rational constraints placed on their lives.

The women who frequented the salons were constantly seeking innovative ways to express their needs and to embellish the forms and style of speech and communication that they shared. Given the fact that they had all been exposed to folk tales as children and that they entertained themselves with conversational games that served as models for the occasional lyric and the serial novel, it is not by chance that they turned to the folk tale as a source of amusement. Around the middle of the seventeenth century the aristocratic women started to invent parlor games based on the plots of tales with the purpose of challenging one another in a friendly fashion to see who could create the more compelling narrative. Such challenges led the women, in particular, to improve the quality of their dialogues, remarks, and ideas about morals, manners, and education, and at times to question male standards that had been set to govern their lives. The subject matter of the conversations consisted of literature, mores, taste, love, and etiquette, whereby the speakers all endeavored to portray ideal situations in the most effective oratory style that would gradually be transformed into literary forms and set the standards for the *conte de fée*, or what we now call the literary fairy tale.

By the 1670s there were various references in letters about the fairy tale as an acceptable *jeux d' esprit* in the salons. In this type of game, the women would refer to folk tales and use certain motifs spontaneously in their conversations. Eventually, they began telling the tales as a literary *divertimento, intermezzo*, or as a kind of after-dinner dessert that one would invent to amuse listeners. This social function of amusement was complemented by another purpose, namely, that of self-portrayal and representation of proper aristocratic manners. The telling of fairy tales enabled women to picture themselves, their social manners, and their relations in a manner that represented their interests and those of the aristocracy. Thus, they placed great emphasis on certain rules of oration, such as naturalness and spontaneity, and themes, such as freedom of choice in marriage, fidelity, and justice. The teller of the tale was to make it "seem" as though the tale were made up on the spot and as though it did not follow prescribed rules. Embellishment, improvisation, and experimentation with known folk or literary motifs were stressed. The procedure of telling a tale as *bagatelle* (trinket or trifle) would work as follows: The narrator would be requested to think up a tale based on a particular motif; the adroitness of the narrator would be measured by the degree with which she was inventive and natural; the audience would respond politely with a compliment; then another member of the audience would be requested to tell a tale, not in direct competition with the other teller, but in order to continue the game and vary the possibilities for invention and symbolic expression that often used code words such as *galanterie, tendresse*, and *l'esprit* to signal the qualities that distinguished their protagonists.

By the 1690s the "salon" fairy tale became so acceptable that women and men began writing their tales down to publish them. The "naturalness" of the tales was, of course, feigned since everyone prepared tales very carefully and rehearsed them before participating in a particular salon ritual. Most of the notable writers of the fairy tale learned to develop this literary genre by going to the salons or homes of women who wanted to foster intellectual conversation. And some writers, such as Mme d'Aulnoy, Mme de Murat, and Mlle Lhéritier even had their own salons. Moreover, there were festivities at King Louis XIV's court and at aristocratic homes, especially during the Carnival period, that people attended dressed as nymphs, satyrs, fawns, or other fairy-tale figures. There were spectacular ballets and plays that incorporated fairy-tale motifs, as in the production of Molière and Corneille's *Psyché* (1671), which played a role in the development of the beauty and the beast motif in the works of Mme d'Aulnoy. In this regard, the attraction to the fairy tale had a great deal to do with Louis XIV, the Sun King's desire to make his court the most splendid and radiant in Europe, for the French aristocracy and bourgeoisie sought cultural means to translate and represent this splendor in form and style to themselves and the outside world. Thus, the peasant contents and the settings of the oral folk tales were transformed to appeal to aristocratic and bourgeois audiences.

The transformation of the oral folk tale into a literary fairy tale was not superficial or decorative. The aesthetics that the aristocratic women developed in their conversational games and in their written tales had a serious aspect to it: Though they differed in style and content, these tales were all anticlassical and were implicitly written in opposition to the leading critic of the literary establishment, Nicolas Boileau, who championed Greek and Roman literature in the famous "Quarrel of the Ancients and Moderns" (1687–96) as the models for French writers to follow at that time. Instead, the early French fairy-tale writers used models from the Italian literary tradition (Straparola and Basile), French folklore, and the medieval courtly tradition. In addition, since the majority of the writers and tellers of fairy tales were women, these tales displayed a certain resistance toward male rational precepts and patriarchal realms by conceiving pagan worlds in which the final "say" was determined by female fairies, extraordinarily majestic and powerful fairies, if you will. To a certain extent, *all* the French writers of fairy tales, men and women, continued the "modernization" of an oral genre (begun by Straparola and Basile) by institutionalizing it in literary form with utopian visions that emanated from their desire for better social conditions than they were experiencing in France at that time.

Despite the fact that their remarkable fairy tales set the tone and standards for the development of most of the memorable literary fairy

tales in the West up to the present, they and their utopian visions are all
but forgotten, not only in English-speaking countries but also in France
itself. If anyone is known today and represents this genre, it is Charles
Perrault, who published the verse fairy tales "Donkey-Skin" and "The
Foolish Wishes" in 1694, and a slim volume of six prose fairy tales, *Histoires ou contes du temps passé*, in 1696. Perrault (1628–1703) was born in
Paris into one of the more distinguished bourgeois families of that time.
His father was a lawyer and member of Parliament, and his four brothers
— he was the youngest — all went on to become renown in such fields
as architecture and law. In 1637, Perrault began studying at the Collège
de Beauvais (near the Sorbonne), and at the age of fifteen he stopped
attending school and largely taught himself all he needed to know so
he could later take his law examinations. After working three years
as a lawyer, he left the profession to become a secretary to his brother
Pierre, who was the tax receiver of Paris. By this time Perrault had
already written some minor poems and began taking more and more
of an interest in literature. In 1659, he published two important poems,
"Portrait d'Iris" and "Portrait de la voix d'Iris," and by 1660 his public
career as a poet received a big boost when he produced several poems
in honor of Louis XIV. In 1663, Perrault was appointed secretary to Jean
Baptiste Colbert, controller general of finances, perhaps the most influential minister in Louis XIV's government. For the next twenty years,
until Colbert's death, Perrault was able to accomplish a great deal in the
arts and sciences due to Colbert's power and influence. In 1671, he was
elected to the French Academy and was also placed in charge of the
royal buildings. He continued writing poetry and took an active interest
in cultural affairs of the court. In 1672, he married Marie Guichon, with
whom he had three sons. She died giving birth in 1678, and he never
remarried, supervising the education of his children by himself.

When Colbert died in 1683, Perrault was dismissed from government service, but he had a substantial pension and was able to support
his family until his death. Released from governmental duties, Perrault
could concentrate more on literary affairs. In 1687, he inaugurated
the famous "Quarrel of the Ancients and the Moderns" (*Querelle des
Anciens et des Modernes*) by reading a poem titled "Le Siècle de Louis le
Grand." Perrault took the side of modernism and believed that France

and Christianity — here he sided with the Jansenists — could only progress if they incorporated pagan beliefs and folklore and developed a culture of Enlightenment. On the other hand, Nicolas Boileau, the literary critic, and Jean Racine, the dramatist, took the opposite view-point and argued that France had to imitate the great empires of Greece and Rome and maintain stringent classical rules in respect to the arts. This literary quarrel, which had great cultural ramifications, lasted until 1697, at which time Louis XIV decided to end it in favor of Boileau and Racine. However, this decision did not stop Perrault from trying to incorporate his ideas into his poetry and prose.

Perrault had always frequented the literary salon of his niece Mlle Lhéritier, in addition to those of Mme d'Aulnoy, and other women, and he had been annoyed by Boileau's satires written against women. Thus, he decided to write three verse tales — "Griseldis" (1691), "Les Souhaits Ridicules" ("The Foolish Wishes," 1693), and "Peau d'Ane" ("Donkey Skin," 1694) — along with a long poem "Apologie des femmes" (1694) in defense of women. Whether these works can be considered pro-women today is another question. However, Perrault was definitely more enlight-ened in regard to this question than either Boileau or Racine, and his poems make use of a highly mannered style and folk motifs to stress the necessity of assuming an enlightened moral attitude toward women and exercising just authority. In 1696, Perrault embarked on a more ambi-tious project of transforming several popular folk tales with all their superstitious beliefs and magic into moralistic tales that would appeal to children and adults and demonstrate a modern approach to literature. He also invented two or three of the tales and used literary sources. He had a prose version of "Sleeping Beauty" ("La Belle au Bois Dormant") printed in the journal *Mercure Galant* in 1696, and in 1697 he published an entire collection of tales titled *Histoires ou contes du temps passé*, which consisted of new literary versions of "La Belle au Bois Dormant," "Le Petit Chaperon Rouge" ("Little Red Riding Hood"), "Barbe Bleue" ("Blue Beard"), "Cendrillon" ("Cinderella"), "Le Petit Poucet" ("Tom Thumb"), "Riquet à la Houppe" ("Ricky with the Tuft"), "Le Chat Botté" ("Puss in Boots"), and "Les Fées" ("The Fairies"). All of these fairy tales, which are now considered "classical," were based on oral and literary motifs that had become popular in France, but Perrault transformed the stories to address social and political issues as well as the manners and mores of the upper classes. Moreover, he added ironic verse morals to provoke his readers to reflect on the ambivalent meaning of the tales. Although *Histoires de contes du temps passé* was published under the name of Pierre Perrault Darmancour, Perrault's son, and some critics have asserted that the book was indeed written or at least coauthored by his son, recent evidence has shown clearly that this could not have been the case, especially since his son had not published anything up to that point. Perrault was simply using his son's name to mask his own identity so that he would not be blamed for reigniting the "Quarrel of the Ancients and the Moderns." Numerous critics have regarded Perrault's tales as written directly for children, but they overlook the facts that at that time there was no children's literature per se, and most writers of fairy tales were composing and reciting their tales for their peers in the literary salons. Certainly, if Perrault intended them to make a final point in the "Quarrel of the Ancients and the Moderns," then he obviously had an adult audience in mind who would understand his humor and the subtle manner in which he transformed folklore superstition to convey his position about the "modern" development of French civility.

There is no doubt that, among the writers of fairy tales during the 1690s, Perrault was the greatest stylist, which accounts for the fact that his tales have withstood the test of time. Furthermore, Perrault claimed that literature must become modern, and his transformation of folk motifs and literary themes into refined and provocative fairy tales still speaks to the modern age, ironically in a way that may compel us to ponder whether the age of reason has led to the progress and happiness promised so charmingly in his narratives. Though finely wrought, his tales are not indicative of the great vogue that took place, nor are they representative of the utopian (and sometimes dystopian) verve of the tales. In his recent, superb study, *Seeing through the Mother Goose Tales: Visual Turns in the Writings of Charles Perrault*, Philip Lewis examines the linguistic rigor of Perrault's writing and demonstrates convincingly how Perrault elaborated Cartesian thought in favor of the visual in his tales. What makes Perrault's tales so unique is that the rational structure is always thrown into doubt because, as Lewis argues, there is a certain necessary inconceivability or irrepresentability with the conceptual knowledge that he extols. Thus the protagonists of all his tales — Tom Thumb, Bluebeard, the master cat, the wolf, the princes — all exhibit dubious motives and compromise an ambivalent civilizing process that rationalizes phallocentric power. To appreciate the value of Perrault's tales and how different they are, it is important to see them in their historical context.

There were approximately three waves of the French fairy-tale vogue: (1) the experimental salon fairy tale, 1690–1703; (2) the Oriental tale, 1704–20; and (3) the conventional and comical fairy tale, 1721–89. These waves overlap somewhat, but if we understand the reasons for their origins and changes, we can grasp some of the underlying meanings in the symbols of the tales that are not apparent without history in mind.

THE SALON FAIRY TALE

When Marie-Catherine d'Aulnoy included the fairy tale "The Island of Happiness" in her novel *Histoire d'Hippolyte, comte de Duglas* in 1690, she was not aware that she was about to set a trend in France. Within five years, the *literary* fairy tale became the talk of the literary salons, or what had been the talk in these salons now came to print: Her tales were followed by Mlle Lhéritier's *Oeuvres Meslées* (1696); Mlle Bernard's *Inès de Cordoue* (1696), a novel that includes "Les Enchantements de l'Eloquence" and "Riquet à la houppe"; Mlle de la Force's *Les Contes des Contes* (1698); Perrault's *Histoires ou contes du temps passé* (1697); Mme d'Aulnoy's *Les Contes des fées*, 4 vols. (1697–98); Chevalier de Mailly's *Les Illustres Fées, contes galans* (1698); Mme de Murat's *Contes de fées* (1698); Nodot's *Histoire de Mélusine* (1698); Sieur de Prechac's *Contes moins contes que les autres* (1698); Mme Durand's *La Comtesse de Mortane* (1699); Mme de Murat's *Histoires sublimes et allégoriques* (1699); Eustache Le Noble's *Le Gage touché* (1700); Mme d'Auneuil's *La Tyrannie des fées détruite* (1702); and Mme Durand's *Les Petits Soupers de l'été de l'année 1699* (1702).

The main reason for the publication of these tales — and perhaps the stress should be on making the tales *public*, or letting a greater

public outside the salons know about the tales that were told in them
— is that France had entered a major crisis in 1788 and conditions
of living began to deteriorate on all levels of society. Indeed, even the
aristocracy and haute bourgeoisie were not exempt. Due to the fact that
Louis XIV continued to wage costly wars and sought to annex more
land for France, the taxes for all classes became exorbitant. At various
times during the latter part of Louis XIV's reign there were years of bad
crops due to terrible weather and devastation of human lives due to the
wars. The steady increase of debt, taxation, and poor living conditions
resulted in extreme misery for the peasantry and an austere life for the
bourgeoisie and aristocracy. Moreover, this was the period when Louis
XIV turned more orthodox in his devotion to Catholicism under the
influence of Madame de Maintenon, became more rigid in his cultural
taste, and became more arbitrary and willful as an absolutist king. His
reign, which had begun during the age of reason, turned reason against
itself to justify his desires, tastes, and ambition for glory. This solipsism
led to irrational policies that were destructive for the French people and
were soundly criticized by the highly respected Fénelon, the Archbishop
of Cambrai, who in some ways became the moral conscience of the
ancien régime during its decline.

Given the "dark times" and the fact that writers were not allowed to
criticize Louis XIV in a direct way due to censorship, the fairy tale was
regarded as a means to vent criticism, and, at the same time, writers
began cultivating it to project some hope for a better world. The very
first fairy tale that Mme d'Aulnoy wrote in 1690 is a good example of how
writers regarded the fairy tale as a narrative strategy to criticize Louis
XIV and to elaborate a code of integrity, for many French writers were
intent at that time to establish standards of manners, correct speech,
justice, and love. For example, in d'Aulnoy's "The Island of Happiness,"
Adolph fails to attain complete happiness because he sacrifices love for
glory in war. It is because he does not know how to esteem the tenderness of Princess Felicity, or how to behave and remain faithful, that he
destroys himself. "The Island of Happiness" is a utopian tale because it
confronts male desire as a destructive force and suggests that there is
something missing in life, something that women can provide if utopia
is to be attained and maintained. Paradise, which is associated with the

Princess Felicity, will remain beyond our reach, and it is this longing for paradise, for a realm that is just and allows for natural feelings to flow, that formed the basis for most of the literary fairy tales produced during the 1690s in France. In this sense, the utopian impulse was not much different from the utopian impulse that led peasants to tell their folk tales. But the wish fulfillment in the oral tales of the peasants arose out of completely different circumstances of oppression and hope. The salon tales were marked by the struggles within the upper classes for recognition, sensible policies, and power.

Interestingly, almost all of the major fairy-tale writers of the 1690s were on the *fringe* of Louis XIV's court and were often in trouble with him or the authorities. For instance, Mme d'Aulnoy had been banished from the court in 1670, returned to Paris in 1690, and became involved in a major scandal when one of her friends killed her husband. Mme de Murat was banished from the court in 1694 when she published a political satire about Mme de Maintenon, Scarron, and Louis XIV. Mlle de la Force was sent to a convent in 1697 for publishing impious verses. Catherine Bernard was not accepted at court and remained single to maintain her independence. The Chevalier de Mailly was an illegitimate son of a member of the de Mailly family and, though accepted at court, caused difficulties by insisting that his bastard status be recognized as equal to that of the legitimate sons of the de Mailly family. Even Charles Perrault, who had been a loyal civil servant as long as his protector Jean Baptiste Colbert, controller general of finances, was alive, fell into disfavor in 1683, and opposed the official cultural policy of Louis XIV until his death in 1701.

It would be an exaggeration to say that the first wave of salon fairy-tale writers were all malcontents and totally opposed to Louis XIV's regime, for they all mixed in the best circles and were considered highly respectable and talented writers. Nevertheless, with the exception of Perrault, they were not part of the literary establishment and made names for themselves in a new genre that was looked upon with suspicion. Even the respectable Fénelon, who was a member of the Court's inner circle and the preceptor of the Duke de Bourgogne, Louis XIV's grandson, wrote fairy tales in the 1690s in an experiment to expand the Dauphin's mind through pleasurable reading, but did not publish these tales until the 1730s. In other words, there was something inherently suspicious and perhaps subversive about the development of the literary fairy tale, and the French writers always felt compelled to apologize somewhat for choosing to write fairy tales. Though apologetic, they knew what they were doing.

Most of the early writers came to Paris from the provinces and were steeped in the folklore of their region. Before they published their tales, we must remember, they first practiced them orally and recited them in the salons. Whenever they wrote them down, they circulated them among their friends — they all knew each other and moved in the same circles — and made changes before the tales were printed. Some of them, like Perrault and Mlle Lhéritier, were related and exchanged ideas. It is clear that Perrault also had contact with Catherine Bernard; their different versions of "Riquet with the Tuft" reveal mutual interests. In particular, the writers shared their ideas for their tales and discussed their dreams and hopes with each other in private and in their letters. When Mme de Murat was banished to the provinces, she used to stay up into the early hours of the morning, telling tales to her friends, among whom was Mlle de la Force, who used to distribute her tales among her friends and discuss them before she was placed in a convent.

All the writers revised their tales to develop a *précieux tone*, a unique style, which was not only supposed to be gallant, natural, and witty, but inventive, astonishing, and "modern." Their tales are highly provocative, extraordinary, bizarre, and implausible. They wrote in hyperbole to draw attention to themselves and their predicaments. They were not afraid to include sadomasochistic elements and the macabre in their tales.

Many critics and educators have often complained that the Grimms' tales are too harsh and cruel to be read to children, and some have even gone so far as to maintain that German fairy-tale writers indulged themselves in violence. But, in fact, the salon tales of the refined French ladies make the Grimms' tales look prudish. In particular, Mme d'Aulnoy was a genius in conceiving ways to torture her heroines and heroes. She had them transformed into serpents, white cats, rams, monkeys, deer, and birds. Two of her most famous fairy tales, "Green Serpent" (fig. 3) and "The Ram," derived from the beast/bridegroom oral and literary traditions, appear to take pleasure in the tormenting of the princes as

Figure 3. "The Green Serpent." From D'Aulnoy's Fairy Tales. Trans. J. R. Planché. Illustr. Gordon Browne and Lydia F. Emmet. London: Routledge, 1865.

beasts, and are strange anticipations of the more sedate "Beauty and the Beast." Some of her heroines are whipped, incarcerated, and tantalized by grotesque fairies or sinister princes. Some of her heroes are treated brutally by ugly fairies who despise them because they want to marry an innocent, beautiful princess. Many of her tales end tragically because the protagonists cannot protect themselves from those forces undermining their natural love.

The cruel events, torture, and grotesque transformations in d'Aulnoy's tales were not exceptional in the fairy tales written by women. In "The Discreet Princess" (1695) Mlle Lhéritier has Finette brutalize the prince on three different occasions before she mercifully allows him to die. In "Ricky with the Tuft" (1696) Mlle Bernard ends her tale by placing her heroine in a most cruel dilemma with two ugly gnomes. Mlle de la Force depicts a cruel king as murderer in "The Good Woman" (1697), and his ferociousness knows no bounds, while in "Fairer than a Fairy" (1697) she has a prince and princess demeaned and compelled to perform arduous tasks before they can marry and live in peace. Finally, Mme de Murat has a sadistic sprite place two lovers in an unbearable situation at the end of "The Palace of Revenge" (1698), and she often has sets of lovers deceive and maltreat each other, as in "Anguillette" (1698) and "Perfect Love" (1698).

However, women were not the only writers of fairy tales who wove violence and brutality into their tales. Perrault dealt with incest in "Donkey-Skin" (1794) and portrayed an ogre cutting the throats of his own daughters in "Tom Thumb" (1796). The Chevalier de Mailly had a penchant for transforming his protagonists into beasts, and in "The Queen of the Island of Flowers" (1798) he has a princess persecuted in a sadistic manner.

The brutality and sadomasochism in French fairy tales can be interpreted in two ways. On the one hand, it is apparent that the protagonist, whether male or female, had to suffer in order to demonstrate his or her nobility and tendresse. Therefore, a cruel trial or suffering became a conventional motif in the tales, part of the compositional technique to move the reader to empathize with the protagonist. On the other hand, much of the cruelty in the tales is connected to forced marriage or the separation of two lovers, who come together out of tender feelings for each other and not because their relationship has been arranged. Since many of the female writers had been victims of forced marriages or refused to marry in order to guard their independence, there is an apparent comment on love, courtship, and marriage in these tales that, despite all the sentimentality, was taken very seriously by the writers and their audiences.

In general, the fairy tales of the first phase of the vogue were very serious in tone and intent. Only here and there in the works of d'Aulnoy and Perrault do we find ironic and humorous touches. The fairy tales were meant to make readers realize how deceived they were if they compared their lives to the events of the fairy tales. There was no splendid paradise in Louis XIV's court, no genuine love, no reconciliation, no tenderness of feeling. All this could be, however, found in fairy tales, and in this regard the symbolic portrayal of the impossible was a rational endeavor on the part of the writers to illuminate the irrational and destructive tendencies of their times.

THE ORIENTAL FAIRY TALE

The second phase of the fairy-tale vogue was only partially connected to the utopian critique of the first phase. The major change, the attraction to Oriental fairy tales, was due to the fact that the salons had abandoned the fairy-tale games, and the major writers of fairy tales had either died or been banished from Paris by 1704. To fill the gap, so to speak, some writers began to turn toward Oriental literature. (It is interesting to note that the classical literature of Greece and Rome was ignored again.) The most significant work of this period was Antoine Galland's translation *Les Mille et Une Nuits* (1704–17) of the Arabian collection of *The Thousand and One Nights*. Galland (1646–1715) had traveled and lived in the Middle East and had mastered Arabic, Hebrew, Persian, and Turkish. After he published the first four volumes of *The Thousand and One Nights*, they became extremely popular, and he continued translating the tales until his death. The final two volumes were published posthumously. Galland did more than translate. He actually adapted the tales to suit the tastes of his French readers, and he invented some of the plots and drew material together to form some of his own tales. His example was followed by Pétis de La Croix (1653–1713), who translated a Turkish work by Sheikh Zadah, the tutor of Amriath II, titled *L'Histoire de la Sultane de Perse et des Visirs. Contes turcs (The Story of the Sultan of the Persians and the Visirs. Turkish Tales)* in 1710. Moreover, he also translated a Persian imitation of *The Thousand and One Days*, which borrowed material from Indian comedies. Finally, there was the Abbé Jean-Paul Bignon's collection *Les Aventures d'Abdalla, fils d'Anif* (1712–14), which purported to be an authentic Arabic work in translation but was actually Bignon's own creative adaptation of Oriental tales mixed with French folklore.

Why all this interest in Oriental fairy tales?

One explanation is that the diminishing grandeur of King Louis XIV's court and the decline of France in general compelled writers to seek compensation in portrayals of exotic countries. Certainly, for the readers of that time, the Oriental tales had a unique appeal because so little was known about the Middle East. Of course, the men who stimulated the interest in the Oriental fairy tales were scholars; their reason for turning to Arabic, Persian, and Turkish folklore had more to do with their academic interests than with compensation for the decline of French glory. Whatever the reason for the second phase, it is important to point out that women stopped playing the dominant role and that the tales were no longer connected to the immediate interests of the aristocracy and haute bourgeoisie.

The Comic and Conventional Fairy Tale

By 1720, the interest in the literary fairy tale had diminished so that writers began parodying the genre, developing it along conventional lines or utilizing it for children's literature. Anne-Claude-Philippe de Caylus's tales in *Féerie novelles* (1741) and *Contes orientaux tirés des manuscrits de la bibliothèque du roi de France* (1743) are indicative of the endeavor to poke fun at the fairy-tale genre. De Caylus is not overly sarcastic but he does reverse the traditional courtly types to reveal how ridiculous they and the court are. Most of his narratives are short, dry, and witty and are connected to the style of caricature that he was developing at that time. Actually, his work had been preceded by Antoine Hamilton (c. 1646–1720), who had earlier written much longer burlesques of the Oriental trend in such tales as "Fleur d'Epine" and "Les Quatre Facardins," which were published posthumously after his death in 1730.

In a more serious vein, Mlle Lubert and Mme de Villeneuve carried on the salon tradition. For instance, Mlle Lubert, who rejected marriage in order to devote herself to writing, composed a series of long, intricate fairy tales from 1743 to 1755. Among them, "Princesse Camion" (1743) is a remarkable example of a sadomasochistic tale that is intriguing because of the different tortures and transformations that she kept inventing to dramatize the suffering of her protagonists. Mlle de Villeneuve's major contribution to the fairy tale had more to do with her ability to transcribe a discourse on true love and class differences in marriage into a classic fairy tale, "Beauty and the Beast" (1740), than with writing a horror fairy tale like Mlle de Lubert. Mme de Villeneuve's tale employs almost all the traditional fairy-tale and folklore motifs in a conventional manner, but to her credit, she was the first writer to develop the plot of "Beauty and the Beast" as we generally know it today. Her addition of dream sequences was an innovative touch that later writers of fairy tales such as Novalis and E. T. A. Hoffmann were able to develop more fully.

The "conventionalization" of the salon tale meant that the genre had become part of the French cultural heritage and was open to parody, as we have seen, but also open to more serious cultivation, as in the works of Mlle de Lubert and Mme de Villeneuve. More important, it meant that the literary fairy tale could convey standard notions of propriety and morality that reinforced the socialization process in France. What might have been somewhat subversive in the salon fairy tale was often "conventionalized" to suit the tastes and values of the dominant classes and the regime by the middle of the eighteenth century. This was the period when there was a great debate about the meaning of *civilité*, and literature was regarded as a means of socialization through which norms, mores, and manners were to be diffused. Therefore, it is not by chance that the literary fairy tale for children was actually established during the eighteenth century by Mme Leprince de Beaumont, not by Mme d'Aulnoy or Perrault. Both the debate about civility and the acceptance of the fairy tale as a proper literary genre had to reach a certain stage before the tale could be conventionalized as children's literature.

It is extremely important to note that Mme Leprince de Beaumont's shorter version of Mme de Villeneuve's "Beauty and the Beast" was published in an educational book titled *Magasin des Enfans* in 1757. In fact, she published several fairy tales in this volume, all with the didactic purpose of demonstrating to little girls how they should behave in different situations. Therefore, her "Beauty and the Beast" is one that preaches domesticity and self-sacrifice for women, and her "Prince Désir" and "Princess Mignone," based on an old Breton folk tale, is one that teaches a lesson about flattery and narcissism. Mme Leprince de Beaumont's conventionalizing the fairy tale for pedagogic purposes led to the undermining of the subversive and utopian qualities of the earlier tales. However, conventionalization did not necessarily bring about a total watering down and depletion of the unusual ideas and motifs of the literary fairy tale and folk tale. It actually led to a more general acceptance and institutionalization of the literary fairy tale as a genre for all ages and classes of readers. Such institutionalization set the framework within which other writers would create and play with those motifs, characters, and topoi that had been developed, and revise them in innovative ways to generate new forms, ideas, and motifs.

For instance, as I already mentioned in the previous chapter, many of the literary fairy tales of the 1690s and early part of the eighteenth century found their way into very cheap popular books published in a series called the *Bibliothèque Bleue* (known in England as chapbooks) and distributed by traveling book peddlers called colporteurs. The tales were rewritten (often drastically) and reduced in a more simple language so that the tales, when read in villages, were taken over by the peasants again and incorporated into the folklore. These tales were told and retold thousands of times and reentered the literary fairy-tale genre through fairy-tale writers exposed to this amalgamated "folklore." The interaction between the oral and literary retellings of tales became one of the most important features in the development of the literary genre as it was institutionalized in the eighteenth century. The most obvious sign that the literary fairy tale had become an institution in France was the publication by Charles Mayer of *Le Cabinet des fées* (1785–89), a forty-one-volume set of the most well-known salon fairy, comical, and conventional fairy tales of the preceding century. From this point on, the French literary fairy tales were disseminated and made their mark through translations in most of the Western world.

In point of fact, then, though the original French fairy tales are no longer read, they have never been forgotten. They have come down to us in various forms and have inspired writers including Goethe, the Brothers Grimm, Andersen, George Sand, and numerous others. The literary fairy tale keeps thriving and makes itself felt not only through literature in remarkable works by such contemporary authors as Angela Carter, Margaret Atwood, Michel Tournier, Michael Ende, A. S. Byatt, Jane Yolen, and others, but also through stage adaptations, radio programs, films, television shows, and Internet sites. The best of the contemporary fairy tales also keep alive the utopian quest and the questioning spirit of the earlier salon tales. Written out of dissatisfaction with their times, these fairy tales still have a unique charm, something captivating that is not confined to the particular historical period in which they were conceived and written. They embrace the future. They anticipate hopes and wishes that we ourselves have yet to fulfill. In that sense, they are still modern, and — who knows? — may even open up alternatives to our postmodern dilemmas.

three

The Splendor of the Arabian Nights

No other work of Oriental literature has had such a profound influence on the Western world as *The Thousand and One Nights*. First translated into French between 1704 and 1717 by Antoine Galland (1646–1715), a gifted Orientalist, the *Nights* spread quickly throughout Europe and then to North America. The amazing success of the *Nights* was due largely to the remarkable literary style of Galland's work, which was essentially an adaptation of an Arabic manuscript of Syrian origins and oral tales that he recorded in Paris from a Maronite Christian Arab from Aleppo named Youhenna Diab or Hanna Diab. Galland was born in Picardy and studied at the Collège du Plessis in Paris. His major field of study was classical Greek and Latin, and in 1670, thanks to his command of these languages, he was called upon to assist the French ambassador in Greece, Syria, and Palestine. After a brief return to Paris in 1674, he worked with the ambassador in Constantinople from 1677 to 1688 during which time he perfected his knowledge of Turkish, modern Greek, Arabic, and Persian. In addition he collected valuable manuscripts and coins for the ambassador. Back in Paris, he devoted the rest of his life to Oriental studies and published historical and philological works such as *Paroles remarkables, bons mots et maximes des Orientaux* (*Remarkable Words, Sayings and Maxims of the Orientals*, 1694). One of his great achievements was to assist Barthélemy d'Herbelot compile the *Bibliothèque orientale*, which was the first major encyclopedia of Islam with more than eight thousand entries about Middle Eastern people, places, and things. When d'Herbelot died in 1695, Galland continued his work and published the completed dictionary in 1697. But, by far, Galland's major contribution to European and Oriental literature was his translation or, one could say, "creation" of the *Nights*, which began during the 1690s when he obtained a manuscript of "The Voyages of Sinbad" and published the Sinbad stories in 1701 (fig. 4). Due to the success of this work, he began translating and adapting a four-volume Arabic manuscript in French and added such stories as "Prince Ahmed and the Fairy Pari-Banou," "Aladdin," "Ali Baba," and "Prince Ahmed and His Two Sisters." By the time the last volume of his *Nights* was published posthumously in 1717, he had fostered a vogue for Oriental literature and had altered the nature of the literary fairy tale in Europe and North America.

In addition to this literary vogue, the enormous European interest and curiosity about the Orient, stimulated through trade and travel reports, contributed to the popularity of the *Nights*. At first the tales were famous chiefly among the literate classes, who had direct access to the different English, German, Italian, and Spanish translations of Galland's work. However, because of their exotic appeal, there were many cheap and bowdlerized editions of the *Nights* in the eighteenth century that enabled the tales to be diffused among the common people and become part of their oral tradition. Moreover, they were also sanitized and adapted for children so that, by the end of the nineteenth century, the *Arabian Nights* had become a household name in most middle-class families in Europe and North America, an important source of knowledge about Arabic culture for intellectuals, and known by word of mouth among the great majority of the people.

The development of the *Nights* from the Oriental oral and literary traditions of the Middle Ages into a classical work for Western readers is a fascinating one. The tales in the collection can be traced to three ancient oral cultures — Indian, Persian, and Arab — and they probably circulated in the vernacular hundreds of years before they were written down some time between the ninth and fourteenth centuries. The apparent model for the literary versions of the tales was a Persian book

Figure 4. "*Sinbad.*" From The Arabian Nights' Entertainments. *Illustr. Louis Rhead. New York: Harper, 1916.*

titled *Hezâr afsân* (A Thousand Stories), translated into Arabic in the ninth century as *Alf laylah wa-laylah* (A Thousand and One Nights), for it provided the framework story of a caliph who kills his wife because she betrays him. Then, for the next three years, he takes a new wife and slays her each night after taking her maidenhead to avenge himself on women. He is finally diverted from this cruel custom by a vizier's daughter, assisted by her slave-girl. During the next seven centuries, various storytellers, scribes, and scholars began to record the tales from this collection and others and to shape them either independently or within the framework of the Sheherezade/Shahriyâr narrative. The tellers and authors of the tales were anonymous, and their styles and language differed greatly; the only common distinguishing feature was the fact that they were written in a colloquial language called Middle Arabic that had its own peculiar grammar and syntax. By the fifteenth century there were three distinct layers that could be detected in the collection of those tales that formed the nucleus of what became known as *The Thousand and One Nights*: (1) Persian tales that had some Indian elements and had been adapted into Arabic by the tenth century; (2) tales recorded in Baghdad between the tenth and twelfth centuries; and (3) stories written down in Egypt between the eleventh and fourteenth centuries. By the nineteenth century, the time of Richard Burton's unexpurgated translation, *The Book of the Thousand Nights and a Night* (1885–86), there were four "authoritative" Arabic editions, more than a dozen manuscripts in Arabic, and the Galland work, which one could draw from and include as part of the tradition of the *Nights*. The important Arabic editions are as follows:

> *Calcutta I*, 1814–18, 2 vols. (also called the Shirwanee Edition)
> *Bulak*, 1835, 2 vols. (also called the Cairo Edition)
> *Calcutta II*, 1839–42, 4 vols. (also called the W. H. Macnaghten Edition)
> *Breslau*, 1825–38, 8 vols. (edited by Maximilian Habicht)

In English, the Burton translation became the basis for numerous books for adults and children in the twentieth century. Considered one of the greatest scholar-explorers of the nineteenth century, Burton (1821–90) was the son of a retired lieutenant colonel and educated in France and Italy during his youth. By the time he enrolled at Trinity College, Oxford, in 1840, he could speak French and Italian fluently, along with the Béarnais and Neapolitan dialects, and he had an excellent command of Greek and Latin. In fact, he had such an extraordinary gift as a linguist that he eventually learned twenty-five other languages and fifteen dialects. Yet, this ability was not enough to help him adapt to life and the proscriptions at Oxford. He soon encountered difficulties with the Oxford administration and was expelled in 1842. His troubles there may have been due to the fact that he was raised on the Continent and never felt at home in England. Following in his father's footsteps, he enlisted in the British army and served eight years in India as a subaltern officer. During his time there, he learned Arabic, Hindi, Marathi, Sindhi, Punjabi, Teugu, Pashto, and Miltani, which enabled him to carry out some important intelligence assignments. He was eventually forced to resign from the army because some of his espionage work became too controversial. After a brief respite (1850–52) with his mother in Boulogne, France, during which time he published four books on India, Burton explored the Nile Valley and was the first Westerner to visit forbidden Muslim cities and shrines. In 1855 he participated in the Crimean War, then explored the Nile again (1857–58), and took a trip to Salt Lake City, Utah (1860), to do research for a biography of Brigham Young. In 1861, Burton married Isabel Arundell, the daughter of an aristocratic family, and accepted a position as consul in Fernando Po, a Spanish island off the coast of West Africa, until 1864. Thereafter, he was British consul in Santos, Brazil (1864–68), Damascus, Syria (1868–71), and finally Trieste, Italy, until his death in 1890. Wherever he went, Burton wrote informative anthropological and ethnological studies such as *Sindh, and the Races that Inhabit the Valley of the Indus* (1851) and *Pilgrimage to El-Medinah and Mecca* (1855–56), composed his own poetry such as *The Kasidah* (1880), translated unusual works of erotica, such as *Kuma Sutra of Vatsyayana* (1883), as well as collections of folk tales such as Giambattiste Basile's *The Pentamerone* (1893). Altogether he published forty-three volumes about his explorations and travels, more than one hundred articles, and thirty volumes of translations.

Burton's *Nights* is generally recognized as one of the finest *unexpurgated* translations of William Hay Macnaghten's *Calcutta II Edition* (1839–42). The fact is, however, that Burton "plagiarized" a good deal of his translation from John Payne's *The Book of the Thousand Nights and One Night* (1882–84) so that he could publish his book quickly and acquire the private subscribers to Payne's edition. Payne (1842–1916), a remarkable translator and scholar of independent means, had printed only five hundred copies of his excellent unexpurgated edition, for he had not expected much of a demand for the expensive nine-volume set. However, there were one thousand more subscribers who wanted his work, and since he was indifferent with regard to publishing a second edition, Burton received Payne's permission to offer his "new" translation to these subscribers about a year after Payne's work had appeared. Moreover, Burton profited a great deal from Payne's spadework (apparently with Payne's knowledge). This is not to say that Burton's translation (which has copious anthropological notes and an important "Terminal Essay") should not be considered his work. He did most of the translation by himself, and only toward the end of his ten volumes did he apparently plagiarize, most likely without even realizing what he was doing. In contrast to Payne, Burton was more meticulous in respecting word order and the exact phrasing of the original; he included the division into nights with the constant intervention of Sheherezade and was more competent in translating the verse. Moreover, he was insistent on emphasizing the erotic and bawdy aspects of the *Nights*. As he remarked in his introduction, his object was "to show what *The Thousand Nights and a Night* really is. Not, however, for reasons to be more full stated in the 'Terminal Essay,' by straining *verbum reddere verbo*, but by writing as the Arab would have written in English."

The result was a quaint, if not bizarre and somewhat stilted, English that makes for difficult reading today. Even in his own day his language was obsolete, archaic, and convoluted. Although Burton and John Payne, whose translation preceded Burton's, relied on the *Calcutta II* and *Breslau* editions for their translations, neither these two nor the other editions can be considered canonical or definitive. There was never a so-called finished text by an identifiable author or editor. In fact, there were never 1,001 nights or stories; the title was originally *One Thousand Stories*, and the Persian term *hazâr* only indicated an exceedingly large number. When and why the tales came to be called *The Thousand and One Nights* in Arabic is unclear. The change in the title may stem from the fact that an odd number in Arabic culture is associated with luck and fortune. The editions vary with regard to contents and style, and though there is a common nucleus, as Hussain Haddawy has demonstrated in what are the two best contemporary translations, *The Arabian Nights* (1990) and *The Arabian Nights II* (1995), the versions of the same tale are often different. Nevertheless, together the various editions, along with the manuscripts and Galland's work, can be considered to constitute what has become accepted in the West as *The Thousand and One Nights*. In sum, as Robert Irwin pointed out in *The Arabian Nights: A Companion*, "the *Nights* are really more like the New Testament, where one cannot assume a single manuscript source, nor can one posit a fixed canon. Stories may have been added and dropped in each generation," including today.

As already mentioned, the tales of the *Nights* have been published in all Western languages either separately or in collections of different kinds ever since the eighteenth century. However, as Burton remarked — and without trying to sound like a purist — "the *Nights* are nothing without the nights." That is, the Sheherezade framework is essential for the collection, and Sheherezade sets the tone for the employment of the narratives, even though they were probably created by different authors: It is she who provides the raison d'être for the tales, the driving impulse, and without comprehending why she was "invented," the *Nights* cannot be understood.

Given the patriarchal nature of Arabic culture, it would seem strange that Sheherezade assumed the key role in the *Nights*. Yet, a woman exercised more power in Muslim culture during the Middle Ages in Baghdad and Cairo than is commonly known. Not only did she receive a dowry when she married and shared in the disposition of the property with her husband, but she also was the absolute ruler of the home, children, and slaves. In particular, she was responsible for the children's early education, choice of faith, marriage, and profession. Perhaps most important, sexual initiation was a major part of her responsibility. In short, the wife was in charge of civilizing the children of a family more than the husband, and if we consider that the *Nights* are primarily concerned with the acquisition of manners and mores, it is clear why Sheherezade should exercise such a pivotal role in the collection: Not only does she cure Shahriyâr's madness, ostensibly caused by another woman (perhaps even his mother, as some psychologically minded critics have suggested), but she also produces an entertaining manual for listeners who will not survive or become humane without learning the Muslim social code of that time. Far from being a "feminist" prototype, she plays an exemplary conservative role in the *Nights*. As Robert Irwin points out in his essay "Political Thought in the Nights," "Submission to God, submission to Fate, and submission to the ruler dominate rather a large number of the stories. The political direction is determined at the outset, when Sheherezade, rather than thinking of how to overthrow the tyrant Shahriyâr, instead proceeds to entertain him with stories." Yet, as Sadhana Naithani clarifies in her perceptive article "The Teacher and the Taught: Structures and Meaning in the *Arabian Nights* and the *Panchatantra*":

> Shahrazâd [Sheherezade] does not have the opportunity of formalized teaching to present high and lofty goals in an authoritative manner but the power to informally relativize the listener's place in this world. She not only makes him see himself with reference to the others but also to accept and respect another — a woman — as "teacher" and thereby himself as the taught. She erases distortion not by justification but by replacing it with a realistic image. ... Shahrazâd is not a magician but a teacher, who reveals the true purpose of her magic without fearing that its effect may evaporate. Shahrazâd practices what Vishnu Sharma had set out to teach: the intelligent art of living.

The listener is not just the fictitious Shahriyâr, but also Dunazade and the implicit readers of the texts, then and now. That is, the figure of Sheherezade has a threefold purpose in telling her tale: (1) She wants to reeducate Shahriyâr and return him to the world of civilization and humanity. His reaction to his wife's betrayal has been so extreme and his wound so deep that he has apparently been reacting to some traumatic experience suffered during his childhood. In other words, he may have been abused by his mother or other women during his youth, and Sheherezade's narrative is the means through which he can regain trust in women and come to see that they have many different sides to them. (2) Sheherezade's other major auditor is her younger sister, Dunazade, and she obviously wants to relate all her wisdom through the tales to her so that Dunazade will know how to fend for herself in the years to come. Like Sheherezade, Dunazade has witnessed the three-year reign of terror by Shahriyâr, but unlike Sheherezade, who is a most accomplished scholar and confident woman, she does not have the means to contend with the caliph and his autocratic rule. Through listening to her sister's tales as the representative of other young Muslim virgins, she will be prepared to cope with men like Shahriyâr and to turn a male social code to her advantage. In fact, Sheherezade teaches Dunazade how to plot and narrate her own destiny to achieve an autonomous voice, which receives due respect from Shahriyâr at the conclusion of all the tales. (3) Aside from educating her sister and Shahriyâr, the two fictitious listeners, Sheherezade's function as storyteller is to socialize the Muslim readers/listeners of her time and all future readers, who may be unaware of Muslim custom and law. That is, once the frame was invented that allowed for the incorporation of different narratives, the anonymous editors of the *Nights* consistently and purposely chose a core of forty-two tales that continually reappeared in the four different Arabic editions and Galland's work. Without disregarding the entertaining and humorous aspects of these stories, they are primarily *lessons* in etiquette, aesthetics, decorum, religion, government, history, and sex. They have urban settings and bring together criminals, confidence men, and members of the wealthy classes. Together they represent a compendium of the religious beliefs and superstitions of the time. They also convey the aspirations and wishes of a strong middle class, for most of the tales concern merchants and artisans, who, like Sinbad and Junar, continually take risks to make their fortune. Since they are daring and adventurous, they can only survive through cunning, faith in Allah, and mastery of words. That is, there is an artistic side to them. Like Sheherezade, most of the protagonists are creative types, who save themselves and fulfill their destiny because they can weave the threads of their lives together in narratives that bring their desires in harmony with divine and social laws. Narration is raised to an art par excellence, for the nights are paradoxically moments of light, epiphanies, through which the listeners gain insight into the mysteries and predicaments that might otherwise overwhelm them and keep them in darkness.

Four of the major tales, "The Merchant and the Jinnee," "The Fisherman and the Jinnee," "The Tale of the Three Apples," and "The Hunchback,"

of different genres, some with lessons commensurate with Sheherezade's task of educating Shahriyâr and Dunazade; others with representations of the conditions and mores of medieval Oriental culture in the broadest sense. "The Ebony Horse" and "Julnar the Mermaid" are remarkable fairy tales that make use of numerous folk from different social classes and are based on the traditional plot of the young prince compelled to undergo arduous tasks before he is allowed to marry the princess of his choice. "Prince Behram and the Princess Al-Datma" is a delightful example of one of the early folk versions of *The Taming of the Shrew* that found its German expression later in the Grimms' "King Thrushbeard." Whereas a haughty woman is put in her place here, "The Wily Dalilah" is a hilarious anecdote about a crafty woman and her daughter who put an entire city of men in their place. Like "The Tale about the Thief of Alexandria and the Chief of Police," it mocks the judicial system in Egypt and expresses sympathy with those who dare to break the law, especially when the law itself is ridiculous. There is also a subversive quality to the fables and parables contained in "The Hedgehog and the Pigeons," whereas such tales as "Judar and His Brothers" and "Sinbad the Seaman and Sinbad the Landsman" are much more serious in the themes centered on humility. Both are fairy tales that draw their material from Egyptian, Persian, and Greek oral traditions and celebrate the rise of the mercantile classes. At the very least, the dreams of the merchant classes are fulfilled. Judar, though poisoned by his evil brothers, rises to become a great caliph, while Sinbad becomes as wealthy as the caliph of Baghdad.

The constant appeal to Allah in all the tales indicates that the characters have little faith in the temporal order that is either unjust or breaks down. Despite the long period of congestion and the different authors/editors, the tales are consistent in the way they live, from the tension between individual desire and social law. As Burton recognized, despite the fantastical elements, the tales tell life as it is; they expose hypocrisy, deceit, and, most of all, despotism. In fact, in the figure of Sheherezade, they favor the oppressed who live according to the high standards of the social code. Thus, thanks to Allah or Fortune, their deepest desires are fulfilled in ways they had thought were unimaginable. Yet, everything is imaginable in the *Nights*, and it is no doubt the miraculous realization of the unimaginable in the tales that drew and still draws readers to the *Nights* today.

In regard to the development of the fairy tale as genre in the West, *The Thousand and One Nights* played and continues to play a unique role. From the moment Galland translated and invented his *Nights*, the format, style, and motifs of the so-called Arabian tales had a profound effect on how other European writers were to define and conceive fairy tales. In some respects, the *Nights* are more important and famous in the West than they are in the Orient. Robert Irwin discusses this point in his chapter on the European and American "children of the nights" in his critical study. He shows how numerous authors were clearly influenced by *The Thousand and One Nights*: in France, Antoine Hamilton, Thomas Simon Guellette, Crébilon fils, Denis Diderot, Jacques Cazotte Voltaire; in England, Joseph Addison, Samuel Johnson, William Beckford, Horace Walpole, Robert Southey, Samuel Coleridge, Thomas De Quincey, George Meredith, and Robert Louis Stevenson; in Germany, Wilhelm Heinrich Wackenroder, Friedrich Schiller, Wilhelm Hauff, and Hugo von Hofmannsthal; in America, Washington Irving, Edgar Allan Poe, and Herman Melville. In recent times such gifted writers as John Barth, Jorge Luis Borges, Steven Millhauser, and Salman Rushdie have given evidence of their debt to the *Nights*. In particular it was Borges, who in his essay, "The Translators of the 1001 Nights," superbly summed up the ironic significance that the Arabian tales had and will continue to have for the literary fairy tale and readers of fairy tales in the West: "Enno Littmann observes that *The 1001 Nights* is, more than anything, a collection of marvels. The universal imposition of that sense of the marvelous on all Occidental minds is the work of Galland. Let there be no doubt of that. Less happy than we, the Arabs say they have little regard for the original; they know already the men, the customs, the talismans, the deserts, and the demons that those histories reveal to us."

four

Once There Were Two Brothers Named Grimm

Many are the fairy tales and myths that have been spread about the Brothers Grimm, Jacob and Wilhelm. For a long time it was believed that they had wandered about Germany and gathered their tales from the lips of doughty peasants and that all their tales were genuinely German. Although much of what had been believed has been disproved by recent scholarship, new rumors and debates about the Grimms keep arising. For instance, one literary scholar has charged them with manufacturing the folk spirit of the tales in order to dupe the general public in the name of nationalism. Other critics have found racist and sexist components in the tales that they allege need expurgation, while psychologists and educators battle over the possible harmful or therapeutic effects of the tales. Curiously, most of the critics and most of the introductions to the English translations of the Grimms' tales say very little about the brothers themselves or their methods for collecting the tales — as though the Grimms were incidental to their tales. Obviously, this is not the case, and there is a story here worth telling.

Just who were the Brothers Grimm and how did they discover those tales, which may be the most popular in the world today? Why and how did the brothers change the tales? And what is the significance of the magic of those tales today?

I

A fairy-tale writer could not have created a more idyllic and propitious setting for the entrance of the Brothers Grimm into the world. Their father, Philipp Wilhelm Grimm, a lawyer, was ambitious, diligent, and prosperous, and their mother, Dorothea (née Zimmer), daughter of a city councilman in Kassel, was a devoted and caring housewife, even though she tended at times to be melancholy. Initially they settled in the quaint village of Hanau, and during the first twelve years of their marriage, there were nine births, out of which six children survived: Jacob Ludwig Grimm (1785–1863), Wilhelm Carl Grimm (1786–1859), Carl Friedrich Grimm (1787–1852), Ferdinand Philipp Grimm (1788–1844), Ludwig Emil Grimm (1790–1863), and Charlotte Amalie (Lotte) Grimm (1793–1833). By 1791 the family had moved to Steinau, near Kassel, where Philipp Grimm had obtained an excellent position as district judge (*Amtmann*) and soon became the leading figure of the town. He and his family lived in a large comfortable home there and had servants to help with the domestic chores. As soon as the children were of age, they were sent to a local school, where they were given a classical education. They also received strict religious training in the Reform Calvinist Church. Both Jacob and Wilhelm were bright, hardworking pupils and were distinctly fond of country life. Their familiarity with farming, nature, and peasant customs and superstitions would later play a major role in their research and work in German folklore. At first, though, both boys appeared destined to lead comfortable lives, following in the footsteps of their father, whose seal was *Tute si recte vixeris* — "Honesty is the best policy in life." To be sure, this was the path that Jacob and Wilhelm took, but it had to be taken without the guidance of their father.

Philipp Grimm died suddenly in 1796 at the age of forty-four, and his death was traumatic for the entire family. Within weeks after his death, Dorothea Grimm had to move out of the large house and face managing the family of six children without servants or much financial support. From this point on, the family was totally dependent on outside help, particularly on Henriette Zimmer, Dorothea's sister, who was a lady-in-waiting for the princess of Hessia-Kassel. Henriette arranged for Jacob and Wilhelm to study at the prestigious Lyzeum (high school) in Kassel and obtained provisions and funds for the family.

Although the brothers were different in temperament — Jacob was more introverted, serious, and robust; Wilhelm was outgoing, gregarious, and asthmatic — they were inseparable and totally devoted to each other. They shared the same room and bed and developed the same work habits: In high school the Grimms studied more than twelve hours a day and were evidently bent on proving themselves to be the best students at the Lyzeum. That they were treated by some teachers as socially inferior to the other "high-born" students only served to spur their efforts to distinguish themselves as young scholars. In fact, the Grimms had to struggle against social slights and financial deprivation during a good part of their lives, but they never forgot their father's motto, *Tute si recte vixeris*, and they became famous not only because of their extraordinary scholarship but also because of their great moral integrity.

Although each one graduated from the Lyzeum at the head of his class, Jacob in 1802 and Wilhelm in 1803, they both had to obtain special dispensations to study law at the University of Marburg because their social standing was not high enough to qualify them. Once at the university they had to confront yet another instance of injustice, for most of the students from wealthier families received stipends, while the Grimms had to pay for their own education and live on a small budget. This inequity made them feel even more compelled to prove themselves, and at Marburg they drew the attention of Professor Friedrich Karl von Savigny, the genial founder of the historical school of law. Savigny argued that the spirit of a law could be comprehended only by tracing its origins to the development of the customs and language of the people and by paying attention to the changing historical context in which laws developed. Ironically, it was Savigny's emphasis on the philological aspect of law that led Jacob and Wilhelm to dedicate themselves to the study of ancient German literature and folklore. This decision was made in 1805 after Savigny had taken Jacob to Paris to assist him in research on the history of Roman law. Upon returning to Germany in 1806, Jacob left the university and rejoined his mother, who had moved to Kassel. Given the pecuniary situation of the family, it was Jacob's duty, as head of the family now, to support his brothers and sister, and he found a position as secretary for the Kassel War Commission, which made decisions pertaining to the war with France. Fortunately for Jacob, he was able to pursue his study of old German literature and customs on the side while Wilhelm remained in Marburg to complete his legal studies.

The correspondence between Jacob and Wilhelm during this time reflects their great concern for the welfare of their family. With the exception of Ludwig, who later became an accomplished painter and also illustrated the fairy tales, the other children had difficulty establishing careers for themselves. Neither Carl nor Ferdinand displayed the intellectual aptitude that the two oldest brothers did or the creative talents of Ludwig. Carl eventually tried his hand at business and ended up destitute as a language teacher, while Ferdinand tried many different jobs in publishing and later died in poverty. Lotte's major task was to assist her mother, who died in 1808. After that, Lotte managed the Grimm household until she married a close friend of the family, Ludwig Hassenpflug, in 1822. Hassenpflug became an important politician in Germany and eventually had a falling out with Jacob and Wilhelm because of his conservative and opportunistic actions as statesman.

While Ludwig, Carl, Ferdinand, and Lotte were young, they were chiefly the responsibility of Jacob, who looked after them like a stern father. Even Wilhelm regarded him as such and acknowledged his authority, not only in family matters, but also in scholarship. It was during the period from 1806 to 1810, when each of the siblings was endeavoring to make a decision about a future career and concerned about the stability of their home, that Jacob and Wilhelm began systematically gathering folk tales and other materials related to folklore. Clemens Brentano, a gifted romantic writer and friend, had requested that the Grimms help him collect tales for a volume that he intended to publish some time in the future. The Grimms responded by selecting tales from old books and recruiting the help of friends and acquaintances in Kassel. However, the Grimms were unable to devote all their energy to their research. Jacob lost his job on the War Commission in 1807, when Kassel was invaded by the French and became part of the Kingdom of Westphalia under the rule of Jerome Bonaparte. Soon thereafter, the Grimms' mother died, and it was imperative that Jacob find some new means of supporting the family. Although he had a strong antipathy to the French, he applied for the position of King Jerome's private librarian in Kassel and was awarded the post in 1808. This job enabled him to pursue his studies and help his brothers and sister. Meanwhile, Wilhelm had to undergo treatment for a heart disease in Halle. Ludwig began studying art at the Art Academy in Munich, and Carl began working as a businessman in Hamburg. From 1809 to 1813 there was a period of relative stability and security for the Grimm family, and Jacob and Wilhelm began publishing the results of their research on old German literature: Jacob wrote *On the Old German Meistergesang*, and Wilhelm, *Old Danish Heroic Songs*, both in 1811. Together they published in 1812 a study of the *Song of Hildebrand* and the *Wessobrunner Prayer*. Of course, their major publication at this time was the first volume of the *Kinder- und Hausmärchen* (*Children's and Household Tales*) with scholarly annotations, also in 1812.

The Napoleonic Wars and French rule had been upsetting to both Jacob and Wilhelm, who were dedicated to the notion of German unification. Neither wanted to see the restoration of oppressive German princes, but they did feel a deep longing to have the German people united in one nation through customs and laws of their own making. Thus, in 1813 they celebrated when the French withdrew from Kassel and the French armies were defeated throughout Central Europe. Jacob was appointed a member of the Hessian Peace Delegation and did diplomatic work in Paris and Vienna. During his absence Wilhelm was able to procure the position as secretary to the royal librarian in Kassel and to concentrate on bringing out the second volume of the *Children's and Household Tales* in 1815. When the peace treaty with the French was concluded in Vienna, Jacob returned home and was disappointed to find that the German princes were seeking to reestablish their narrow, vested interests in different German principalities and to discard the broader notion of German unification.

After securing the position of second librarian in the royal library of Kassel, Jacob joined Wilhelm in editing the first volume of *German Legends* in 1816. During the next thirteen years, the Grimms enjoyed a period of relative calm and prosperity. Their work as librarians was not demanding, and they could devote themselves to scholarly research and the publication of their findings. Together they published the second volume of *German Legends* (1818) and *Irish Elf Tales* (1826), while Jacob wrote the first volume of *German Grammar* (1819) and *Ancient German Law* (1828) by himself, and Wilhelm produced *The German Heroic Legend* (1829).

In the meantime, there were changes in the domestic arrangement of the Grimms. Lotte moved out of the house to marry Ludwig Hassenpflug in 1822, and a few years later, in 1825, Wilhelm married Dortchen Wild, the daughter of a pharmacist in Kassel. She had known both brothers for over twenty years and had been part of a group of storytellers who had provided the Grimms with numerous tales. Now it became her task to look after the domestic affairs of the brothers, for Jacob did not leave the house. Indeed, he remained a bachelor for his entire life and had very little time for socializing. The Grimms insisted on a quiet atmosphere and a rigid schedule at home so they could conduct their research without interruptions. Although Wilhelm continued to enjoy company and started a family — he had three children with Dortchen — he was just as much married to his work as Jacob was. Since Dortchen had been well acquainted with the brothers before her marriage, when she assumed her role in the family she fully supported their work and customary way of living.

In 1829, however, when the first librarian died and his position in Kassel became vacated, the Grimms' domestic tranquillity was broken. Jacob, who had already become famous for his scholarly publications, had expected to be promoted to this position. But he did not have the right connections or the proper conservative politics and was overlooked. In response to this, he and Wilhelm resigned their posts and, one year later, traveled to Götttingen, where Jacob became professor of old German literature and head librarian, and Wilhelm, librarian and, eventually, professor in 1835. Both were considered gifted teachers and broke new ground in the study of German literature, which had only recently become an accepted field of study at the university. Aside from their teaching duties, they continued to write and publish important works: Jacob wrote the third volume of *German Grammar* (1831) and a major study titled *German Mythology* (1835), while Wilhelm prepared the third edition of *Children's and Household Tales*. Although their positions were secure, there was a great deal of political unrest in Germany due to the severely repressive political climate that had developed since 1819. By 1830 many revolts and peasant uprisings had become frequent and began spreading, and a group of intellectuals known as Young Germany (*Jungdeutschland*) pushed for more democratic reform in different German principalities. For the most part, however, their members were persecuted and silenced, just as the peasants too were vanquished. Some leading writers, such as Ludwig Börne, Heinrich Heine, and Georg Büchner, took refuge in exile. The Brothers Grimm were not staunch supporters of the Young Germany movement, but they had always supported the liberal cause throughout Germany and were greatly affected by the political conflicts.

In 1837, when King Ernst August II succeeded to the throne of Hanover, he revoked the constitution of 1833 and dissolved parliament. In his attempt to restore absolutism to the kingdom of Hanover, of which Göttingen was a part, he declared that all civil servants must pledge an oath to serve him personally. Since the king was nominally the rector of the University of Göttingen, the Grimms were obligated to take an oath of allegiance, but instead they, along with five other professors, led a protest against the king and were summarily dismissed. Jacob was compelled to leave Göttingen immediately and returned to Kassel, where Wilhelm joined him a few months later.

Once again, they were in desperate financial straits. Despite the fact that they had received funds and support from hundreds of friends and admirers who supported their stand on academic freedom, the ruling monarchs of the different principalities prevented them from teaching at another university. It was during this time that Jacob and Wilhelm decided to embark on writing the *German Dictionary*, one of the most ambitious lexicographical undertakings of the nineteenth century. Though the income from this project would be meager, they hoped to support themselves through other publishing ventures as well. In the meantime, Bettina von Arnim, Friedrich Karl von Savigny, and other influential friends were trying to convince the new king of Prussia, Friedrich Wilhelm IV, to bring the brothers to Berlin. Finally, in November 1840, Jacob and Wilhelm received offers to become professors at the University of Berlin and to do research at the Academy of Sciences. It was not until March 1841, however, that the Grimms took up residence in Berlin and were able to continue their work on the *German Dictionary* and their scholarly research on other subjects. In addition to teaching, the Grimms played an active role in the institutionalization of German literature as a field of study at other universities and entered into political debates. When the Revolution of 1848 occurred in Germany, the Grimms were elected to the civil parliament, and Jacob was considered to be one of the most prominent men among the representatives at the National Assembly held in Frankfurt am Main. However, the brothers' hopes for democratic reform and the unification of the German principalities dwindled as one compromise after another was reached with the German monarchs. Both brothers retired from active politics after the demise of the revolutionary movement. In fact, Jacob resigned from his position as professor in 1848, the same year he published his significant study titled *The History of the German Language*. Wilhelm retired from his post as professor in 1852. For the rest of their lives, the Grimms devoted most of their energy to completing the monumental *German Dictionary*, but they got only as far as the letter F. Though they did not finish the *Dictionary*, a task that had to be left to scholars in the twentieth century, they did produce an astonishing number of remarkable books during their lifetimes: Jacob published twenty-one and Wilhelm fourteen. Together they produced eight. In addition, there are another twelve volumes of their essays and notes and thousands of important letters. The Grimms made scholarly contributions to the areas of folklore, philology, history, ethnology, religion, jurisprudence, lexicography, and literary criticism. Even when they did not work as a team, they shared their ideas and discussed all their projects together. When Wilhelm died in 1859, the loss affected Jacob deeply; he became even more solitary but did not abandon the projects he had held in common with his brother. In addition, the more he realized that his hopes for democratic reform were being dashed in Germany, the more he voiced his criticism of reactionary trends in Germany. Both Jacob and Wilhelm regarded their work as part of a social effort to foster a sense of justice among the German people and to create pride in the folk tradition. Jacob died in 1863, after completing the fourth volume of his book *German Precedents*. In German the title *Deutsche Weistümer* connotes a sense of the wisdom of the ages that he felt should be passed on to the German people.

II

Though the Grimms made important discoveries in their research on ancient German literature and customs, they were neither the founders of folklore as a study in Germany, nor the first to begin collecting and publishing folk and fairy tales. In fact, from the beginning their principal concern was to uncover the etymological and linguistic truths that bound the German people together and were expressed in their laws and customs. The fame of the Brothers Grimm as collectors of folk and fairy tales must be understood in this context, and even here, chance played a role in their destiny.

In 1806, Clemens Brentano, who had already published an important collection of folk songs titled *Des Knaben Wunderhorn* (*The Boy's Magic Horn*, 1805) with Achim von Arnim, was advised to seek out the aid of Jacob and Wilhelm Grimm because they were known to have a vast knowledge of old German literature and folklore. They were also considered to be conscientious and indefatigable workers. Brentano hoped to use whatever tales they might send him in a future publication of folk tales, and he was able to publish some of the songs they gathered in the second and third volumes of *Des Knaben Wunderhorn* in 1808. The Grimms believed strongly in sharing their research and findings with friends and congenial scholars, and between 1807 and 1812 they began collecting tales with the express purpose of sending them to Brentano, as well as of using them as source material for gaining a greater historical understanding of the German language and customs.

Contrary to popular belief, the Grimms did not collect their tales by visiting peasants in the countryside and writing the tales they heard. Their primary method was to invite storytellers to their home and then have them tell the tales aloud, which the Grimms either noted on first hearing or after a couple of hearings. Most of the storytellers during this period were educated young women from the middle class or aristocracy. For instance, in Kassel a group of young women from the Wild family (Dortchen, Gretchen, Lisette, and Marie Elisabeth), their mother (Dorothea), and the Hassenpflug family (Amalie, Jeanette, and Marie) used to meet regularly to relate tales they had heard from their nursemaids, governesses, and servants. In 1808, Jacob formed a friendship with

Werner von Haxthausen, who came from Westphalia, and in 1811, Wilhelm visited the Haxthausen estate and there became acquainted with
a circle of young men and women (Ludowine, Marianne, and August
von Haxthausen, and Jenny and Annette von Droste-Hülfshoff), whose
tales he noted. Still, the majority of the storytellers came from Hessia:
Dorothea Viehmann, a tailor's wife from nearby Zwehrn who used to
sell fruit in Kassel, would visit the Grimms and told them a good many
significant tales; and Johann Friedrich (Wachtmeister) Krause, an old
retired soldier, gave the brothers tales in exchange for some of their old
clothes. Many of the tales the Grimms recorded had French origins
because the Hassenpflugs were of Huguenot ancestry and spoke French
at home. Most of the brothers' informants were familiar with both oral
and literary traditions and would combine motifs from both sources. In
addition to the tales of these storytellers and others who came later, the
Grimms took tales directly from books and journals and edited them
according to their taste.

In 1810, when Brentano finally requested the Grimms' collection of
tales, the brothers had copies made and sent forty-nine texts to him.
They had copies made because they felt Brentano would take great
poetic license and turn them into substantially different tales, whereas
they were intent on using the tales to document basic truths about the
customs and practices of the German people, and on preserving their
authentic ties to the oral tradition. Actually, the Grimms need not have
worried about Brentano's use of their tales, for he never touched them
but abandoned them in the Ölenberg Monastery in Alsace. Only in
1920 were the handwritten tales rediscovered and published in different
editions in 1924, 1927, and 1974. The last publication by Heinz Rölleke
is the most scholarly and useful, for he has carefully shown how the
Grimms' original handwritten manuscripts can help us to document
their sources and reveal the great changes the brothers made in shaping
the tales.

As it happened, after the Grimms sent their collected texts to
Brentano, who was unreliable and was going through great personal
difficulties, they decided to publish the tales themselves and began
changing them and preparing them for publication. They also kept
adding new tales to their collection. Jacob set the tone, but the

brothers were very much in agreement about how they wanted to alter and stylize the tales. This last point is significant because some critics have wanted to see major differences between Jacob's and Wilhelm's approaches to editing the tales. These critics have argued that there was a dispute between the brothers after Wilhelm assumed major responsibility for the editing of the tales in 1815, and that Wilhelm transformed them against Jacob's will. There is no doubt that Wilhelm was the primary editor after 1815, but Jacob established the framework for their editing practice between 1807 and 1812, and even edited the majority of the tales for the first volume. A comparison of the way Jacob and Wilhelm worked both before and after 1815 does not reveal major differences, except that Wilhelm did take more care to refine the style and make the contents of the tales more acceptable for a children's audience or, really, for adults who wanted the tales censored for children. Otherwise, the editing of Jacob and Wilhelm exhibits the same tendencies from the beginning to the end of their project: the endeavor to make the tales stylistically smoother; the concern for clear sequential structure; the desire to make the stories more lively and pictorial by adding adjectives, old proverbs, and direct dialogue; the reinforcement of motives for action in the plot; the infusion of psychological motifs; and the elimination of elements that might detract from a rustic tone. The model for a good many of their tales was the work of the gifted artist Philipp Otto Runge, whose two stories in dialect, "The Fisherman and His Wife" and "The Juniper Tree," represented in tone, structure, and content the ideal narrative that the Grimms wanted to create.

And create they did. The Grimms were not merely collectors. In fact, their major accomplishment in publishing their two volumes of 156 tales in 1812 and 1815 was to create an ideal type for the literary fairy tale, one that sought to be as close to the oral tradition as possible, while incorporating stylistic, formal, and substantial thematic changes to appeal to a growing middle-class audience. By 1819, when the second edition of the tales, now in one volume that included 170 texts, was published and Wilhelm assumed complete charge of the revisions, the brothers had established the form and manner through which they wanted to preserve, contain, and present to the German public what they felt were profound truths about the origins of civilization. Indeed, they saw the "childhood of humankind" as embedded in customs that Germans had cultivated; the tales were to serve as reminders of such rich, natural culture.

After 1819 there were five more editions and sixty-nine new texts added to the collection, with twenty-eight original texts omitted. By the time the seventh edition appeared in 1857, there were 211 texts in all. Most of the additions after 1819 were from literary sources, and the rest were either sent to the brothers by informants or recorded from a primary source. Indeed, the chief task after 1819 was largely one of refinement: Wilhelm often changed the original texts by comparing them to different versions he had acquired. Although he evidently tried to retain what he and Jacob considered the essential message of the tale, he tended to make the tales more proper and prudent for bourgeois audiences. Thus it is crucial to be aware of the changes both brothers made between the original handwritten manuscript and the last edition of 1857. Compare the following, for example:

"Snow White" — Ölenberg Manuscript (1810)

When Snow White awoke the next morning, they asked her how she happened to get there. And she told them everything, how her mother, the queen, had left her alone in the woods and gone away. The dwarfs took pity on her and persuaded her to remain with them and do the cooking for them when they went to the mines. However, she was to beware of the queen and not to let anyone into the house.

"Snow White" — 1812 Edition

When Snow White awoke, they asked her who she was and how she happened to get into the house. Then she told them how her mother had wanted to have her put to death, but the hunter had spared her life, and how she had run the entire day and finally arrived at their house. So the dwarfs took pity on her and said, "If you keep house for us and cook, sew, make the beds, wash and knit, and keep everything tidy and clean, you may stay with us, and you will have everything you want. In the evening, when we come home, dinner must be ready. During the day we are in the mines and dig for gold, so you will be alone. Beware of the queen and let no one into the house."

"Rapunzel" — 1812 Edition

At first Rapunzel was afraid, but soon she took such a liking to the young king that she made an agreement with him: he was to come every day and be pulled up. Thus they lived merrily and joyfully for a certain time, and the fairy did not discover anything until one day when Rapunzel began talking to her and said, "Tell me, Mother Gothel, why do you think my clothes have become too tight for me and no longer fit?"

"Rapunzel" — 1857 Edition

When he entered the tower, Rapunzel was at first terribly afraid, for she had never laid eyes on a man before. However, the prince began to talk to her in a friendly way and told her that her song had touched his heart so deeply that he had not been able to rest until he had seen her. Rapunzel then lost her fear, and when he asked her whether she would have him for her husband, and she saw that he was young and handsome, she thought, He'll certainly love me better than old Mother Gothel. So she said yes and placed her hand in his.

"I want to go with you very much," she said, "but I don't know how I can get down. Every time you come, you must bring a skein of silk with you, and I'll weave it into a ladder. When it's finished, then I'll climb down, and you can take me away on your horse."

They agreed that until then he would come to her every evening, for the old woman came during the day. Meanwhile, the sorceress did not notice anything, until one day Rapunzel blurted out, "Mother Gothel, how is it that you're much heavier than the prince? When I pull him up, he's here in a second."

"The Three Spinners" — 1812 Edition

In olden times there lived a king who loved flax spinning more than anything in the world, and his queen and daughters had to spin the entire day. If he did not hear the wheels humming, he became angry. One day he had to take a trip, and before he departed, he gave the queen a large box with flax and said, "I want this flax spun by the time I return."

"The Three Spinners" — 1857 Edition

There once was a lazy maiden who did not want to spin, and no matter what her mother said, she refused to spin. Finally, her mother became so angry and impatient that she beat her, and her daughter began to cry loudly. Just then the queen happened to be driving by, and when she heard the crying, she ordered the carriage to stop, went into the house, and asked the mother why she was beating her daughter, for her screams could be heard out on the street. The woman was too ashamed to tell the queen that her daughter was lazy and said, "I can't get her to stop spinning. She does nothing but spin and spin, and I'm so poor that I can't provide the flax."

"Well," the queen replied, "there's nothing I like to hear more than the sound of spinning, and I'm never happier than when I hear the constant humming of the wheels. Let me take your daughter with me to my castle. I've got plenty of flax, and she can spin as much as she likes."

As is evident from the above examples, the Grimms made major changes while editing the tales. They eliminated erotic and sexual elements that might be offensive to middle-class morality, added numerous Christian expressions and references, emphasized specific role models for male and female protagonists according to the dominant patriarchal code of that time, and endowed many of the tales with a "homey," or *biedermeier*, flavor by the use of diminutives, quaint expressions, and cute descriptions. Moreover, though the collection was not originally printed with children in mind as the primary audience — the first two volumes had scholarly annotations, which were later published separately — Wilhelm made all the editions from 1819 on more appropriate for children, or rather, to what he thought would be proper for children to learn. Indeed, some of the tales, such as "Mother Trudy" and "The Stubborn Child," are intended to be harsh lessons for children. Such didacticism did not contradict what both the Grimms thought the collection should be, namely an *Erziehungsbuch*, an educational manual. The tendency toward attracting a virtuous middle-class audience is most evident in the so-called *Kleine Ausgabe* (*Small Edition*), a selection of fifty tales from the *Grosse Ausgabe* (*Large Edition*). This *Small Edition* was first published in 1825 in an effort to popularize the larger work and to create a best seller. There were ten editions of this book, which contained the majority of the *Zaubermärchen* (the magic fairy tales), from 1825 to 1858. With such tales as "Cinderella," "Snow White," "Sleeping Beauty," "Little Red Riding Hood," and "The Frog King," all of which underline morals in keeping with the Protestant ethic and a patriarchal notion of sex roles, the book was bound to be a success.

III

The magic fairy tales were the ones that were the most popular and acceptable in Europe and America during the nineteenth century, but it is important to remember that the Grimms' collection also includes unusual fables, legends, anecdotes, jokes, and religious tales. The variety of their tales is often overlooked because only a handful have been selected by parents, teachers, publishers, and critics for special attention. This selective process is generally neglected when critics talk about the effects of the tales and the way they should be conveyed or not conveyed to children (fig. 5).

The Grimms' collection *Children's and Household Tales* was not an immediate success in Germany. In fact, Ludwig Bechstein's *Deutsches Märchenbuch* (*German Book of Fairy Tales*, 1845) was more popular for a time. However, by the 1870s the Grimms' tales had been incorporated into the teaching curriculum in Prussia and other German principalities, and they were also included in primers and anthologies for children throughout the Western world. By the beginning of the twentieth century, the *Children's and Household Tales* was second only to the Bible as a best seller in Germany and has continued to hold this position. Furthermore, there is no doubt that the Grimms' tales, published either together in a single volume or individually as illustrated books, enjoy the same popularity in the English-speaking world.

Such popularity has always intrigued critics, and advocates of various schools of thought have sought to analyze and interpret the "magic" of the Grimms' tales. Foremost among the critics are the folklorists, educators, psychologists, and literary critics of different persuasions, including structuralists, literary historians, semioticians, and Marxists. Each group has made interesting contributions to the scholarship on the Grimms' tales, although there are times when historical truths about the Grimms' work are discarded or squeezed to fit into a pet theory.

The efforts made by folklorists to categorize the Grimms' tales after the nineteenth century were complicated by the fact that numerous German folklorists used the tales to explain ancient German customs and rituals, under the assumption that the tales were authentic documents of the German people. This position, which overlooked the French and

Figure 5. "*Hansel and Gretel*." *From* Fairy Tales of the Brothers Grimm. *Trans. Mrs. Edgar Lucas. Illustr. Arthur Rackham. London: Constable, 1910.*

other European connections, led to an "Aryan" approach during the 1920s, 1930s, and 1940s, which allowed many German folklorists to interpret the tales along racist and elitist lines. Such an approach had always been contested by folklorists outside Germany, who viewed the tales as part of the vast historical development of the oral tradition, wherein the Grimms' collection is given special attention because of the mixture of oral and literary motifs. These motifs have been related by folklorists to motifs in other folk tales in an effort to find the origin of a particular motif or tale type and its variants. By doing this kind of research, folklorists have been able to chart distinctions in the oral traditions and customs of different countries.

Educators have not been interested in motifs so much as in the morals and the types of role models in the tales. Depending on the country and the educational standards in a particular historical period, teachers and school boards have often dictated which Grimms' tales are to be used or abused. Generally speaking, such tales as "The Wolf and the Seven Young Kids," "Cinderella," "Little Red Cap," and "Snow White" have always been deemed acceptable because they instruct children through explicit warnings and lessons, even though some of the implicit messages may be harmful to children. Most of the great pedagogical debates center around the brutality and cruelty in some tales, and the tendency among publishers and adapters of the tales has been to eliminate the harsh scenes. Consequently, Cinderella's sisters will not have their eyes pecked out; Little Red Cap and her grandmother will not be gobbled up by the wolf; the witch in "Snow White" will not be forced to dance in red-hot shoes; and the witch in "Hansel and Gretel" (fig. 5) will not be shoved into an oven.

Such changes have annoyed critics of various psychoanalytical persuasions, because they believe that the violence and conflict in the tales derive from profound instinctual developments in the human psyche, and hence represent symbolical modes by which children and adults deal with sexual problems. Most psychoanalytical critics take their cues from Freud, even if they have departed from his theories and have joined another school of analysis. One of the first important books about the psychological impact of the Grimms' tales was Josephine Belz's *Das Märchen und die Phantasie des Kindes* (*The Fairy Tale and the Imagination of the Child*, 1919) in which she tried to establish important connections between children's ways of fantasizing and the symbols in the tales. Later, Carl Jung, Erich Fromm, and Gerza Roheim wrote valuable studies of fairy tales that sought to go beyond Freud's theories. In the period following World War II, Aniela Jaffé, Joseph Campbell, and Maria von Franz charted the links between archetypes, the collective unconscious, and fairy tales, while Julius Heuscher and Bruno Bettelheim focused on Oedipal conflicts from neo-Freudian positions in their analyses of some Grimms' tales. Finally, André Favat published an important study, *Child and the Tale* (1977), which uses Piaget's notions of child development, interests, and stages of understanding to explore the tales and their impact. Although the various psychoanalytical approaches have shed light on the symbolical meanings of the tales from the point of view of particular schools of thought, the tales have often been taken out of context to demonstrate the value of a psychoanalytical theory, rather than to render a cultural and aesthetic appreciation and evaluation of the text.

Literary critics have reacted to the psychoanalytical approach in different ways. Influenced by the theories of Vladimir Propp (*Morphology of the Folktale*, 1968) and Max Lüthi (*Once Upon a Time*, 1970), formalists, structuralists, and semioticians have analyzed individual texts to discuss the structure of the tale, its aesthetic components and functions, and the hidden meanings of the signs. Literary historians and philologists such as Ludwig Denecke and Heinz Rölleke have tried to place the Grimms' work in a greater historical context in order to show how the brothers helped develop a mixed genre, often referred to as the *Buchmärchen* (book tale), combining aspects of the oral and literary tradition. Sociological and Marxist critics such as Dieter Richter, Christa Bürger, and Bernd Wollenweber have discussed the tales in light of the social and political conditions in Germany during the nineteenth century, and have drawn attention to the racist and sexist notions in the tales. In the process, they have added fuel to the debate among educators, and the use and abuse of the Grimms' tales remains a key issue even today among educators, psychologists, folklorists, and literary critics.

Though there were debates about the value of the tales during the Grimms' own lifetime, if they were alive today, they would probably be surprised to see how vigorous and violent some of the debates are and how different the interpretations tend to be. To a certain extent, the intense interest in their tales by so many different groups of critics throughout the world is a tribute to the Grimms' uncanny sense of how folk narratives inform cultures. They were convinced that their tales possessed essential truths about the origins of civilization, and they selected and revised those tales that would best express these truths. They did this in the name of humanity and *Kultur*: the Grimms were German idealists who believed that historical knowledge of customs, mores, and laws would increase self-understanding and social enlightenment. Their book is not so much a book of magic as it is a manual for education that seeks to go beyond the irrational. It is in their impulse to educate, to pass on the experiences of a variety of people who knew the lore of survival, that we may find the reasons why we are still drawn to the tales today. Though the Grimms imbued the tales with a heavy dose of Christian morality, the Protestant work ethic, and patriarchalism, they also wanted the tales to depict social injustices and possibilities for self-determination. Their tales reflect their concerns and the contradictions of their age. Today we have inherited their concerns and contradictions, and their tales still read like innovative strategies for survival. Most of all they provide hope that there is more to life than mastering the art of survival. Their "once upon a time" keeps alive our utopian longing for a better world that can be created out of our dreams and actions.

five

The "Merry" Dance of the Nutcracker

Discovering the World through Fairy Tales

how does a wooden nutcracker, decorated as an old-fashioned soldier, manage to conquer the world of ballet during Christmas time in America and many other countries every year? Who created this odd nutcracker? What is the real story behind this mysterious inanimate figure that comes alive to fight a wicked mouse?

I

In her illuminating book *"Nutcracker" Nation*, Jennifer Fisher explains in great detail how an old-world ballet from Russia became a modern Christmas ritual in the new world of America. Beginning with an account about the 1890 collaboration between Marius Petipa, a masterful choreographer, and Pyotr Ilich Tchaikovsky, the renowned Russian composer, she describes how Tchaikovsky unwillingly wrote the music to the choreography and libretto of Alexandre Dumas's "L'histoire d'un casse-noisette" ("The Story of a Nutcracker," 1845), which was an adaptation of E. T. A. Hoffmann's more famous tale "Der Nußknacker und der Mausekönig" ("The Nutcracker and the Mouse King," 1816) (fig. 6). Tchaikovsky was never satisfied with the libretto by Petipa and Ivan Alexandrovitch Vsevolojsky, who had used Dumas's sweetened version as the model for the story, and he had major difficulties with Petipa's choreography and felt it lacked cohesion. While writing the music, he took a trip to America to conduct several concerts and during that time his sister died, causing him grief and stress. Petipa took ill just as the rehearsals began, and his assistant Lev Ivanov assumed control of the ballet and made changes in the choreography. The premiere of the ballet at the St. Petersburg Imperial Theater in 1892 received mixed reviews, and though it continued to be performed in the early part of the twentieth century throughout Europe, *The Nutcracker* was not all that popular with audiences or with dancers. Nor had it ever been considered a favorite of children or families. The libretto, which was already an adulteration of the tales by Dumas and Hoffmann, was often shortened, altered, and choreographed anew by the different companies that performed the ballet, and the full ballet was rarely performed.

It was not until 1944, when Willam Christensen produced the first full-length production of *The Nutcracker* in San Francisco, that the ballet began to receive the attention it needed to become the classical ritual it is today. Christensen had been in touch with the brilliant Russian choreographer George Balanchine, who had advised him to stage the entire ballet in his original way, and Christensen soon realized its potential as a money-maker and crowd pleaser for families. He gradually began repeating it annually during the Christmas period. Balanchine followed suit in 1954 with his own unique spectacle in New York, and since that time there is not a winter season that goes by when *The Nutcracker* is not performed throughout the United States and other countries in various formats. Not only has the ballet been adopted by Americans for their Christmas celebration as a ritual for middle-class audiences, especially young girls, as has Charles Dickens's *The Christmas Carol*, but it has also been adapted for animated and live-action films, and there are numerous video cassettes and DVDs that offer recordings of live performances by famous European and American companies. All sorts of artifacts representing the wooden nutcracker have been manufactured, and the nutcracker has been transformed into a charming secular icon representing the joyful advent of the yuletide season.

Figure 6. "The Nutcracker and the Mouse King," illustrated by Theodor Hosemann in E.T.A. Hoffmann's Gesammelte Schriften, Berlin: Reimer, 1844–45.

II

But this brief story does not reveal fully how the wooden nutcracker became so famous. There is much more to tell, for the nutcracker's fame is not what E. T. A. Hoffmann (1776–1822) intended, or what he might have expected from his unusual fairy tale.

A gifted musician and writer, Hoffmann, who was the creator of the peculiar wooden nutcracker, certainly would have been pleased by Tchaikovsky's music, but he might have also been disappointed if not upset by the libretto and choreography. Hoffmann, a contemporary of the Grimms, sought to revolutionize the fairy-tale genre and wanted his readers to envision the world in a light different from how they normally saw it. His fairy tale was a provocation and a radical attempt to change the genre of the fairy tale for children. (Incidentally, he had already begun radicalizing the genre for adults with the publication of "The Golden Pot" in 1815.) Most of all he wanted to express his dissatisfaction with the neatly trimmed bourgeois conventions of his time and the overly rational and disciplinary way in which children were being raised. Indeed, it is ironic that "The Nutcracker and the Mouse King" has now been fully appropriated in another culture as a conventional, if not "exquisite" American ballet and ritual by the middle class, drained of its irony and satirical barbs. Through most of his life Hoffmann endeavored to break with the propriety fostered by a pretentious class society. Yet, he could never fully discard his social conditioning to become the free-spirited artist he desired to become. Interestingly, his personal "failure" led to his development as one of the most imaginative if not bizarre writers of his time, who desperately tried to transform life into art.

Hoffmann is the type of artist about whom biographers and critics have loved to build legends, or to explode old legends by creating new ones. As early as 1827, Sir Walter Scott published in the *Quarterly Review* a review of Julius Hitzig's biography of Hoffmann, titled "On the Supernatural in Fictitious Composition." Scott commented on Hoffmann's unusual stories: "It is impossible to subject tales of this nature to criticism. They are not the visions of a poetical mind; they are scarcely even the seeming authenticity which the hallucinations of lunacy convey to the patient; they are the fevrish dreams of a lightheaded patient, to which, though they may sometimes excite by their peculiarity, or surprise by their oddity, we never feel disposed to yield more than a momentary attention." Scott condemns Hoffmann largely on the basis of reading Hitzig's biography without questioning the German's interpretation of Hoffmann's life. Hitzig was, in fact, a good friend of Hoffmann, but he was also a prude and overly serious civil servant who never fully understood Hoffmann. He criticized Hoffmann's life on traditional moral grounds and spurred Scott to conclude that, if Hoffmann had not led such a dissolute life, he might have written supernatural stories handled with delicacy, not macabre stories that appear incredible. Like Goethe, Scott believed that Hoffmann was sick — mentally deranged — and, consequently he could not approve of the grotesque and absurd elements in his stories.

It is true that Hoffmann was sick during the latter part of his life — physically sick due to atrophy of the liver that caused a slow paralysis of his body. Even here we have a legend. As late as 1966, Gabrielle Wittkop-Ménardeau continued to spread a myth about the cause of Hoffmann's death and attributed it to his sex life and syphilis, a rumor that an Internet encyclopedia ignorantly continues to spread in the twenty-first century. He is even labeled a notorious philanderer and impecunious alcoholic. But to argue that Hoffmann was mentally disturbed, sexually promiscuous, and immoral is to overlook the fact that Hoffmann was a responsible civil servant and judge for a good part of his life; that he was an aspiring and diligent opera conductor in Bamberg, Leipzig, and Dresden; and was respected by some of the great minds of his time — doctors, judges, poets, actors, musicians, and administrators. Hoffmann was by no means a saint: He was overly fond of wine and may have had an affair after his marriage. But he was certainly not the demented eccentric that some biographers try to make him out to be. He was a profound thinker, avant-garde in all that he attempted, and hence suspect in the eyes of the establishment, and especially in the eyes of the "philistines." This was a common term that Hoffmann and many others at that time used to describe those people who approached life with a utilitarian and rationalistic mentality, who followed life according to arbitrary precepts, and who had a narrow if not uninformed appreciation of the arts. In short, they were superficial people who lacked any true appreciation of the imagination and the arts. Hoffmann detested the utilitarian nature of the philistines and mocked them in his tales whenever he could. His concepts of insanity, genius, music, hypnotism, dream, and reality formed a modern aesthetic theory, and he explored his unique ideas in other worlds that, he insisted, could be found in everyone's imagination. The discovery of these worlds, so he thought, could open up new vistas that would enable people to gain a deeper pleasure of reality. Hoffmann was a man ahead of his times, an amoral man, an aesthete, but not a man without a sense of justice. As a matter of fact, his idea of society and justice was so fine and idealistic that his experience with real society and justice as an expert in legal affairs and as judge and councilor "sickened" him, and engendered the duality in his life that he recorded in his writings. Hoffmann longed to live his life primarily for art, and he could barely tolerate the banal conditions, morals, and ethics of the social and political order that he virtually served as a civil servant. He led a double life and created the doppelgänger or double so that he might resolve the split he corporeally experienced. Hoffmann dreamed of an earthly paradise, a utopia, a millennium, in which man as *homo ludens* might create (free from repression) the kind of happiness which we associate with beauty and the sublime. The man who risks his life for the sublime in an age of banality — this is how Hoffmann tried to realize his own life and art.

Let us try to counter some of the legends from the beginning: Hoffmann drank but he was not an alcoholic. He enjoyed wine and champagne and consumed alcohol in abundance, but we have no proof that he wrote while under the influence. In fact, his stories and novels are so complicated that they demanded great concentration on his part and the full use of his conscious powers as a writer. Hoffmann easily became infatuated with young innocent women, but he rarely if ever had an extramarital affair. In his writings women represented the ideal priestess or goddess of the arts, and he especially idealized young women. As a talented writer, musician, and painter, he lived for the arts not for sex. Though he spoke his mind and loved to play pranks, Hoffmann was a true friend and never betrayed anyone or committed a crime. In fact, as judge, he came to the rescue of numerous people who were charged with crimes by corrupt politicians.

III

Hoffmann was born on January 24, 1776, in Königsberg (now Russian Kalingrad), a city of some 40,000 inhabitants. His father, Christoph Ludwig Hoffmann, and mother, Luisa Albertine Doerffer, were cousins. His father was a lawyer, somewhat eccentric and imaginative and unreliable as a breadwinner. His mother was orderly and anxious and lacked confidence in herself. Before Hoffmann was born, his parents had two other sons. One died and the second was taken away by the father when he separated from his wife in 1779 and moved to another city. Thereafter, Hoffmann's father and brother disappeared completely from his life. Perhaps this is why friendship and the father figure, often portrayed as an omniscient adviser or devil's emissary, play such important roles in his writings. This may also be why Hoffmann had such a disdain for the orderly philistine life that seemed to threaten his well-being and his artistic and imaginative pursuits.

After his father's separation from his mother, she returned to her family home, run by her dominating widowed mother, two strange aunts, and an incompetent uncle. She virtually abandoned her son to her own mother's care and did not develop an affectionate relationship with him. (Hoffmann made no mention of her or his father in his diaries or letters when they died during the 1790s.) The Doerffer household was a respectable middle-class family that had fallen on hard times, and Hoffmann was raised strictly with a view to making him into a lawyer or civil servant who might restore the standing of the family. As was the custom during this time, he was provided with music lessons and was expected to be well versed in all the arts. His mode of dress, speech, and behavior were governed by set social rules, which his pedantic uncle tried to enforce, and Hoffmann was constantly obliged to comply with social and familial precepts. At the same time, he was aware of the shortcomings of the odd household of domineering women and a foolish dogmatic uncle, and found ways to subvert their plans to regulate his life. Very early Hoffmann came to resent and criticize the Doerffer family and sought an escape through music and writing. During his teenage years he formed a strong bond with a fellow student named Theodor Hippel and shared all his intimate dreams with him. Together they conceived numerous artistic projects and planned adventurous trips and other outings. However, their paths diverged by the time they began attending the university. Hippel, whose family was very wealthy and had been granted nobility in 1790, followed a straight and "normal" path through the university to become a civil servant, administrator, and politician with a good deal of power. As the friends grew older, Hippel often interceded in Hoffmann's behalf, lent him money, and tried to "stabilize" his life by giving sound advice. But it was to no avail.

Hoffmann, who also studied law at the university, took a more zigzag course through life and realized that social class differences would keep him apart from Hippel. Moreover, Hoffmann's demeanor and dedication to art would cause rifts. He began writing novels and musical compositions as a young man and had his first love affair in 1794 with Cora (Dora) Hatt, a woman who was ten years older than he and married to a brewery owner. It was this turbulent and passionate affair that caused him to leave Königsberg in 1796. By this time Hoffmann, who had enrolled at the university at sixteen, had passed his first law examinations and was employed by the municipal government at Glogau in Silesia, where he benefited from the connections of another uncle, Johann Ludwig Doerffer. Hoffmann lived in his uncle's house, and apparently he decided that, to support himself and to pursue an artistic career at the same time, he had to prove himself as a jurist and civil servant and lead a respectable life. Part of his plan to settle down and forget Dora Hatt involved an engagement to his uncle's daughter Minna. It was clear that, from the beginning, he was not in love with her and acted opportunistically to please her father and his own family in Königsberg. When his uncle Johann was promoted, the Doerffers moved from Glogau to Berlin in 1798; Hoffmann accompanied them and continued to work for the Prussian government. During the next two years he reveled in the cultural life of Berlin, attending the theater and opera and visiting museums. In addition he began writing increasingly more musical compositions and endeavored to have some of his work published or performed without much success. In the meantime, he kept studying for his final law examination, for he knew that, once he passed it, he would receive a permanent position as a civil servant in the Prussian government and would become financially independent.

By March 1800, he had passed the exams with honors and was assigned a post in Posen, a small provincial city in Poland about two hundred miles east of Berlin, that had become part of Prussia. Hoffmann chose this opportunity to spread his wings. Within a short period of time, he not only broke his engagement to Minna, but also damaged his relations with the entire Doerffer family.

Hoffmann lived a convivial bachelor's life for a while, enjoying what little cultural life there was in Posen, and soon married a beautiful Polish woman, Maria Thekla Michaelina Rohrer, whom Hoffmann called Mischa. She came from a humble middle-class family and was not particularly well-educated. But Hoffmann, despite his infatuation with other women, remained devoted to her for the rest of his life. Soon after this marriage, he became involved in a scandal during carnival season by drawing comical sketches of some of the aristocratic Prussian officers, thereby causing his transfer to the tiny town of Plock (now called Plozk) in the Polish provinces. The only possibility for Hoffmann to survive in Plock was to throw himself into music by studying the great composers and writing his own compositions and essays about music. He even had his first article about music published in a German magazine, and this publication gave him confidence to continue his study of music with greater dedication. For the most part, he felt himself bored and isolated and applied for jobs in other cities. Thanks to his friend Hippel, who had many important political connections by now, Hoffmann was able to obtain a governmental position in Warsaw, which was under Prussian control.

In 1804, Hoffmann and Mischa moved to Warsaw, where he soon became the center of the musical life in the city. Not only did he compose a singspiel called "The Merry Musicians," but he also formed a music society and conducted and performed at various concerts. At the same time Mischa gave birth to their daughter Cäcilia. Hoffmann would have been content to remain in Warsaw, but Prussia joined the Allies in their battles against Napoleon, and the French troops invaded the city. Hoffmann lost his position, and to protect his family, he sent his wife and daughter to Posen to stay with Mischa's family, while he tried to find some way to continue to make a living in Warsaw. However, he failed and soon moved to Berlin, where he hoped Julius Hitzig, another Prussian civil servant whom he had befriended in Warsaw, might help him. However, despite Hitzig's family connections — he came from a very wealthy and established Berlin family — there was little Hitzig could do, and by the middle of August 1807, Hoffmann, who was very depressed, was further saddened to learn of the death of his two-year-old daughter Cäcilia. At times starving and unemployed, Hoffmann shifted gears, abandoned the civil service, and tried to find a job as a music conductor, though he had very little experience. Fortunately, he was offered a position as director of the music theater in Bamberg in southern Germany, and by the fall of 1808 he had moved there with Mischa.

No sooner did he make his debut in Bamberg than he lost his job. His lack of experience showed immediately. However, he and Mischa decided to stay in Bamberg, where he made his living by giving music lessons to the children of wealthy families and by writing compositions for the theater. He also started writing short stories, and his first tale, "The Knight Gluck" ("Ritter Gluck)" was published in 1809. The following year the new director of the Bamberg Theater hired him to work as his assistant, dramaturg, and composer. It appeared that conditions in Bamberg might now allow him to flourish as the versatile artist that he was. Indeed, Hoffmann helped stage some of the memorable plays by Calderon, Schiller, Lessing, and Shakespeare and operas by Mozart and Weber. He changed one of his middle names to Amadeus out of admiration for Mozart's accomplishments, and began writing music reviews for various journals, as well as short stories about a tormented musical genius by the name of Johannes Kreisler. Everything seemed to be going well for Hoffmann until, in 1811, he fell in love with one of his students, Julia Marc, a thirteen-year-old singer who had a voice like an angel. Hoffmann could not control himself, and although he never had an affair with her, his obsession eventually became public by 1812, causing a scandal in Bamberg. Since it was impossible for him to live and work there anymore, he had to search for a new position. It was during this time that he turned more and more to writing fantasy stories, while also composing his opera *Undine*, based on the fairy tale by his friend Friedrich de la Motte Fouqué.

In 1813 Hoffmann was fortunate to find a position as the conductor for an opera company stationed in Leipzig and Dresden. During the next sixteen months he conducted over thirty-five operas and singspiele while finishing *Undine* and collaborating with Fouqué, who wrote the libretto. In addition, he published two volumes of short stories, *Fantasy Pieces* (*Phantasie Stücke*, 1814), and wrote his most famous fairy tale "The Golden Pot" ("Der goldene Topf"). However, the stress caused by the war and disagreements at the opera took their toll, and Hoffmann was dismissed as conductor by the director of the company, Joseph Seconda. The loss of a secure income caused great difficulty for Hoffmann and Mischa. By chance, however, his friend Hippel appeared in Leipzig and encouraged him to resume his career in the civil service. Indeed, once again Hippel came to his rescue and procured a position for Hoffmann at the justice ministry in Berlin.

In September 1814, Hoffmann arrived in Berlin, and much to his surprise, he was greeted as a minor celebrity. His fantasy stories and fairy tales had been extremely well received by literary circles throughout Germany, and for the next eight years until his death in 1822, Hoffmann's stories were very much in demand by the publishers of ladies magazines, which were very popular at that time. In addition to these publications, he wrote two intriguing novels *The Devil's Elixirs* (*Die Elixiere des Teufels*, 1815–16) and *Tom Cat's Views on Life* (*Die Lebensansichten des Kater Murrs*, 1819–21); published "The Nutcracker and the Mouse King" and "The Strange Child" ("Das fremde Kind") in two volumes, *Children's Fairy Tales* (*Kinder-Märchen*, 1816–17), which included stories by Fouqué and Carl Wilhelm Salice Contessa; and collected his fairy tales, novellas, and fantasy stories in two volumes with the title *Night Pieces* (*Nachtstücke*, 1815–17), and in four volumes with the title *The Serapion Brothers* (*Die Serapionsbrüder*, 1819-–22).

No sooner did he settle down in Berlin than he began to hold weekly meetings at a nearby tavern with some of the leading writers and artists of the day. They would gather together, discuss cultural and political events, drink and eat, and conceive projects together. Among the writers who would appear on a regular and irregular basis were Fouqué, Contessa, Adelbert von Chamisso, Ludwig Tieck, Clemens Brentano, and David Ferdinand Koreff, as well as the famous actor Ludwig Devrient and his friend Hitzig, who worked at the same ministry that he did. As time went on, the gatherings became less frequent, until Hoffmann called a formal meeting of many of the "members" of the group on November 14, 1818, the saint's day of the holy Serapion, to renew their association and discussions. The friends and writers of this group were depicted fictitiously in the framework of The Serapion Brothers, but there is no clear identification of one particular character with a real person. Actually Hoffmann played all the roles in this framework collection, and conducted a multidimensional discourse about the imagination, fantasy works, music, and devotion to art. The manner in which he conceived this book basically shows how Hoffmann was inspired by his friends just as he was inspired by the plays, concerts, and operas he attended in Berlin. When his own opera, Undine, finally had been performed in 1816, he became even more famous, and was constantly invited as an honored guest to attend literary salons and other cultural events.

But it would be wrong to focus on Hoffmann solely as the accomplished artist who had become a gallant man about town. Hoffmann was a disciplined writer, constantly creating new types of tales and novels. His production and dedication to his writing damaged his health, and he was often sick. Moreover, there was always stress at the justice ministry. He began as a minor civil servant and was eventually promoted to the rank of councilor and judge. Along with promotions came merit increases in his salary because of his scrupulous work. However, his scruples also landed him in trouble. By 1818, Prussia, Russia, Austria, and England had formed the Holy Alliance, and there was a conservative and repressive political movement in all these countries that caused protests by liberal groups, especially students.

The leaders of the German principalities issued decrees that called for the punishment of anyone suspected of subversive activities. Because of Hoffmann's reputation as a fair and ethical judge, he was appointed to a special commission (the Prussian Intelligence Committee against High Treason) to investigate subversive activities (somewhat like the House Committee on Un-American Activities during the 1940s and 1950s). In many cases, Hoffmann brought about the release of people with liberal ideas who had been falsely charged with illegal activities. Hoffmann consistently defended the civil rights of the accused. The most important case involved the famous Friedrich Ludwig Jahn, founder of gymnastics, who had been in prison for eight months. Karl Albert von

Kamptz, the notorious commissioner of police in the Department of Interior, who belonged to the Ministerial Commission, had Jahn sent to the fortress of Kolberg, announcing that Jahn had been proven guilty, something that was untrue. Hoffmann wanted Kamptz brought before the courts, but was prevented from doing so by the king of Prussia himself. Hoffmann served on this committee for two years (1819–21), and in 1822 he satirized Kamptz as Knarrpaxiti in one of his last stories, "Master Flea" ("Meister Floh"), and then boasted about it. Once Kamptz knew about this, he prevented the publication of the story in Frankfurt and pressed charges against Hoffmann, who by this time was dying from a liver disease. Hoffmann was ordered to attend the court proceedings, but he had become so ill he could not leave his bed. Once again his friend Hippel intervened. Hoffmann was allowed to prepare a masterful defense of his case, and the king let him off with a reprimand. Soon after, "Master Flea" was published with certain portions extracted. It was Hoffmann's last laugh at the corrupt bureaucracy that he had so loyally served. By now he had atrophy of the liver and degeneration of the spinal marrow. He was in great pain, but kept writing until his throat became paralyzed. He died at the age of forty-six on June 25, 1822, and was buried in Berlin. His wife, Mischa, left Berlin and went to Posen until 1835. Although she was looked after by Hoffmann's loyal friend Hitzig, she died in poverty in the small city of Warmbrunn on January 27, 1859.

IV

Hoffmann was a late bloomer as a writer, but once he discovered his extraordinary talent, he became almost obsessed by his writing and demanded total dedication of himself to his craft. He often demanded the same of the protagonists in his stories, who often collapsed or died because they could not maintain their dedication or find a way to balance the dedication to art with the crass demands of their mundane existence. This was the major conflict in many of Hoffmann's stories, life in the paradise of art versus life in the humdrum world of the philistines. It was clearly expressed in his first major fairy tale, "The Golden

Pot," which is subtitled "A Fairy Tale from the New Time," a signal that Hoffmann was about to use the fairy tale in an unusual modern way to address readers with a new sensibility. To a certain degree, Hoffmann carried the romantic experiments of Wilhelm Heinrich Wackenroder, Ludwig Tieck, Novalis, Brentano, and Chamisso to their logical end with his intricate tales of magical realism. Not only is "The Golden Pot" the culmination of the innovative fairy tales produced by the romantic writers, it is also the pioneer work of European magic realism. Hoffmann developed an uncanny narrative style of reportage, and often began his tales as though he were writing an article for a newspaper or preparing a dry historical chronicle. After a few paragraphs, however, he conflates reality with fantasy, and the boundaries between the two disappear. Both reader and protagonist must find their way through a labyrinth of events, and in the course of the narrative, they must also learn to position themselves to see anew, to perceive their worlds with greater sensitivity and acumen, and to delight in their imaginations.

This is the ultimate message of "The Nutcracker and the Mouse King," but there is more to this story and its background than meets the eye. Hoffmann wrote this fairy tale in 1816, ostensibly for the children of Julius Hitzig, but in reality it was a tale *about* the Hitzig family and their social class and how children were being raised. Though Hoffmann himself led an eminently bourgeois life, he was personally unconventional and somewhat eccentric, while Hitzig was serious and proper and felt there was something immoral about Hoffmann's lifestyle. In Hitzig's eyes, Hoffmann was somewhat weird. Nevertheless, they were good friends, and Hitzig attended Hoffmann's weekly Serapion meetings, while Hoffmann was a welcome guest in the Hitzig house. By 1816 the Hitzigs had two children, Marie and Fritz, six and eight, and Hoffmann had great affection for them, although he was known never to caress the children or physically demonstrate his feelings. Rather, he showed his affection through gifts and stories. In 1815 he had given the Hitzig children an illuminated castle that he himself had built, and he told them the story of "Undine" and other tales. Hoffmann was an energetic, small, wiry man with a twinkle in his eyes that often blitzed like lightning. He was not particularly handsome, but when he began speaking or playing music, he could be captivating. There was magic about Hoffmann that drew all kinds of people to him, and there is no doubt that the figure of Drosselmeier in "The Nutcracker and the Mouse King" bears some of his characteristics, just as the children are related to a certain degree to Marie and Fritz Hitzig. But it would be misleading to interpret "The Nutcracker and the Mouse King" from a simple autobiographical perspective. After all, his tale was a radical fairy tale intended, like "The Golden Pot," to give a new form to fairy tales written for children; and indeed, Hoffman was preparing the way for many writers of modern fairy tales, like Hans Christian Andersen, who would owe Hoffmann a great debt.

Hoffmann was not all that conversant with children's literature at the beginning of the nineteenth century, but he knew from his own experience and from observing the children of proper and decent bourgeois families that their lives were overly regulated. In keeping with the rationalism of the times, they were "drilled" to behave according to moral and ethical principles that were intended to curb their imaginations. Hoffmann himself had never been able to abandon these principles altogether. Although he felt comfortable and needed the security of a settled middle-class life, he had always felt confined by the conventions and constantly sought alternatives to them in his tales, if not in his own life. He could be abrasive yet gentle in his ironical critique of the neat and homey bourgeois customs. But he never abandoned championing the imagination with all his critical powers.

In 1816, when he proposed the collaboration on a book of fairy tales for children to Fouqué and Contessa, he already knew that his own contribution would be a kind of manifesto about a new form of the fairy tale. He had announced his "radical" intentions in "The Golden Pot," a complex fairy tale for adults, and he wanted to do the same for children with "The Nutcracker and the Mouse King" and "The Strange Child." This became much clearer when he reprinted "The Nutcracker and the Mouse King" and "The Strange Child" in *The Serapion Brothers* in 1819, framed by a discussion about the merits of the imagination and irony and about what makes an appropriate fairy tale for children. Hoffmann indicated that his fairy tales were for children with lively imaginations and also for adults. Indeed, both his tales incorporate what he called the guiding Serapion principle that was to determine the value of all the stories told by the friends in *The Serapion Brothers*.

Each one of us is to test whether he really has seen what he seeks to communicate before he dares to say it aloud. At the very least, each one of us is to seek as earnestly as possible to capture the exact image, which arises within him, with all its shapes, colors, lights, and shadows, and then, when he feels himself ignited by all of this, to transmit this portrayal to the outside world.

"The Nutcracker and the Mouse King" is all about igniting the imagination of Marie so that she can act and realize her inner dreams and desires in opposition to a conventional and prescriptive upbringing. It is not by chance that the household in which most of the action takes place is called "Stahlbaum" or steel tree. The parents of Marie and Fritz are truly solid and tough as steel, and they are somewhat anxious that Drosselmeier, even though a friend, might contaminate Marie's mettle with his toys and foolish stories. He might even break the "steel encasement" in which Marie is placed to learn about proper manners and good behavior.

The question that Hoffmann asks in this tale, and also in "The Strange Child," is how to infiltrate a good and proper bourgeois home to free the children's imagination so that they can recognize and fulfill their desires. In this regard, the title of Hoffmann's fairy tale is misleading. The story is not about the Nutcracker and the Mouse King; rather, it is about the curious child Marie and the ambivalent somewhat threatening figure of Drosselmeier, the mysterious artist and teacher. Hoffmann positions Marie as the learner, who grasps that she must use her imagination to see the world as it really is. Drosselmeier provides the spark for her imagination and tests her through his remarks and stories to see whether she will remain true to her inner desires and imagination before he will help her reconcile what she sees inside herself and around her. From the point of view of Marie's parents and her brother Fritz and sister Luise, she is delirious and talks nonsense. But Drosselmeier sees Marie differently: He is struck by the way that she associates her visions and imaginings with the world around her, and how she combines them to enrich her daily existence. Consequently, Drosselmeier does his best to assist her almost magically to uncover the potential of objects and symbols to become alive and to animate her modus vivendi.

At the same time that Hoffmann depicts Marie developing insights and a new mode of perceiving herself in the world, he also prompts readers to read differently and to change their attitudes toward the fairy tale. This transformation is not imposed, but emanates from the mixture of narrative modes and genres and the creation of a labyrinthic narrative structure, doubling of characters, and an ironic omniscient narrator. Hoffmann's fairy tale does not begin with the traditional "once upon a time;" rather the beginning is a dry realistic description of the somewhat customary preparations for a Christmas eve celebration in the home of a typical German bourgeois family at the beginning of the nineteenth century.

> For the entire twenty-fourth of December, the children of Medical Officer Stahlbaum were not permitted to step inside the intermediary room, much less the magnificent showcase next door. Fritz and Marie sat huddled together in a corner of the back room. The deep evening dusk had set in, and the children felt quite eerie because, as was usual on this day, no light had been brought in. Fritz quite secretly whispered to his younger sister (she had just turned seven) that he had heard a rustling and murmuring and soft throbbing in the locked rooms since early that morning. Also, not so long ago (Fritz went on), a short, dark man with a large casket under his arm had stolen across the vestibule. However, said Fritz, he knew quite well that it was none other than Godfather Drosselmeier.

The narrator is formal, often tongue in cheek, toying with the readers because he will soon use his careful realistic mode to depict the inner world of Marie as though she were actually experiencing everything that she sees, whether it be in her mind or outside her.

The shifts in the narration are challenging for readers of any age, but they are clearly aimed at bringing all readers to realize that there is no phenomenological difference between the life of the mind and physical reality. The significance of Drosselmeier's satirical fairy tale "The Hard Nut" is determined by the doubling effect that allows Marie to have a more profound understanding of things that her immediate family cannot see, and to determine how to fulfill her dreams. Like "The Nutcracker and the Mouse King," itself, "The Hard Nut" is an antifairy tale, that is, it is an antitraditional fairy tale or folk tale because it is unsettling, macabre, and provocative. The king and queen are fops; their daughter is spoiled. The mice, who substitute for witches, fairies, and ogres, are ridiculous creatures. The horror and threats of the mice are ludicrous. Hoffmann

creates a parody of the court life of his times. Food and the appetite are
the most important matters for the king and queen, and they can also
arbitrarily execute anyone they desire if their subjects displease them. The
narrator Drosselmeier enters the story as artistic inventor, whose life is
endangered because he inadvertently causes the princess to become ugly,
and as one of the main protagonists of the story, he introduces the double
of his real nephew who is also to become the nutcracker. The fairy tale
ends unhappily, because it can only be completed happily by Marie, both
in her imagination when she saves the Nutcracker, and later when she
marries Drosselmeier's real nephew from Nuremburg.

The reconciliation of real and imaginative realms that Marie experiences and the emphasis placed on following one's natural instincts are
developed more didactically and theoretically in "The Strange Child,"
which was published in the second volume of Children's Fairy Tales (1817).
Hoffmann had read Jean-Jacques Rousseau's works as a young student
and was strongly influenced by them, especially Rousseau's notions of a
natural education that would enable children to flower. Hoffmann never
forgot Rousseau's "lessons," and in "The Strange Child," he depicted two
children, Felix and Christlieb, living in the country with their parents,
Count and Countess von Brakelheim. The setting is idyllic, and despite
the fact the Brakelheims have very little money and live like common
farmers in a dilapidated house, the family is content. However, this harmony is broken by the "distinguished" visit of a wealthy and pompous
uncle, his wife, and his dainty, disciplined children, who can spout their
memorized lessons like automatons. The uncle is distressed by the lack of
academic knowledge and poor manners of carefree Felix and Christlieb
and offers to send a private tutor so that they might live up to the aristocratic reputation of the family. After his departure, Felix and Christlieb
take the artificial toys that had been given to them as gifts by their rich
relatives into the forest, only to realize how useless and boring they are.
The next day in the forest they meet a "strange child," somewhat like an
alien creature, who unveils the magic of nature to them so that they feel
liberated and inspired by everything they encounter. The androgynous
child has magical powers and refuses to reveal its sex. Felix and Christlieb
tell their parents about their encounters with the strange child, and the
parents, though concerned, are happy that the children are at one with

nature. Yet, when the private tutor named Master Tinte (ink), sent by the rich uncle, arrives and begins to control their lives with his pedantry, they lose their contact with the strange child. Fortunately, as Master Tinte begins to take over the family and oppress the children, they flee into the forest, where they once again encounter the strange child, who reveals how they can banish the private tutor from their lives. Soon thereafter, however, their father becomes ill and tells his children that he, too, had met a strange child during his childhood and that they should endeavor to stay loyal to this child. The father dies. His wife and children are forced to leave their home in nature. But because Fritz and Christlieb keep the strange child alive in their hearts, they continue to see the marvelous things that the strange child brings to them from his realm.

This short summary does not do justice to Hoffmann's remarkable fairy tale that prefigures the science fiction/fantasy film *E. T.* by some 150 years. Whereas E. T., the alien, comes from outer space to help young children learn to empathize with and tolerate strangers in their lives and then departs, Hoffmann's strange child enters the lives of Felix and Christlieb to remain there forever. Hoffmann insists on keeping the child in us alive until we die. Without imagination we can become instrumentalized and exploited. By no means was Hoffmann a devout follower of Rousseau's precepts concerning the importance of raising children in nature without books. Through his fairy tales and fantasies, he sought to bring about a deeper understanding about the mysteries of the imagination and an appreciation of how our inner and outer natures cannot be divided. These were deeply held convictions, and he embodied them in his own life so that it is at times difficult to distinguish where Hoffmann's life ends and his art begins. The ambivalent and enchanting figures of Drosselmeier, Marie, Felix, and Christlieb are good examples of how it is possible to discover the world through fairy tales and to blend all kinds of ontological phenomena to develop one's identity.

V

But the same cannot be said of Alexandre Dumas's Drosselmayer and Marie in "The Story of a Nutcracker," the 1845 French adaptation of

Hoffmann's fairy tale. Dumas (1802–70), born in the small town of Villers-Cotterêts outside of Paris, desired to become a great writer in his youth. He moved to Paris in 1823, and within six years, he made a name for himself with his historical play *Henri III*, and went on to become the most famous playwright in France during the nineteenth century. Moreover, he also was regarded as one of the finest novelists of his times with such works as *The Three Musketeers* (1844), *The Count of Monte Cristo* (1846), and *The Man in the Iron Mask* (1848–50). Unlike Hoffmann, Dumas became a celebrity as a young man and was amazingly prolific, in part because he collaborated with many writers, who supplied him with drafts and sketches for his works. Nor did he worship art in the same manner as Hoffmann, who lived for his art. Dumas lived for his public and the growing commercial market for cultural goods, and churned out plays, stories, dramas, novellas, and novels at a fast rate in newspapers and magazines, and in book form. He wrote to entertain, rarely to teach or to theorize. He popularized history and wanted the populace to read his works, which they did. Why and how he translated Hoffmann's "The Nutcracker and the Mouse King" is somewhat of a mystery. We do know, however, that he was familiar with Hoffmann's tales and admired him. He even wrote a tale, "La Femme au Collier de velours" ("The Woman with the Velvet Necklace," 1851), which features Hoffmann, who falls in love with a dancer. But Dumas had no facility with the German language, and it is unclear whether he translated "The Nutcracker and the Mouse King" or whether he had the tale translated for him to adapt.

The cultural significance of Dumas's adaptation is minimal. Though it is somewhat popular in the field of French children's literature, this popularity may have more to do with the popularity of Hoffmann and the Russian ballet. Not that Dumas's tale is poorly written, but it lacks the irony and complexity of Hoffmann's original. Dumas transformed "The Nutcracker and the Mouse King" into a charming tale intended to entertain a group of rowdy children who tie up the author when he falls asleep in a boudoir. The comical frame allows the author to introduce Hoffmann as the real author of the tale and begin addressing his captors in a didactic tone to enable the implied readers, young French children, to grasp a story that he sets in Nuremburg in the eighteenth century. There are several religious references that Hoffmann would not have welcomed; the name of the Stahlbaum family is changed to Silberhaus (Silver House), and Godfather Drosselmayer is said to adore the Silberhaus children, instead of maintaining an ambivalent attitude toward them. The sister Luise disappears from Dumas's story, and a governess by the name of Mademoiselle Trudchen (originally a doll) is added for comic effect. After introducing the main characters, Dumas more or less sticks to the same plot, but there is less emphasis placed on the bizarre nature of Drosselmayer and the significant learning experience of Marie. Dumas appropriates the "German" tale *à la français* for young French readers, and often has his author explain incidents where Hoffmann created enigmas. It is strange that Dumas abandons the frame that he set at the beginning of his tale. It is almost as if he had forgotten it, for we never learn what happens to the author, who was telling the tale to liberate himself, whereas Hoffmann's narrator maintains his presence and manipulation to the very end. Dumas simply embellishes the proposal and marriage scene and closes the tale sweetly by writing:

> At this hour, Marie is still queen of the gorgeous kingdom, where we see brilliant Christmas Forests everywhere, rivers of orangeade, orgeat, and attar of roses, diaphanous palaces of sugar finer than snow and more transparent than ice. And finally, all kinds of magnificent and miraculous things — provided your eyes are sharp enough to see them.

Hoffmann's version reads:

> Marie supposedly is still queen of a land where you can see sparkling Christmas Forests everywhere as well as translucent Marzipan Castles — in short, the most splendid and most wondrous things, if you only have the right eyes to see them with.

Both endings emphasize eyes and the perception of wonder, and clearly the question of vision is one that "haunted" Hoffmann during his entire life: how to envision and realize desire and not dampen curiosity as one matures within the confines of an orderly middle-class society. Freud recognized the significance of Hoffmann's reflections about vision and repression in his essay on "The Uncanny," in which he analyzed Hoffmann's famous fantasy story, "The Sandman." In that eerie tale the young protagonist Nathaniel is more or less driven to suicide because he cannot reconcile his imaginative projections with the rational approach to reality that his friends and family maintain. His eyesight is jarred, so to speak, and he becomes desperate and virtually loses his mind. Freud explains that Nathaniel had suffered from a traumatic wound in his childhood that he repressed, and because he never heals the wound, it returns to terrorize him. Insight into this dilemma, perhaps, might have saved him. It is difficult to say, but what Hoffmann kept proposing insistently in all his fairy tales and fantasies was that if one kills the imagination in the child and does not revere it, the child will lose sight of his or her potential, and the imagination will take its revenge by abandoning the child in a banal, lifeless world as an adult. In fact, the imagination might even kill the child, because if it is betrayed, the betrayal might lead to death-in-life. This is how Hoffmann celebrated the power of the imagination.

VI

But, is this why his tale, transformed into a ballet, mediated by Dumas, Tchaikovsky's music, and the choreography of numerous artists, has become so mythic and captivating? Does the enchantment of the ballet have something to do with the liberation of our imaginations and our nostalgia for a time when we perceived everything around us and in us as alive? It is very difficult to talk about the meaning of *The Nutcracker* as ballet because Hoffmann's text has been "destabilized" by Dumas and other adaptations, just as the original libretto by Vsevolojsky and Petipa has been changed and altered hundreds of times throughout the world. However, despite the diverse interpretations of the ballet that often clash with one another, there is a basic plot to the movement of the ballet that recalls the Hoffmann tale.

> Act I, Scene 1 — The Christmas Party. The Silberhaus or Stahlbaum family prepares for a Christmas Eve party. The guests arrive. The two children Clara and Franz are excited. Uncle Drosselmeyer, a peculiar gentleman, who is Clara's godfather, appears almost magically and brings with him three mechanical dolls to display: a lovely ballerina, a dancing doll that blows kisses, and a marching soldier. Sometimes Clara is called Marie or Masha, and sometimes the mechanical dolls represent other

figures. The guests are enchanted by his inventions. Franz receives a toy sword or a wooden horse, and Clara, a funny looking nutcracker, which the jealous and raucous Franz breaks. However, either Drosselmeyer or Drosselmeyer's nephew, manages to repair the nutcracker and place it beneath the Christmas tree in a bed. Afterward there is some dancing, and then the guests leave, while the children get ready for bed.

Act I, Scene 2 — The Battle Scene. Clara cannot sleep because she is concerned about the nutcracker. She returns to the room in which the nutcracker has been placed beneath the Christmas tree, but strange things begin to happen. The grandfather clock turns into Uncle Drosselmeyer, and mice come from all four corners of the room to attack the Nutcracker, who has come alive and assembles Franz's toy soldiers to assist him. The dreadful Mouse King leads the vicious mice. There is a fierce battle, and it appears that the mice will be victorious until Clara throws her slipper at the Mouse King, allowing the Nutcracker to take advantage of the rodent and kill him. Sometimes the Mouse King is simply knocked unconscious and is carried away by his troops. All at once the Nutcracker turns into a handsome prince.

Act II — The Land of Sweets. Now the Nutcracker Prince leads Clara to the Land of Sweets ruled by the Sugar Plum Fairy. Sometimes the bed is transformed into a sleigh, and they ride through a winter wonderland. Snow flakes dance. Once they arrive in the Land of the Sweets, they are treated like royalty, and the Sugar Plum Fairy invites them to enjoy a lavish festival. The sweets, drinks, and flowers dance in their honor. They present a suite of dances from other lands — China, Russia, Arabia. There may also be a large Mother Ginger with offspring or a Shepherdess with her lambs. Finally, the stunning Sugar Plum fairy dances a pas de deux with her handsome cavalier. Thereafter, everyone dances in a grand celebration that appears to be a dream. Sometimes the ballet ends after this dance, and sometimes Clara awakens back home under the Christmas tree or in her own bed.

Depending on the choreographer and the production, Hoffmann's emphasis in his original tale, keeping the imagination alive, is maintained through a diverting spectacle. But gone are the more serious issues of his artwork, such as the conflict between the philistine method of raising children that curbs the imagination and Hoffmann's innovative use of a double antifairy tale that enables young Marie to discover the miracles of life and realize her dreams. The ballet is more about the coziness of home, hominess, and the taming of the imagination. The episodes in the ballet take place in one night; the transitions are elegant and smooth. The ballet masks the difficult struggle that Marie (Clara) undergoes over a period of days in Hoffmann's tale, and it is not clear whether her miraculous adventure will change her life. There are only faint echoes of Hoffmann, the provocateur, in the music and behavior of the strange godfather Drosselmeyer, whose role is more or less effaced in the ballet after the first act. Indeed, Hoffmann's tale is more or less destroyed after the battle scene. The second act is all fluff without much meaning except to show off the talents of the dancers. Clara (Marie) is made into a mere spectator, just as children today are more and more expected to remain spectators and consumers of spectacles. Hoffmann's tale has been made into a candy-coated entertainment that wraps up the imagination instead of setting the imagination of audiences free to lead the lives of their dreams.

In Hoffmann's time there was a much different attitude toward children, family life, and the imagination, and fairy tales, in particular, were looked upon with suspicion because they might spark children to think in the "wrong" way. Gradually, thanks to the romantics like Hoffmann, imaginative stories for children have become acceptable for "good" middle-class children. But fantasy works also became domesticated in the Western world, and *The Nutcracker* as ballet represents such domestication. Yet, as Freud has explained in his interpretation of the uncanny in Hoffmann's works, there is always a return of the repressed, and even as *The Nutcracker* merrily dances on, it carries within it the wound that it has caused to the power of the imagination in Hoffmann's tale, and who knows how viewers and participants will perceive and feel this wound. They might even be impelled to respond to the damage in their own fantastic ways.

six

I'm Hans Christian Andersen

L ong before publishers knew how to market their authors with dexterity to sell their books, long before Walt Disney made his name into an international logo, Hans Christian Andersen knew how to create himself as a celebrity and to glorify his name, despite the fact that he was a writer with limited talents. As a young country boy, perhaps one could even say, a country bumpkin, poor as a church mouse, Andersen tried to take Copenhagen by storm in 1819, when he was only fourteen years old, and very few people would have wagered at that time that he would become the most famous fairy-tale writer of the nineteenth century, even more famous than the Brothers Grimm. But his fame was also tainted. Andersen was a nuisance, a pest, a demanding intruder, and a clumsy actor, whose greatest desire was to write plays and star in them. He never fully realized this ambition, but he did become an inventive and innovative writer of fairy tales, and used his tales therapeutically to come to terms with the traumas and tensions in his life. This led to the formation of an extraordinary personality, for Andersen was one of the greatest mythomaniacs, hypochondriacs, and narcissists of the nineteenth century. He custom-made his life into a fairy tale that he sold successfully from the moment he arrived in Copenhagen, and it is impossible to grasp him or any of his tales without knowing something about the reality of his life and his strategies for survival.

But, how is it possible to know the reality of Andersen's life when he consciously concealed many vital facts and incidents in the three autobiographies that he wrote? How is it possible to relate his unusual autobiographical tales to his life when they are so fantastic and can be interpreted in many different ways and on many levels? Andersen appears to defy definition and categorization, and it may not even be necessary to know something about his life to appreciate his tales. Yet, because he wove himself so imaginatively into his narratives, and because there are so many misunderstandings about his life and the meaning of his tales, it is crucial to try to sort through the myths about him and investigate how his tales came into existence so that we can have a fuller and clearer appreciation of the difficulties he overcame to achieve the success he did. Moreover, it is important to realize how diverse his stories are, for they were not all fairy tales about his life. Nor were they written for children. Nor did they always end happily. There is something uncanny and often chilling about Andersen's tales, a bitter irony that makes us wonder whether the pursuit of happiness and success is worth all the effort.

I. The Hans Christian Andersen We Never Knew

Andersen was born on April 2, 1805, into a dirt-poor family in Odense, in a squalid section of the provincial town of about fifteen thousand people. His father, Hans, was a shoemaker, several years younger than his wife, Anne Marie Andersdatter, a washerwoman and domestic. His parents suffered from poverty all their lives; his father became so desperate at one point that he took money from a rich merchant as an inducement to replace this man as a soldier in the military draft. Consequently, Andersen's father had to fight for two years in the Danish army during the Napoleonic Wars. Overly sensitive about his family's poverty and his own homely appearance, Andersen kept to himself as a young boy. When he was seven, his parents took Andersen to the theater, and a new, fantastic world exploded before his eyes. From this point on, theater life came to represent a glorious realm of freedom, and he hoped to become a great writer involved with the stage. But there was a lot of misery to overcome: His father, a sick and broken man, died in 1816, two years after he returned from the wars; his mother was afflicted by alcoholism; the adolescent Andersen was often humiliated at work by older boys and men; he was haunted by the insanity that ran in the family and felt shame about an aunt who ran a brothel in Copenhagen. The traumas of his youth cast him into the role as an outsider, and they undoubtedly led him to imagine how he might abandon Odense and create a different life for himself as an actor or writer. Indeed, he showed an early proclivity toward reading and writing, even though his schooling was modest, and he believed deeply that he belonged elsewhere. Perhaps he was the son of a royal couple, he imagined. Clearly, his imagination was fertile, but his drive and ambition were just as important.

Andersen's immense desire to become a famous writer or actor drove him to transcend his poor start in life and his lowly social status. In 1819, when he was only fourteen, he convinced his mother to allow him to travel to Copenhagen to pursue his dreams. But once he arrived, he again faced one trial after the next. At that time Copenhagen was a relatively small port city of 120,000 inhabitants, and Danish society, dominated by the aristocracy and upper middle classes, was highly stratified. Armed with a letter of introduction to a famous solo dancer at the Royal Theatre, Andersen made numerous attempts to impress people with his talent, but he was too raw and uncouth to be accepted into the art world. To rectify the situation he took singing and acting lessons and even had a bit part as a troll in a play performed at the Royal Theatre. In addition he endeavored to write plays that he continually submitted to the theater management, which always rejected them. Finally, a wealthy legal administrator by the name of Jonas Collin took him under his wing and sent him to a private boarding school to fine-tune him for polite society. From 1822 to 1827, Andersen was indeed trained and retooled, largely by a neurotic taskmaster by the name of Simon Meisling, first in Slagelse, a provincial town fifty miles from Copenhagen, and later in Helsingør. Andersen, who was several years older and much taller than his classmates, was instructed to forget all ideas of becoming a writer or poet, and Meisling, a notable scholar but a notorious teacher, tried which he introduced in his very first fairy tale, "The Tinderbox." Andersen had to prove that he was a soldier of fortitude who had the makings of a king, or that he was an oppressed and awkward fowl who would develop into an elegant swan. This is the story he repeated to himself and formed the basis of three autobiographies he wrote. At the same time, Andersen learned how to market himself as the Lord's chosen writer whenever he traveled abroad — he made more than thirty trips throughout Europe and the Middle East during his lifetime. Beginning with his first major trip to Germany in 1831, he sent his books to famous authors and wealthy people in advance of his arrival, implying that he was a kind of poetic genius, who was stunning the world and worth meeting and befriending. Indeed, Andersen did have a peculiar charm that made him an odd performer for court societies and middle-class salons always on the lookout for "sensational" entertainment.

Andersen knew exactly what he had to do and wanted to do to maintain his early success: He had to forge a name for himself, influence and cater to the public, and become a respectable member of the upper classes through marriage. From 1831 to 1840, he worked hard in both the artistic and social domains, succeeding in art and failing only in his plan to wed a proper wife. After his trip to Germany, where he met two of the great romantic writers, Ludwig Tieck and Adelbert von Chamisso, Andersen published *Shadow Pictures*, which described his journey, and the long dramatic poem *Agnete and the Merman* (1833), which served as the basis for his fairy tale "The Little Mermaid." At the same time, he wrote a short autobiography that only circulated among his closest friends; it was first published much later in 1926. Instead of the autobiography, he did produce an autobiographical novel, *The Improvisatore* in 1835, and this work was so successful that it was immediately translated into German. The year 1835 was also important because it marked the publication of his first two pamphlets of fairy tales inserted into books: "The Tinderbox," "Little Claus and Big Claus," "The Princess on the Pea," "Little Ida's Flowers," "Thumbelina," and "The Naughty Boy." In 1836, he published his second autobiographical novel, *O.T. Life in Denmark,* and his third, *Only a Fiddler,* in 1837, the same year he added "The Little Mermaid" (fig. 7) and "The Emperor's New Clothes" to his collection of fairy tales. Finally, two of his plays, *The Mulatto, A Comedy in Green* and *The*

Figure 7. *"The Little Mermaid." From* Fairy Tales *by Hans Christian Andersen. Illustr. Harry Clarke. New York: Brentano's, c. 1900.*

Moorish Maiden, were performed at the Royal Theatre in Copenhagen during 1840. All these different works led to Andersen's receiving an annual grant from the king of Denmark in 1838, and this grant, which was raised from time to time, enabled Andersen to live as a freelance writer for the rest of his life.

Although the 1830s were highly productive and successful years for his artistic career, there were some personal setbacks. He proposed to Riborg Voigt, the sister of a schoolmate, in 1830, and courted Louise Collin, daughter of his patron, in 1832. Both young women rejected his advances, as did Jenny Lind, the famous Swedish singer, in 1843. Andersen was never able to achieve the "happy" married life he ostensibly sought because he was never fully acceptable in upper class society, and because he felt strong attractions toward men. For most of his life, he was in love with Edvard Collin, the son of his patron Jonas Collin, and his diaries and papers reveal that he often used women to draw closer to men, or that he favored the company of young men. Some critics have argued that Andersen was a homosexual, who had an occasional relationship and veiled his sexual preferences his entire life. Others maintain that Andersen may have been gay or bisexual, but he never had any sexual affair whatsoever because he was painfully afraid of sex, often fearful he would contract a venereal disease, and thus he repressed his urges. Whatever the case may be, his diaries and letters reveal just how confused and frustrated, if not tortured, Andersen was because he could not fulfill his sexual desires. Throughout his life he suffered from migraine headaches, paranoia, hypochondria, and other neuroses that might be attributed to the repression of his sexual drives. Ironically, all this suffering also played a significant role in his producing some of the greatest fairy tales and stories in Western literature.

By 1840 Andersen had become famous throughout Europe, and his fame rested more on his fairy tales and stories than any of the other works he continued to produce. Although the title of his first collection was *Fairy Tales Told for Children* (*Eventyr, fortalte for Børn*), Andersen had not had much contact with children and did not tell tales to children at that point. He basically intended to capture the tone and style of a storyteller as if he were telling tales to children. Indeed, he thrived on the short narrative form. Although his novels and plays were sometimes well received, it was evident that his writing was not suited for these forms. Andersen's novels, plays, and even his poetry are flaccid, conventional, sentimental, and imitative and are barely readable today, if they are even read. On the other hand, he had an extraordinary gift for writing short narratives, and during the 1840s he continued to produce some of his best tales, such as "The Ugly Duckling" (1843), "The Nightingale" (1843) (fig. 8), "The Snow Queen" (1844), and "The Shadow" (1846). By this time Andersen no longer made the pretense that his tales were addressed to children. He eliminated the phrase "for children" in the title of his collection, and many of the tales became more complex. For instance, "The Shadow" was purposely written to address the hurt and humiliation that Andersen felt because his beloved Edvard Collin refused throughout his life to speak to him with the familiar "*du*" in Danish. Instead, Collin kept Andersen at a distance by using the formal "*de*." In "The Shadow" Andersen reveals the feelings of obliteration caused by this relationship, which, as a story, is also a brilliant reflection of the master/slave relationship and the condition of paranoia.

It was clearly due to the appreciation of adults that Andersen became immensely successful by the 1840s. Not only were his tales well received, but he published his first official autobiography, *The True Story of My Life*, in 1846, the same year his stories were translated into English. The next year he planned and organized his first trip to England, where he was treated as a celebrity. He wrote a patriotic novel, *The Two Baronesses*, in 1848, and although he felt drawn to the Germans, he defended Denmark in the conflict between his country and Prussia from 1848–51. In fact, Andersen's loyalties were split because he felt more comfortable in foreign countries, especially when he was hosted by rich aristocratic families there, and sorely mistreated and unrecognized in Denmark. In 1846 he wrote the following letter to his patron, Jonas Collin, from Berlin:

> You know, of course, that my greatest vanity, or call it rather joy, resides in the knowledge that you consider me worthy of you. I think of you as I receive all this recognition. Yet I am truly loved and appreciated abroad; I am — famous. Yes, you may well smile. But the foremost men fly to meet me, I see myself welcomed into all their families. Princes, and the most talented of men pay me the greatest courtesies. You should see how they flock around me in the so-called important circles. Oh, that's not

Figure 8. "The Nightingale." From Fairy Tales *by Hans Christian Andersen. Illustr. Harry Clarke. New York: Brentano's, c. 1900.*

something any of all those people back home think about, they overlook me completely and no doubt they would be happy with a droplet of the tribute I receive. Yet my writings must have greater merit than the Danes give them. (Jens Andersen, *Hans Christian Andersen*, 114)

Andersen could never reconcile himself to the fact that he was not praised unconditionally by the Danish critics and public. He had an enormous ego and insatiable need for compliments and special treatment. The more he wrote from 1850 until his death in 1875, the more he tended to repeat the plots and styles of his earlier tales; and although some like "Clod Hans" (1855), "Father's Always Right" (1861), and "The Gardener and the Gentry" (1872) were masterful works of art, most waxed pale in comparison to those that preceded them. His last two novels, *To Be or Not to Be* (1857) and *Lucky Peter* (1870), were poorly conceived and boring to read. His plays were performed but were not very successful. If anything, it was not Andersen's unusual talents as a storyteller that grew in the latter part of his life, but rather his vanity, so that he was often a burden on others. For instance, when he returned to England in 1857 and spent five weeks with Charles Dickens and his family, they could not wait to see him leave because he was too nit-picky and overbearing. Wherever he went — and he continued to make annual excursions to other countries and cities — Andersen insisted on being coddled and pampered. At the same time, he sought close male friendships, often amorous, but never fulfilled in the way he desired. The older he became, the more lonely he felt, and the more he needed some kind of warm family life to replace the Collins, who continued to assist him and manage his affairs, but kept their distance. In 1865, Andersen began a very close friendship with two wealthy Jewish families, the Melchiors and the Henriques, who became his dedicated supporters. Although he maintained a residence in Copenhagen and went abroad to visit the World Exposition in Paris and such countries as Spain, Germany, and Switzerland in 1867, Andersen often stayed at their estates. By 1873, it was clear that he was suffering from cancer of the liver, and although he courageously fought the disease and even made a few trips and attended social functions during the next two years, he finally succumbed to the cancer on August 4, 1875.

Most anthologies of Andersen's fairy tales and stories tend to publish them chronologically according to the dates they first appeared in
Danish. This type of organization enables readers to follow Andersen's
development as a writer and to draw parallels with the events in his life.
It also has a disadvantage, because many critics and readers interpret
the tales autobiographically and tend to trace biographical details in his
tales. For example, "The Ugly Duckling" is generally regarded as a representation of the trials and tribulations of the outsider Andersen, who
had to overcome obstacles to reveal his aristocratic nature as a swan.
"The Little Mermaid" has frequently been interpreted as a reflection of
the unrequited love that Andersen felt for Edvard Collin. "The Nightingale" mirrors the tenuous relationship between Andersen the artist
and his patron the king of Denmark. There is undoubtedly some truth
to these interpretations. All writing has psychological and biographical
dimensions. But to constantly view most of Andersen's tales as symbolical stories about his own life and experiences can diminish the depth
and originality of many of his narratives. At his best, Andersen was an
unusually creative and sensitive writer whose imagination enabled him
to transform ordinary occurrences and appearances into extraordinary
stories that open new perspectives on life. He was not a profound philosophical thinker, but he had a knack of responding spontaneously and
naively to the world around him, and a talent to convey his wonder
about the miracles of life through short narrative prose that could be
awe-inspiring. Moreover, because he always felt oppressed, dominated,
and misrecognized, he sought to assess and grasp the causes of suffering
and offered hope to his readers — a hope that he himself needed to
pursue his dreams.

It therefore makes eminent sense to try to "categorize" Andersen's
tales in a nontraditional, that is, nonchronological manner to try to
appreciate some of the common themes that bind them together and
that he tried to weave into his narratives time and again from 1835 to
1875. Though it is admittedly difficult to typify all his tales, I believe
that their common themes will allow for a broader and more critical appreciation of his works, and might make some of his intentions
clearer. Therefore, I have divided the tales into the following categories:
the artist and society; the adaptation of folklore; original fairy tales;

evangelical and religious tales; the anthropomorphization of animals and nature; the humanization of toys and objects; and legends. There are, of course, overlapping themes and motifs, and a tale in one category could possibly be included in another. Yet, looked at from the vantage point of these categories, Andersen's tales may assume more relevance in a sociocultural context.

The Artist and Society

One of Andersen's most insightful and profound fairy tales, one that fully addresses his philosophy of art and the artist, is "The Nightingale" (1844), and in my opinion, it deserves to be placed first in any anthology of Andersen's tales, followed by "The Gardener and the Gentry" (1872). The first is clearly a fairy-tale allegory about the relationship of the artist to his patron, and the second is a bitter ironic story, also about patronage, but more specifically about folklore and the artist's role in Denmark. Although it is difficult to claim which category of Andersen's tales is the most important, it is clear that there was an overriding concern in all his tales about the virtue of art and the genuine storyteller as cultivator of the social good. Andersen was writing at a time when the status of the professional and independent writer was in the process of being formed. As I have already mentioned, in Denmark and most of Europe it was virtually impossible to earn a living as a professional writer from the profits of one's publications. Therefore, a writer either had to have an independent income, trade, and profession, or he had to have a wealthy patron to support his art work. At this time in Europe there was no copyright law, so a writer's works were not fully protected. If a writer were dependent on a patron, he would be obliged to respect and pay attention to the expectations of his benefactor. In both "The Nightingale" and "The Gardener and the Gentry," Andersen depicts the quandary of the artist, who must suffer the indignities of serving upper-class patrons because they do not appreciate his great accomplishments. In each case, the artist is a commoner or is common looking, but capable of producing uncommon art. For Andersen, uncommon art was "authentic" and "true" and stemmed from nature, that is, the natural talents of the artist. True art is also essential and therapeutic, for humankind cannot do without it. In "The Nightingale," the artist/

bird heals the emperor, who realizes that mechanical art is artificial. In "The Gardener and the Gentry," Andersen is more cynical and depicts an arrogant rich couple, unable to appreciate the originality of their innovative artist/gardener. Despite their ignorance and closed minds, true art succeeds, indicating Andersen's strong belief that the artist who is naturally endowed will somehow shine forth. One can always distinguish the true art from the false, and all the other tales in the section of the artist and society reflect how Andersen constantly reexamined the nature of storytelling and the salvation it offered all people. In one of his very last tales, "The Cripple" (1872), it is the fairy tale that enables a sick boy to regain his health, a personal wish fulfillment that transcends the personal condition to become a universal narrative about art's wondrous powers.

The Adaptation of Folklore

Many famous writers of fairy tales have made and continue to make extraordinary use of folk tales that were spread by word of mouth, and Andersen was no exception. In fact, most of Andersen's early tales such as "The Tinderbox" (1835), "Little Claus and Big Claus" (1835), "The Princess on the Pea" (1835), and "The Traveling Companion" (1835) are based on Danish folk tales that he heard or read. He may have even used German and European tales collected by the Brothers Grimm as his sources. For instance, "The Tinderbox" and "Little Claus and Big Claus" are closely related to the Grimms' "The Blue Light" and "The Little Farmer," respectively, and some other tales show the influence of the Grimms. Knowing the sources enables us to study how Andersen appropriated and enriched these tales to reflect upon conditions in Danish society and upon the trajectory of his life. "The Traveling Companion" is a good example, for it is an oral tale that was widespread in the Scandinavian countries and most of Europe. Folklorists refer to it as a tale type about "the grateful dead," in which a dead man, whose corpse is maltreated, rises to help a young man, who kindly protects the corpse from abuse. What is interesting in Andersen's version is that the young man is devout and trusts the Lord and his dead father in Heaven to guide him through life. Andersen combines pagan and Christian motifs to illustrate the rise of a poor naive man, whose goodness enables him to marry a princess. As in many of his other tales that stem from folklore, Andersen colored them with his personal experience while also using the folk perspective to expose the contradictions of the aristocratic class, as in "The Swineherd" (1842). Here he remains close to the folk perspective that he also developed in some of his original fairy tales, such as "The Emperor's New Clothes" (1837). His early adaptations of folklore reveal that Andersen was in an "apprentice" phase as a writer of short prose. He relied on the structure and contents of these tales to develop his own style and tone that was fermented by the simple folk mode of storytelling. Andersen's style is really not so much "childlike" as it is "folksy," and it is this blend of the intimate down-to-earth storyteller with folk motifs and literary themes that gave rise to some of his most significant fairy tales.

Original Fairy Tales

It is perhaps an exaggeration to assert that Andersen's fairy tales are "original" because all his narratives reveal how much he borrowed from literature and from the folklore tradition. Nevertheless, he endowed them with his own original touch and personal experiences that, even today, make them somewhat unique narratives. This is the major feature of his original literary fairy tales: He turned known literary motifs into provocative and uncanny stories that challenged conventional expectations and explored modes of magic realism that he learned from the German romantics, especially E. T. A. Hoffmann. Two of his greatest fairy tales, "The Shadow" (1847) and "The Little Mermaid" (1837), demonstrate his talent for transforming known folk and literary motifs into highly complex narratives about identity formation. "The Shadow," which is clearly based on the German writer Adelbert von Chamisso's novella *Peter Schlemihl* (1813), in which a man sells his shadow to the devil, can also be traced to E. T. A. Hoffmann's tale "The New Year's Adventure" (1819), in which a man gives up his reflection for love. For Andersen, this loss of a shadow or reflection is transformed into a problematic psychological conflict in which unconscious forces debilitate and eventually destroy a strong ego. The learned man's identity is literally effaced by his shadow. In "The Little Mermaid," another tale based on Friedrich de la Motte Fouqué's novella *Undine* (1816), Andersen depicts the quest for identity in a more positive light. There are strong religious overtones in this narrative in which a young girl learns that to become human involves self-sacrifice, humility, and devotion. Christian redemption is promised if the mermaid wants to fulfill her destiny. This is often the case in others of Andersen's fairy tales, such as "The Bronze Pig" (1842) and "Ib and Little Christina" (1855). However, many reflect Andersen's desire to uncover social contradictions. What often makes his original tales original is their irony, a key element in "The Shadow," but even more pronounced in "The Emperor's New Clothes" (1837) and "The Naughty Boy" (1835). Andersen used the metaphorical mode of the fairy tale to expose social hypocrisy, and in the best of his original fairy tales, he left his readers not with happy endings, but with startling endings aimed at prompting them to reflect upon ethical and moral behavior.

Evangelical and Religious Tales

Andersen is not commonly thought of as a religious writer, and yet, if one studies the entire corpus of his tales, it is apparent that religious motifs and themes run through a majority of them. This is indeed one of the reasons that Andersen became so popular in the nineteenth century: He "tamed" the pagan or secular aspects of the folk- and fairy-tale tradition and made them acceptable to a nineteenth-century European and American reading public. To a certain extent, some of his tales fit the standards of evangelical literature that was very prevalent and popular throughout Europe and North America. "The Snow Queen" (1845) and "The Red Shoes" (1845) are good examples. Both depict young girls who place their lives in the hands of God and are saved because they trust in the Lord's powers of redemption. In "The Snow Queen," it becomes clear by the end of the tale that Gerda will need the assistance of angels and the Lord to save Kai. The very beginning of this tale establishes the connection between the devil and the snow queen, so that the narrative develops into a Christian conflict between good and evil. In "The Red Shoes," the unfortunate Karen is mercilessly punished for her pride, and she must have her feet cut off and learn Christian humility before she can be accepted into Heaven. Andersen tended to chastise girls or use them as examples in Christian allegorical fairy tales that celebrated the intelligent design of God. Whether the girl is reprimanded, as in

"The Girl Who Stepped on Bread" (1859), or elevated to the level of a saint, as in "The Little Match Girl" (1845), Andersen insisted that they become self-sacrificial and pious. It was not much different for the male characters in Andersen's tales, but interestingly, he did not treat them as harshly as he did girls. Whatever the case may be, almost all of Andersen's religious tales and many of his others indicate that the only way to fulfill one's destiny is to place one's trust in the Lord's hands.

The Anthropomorphization of Animals and Nature

Placing one's faith in God is an undercurrent in Andersen's most famous fairy tale "The Ugly Duckling" (1844). Although there are no Christian references in this narrative, Andersen uses the tradition of animal tales to demonstrate that there is such a thing as intelligent design. The duckling must have faith to overcome all the obstacles in his life so that he can triumph in the end. As in the traditional tales in which animals, insects, and plants speak and come to life, Andersen conveys didactic morals. They are not always religious. In fact, Andersen enjoys poking fun at human foibles such as pomposity in "The Spruce Tree" (1845) and "The Dung Beetle" (1861). His short tales are pungent and often bitterly ironic. They stand in the tradition of Aesop's fables and reflect Andersen's notions of "survival of the fittest." Though he rejected Darwin's ideas, many of Andersen's tales that deal with anthropomorphic animals and plants are concerned with intense social and natural conflict. He understood the fierce battles waged in the European societies of his day, but instead of recounting these conflicts in realistic stories, Andersen anthropomorphized animals and nature to comment critically on delicate issues and taboo subjects of his times.

The Humanization of Toys and Objects

Much in the same way that he used animals and nature, Andersen "humanized" toys and inanimate objects to comment on social issues and human weaknesses. Here his model was E. T. A. Hoffmann, who had experimented with this narrative mode in such tales as "The Nutcracker and the Mouse King" (1816). The influence can be seen in Andersen's "The Steadfast Tin Soldier" (1838). But perhaps more important is his tale "The Shepherdess and the Chimney Sweep" (1845), in which Andersen uses porcelain figures to ruminate philosophically on the fear of freedom. What is intriguing in Andersen's tales about toys and objects is the realistic description. He had a great eye for detail and depicted the toys, objects, and their settings carefully and precisely so that it almost seems natural that they would come to life. Tiny incidental and neglected objects, such as a darning needle or rags, served as the subject matter for serious philosophical and social concerns that involve survival and immortality.

Legends

Andersen was also concerned about traditions, and although he became very cosmopolitan and developed a hate-love relationship with Denmark, he sought to mine the Danish soil, so to speak, to celebrate its richness. Throughout his tales there are references to Danish legends and proverbs, and he relied on them to add local color to his narratives. He often heard local legends on his trips in Denmark, or he saw something legendary that inspired his imagination. Two good examples are "Holger the Dane" (1845) and "Everything in Its Right Place" (1853). Although the tale about the legendary king who rises from the dead to save his country can be found in other cultures, Andersen based his tale on Danish lore and wrote at a time when Denmark was engaged in a conflict with Prussia. Thus, it contains patriotic elements, something unusual for Andersen, who was a loyal Danish citizen but never really patriotic. More typical of Andersen is "Everything in Its Right Place," in which he invents his own local legend about a family's history and its house to comment on class conflict. Houses and mansions abound in Andersen's stories, and although he knew some of their legendary histories, he was at his best when he invented their legends. They were always bound up with his real experiences and realistic appraisal of Danish society.

Andersen's range as a short-story writer was great. Not only did he experiment with a variety of genres, but he also dealt with diverse social and psychological problems in unusual narrative modes. He was a master of self-irony and often employed the first-person narrative to poke fun at himself and simultaneously at conceited people who tell stories that reveal their pretentiousness without their realizing it. Some of his more imaginative fairy tales are told in a vivacious colloquial style that appears to be flippant, and then he suddenly introduces serious issues that transform the tale into a complex narrative of survival and salvation. Although he could be overly sentimental, religious, and pathetic, Andersen was deeply invested in the issues that he raised in his tales. It was almost as if life and death were at risk in his short prose, and he needed to capture the intensity of the moment. This is perhaps why he kept trying to write from different vantage points, used different genres, experimented with forms and ideas borrowed from other writers, and kept infusing his own life experiences into the narratives. Little is known in the English-speaking world about the tireless creative experiments of this tormented writer called Hans Christian Andersen. He tried to make a fairy tale out of his life to save himself from his sufferings. Whether he succeeded is open to question, but he did succeed in leaving us fantastic tales that still stun us and compel us to reflect on the human will to survive.

II. CRITICAL REFLECTIONS ABOUT HANS CHRISTIAN ANDERSEN, THE FAILED REVOLUTIONARY

For years the public image of Hans Christian Andersen in North America has been associated with images of Danny Kaye singing "I'm Hans Christian Andersen" in the popular 1952 Samuel Goldwyn film with the title *Hans Christian Andersen*. Happy-go-lucky, adored by children, compassionate, innocent, and modest, the cinematic Andersen is a total fraud, and this is made abundantly clear in the two most recent biographies by Jackie Wullschlager and Jens Andersen, who depict Andersen as a tortured individual. Indeed, as I have already noted, Andersen had very little to do with children and had an enormous but fragile ego. He was anything but naive and pleasant. In fact, as I have already demonstrated, he was very shrewd and calculating and could also be obnoxious. Most of all, he was desperate for love and admiration.

This combined portrayal of the complex-ridden Andersen by Wullschlager and Jens Andersen, who lean over backward to be fair to him, is not new at all. During the past thirty years there have been numerous critical studies of Andersen's life and writings, and in Denmark where he is considered a national literary figure, most Danes are familiar with the dark side of his putative charmed life. What makes the two recent biographies so important is that they, along with the insightful introduction of Diane Crone Frank and Jeffrey Frank to their new translation of Andersen's tales, bring together most of the recent research on Andersen's life, making use of rare documents that enlarge and enrich our picture of the notorious Dane, who lied time and again in his own autobiography *The Fairy Tale of My Life* to recast himself as fortune's child.

However, there are three aspects of Andersen's works that the biographies by Wullschlager and Andersen do not discuss, and if there is a weakness to these two fine works, it is their inability to deal critically and thoroughly with the general mediocrity of his writing and his failure to pursue the revolutionary aesthetic and ideological program that he announced in his initial fairy tales. Here we must remember that Andersen wrote six novels, over thirty plays, several volumes of poetry, five travelogues, and 156 tales. With the exception of ten to fifteen of his stories, practically none of these works are read today, either in Danish or in English. Overall, Andersen was an imitative, eclectic, and sentimental writer who, despite his narcissism, is fascinating more for the way he cut out his own tongue and kowtowed to an upper class elite and religious reading public than he is for his prodigious writings and for transforming the fairy tale. If he has left a legacy for modernism or postmodernism, then it stems more from the compromises he made in his writing, the sublimation of his rage that stemmed from humiliation by the upper classes, and his ambivalent desire to fully expose the arrogance and unjust behavior of the upper classes. The best of Andersen's fairy tales are what a German critic has called *schräg*, which can be translated as oblique, eccentric, or weird, and in my opinion, it is this dubious virtue that renders his stories relevant for our troubled day and age and call out for our attention. But before I discuss how and why they are *schräg*, I want to comment on three aspects of his fairy tales that need to be grasped if we are to understand whether he has really left behind a legacy for our days: his imitation and unique appropriation of the German romantics, his overbearing religiosity, and his ideological compromise with the ruling classes.

The Imitation and Appropriation of the German Romantics

As Jens Andersen makes clear, Andersen more or less "stumbled" upon the fairy tale as a form in which he could best express his sentiments, ideas, and beliefs. "One of Andersen's many literary projects in the spring of 1835 was a handful of tales 'told for children,' as he added to the title page. In May 1835, Andersen still had no idea that this would soon become the strongest playing card of both his life and work; he was thinking more about the money he might earn from these little stories. Yet he was excited about his new attempts in this literary genre" (226).

In a letter to B. S. Ingemann in February of 1835, quoted by Jens Andersen, he states: "Next, I've started on several 'fairy tales *told* for children,' and I think I've made them a success. I've presented a couple of the tales that I myself liked as a child, but which I don't think are known. I've written them exactly as I would tell them to a *child*" (226).

Much has been made of Andersen's unique if not radical transformation of children's literature and the fairy tale in Denmark, and though his tales may have been unusual in Denmark, they were not exceptional if we compare them to fairy tales that had already been produced in Germany, France, and England. Moreover, it is clear from the beginning that Andersen never really intended his tales for a children's reading audience, for there was only a tiny one at that point in history. Nor had he had much experience telling tales to children. Andersen was keenly interested in making tales that he knew, either from his voracious reading or from those he had heard, more childlike and provocative than the normal run-of-the-mill tales in Denmark.

If we look at the first nine fairy tales he produced between 1835 and 1836, more than half of them stem from tales already circulating in print and in the oral tradition. "The Tinderbox," "Little Claus and Big Claus," and "Thumbelina" are similar to the Grimms' "The Blue Light," "Little Farmer," and "Thumbling's Travels," respectively. "The Traveling Companion," "The Princess on the Pea," and "The Emperor's New Clothes" were derived from the oral tradition. "The Little Mermaid" was clearly influenced by Friedrich de la Motte Fouqué's *Undine*, and only "Little Ida's Flowers" and "The Naughty Boy" appear to be Andersen's own inventions. The appropriation of tales from the oral and literary traditions is nothing new, nor is it to be belittled or condemned. In fact, the fairy tale thrives on appropriation up to the present day. The point that I want to make simply is that Andersen was not as "revolutionary" or original as he pretended to be, or as the Danes thought he was. If we compare his tale with those of Ludwig Tieck, Novalis, the Brothers Grimm, Adelbert von Chamisso, Fouqué, and especially E. T. A. Hoffmann, all authors with whom he was familiar, we can readily see that the German romantics had long since experimented with the fairy tale and had brought about major innovations that had transformed the genre so that it became philosophically more profound, encompassed children and adults as potential readers, developed a variety of narrative voices, questioned social norms and customs, and experimented with language. Like many writers of his time, Andersen was imitative and eclectic in his approach to the fairy tale.

To his credit, however, Andersen was among the first writers in Denmark to realize what the German romantics had accomplished, and sought to continue their "revolutionary" approach to the fairy tale by endowing it with a new childlike tone that was close to the oral telling of tales. Incidentally, Wilhelm Grimm had already begun doing this by 1819 in the second edition of the *Children's and Household Tales*, and by 1823 Edgar Taylor had translated some of the Grimms' tales into English, catering to young readers. So, even here, Andersen was not really unique, and it may be one of the reasons why he was so readily accepted and appreciated in Germany and also in England before he finally gained approval in Denmark. Given the provincial and pseudoclassical standards of Danish culture at that time, Andersen's turn to the fairy tale was at first considered strange, unconventional, and alarming, whereas in other countries his style and approach were not so unusual.

Of course, in tales such as "The Tinderbox," "Little Claus and Big Claus," and "The Emperor's New Clothes," there was truly cause for alarm because they are so "revolutionary" in tone, style, and content. In each of these tales, the rich and powerful figures are either overthrown or exposed as conceited, arrogant, and stupid. All three tales have close ties to the peasant oral tradition and can be regarded ideologically and aesthetically as Andersen's challenge to the ruling notions of how such tales should be transformed into startling literary tales and what the contents should be. Andersen's brisk, crisp, and vigorous narrative style conveys a moral and critical perspective from the lower classes — not from a child's viewpoint — that upsets the expectations of upper-class readers in Denmark. I would not consider them childlike, but rather blunt humorous tales that have something of what Mikhail Bakhtin has described as "carnivalesque" to them. For example, in "The Tinderbox," the discharged soldier strides into town after he has killed a witch without a second thought and taken money and the tinderbox with him. He lives life to the hilt, enjoys the princess without her permission, and eventually takes over the kingdom by having the magic dogs topple the king and queen. His "revolution," somewhat individualistic if not solipsistic, can be likened to a declaration by Andersen that he will speak for the underdog and downtrodden, and that he will use a new refreshing language filled with irony and frankness that will disarm the expectations of his readers and perhaps even induce them to have more compassion for those characters who must endure hardship and tyranny.

There is truly a startling quality to the early fairy tales of Andersen, and it is easy to sense his enthusiasm for this genre, as though he had finally found the appropriate mode to address deep personal concerns and channel the feelings of rage that he apparently felt due to the various humiliations he had suffered from his alleged superiors. Certainly, he had already endeavored to criticize them in his novels, poetry, and plays. But the short narrative form demanded that he be more concise, inventive, and provocative as he developed a tone that enabled him to identify with oppressed characters while poking fun at the upper classes. Yet, at the same time that he developed his "revolutionary" program for the fairy tale, he also sowed the seeds for its downfall. Two tales from this initial phase, "The Traveling Companion" and "The Little Mermaid," reveal to what extent Andersen would compromise his revolutionary program with overt religious messages that were in tune with the evangelical spirit of the times in Europe and with an ideological capitulation to the ruling class despite exposing their flaws.

Religiosity

Very few critics have discussed the overt religious nature of his tales, which is rather strange since the majority of the 156 tales in his final collection reveal a strong belief in intelligent design and moralistic evangelicalism. Perhaps the failure to address the religiosity is that the references to God, religion, and divine redemption have often been expunged in English translations, or they are not apparent in the select number of tales that continue to be reprinted. Whatever the case may be, religiosity plays a major role in his tales from the beginning to the very end. Although Andersen's religious beliefs were somewhat unorthodox and far from consistent, there is a common denominator that runs throughout his narratives, and it is connected to what we today associate with intelligent design. As H. Allen Orr has explained in his essay "Devolution: Why Intelligent Design Isn't," the movement of intelligent design's "main positive claim is that there are things in the world, most notably life, that cannot be accounted for by known natural causes and show features that, in any other context, we would attribute to intelligence. Living organisms are too complex to be explained by any natural — or, more precisely, by any mindless — process. Instead, the design inherent in organisms can be accounted for only by invoking a designer, and one who is very, very smart" (40, 48).

Without fully realizing that he was part of a movement of intelligent design, Andersen became a member of this creed early in his life and followed in the footsteps of his father figure and mentor, H. C. Ørsted, whom he met in the 1820s and whose views and book *The Spirit of Nature* (1849–50) had a great influence on him throughout his life. Basically, Ørsted, a major scientist in the nineteenth century, believed that there were natural laws of existence that had parallels in the thoughts of human beings, and that these laws were designed by God. It was therefore incumbent upon human beings to learn how to read the laws of nature to appreciate the Lord's design and to have faith in the "intelligent" way God had organized and arranged the world and each individual's life. Essentially, life is miraculous, but there are very intelligent ways that God has designed the world to benefit humankind. By reading the world scientifically, we can learn more about the divine in our lives. It is the divine miraculous in life that appealed to Andersen, and thus events that appear to be inexplicable could only be explained by believing in God's will and intelligence. For Andersen, to disobey God and to lose faith in what God has ordained are sinful acts and deserve to be severely punished.

In "The Traveling Companion" we have a clear idea of how intelligent design functioned and would function in many of Andersen's tales. The plot is a very simple one: A young man named Johannes, naive, innocent, and pious, is shattered when his father dies. However, when he glances at the sun during the burial, it was as if the sun wanted to say, "'You mustn't be sad, Johannes. See what a beautiful blue the sky is. Your father is up there now, asking the good Lord to see that things go well for you.'

"'I will always be good,' said Johannes. 'Then I'll go up to Heaven to my father. What a joy it will be see each other again! I will have so much to tell him, and he in turn will show me so many things, and teach me about all the splendors in heaven, just as he taught me here on earth. Oh, what a joy that will be!'"

Johannes decides to set out in the world to seek his fortune and says the Lord's Prayer before he departs. Along the way he gives a beggar some money and then saves a corpse from defilement by two nasty debtors. Despite being totally poor, he continues his journey and meets a stranger who asks him where he is going, and he responds, "Out into the wide world. ... I have neither father nor mother. I'm a poor lad, but surely Our Lord will help me." The stranger joins him as his traveling companion and assists him in defeating a troll and marrying a princess. In the end the traveling companion reveals himself as the dead man whom Johannes had helped, and he disappears.

There are so many references to God and piety in this tale that it reads like a moral exemplum or religious tract of the evangelical movement. What is significant about the tale is that it served as a paradigm for the same message that Andersen was to repeat time and again: There are certain young humble men — inevitably it is a male — chosen by God, to struggle and prove their virtuosity so that they will shine in the Lord's light. Their success is a reflection of God's grace and mysterious but intelligent design. There is, of course, an autobiographical aspect to this paradigmatic tale that Andersen told to himself time and again to sanctify his rise from poverty to wealth and fame. All his novels and many of his tales, such as "The Bronze Pig," "The Swineherd," "The Ugly Duckling," "Ib and Little Christina," "Clod Hans," and "The Ice Maiden," are variations on the same theme that can also be found in "The Snow Queen": Trust in God's design, and you will fare well, even if you should die.

This latter point is stressed in "The Little Mermaid," which can be read as a tale of Christian humility and redemption. Of course, there are numerous ways in which this complex tale can be read as Pil Dahlerup has demonstrated in his essay, "Splash! Six Views of 'The Little Mermaid,'" which includes structuralist, feminist, sociological, religious, and other approaches. But the most comprehensive study to date is Nancy Easterlin's Darwinian essay, "Hans Christian Anderson's Fish Out of Water," in which she concludes:

> In the final analysis, Andersen's "Little Mermaid" draws on cultural symbols and forms that derive from innate and universal preoccupations and ways of organizing, and in so doing employs elements that arouse reader/ listener emotion and thus motivate interest. ... But the *meaning* of the tale is another matter. Gazing through the lens of his romantic sensibility, his own essential loneliness and awkwardness and frustrated creativity, Andersen coaxes the colorful and glinting shards into a pattern reminiscent of the little mermaid's garden, delicate and fantastic yet resonant with themes of desire, loss, loneliness, and transcendence. All of these, it seems to me, are related to the twin modern preoccupations of self-completion and communal belonging, and thus derive from our fundamental ambivalence about those others beyond the self, an ambivalence that has become more pronounced with sociocultural complexity. Even as the mermaid herself rises joyously to meet the daughters of the air in the story's conclusion, the adult listener/reader experiences a distinct poignancy, even perhaps a feeling of unfairness, on the mermaid's behalf.

Unfortunately, Easterlin does not pursue the notion of "unfairness," which might also be connected with a feeling of unease. Indeed, as in the Disney film, the religious ending of Andersen's tale in which the good pious mermaid, who has already lost her voice and can barely walk without pain, does not suit the modern temperament because the tale is sexist and promotes a notion of the eternal soul and compliance with spiritual laws that Andersen invents for himself. Easterlin dismisses the idea that Andersen was a misogynist and that the tale is demeaning to women. Her focus is on the ambivalent status of the mermaid as lonely outsider, who seeks a soul and entrance into a civilized world order. Yet, as Easterlin also explains, Andersen's productive work takes place within a male social order, and Andersen seems to never tire of brutally punishing female figures for disrespecting its laws, as "The Red Shoes" and other tales clearly illustrate. The most crucial aspect of this tale concerns self-abnegation. It is only by abandoning herself to God that the Little Mermaid can earn an immortal soul in three hundred years. As the daughters of the air tell her, "For each day that we find a good child who makes his parents happy and deserves their love, God shortens our time of trial. The child doesn't know when we might fly through the room, and if we can smile with joy at the child, one year is subtracted from the three hundred. But if we see a naughty and bad child, then we have to weep tears of sorrow, and every tear adds another year to our time of trial."

Not only is Andersen's tale a spiritualization of a folk tale or legendary tradition of mermaids, as Easterlin correctly points out, but it is a religious and didactic tale that makes children responsible for the moral well-being of the world and their parents. Bluntly speaking, according to Andersen — and this can be traced throughout his tales — children must exhibit a certain purity of the soul and obedience to God's laws to succeed in life and to make their elders content. To overreach and to disrupt the Lord's design can result in a disaster, as it nearly does in "The Little Mermaid." What saves her is a pious act that leads her to deny her own nature and feelings and to accept her humble and minor position within a mystic theological framework based on Andersen's understanding of Christianity.

To be fair to Andersen, he did not organize all his narratives and tales around a Christian notion of self-abnegation and intelligent design, nor were the naughty or uppity girls in his tales the only ones that he views as deserving punishment. There is many a young boy who goes astray in his tales and is brutally reprimanded, but the good bad boy, too, as "The Snow Queen" shows, can be redeemed. In this particular case, it is the young Gerda, who places her faith in the Lord to show her how she can redeem Kai. It appears that children either should not have agency, or, if they have agency, they must carry out God's will, not their own. Their accomplishment is the Lord's accomplishment — a message that is not totally clear in Andersen's very first fairy tales, but this Christian creed of self-abnegation was soon to make many of them ponderous and pathetic. Moreover, it was also the betrayal of his revolutionary philosophy as an artist that hampered him from producing fairy tales that forcefully articulated his views as he first did in "The Tinderbox."

Ideological Compromise

The more Andersen wrote and became successful with a religious and upper-class reading public, the more his tales, with some major exceptions, became conservative, cautious, and conventional. His more extraordinary tales tended to be those that dealt with the tension between the artist and his patrons. The best example is, of course, "The Nightingale" (1844), in which Andersen described the plight of the artist dependent on aristocratic patronage. Although he defends the purity and authenticity of the artist's song in this tale and argues that the upper classes cannot survive without it, Andersen already shows that he has compromised his radical program of "The Tinderbox" by having the nightingale voluntarily return to the dying emperor and maintain his ties to the court. Whereas the king and queen were killed by the magical dogs, and the common soldier became a king in "The Tinderbox," the nightingale does not fully liberate himself from the emperor and become autonomous. Instead, he sets the conditions for his role as court artist, something that can be considered an advance for artists in Andersen's times, but this also represents a compromised position. As the nightingale tells the emperor:

> "I can't live in your palace, but let me come for a visit when I feel like it. In the evening I'll sit on a branch outside your window and sing for you — and bring you joy and wisdom as well. I'll sing about people who are happy and people who are suffering. I'll sing about good and evil, which nobody tells you about. But a little songbird gets around — to the poor fisherman, to the farmer's house, to everyone far away from you and your court. I love your heart more than I love your crown, but still there's something sacred about the crown. I'll come and sing for you, but you have to promise me one thing."

"Anything," the emperor said. He stood there in his imperial robe, which he had put on, and held his heavy gold sword against his heart.

"I'll ask only one thing: Don't let anyone know that a little bird tells you everything. It will be much better that way."

Few if any of the artistic characters in Andersen's fairy tales dare to expose and oppose the aristocracy. They grudgingly comply with upper-class expectations and reflect a servile attitude. Fearful of claiming independence and suffering the repercussions, Andersen's artists retreat, disguise their discontent, and suffer the indignation of misrecognition. Sometimes they even masochistically desire to be effaced. Perhaps the best example of the pitiful state of Andersen's "revolutionary" art program is one of his final tales, "The Gardener and the Aristocrats," also called "The Gardener and the Gentry," which can be read as a bitter testimony about his feelings toward the aristocracy. But, in my opinion, it is a sad commentary on how he failed in his own revolutionary program for the arts. This allegorical tale has a simple plot: An aristocratic family has a talented gardener named Larsen, whom they do not appreciate. Nevertheless, his products gain the attention of other aristocratic families far and wide in the world. Indeed, they profit from the fame of their gardener even as they belittle him because they are traditional and distrust his innovations. When a terrible storm uproots many of the old trees in the garden, Larsen finally has the opportunity to cultivate indigenous plants and brings about a great "revolution" in gardening that attracts national attention. However, his employers think differently:

"People beat the drums for everything that Larsen does," the family said. "He's a lucky man. I guess we really ought to be proud of having him."

But they weren't the least bit proud of having him. They knew that they were the employers and could fire Larsen. But they didn't do it, because they were good people, and there are lots of good people like them — which is a fortunate thing for every Larsen.

Andersen provocatively challenges his readers at the end of the tale to think about it. Of course, he wants his readers to reflect upon how conventional, pompous, and ridiculous the aristocrats are. But if we really think about his tale more comprehensively, we must also consider, as Andersen himself writes, how "faithful and devoted" the gardener is.

Let us recall that wonderfully disturbing comment by Heinrich Heine, recorded by Heinrich Teschner: "Andersen visited me here several years ago. He seemed to me like a tailor. This is the way he really looks. He is a haggard man with a hollow, sunken face, and his demeanor betrays an anxious, devout type of behavior that kings love. This is the reason why they give Andersen such a brilliant reception. He is the perfect representation of all poets, just the way kings want them to be." Heine placed his finger not only on a certain trait in Andersen's behavior, but also in his writing: Andersen's art was intended to bask in the eyes of the upper classes. He desperately sought their approval and felt that art, because it made the ordinary extraordinary, could not be fully recognized unless it was produced within the gardens of the aristocracy, so to speak, and received royal applause. Admittedly, Andersen was not afraid to poke fun at some of the aristocrats, but ultimately he was afraid to upset their expectations and carry forth a drastic change in the nature of the fairy tale or in any of the art forms that he practiced.

The Oblique and the Eccentric

What is left for us to consider from his revolutionary beginnings then is the "*schräg*" quality of his tales — the oblique and eccentric if not weird aspects that compel us to wonder and reflect about disturbing experiences and situations that caught his eye and inspired him to write about them in a candid and truthful manner. If Andersen still has an appeal and meaning for readers in the twenty-first century, it is because *some* of his tales, just a handful, depart from traditional storytelling, self-glorification, and religious conservatism. His most profound and relevant works transform the ordinary into the extraordinary and are disturbing because they reflect a disturbed mind at work that refuses to make concessions to conventional writing and thinking. On the back cover of the German dtv edition of *Schräge Märchen*, there is an interesting description of the contents that is partly hyperbolic and partly true: "In this book the reader will discover an unknown Andersen. What is offered is not mushy baby food, rather something anarchical, aggressive, witty — fairy tales about intoxication and revolt, sexuality and stock deals during the period of the industrial revolution." Michael Maar and Heinrich Detering, who collaborated in producing this German edition, selected thirty-eight tales, anecdotes, excerpts, and legends from Andersen's works that are not usually included in a typical edition of Andersen's short fiction. To be more precise, while a third of the tales are generally available in standard editions, two-thirds have been selected from Andersen's unpublished papers, novels, travel books, poetry, autobiography, and tales, which first appeared in English in *The Riverside Magazine*. I am not certain whether their claim of presenting an unknown Andersen really holds true, because if one reads the 156 tales in Andersen's final collection — and most readers never do — one can easily come to the same conclusion that Maar and Detering would like us to form about Andersen's work: His stories are weird and unsettling, and they are weird and unsettling because Andersen wrote a few radical fairy tales, legends, and anecdotes with a ferocious tone and spirit, along with many saccharine religious tales that drip with sentimentality and banality — and he wrote these types of tales and other strange and mundane narratives at the same time. Though I have tried to categorize Andersen's tales, I must admit that the categories must be fluid and flexible because Andersen could never categorize himself. This is perhaps the major virtue of the collection in *Schräge Märchen*: By selecting stories and commentaries largely intended for an adult readership, Maar and Detering reveal how Andersen could never accommodate himself fully to the position that he believed God had designated for him. If we recall, he began his 1846 autobiography this way: "My life is a pretty fairy tale, very rich and happy. If I had met a powerful fairy when I went out into the world poor and alone and she had said to me, 'Choose your path through life and your goal, and then, according to your spiritual development and the demands of reason in this world, I shall protect and guide you,' — my destiny could not have been happier, smarter, and better directed. My life's story will tell the world, what it says to me: there is a loving God, who directs everything for the best." This announcement, which Maar and Detering include in their collection, is weird because it is a lie, but it is a lie that Andersen constantly told and reiterated in different variants throughout his life. He tried to believe in this lie, but it is because Andersen could not live a false life that he paradoxically told this lie, hoping for God's protection. When he was truthful, he obliquely criticized himself for pretending to be something that he could never be. If

Andersen identified with "The Ugly Duckling," as closely as he did in print and in society during his lifetime, it is because he knew he was not and could not become a white swan. Not only did he suffer from class discrimination throughout his life, but his own inadequacies as a writer were apparent to him, or made apparent to him, and ironically, he was at his best and most oblique when he exposed himself. It is this realization that forms the basis of those *schräg* tales that may continue to resonate into the twenty-first century.

In *Schräge Märchen*, Maar and Detering open their selection with two haunting tales that truly capture Andersen's capacity to reflect critically not only on his condition as a writer, but also on the problematic nature of art and identity, that is, how difficult it is to determine the essence of true art and the authentic person. In the first tale, "The Writer," which was taken from Andersen's posthumous papers and was undated, the very title in Danish ("Skriveren") and German ("Der Schreiber") already indicates Andersen's concern. In both Danish and German, the terms "Digte" and "Dichter" are generally used for great writers. "Skriveren" and "Schreiber" are terms that might be better translated into English as "Scribbler," that is, an ordinary if not mediocre writer. Andersen's bitter tale is about a young man who is hired by a writer who needs someone who has good handwriting because his is bad. When the writer's stories are praised because they appear so charmingly written, the young scribbler feels he deserves all the credit, and he decides to take over the position of the writer. Now this scribbler could have had great success in society, but he wanted to outdo all the writers and wrote about everything he could — music, sculpture, poetry, people — without knowing anything. The most important thing for the scribbler was his beautiful handwriting. In actuality, he only produced junk and nonsense and died because of it. One of his friends who could write fairy tales wanted to write about his life, but even with the best of intentions, this friend could only produce a poor fairy tale. Andersen's unpublished tale reads like a Kafkaesque parable: pungent, enigmatic, and ironic. There is no description; none of the characters have names; the action is intense. A scribbler with no talent wants to transform himself into a grand writer, but his arrogance and lack of talent cause his downfall. He has no understanding of true art. His life constitutes the making

of a bad fairy tale that Andersen artfully uses to write his provocative
tale, which is not a fairy tale. It does not have a moral or a satisfying
ending, but it does have a counterpart in one of the best stories he ever
wrote, "The Shadow," which Detering and Maar position right after
"The Writer."

Almost every critic who has commented on "The Shadow" has
related it to Andersen's complex relationship with Edvard Collin, which
had homoerotic aspects to it. As Diane Crone Frank and Jeffrey Frank
remark in their introduction to *The Stories of Hans Christian Andersen*:

> Perhaps no story in the Andersen canon is as bitter, and personal, as
> "The Shadow" (1847), for it was born of deep enduring hurt: Edvard Col-
> lin, Andersen's closest friend — the son of Jonas Collin, his most impor-
> tant benefactor — rejected Andersen's suggestion that they address one
> another with the familiar "thou" form. Their exchange of letters in 1831
> (when Andersen was twenty-six) did not close the subject for Andersen.
> After "The Shadow" was published sixteen years later, the now-famous
> Andersen wrote to Edvard, "You can see in [an English newspaper],
> along with my picture that I'm 'one of the most remarkable and interest-
> ing man [sic] of his day!' Yet you're still too good to say 'thou' to me."

Certainly, "The Shadow" can be read autobiographically as a testimony to the humiliation that Andersen felt his entire life, and it
also reveals a certain self-hate, perhaps for his inability to confront
the humiliation. But its meaning transcends autobiography. As I have
already pointed out, Andersen was very familiar with the works of
Hoffmann and Chamisso, in particular Hoffmann's use of the double in
"Der Doppelgänger," and Chamisso's in *Peter Schlemihl*. Their exploration of paranoia contributed to Andersen's understanding of this theme,
and in many ways he went beyond them in "The Shadow," for the psychological dilemma, told with bitter irony, recounts the desperation of
a learned writer who loses control of his libido and imagination. The
gradual replacement of the learned man by his own shadow is frightening; not only are his powers usurped and his identity negated, but he is
obfuscated and killed because he cannot contend with a side of himself
that he had undervalued and underestimated.

Even more interesting is Clayton Koelb's interpretation in his essay
"The Rhetoric of Ethical Engagement." He argues that "The Shadow"

is an allegorical tale about the relationship between the artist and his work. The shadow cast by the learned writer can be understood as his own work that eclipses the real producer. As a result, the work on the free market determines its own meaning and takes its own course, and the author has no control over it. The work will continue to live while the author must die. What is horrifying to the author is that he may never be understood for what he accomplished; his intentions and authenticity will have no bearing on the future of what he originally produced. Koelb's stimulating interpretation sheds light on how astutely or intuitively Andersen grasped the situation of the freelance writer, who was not protected by copyright in the nineteenth century. It was practically impossible, especially in Denmark, for a writer to earn an independent living without some kind of patronage, and even as the free market developed, the writer was alienated because he had to sell himself and could not control the meaning and destiny of his works. The situation holds true even today. "The Shadow" does not only speak to the conditions under which writers and academics work, but it can also enable us to understand the crime of "stolen identity" and the trauma that a person feels when his or her identity is taken away. What proof do we have that we are alive other than passports, licenses, and social security numbers? Must we live with the fear that our identity can easily be stolen once some one else knows our numbers? Can we easily be exposed and blackmailed by the shadows we cast? What do we keep in the dark that can threaten us?

These are just some of the questions that Andersen's weird tale provokes today. And there are other *schräg* tales, such as "The Naughty Boy," "The Emperor's New Clothes," "Little Claus and Big Claus," and "The Swineherd," that are open-ended and reverse traditional expectations with biting irony, and perhaps they will play a role in determining Andersen's contested legacy. Indeed, we must ask whether this legacy overshadows the "true" Andersen.

As it now stands, each country in the world has its own Andersen, despite the fact that the government and cultural officials in Denmark have tried to orchestrate the meaning of a homogenized Andersen. In 2005, the commemoration year of Andersen's 200th birthday, Denmark's cultural offices endeavored to market this mediocre *schräg* writer as a

seven

The Flowering of the Fairy Tale in Victorian England

I

In contrast to France and Germany, England did not experience the flowering of the literary fairy tale until the middle of the nineteenth century. This late flowering is somewhat puzzling, for Great Britain had been a fertile ground for folklore in the Middle Ages. Dazzling fairies, mischievous elves, frightening beasts, clumsy giants, daring thieves, clever peasants, cruel witches, stalwart knights, and damsels in distress had been the cultural staple of peasants, the middle class, and aristocracy who told their tales at the hearth, in taverns, at courts, and in the fields throughout the British Isles. Extraordinary characters, miraculous events, superstitions, folk customs, and pagan rituals made their way quickly into the early vernacular of English works by renowned authors such as Chaucer, Spenser, Swift, Marlowe, and Shakespeare — works that became part of the classical British literary tradition. However, the literary fairy tale failed to establish itself as an independent genre in the eighteenth century, when one might have expected it to bloom as it did in France. The fairies and elves seemed to have been banned from their homeland, as if a magic spell had been cast over Great Britain.

Yet it was not magic so much as the actual social enforcement of the Puritan cultural code that led to the suppression of the literary fairy tale in England, while the oral tales still circulated. The domination of Calvinism after the Revolution of 1688 led to a stronger emphasis on preparing children and adults to be more concerned with moral character and conduct in this world, rather than to prepare them for a life hereafter. Through virtuous behavior and industry one would expect to be able to find the appropriate rewards in temporal society. Above all, Christian principles and the clear application of reason were supposed to provide the foundation for success and happiness in the family and at work. Rational judgment and distrust of the imagination were to be the guiding principles of the new enlightened guardians of Puritan culture and utilitarianism for the next two centuries. Despite the fact that the Puritans and later the utilitarians could not be considered as monolithic entities, and despite the fact that they each often viewed the Enlightenment itself as a kind of utopian fantasy, they often assumed the same hostile position toward the fairy tale that bordered on the ridiculous. Here a parallel can be drawn to the situation described in E. T. A. Hoffmann's marvelous tale "Little Zaches Named Zinnober," where a fanatical prime minister representing the new laws of the Enlightenment, which are to be introduced into Prince Paphnutius's realm, argues that fairies are dangerous creatures and capable of all sorts of mischief. Consequently, the pompous prime minister declares:

> Yes! I call them enemies of the enlightenment. They took advantage of the goodness of your blessed dead father and are to blame for the darkness that has overcome our dear state. They are conducting a dangerous business with wondrous things, and under the pretext of poetry, they are spreading uncanny poison that makes the people incapable of serving the enlightenment. Their customs offend the police in such a ghastly way that no civilized state should tolerate them in any way.

Obviously, England after 1688 was not a police state, but the laws banning certain types of amusement in the theater, literature, and the arts had a far-reaching effect on the populace. In particular, the oral folk tales were not considered good subject matter for the cultivation of young souls, and thus the "civilized" appropriation of these tales, which took place in France during the seventeenth and eighteenth centuries, undertaken by eminent writers such as Charles Perrault, Madame d'Aulnoy, Mlle de la Force, Mlle Lhéritier, Madame Leprince de Beaumont, and many others did not occur in England. On the contrary, the stories, poems, and novels written for children were mainly religious and instructional. If literary fairy tales were written and published, then they were transformed into didactic tales preaching hard work and pious behavior. Moreover, most of the fairy tales that circulated in printed form were chapbooks and penny books sold by peddlers to the lower classes. It was not considered proper to defend the fairies and elves — neither in literature for adults nor in literature for children.

The denigration of the fairy tale in England during the seventeenth and eighteenth centuries was in stark contrast to the cultivation of the tale in France and Germany, where it gradually came to express a new middle-class and aristocratic sensibility and flourished as an avant-garde form of art. In Great Britain the literary fairy tale was forced to go underground and was often woven into the plots of novels such as Richardson's *Pamela*. As an oral folk tale it could still dwell comfortably among the lower classes and circulate with disparagement among the upper classes; however, the literary institutionalization of the fairy-tale genre had to wait until the Romantic movement asserted the value of the imagination and fantasy at the end of the eighteenth century. Here it should be stressed that the English utilitarians of the late eighteenth century and the romantics actually shared the same utopian zeal that emanated from the principles of the Enlightenment. However, they differed greatly as to how to realize those principles in the cultural life of English society. The romantics sought to broaden the notions of the Enlightenment so that they would not become narrow and instrumentalized to serve vested class interests. In contrast, the utilitarians did indeed view the romantics as "enemies of the Enlightenment," à la Hoffmann, because they questioned the Protestant ethos and the prescriptions of order conceived by the utilitarians to establish the good society on earth. The questioning spirit of the romantics enabled them to play a key role in fostering the rise of the literary fairy tale in Great Britain, for the symbolism of the tales gave them great freedom to experiment and express their doubts about the restricted view of the utilitarians and traditional religion. Robert Southey, Charles Lamb, Thomas Hood,

Samuel Coleridge, and Hartley Coleridge all wrote interesting fairy tales along these lines, while Blake, Wordsworth, Keats, Byron, and Shelley helped to pave the way for the establishment of the genre and created a more receptive atmosphere for all forms of romance. In time, the return of the magic realm of the fairies and elves was viewed by the romantics and many early Victorians as a necessary move to oppose the growing alienation in the public sphere due to industrialization and regimentation in the private sphere. Indeed, the Victorians became more aware of the subversive potential of the literary fairy tale to question the so-called productive forces of progress and the Enlightenment, for it was exactly at this point that the middle and upper classes consolidated their hold on the public sphere and determined the rules of rational discourse, government, and industry that guaranteed the promotion of their vested interests. Supported by the Industrial Revolution (1830–90), the rise of the middle classes meant regimentation and institutionalization of all forms of life, and this in turn has had severe ramifications to the present day.

We tend to think of the Industrial Revolution mainly in economic and technological terms, but the impact of the Industrial Revolution was much more pervasive than this. It changed the very fabric of society in Great Britain, which became the world's first urban as well as industrial nation. Whereas the landed gentry and the rising middle classes benefited greatly from the innovations in commodities, techniques, and occupations that provided them with unprecedented comfort and cultural opportunities, such "progress" also brought penalties with it. As Barry Supple has pointed out in *The Victorians*, "the impersonalization of factories, the imposition of a compelling and external discipline, the prolonged activity at the behest of machinery, the sheer problem of mass living in cities, the anonymity of the urban community, the obvious overcrowding in the badly built housing devoid of the countryside, the unchecked pollution — all these must have amounted to a marked deterioration in the circumstances and therefore the standards of life for large numbers of people."

Such negative features of the Industrial Revolution did not go unnoticed by early Victorian writers and led to what is commonly called the Condition of England Debate. In actuality, this was not a single debate but a series of controversies about the spiritual and material foundations of English life, and it had a great effect on literary developments. For instance, as Catherine Gallagher has shown in her book *The Industrial Reformation of English Fiction 1832–1867*, disputes about the nature and possibility of human freedom, the sources of social cohesion, and the nature of representation were embraced by the novel and unsettled fundamental assumptions of the novel form. Just as the novel developed a certain discourse and narrative strategies to respond to the Condition of England Debate, the literary fairy tale conceived its own unique aesthetic modes and themes to relate to this debate. Writers like Charles Dickens, Thomas Hood, Thomas Carlyle, John Ruskin, and William Thackeray were among the first to criticize the deleterious effects of the Industrial Revolution. Interestingly, they all employed the fairy tale at one point to question the injustice and inequalities engendered by the social upheaval in England. What is unique about the initial stage of the literary fairy-tale revival in England is that the *form itself* was part of the controversial subject matter of the larger Condition of England Debate. The shifting attitudes toward children, whose imaginations were gradually declared more innocent than sinful, allowed for greater use of works of fancy to educate and amuse them. Even so, despite changing attitudes, German, French, and Danish works of fantasy first had to pave the way for the resurgence of the literary fairy tale and the defense of the imagination in cultural products for children.

As we know, close to two centuries of British educators, writers, and publishers debated the merits of fairy tales, and they were found — at least by the conservative camp, or what would be called the "moral majority" today — useless and dangerous for the moral education of young and old alike. Writers like Mrs. Trimmer and Mrs. Mortimer argued at the end of the eighteenth century that fairy tales made children depraved and turned them against the sacred institutions of society. Their arguments continued to be influential at the beginning of the nineteenth century, although in a somewhat modified form. For instance, one of the champions of the anti-fairy-tale school, Mrs. (Mary Martha) Sherwood rewrote Sarah Fielding's important eighteenth-century work, *The Governess*, or *The Little Female Academy* in 1820, and she stressed:

Instruction when conveyed through the medium of some beautiful story or pleasant tale, more easily insinuates itself into the youthful mind than anything of a drier nature; yet the greatest care is necessary that the kind of instruction thus conveyed should be perfectly agreeable to the Christian dispensation. Fairy-tales therefore are in general an improper medium of instruction because it would be absurd in such tales to introduce Christian principles as motives of action. ... On this account such tales should be very sparingly used, it being extremely difficult, if not impossible, from the reason I have specified, to render them really useful.

One way to oppose the rigid upholders of the Puritan law-and-order school was to import fairy tales from France, Germany, and Scandinavia and to translate them as exotic works of art. This mode of counterattack by the defenders of fairy tales gained momentum at the beginning of the nineteenth century. In 1804, Benjamin Tabart began to publish a series of popular tales, which eventually led to his book *Popular Fairy Tales* (1818) containing selections from *Mother Goose, The Arabian Nights, Robin Hood,* and Madame d'Aulnoy's tales. In 1818, Friedrich de la Motte Fouqué's *Undine* was published and gained acceptance because of its obvious Christian message about the pagan water nymph who leads a virtuous life once she gains a human soul. In 1823 John Harris, an enterprising publisher, who had already produced *Mother Bunch's Fairy Tales* in 1802, edited an important volume titled *The Court of Oberon; or, The Temple of Fairies,* which contained tales from Perrault, d'Aulnoy, and *The Arabian Nights.* Coincidentally, this book appeared in the same year that the most important publication to stimulate an awakened interest in fairy tales for children and adults was issued, namely *German Popular Stories,* Edgar Taylor's translation of a selection from *Kinder- and Hausmärchen* by the Brothers Grimm with illustrations by the gifted artist George Cruikshank. Taylor made an explicit reference to the debate concerning fairy tales in his introduction, in which he aligned himself with the "enemies of the Enlightenment":

The popular tales of England have been too much neglected. They are nearly discarded from the libraries of childhood. Philosophy is made the companion of the nursery: we have lisping chemists and leading-string mathematicians; this is the age of reason, not of imagination; and the loveliest dreams of fairy innocence are considered as vain and frivolous. Much might be urged against this rigid and philosophic (or rather unphilosophic) exclusion of works of fancy and fiction. Our imagination is surely as susceptible of improvement by exercise, as our judgement or our memory; and so long as such fictions only are presented to the young mind as do not interfere with the important department of moral education, a beneficial effect must be produced by the pleasurable employment of a faculty in which so much of our happiness in every period of life consists.

The publication of *German Popular Stories* acted as a challenge to the anti-fairy-tale movement in Britain, and its favorable reception led to a second edition in 1826 and a new wave of translations. For instance, Thomas Carlyle published two volumes titled *German Romances*, which included his translations of fairy tales by Johann Karl August Musäus, Ludwig Tieck, Adelbert von Chamisso, and E.T.A. Hoffmann in 1827. Also his unique book *Sartor Resartus* (1831) was based to a certain extent on Johann Wolfgang von Goethe's "Das Märchen." Various English periodicals carried the translated tales of Otmar, Chamisso, Hoffmann, Tieck, Novalis, and Wilhelm Hauff in the 1830s, and new translations of the Grimm brothers' tales appeared in 1839, 1846, 1849, and 1855. In addition to the significant impact of the German tales, the arrival in 1846 of Hans Christian Andersen's *Wonderful Stories for Children*, translated by Mary Howitt, was a momentous occasion. His unusual tales, which combined fantasy with a moral impulse in line with traditional Christian standards, guaranteed the legitimacy of the literary fairy tale for middle-class audiences. From this point on, the fairy tale flowered in many different forms and colors and expanded its social discourse to cover such different topics as proper comportment for children, free will, social exploitation, political justice, and authoritarian government. The 1840s also saw the translation of the *Arabian Nights* (1840) by Edwin Lane; Felix Summerly's *Home Treasury* (1841–49), which included such works as "Little Red Riding Hood," "Beauty and the Beast," and "Jack and the Beanstalk"; Ambrose Merton's *The Old Story Books of England* (1845); and Anthony Montalba's *Fairy Tales of All Nations* (1849).

The gradual recognition and acceptance of the fairy tale by the middle classes, which had heretofore condemned the genre as frivolous and pernicious, did not mean, however, that the Puritan outlook of the bourgeoisie had undergone a radical change. Indeed, to a certain extent, one can talk about a "co-option" of "the enemies of the Enlightenment." That is, middle-class writers, educators, publishers, and parents began to realize that the rigid, didactic training and literature used to rear their children was dulling their senses and creativity. Both children and adults needed more fanciful works to stimulate their imagination and keep them productive in the social and cultural spheres of British society. Emphasis was now placed on fairy-tale reading and storytelling as recreation, a period of time and a place in which the young could recuperate from instruction and training and re-create themselves, so to speak, without the social pressure calculated to make every second morally and economically profitable. The stimulation of the imagination became just as important as the cultivation of reason for moral improvement. Although many tedious books of fairy tales with didactic lessons were published, such as Alfred Crowquill's *Crowquill's Fairy Book* (1840) and Mrs. Alfred Gatty's *The Fairy Godmothers and Other Tales* (1851), various English writers began to explore the potential of the fairy tale as a form of literary communication that might convey both individual and social protest, as well as personal conceptions of alternative, if not utopian, worlds. To write a fairy tale was considered by many writers a social symbolical act that could have implications for the education of children and the future of society.

In the period between 1840 and 1880 the general trend among the more prominent fairy-tale writers was to use the fairy-tale form in innovative ways to raise social consciousness about the disparities among the different social classes and the problems faced by the oppressed due to the Industrial Revolution. Numerous writers took a philanthropic view of the poor and underprivileged and sought to voice a concern about the cruel exploitation and deprivation of the young. It was almost as though the fairy tales were to instill a spirit of moral protest in the reader — and, as I mentioned, the Victorian writers always had two implied ideal readers in mind: the middle-class parent and child — so that they would take a noble and ethical stand against forces of intolerance and authoritarianism. For instance, John Ruskin's *King of the Golden River* (1841) depicted two cruel brothers who almost destroy their younger brother, Gluck, because of their greed and dictatorial ways (fig. 9). Moreover, they threaten the laws of nature, reminding one of the

Figure 9. "King of the Golden River." From John Ruskin's The King of the Golden River. Illustr. Richard Doyle. London: Smith and Elder, 1851.

cruel materialism of the Industrial Revolution. However, due to Gluck's innocence and compassion, he does not succumb to the brutality of his brothers and is eventually helped by the King of the Golden River to re-create an idyllic realm. Similarly, Francis Edward Paget wrote *The Hope of the Katzekopfs* in 1844 to decry the selfishness of a spoiled prince and convey a sense of self-discipline through the lessons taught by a fairy, an imp, and the old man Discipline. William Makepeace Thackeray composed *The Rose and the Ring* (1855), a delightful discourse on rightful and moral rule in which the humble Prince Giglio and Princess Rosalba regain their kingdoms from power-hungry and materialistic usurpers. Frances Browne also made a significant contribution to the fairy-tale genre with the publication of *Granny's Wonderful Chair* in 1856. Here the wonderful chair provides the framework for a group of connected tales told to the young girl Snowflower, whose virtuous and modest behavior parallels the conduct of the protagonists in the tales. Though poor and orphaned at the beginning of the book, Snowflower's diligence is rewarded at the end. The progression in *Granny's Wonderful Chair* enables the reader to watch Snowflower learn and grow to be the "ideal" Victorian girl. Such is also the case in Charles Kingsley's *The Water Babies* (1863), except that here the model is a boy. To be exact it is Tom, a chimney sweep, who leaves his body behind him to become a water baby in the sea. There he (with others as well) undergoes various adventures and learns all about rewards and punishments for his behavior, especially from Mrs. Bedonebyasyoudid. In the end he realizes that he must take the initiative in being good, for people always tend to reciprocate in kind.

Almost all the fairy tales of the 1840s and 1850s use allegorical forms to make a statement about Christian goodness in contrast to the greed and materialism that are apparently the most dangerous vices in English society. The moralistic tendency is most apparent in such works as Catherine Sinclair's "Uncle David's Nonsensical Story about Giants and Fairies" in *Holiday House* (1839), Clara de Chatelain's *The Silver Swan* (1847), Mark Lemon's *The Enchanted Doll* (1849), Alfred Crowquill's *The Giant Hands* (1856), and Mary and Elizabeth Kirby's *The Talking Bird* (1856). In each case the use of the fairy-tale form as a fanciful mode to delight readers is justified because of the seriousness of the subject matter. Consequently, the fairy tale at mid-century was a manifesto for itself and a social manifesto to blend their regressive urges with progressive social concerns, without succumbing to overt didacticism. The compulsion felt by writers to rationalize their preference for using the fairy tale to express their opinions about religion, education, and progress often undercut their aesthetic experiments. Nevertheless, even the boring allegorical fairy tales were an improvement on the stern, didactic tales of realism that English children had been obliged to read during the first part of the nineteenth century.

Also underlying the efforts of the Victorian fairy-tale writers was a psychological urge to recapture and retain childhood as a paradisiacal realm of innocence. This psychological drive was often mixed with a utopian belief that a more just society could be established on earth. U. C. Knoepflmacher makes the point in his essay "The Balancing of Child and Adult" (1983) that the Victorian writers' "regressive capacity can never bring about a total annihilation of the adult's self-awareness": "Torn between the opposing demands of innocence and experience, the author who resorts to the wishful, magical thinking of the child nonetheless feels compelled, in varying degrees, to hold on to the grown-up's circumscribed notions about reality. In the better works of fantasy of the period, this dramatic tension between the adult and childhood selves becomes rich and elastic: conflict and harmony, friction and reconciliation, realism and wonder, are allowed to interpenetrate and coexist."

Knoepflmacher asserts that the regressive tendency balanced by self-awareness was a major feature of most Victorian fantasies. In his stimulating study, *Ventures into Childland: Victorians, Fairy Tales, and Femininity* (1998), he explores the pursuit of childhood and conceptual differences of femininity between such male authors as George MacDonald, Lewis Carroll, and William Makepeace Thackeray, and such female authors as Jean Ingelow, Christina Rossetti, and Juliana Horatia Ewing. Noting that the male writers tended to seek compensation for the Victorian society's division of the sexes in their yearning for powerful mothers, Knoepflmacher reveals that the women writers reclaimed the fairy tale from male writers in their own unique projections of femininity. Despite the differences, the psychological quests of purity and innocence by both male and female authors share a great deal in common

and can be linked to a conscious social utopian tendency in their writings that paradoxically envisions a return home as a step forward to a
home that must be created, one that is implicitly critical of daily life in
Victorian society. Certainly if we consider the three most important
writers and defenders of fairy tales from 1840 to 1880, Charles Dickens, Lewis Carroll, and George MacDonald, it is apparent that their
quest for a new fairy-tale form stemmed from a psychological rejection
and rebellion against the "norms" of English society that would move
their readers to look forward to change. If the Industrial Revolution had
turned England upside down on the path toward progress, then these
writers believed that English society had to be revolutionized once more
to regain a sense of free play and human compassion. The remarkable
achievement of Dickens, Carroll, and MacDonald lies in their artistic
capacity to blend their regressive urges with progressive social concerns,
without succumbing to overt didacticism.

II

In his essay "Frauds on Fairies" (1853) published in *Household Words*,
Dickens took issue with George Cruikshank and other writers who
sought to tarnish the fairy tale by attaching explicit moral or ethical messages to it. Dickens argued that "in an utilitarian age, of all
other times, it is a matter of grave importance that fairy tales should
be respected. Our English red tape is too magnificently red even to
be employed in the tying up of such trifles, but everyone who has
considered the subject knows full well that a nation without fancy,
without some romance, never did, never can, never will, hold a great
place under the sun." Dickens himself tended to incorporate fairy-
tale motifs and plots primarily in his novels and particularly in his
Christmas Books (1843–45). It is almost as though he did not want
to stain the childlike innocence of the tales that he read as a young
boy — tales that incidentally filled him with hope during his difficult
childhood — by replacing them with new ones. But Dickens did use
the fairy tale to make political and social statements, as in "Prince
Bull" (1855) and "The Thousand and One Humbugs" (1855), and his

regressive longings for the innocent bliss of fairyland are made most evident in his essay "A Christmas Tree" (1850):

> Good for Christmas time is the ruddy color of the cloak, in which — the tree making a forest of itself for her to trip through, with her basket — Little Red Riding-Hood comes to me one Christmas Eve, to give me information of the cruelty and treachery of that dissembling Wolf who ate her grandmother, without making any impression on his appetite, and then ate her, after making that ferocious joke about his teeth. She was my first love. I felt that if I could have married Little Red Riding-Hood, I should have known perfect bliss. But, it was not to be.

What was to be was Dickens's adult quest for fairy bliss in his novels. It is not by chance that one of the last works he wrote was "The Magic Fishbone," part of a collection of humorous stories for children titled *Holiday Romance* (1868). Here Dickens parodied a helpless king as a salaried worker, who is accustomed to understanding everything with his rational mind. He becomes totally confused by the actions of his daughter, Alicia, who receives a magic fishbone from a strange and brazen fairy named Grandmarina. Alicia does not use the fishbone when one would expect her to. Only when the king reveals to her that he can no longer provide for the family does Alicia make use of the magic fishbone. Suddenly Grandmarina arrives to bring about a comical ending in which the most preposterous changes occur. Nothing can be grasped through logic, and this is exactly Dickens's point: His droll tale — narrated from the viewpoint of a child — depends on the unusual deployment of fairy-tale motifs to question the conventional standards of society and to demonstrate that there is strength and soundness in the creativity of the young. The patriarchal figure of authority is at a loss to rule and provide, and the reversal of circumstances points to a need for change in social relations. The realm of genuine happiness that is glimpsed at the end of Dickens's fairy tale is a wish fulfillment that he himself shared with many Victorians who were dissatisfied with social conditions in English society.

Like Dickens, Carroll fought tenaciously to keep the child alive in himself and in his fiction as a critic of the absurd rules and regulations of the adult Victorian world. In *Alice's Adventures in Wonderland* (1865) and *Through the Looking Glass* (1871), Carroll made one of the most radical statements on behalf of the fairy tale and the child's perspective by conceiving a fantastic plot without an ostensible moral purpose. The questioning spirit of the child is celebrated in the Alice books, and Carroll continually returned to the realm of fantasy in his remarkable fairy tale "Bruno's Revenge" (1867), which eventually served as the basis for his Sylvie and Bruno books (1889, 1893). The endeavor to reconcile the fairy world with the world of reality never meant compromising the imagination for Carroll. If anything, reason was to serve the imagination, to allow vital dreams of pleasure to take shape in a world that was threatening to turn those dreams into mere advertisements for better homes and better living, according to the plans of British industrial and urban leaders.

George MacDonald shared Carroll's deep-seated belief in the necessity of keeping alive the power of imagination in children. In fact, after Carroll had completed *Alice's Adventures in Wonderland*, he sent the manuscript to the MacDonald family, who warmly encouraged him to have his fantastic narrative published. Though MacDonald himself was not as "radical" as Carroll in his own fairy tales, he was nonetheless just as pioneering in his endeavors to lend new shape and substance to the fairy-tale genre. In 1867, he published *Dealings with the Fairies*, which contained "The Light Princess," "The Giant's Heart," "The Shadows," "Cross Purposes," and "The Golden Key." Thereafter he continued to write fairy tales for children's magazines and included some in his novels. In fact, he wrote two compelling fairy-tale novels, *The Princess and the Goblin* (1872) and *The Princess and Curdie* (1883), which became classics in his own day. MacDonald stressed the aesthetic reversal of traditional fairy-tale schemes, motifs, and social transformation in all his fairy tales. For instance, his most popular work, "The Light Princess," is a witty parody of Sleeping Beauty that stimulates serious reflection about social behavior and power through comical and unexpected changes in the traditional fairy-tale form and content. Here, a bumbling king and queen give birth to a daughter after many years of sterility, and because they insult one of the fairy godmothers, their daughter is cursed with a lack of gravity. Thus, she can only fly around the court, and her hilarious behavior upsets the absurd conventions of the kingdom. But she is also potentially destructive, because she has no sense of balance and tends to seek to gratify her whims with little concern for other people. Only when she sees a humble prince about to die for her own pleasure does she develop human compassion and gain the gravity necessary for mature social interaction. MacDonald often turned the world upside down and inside out in his fairy tales to demonstrate that society as it existed was based on false and artificial values. He purposely portrayed characters on quests to discover a divine spark within themselves, and self-discovery was always linked to a greater appreciation of other human beings and nature, as in the case of "The Day Boy and the Night Girl" (1882). Domination is opposed by compassion. Magic is power used to attain self-awareness and sensitivity toward others. Fairy-tale writing itself becomes a means by which one can find the golden key for establishing harmony with the world — a utopian world, to be sure, that opens our eyes to the ossification of a society blind to its own faults and injustices.

III

The creation of fairy-tale worlds by British writers moved in two general directions from 1860 until the turn of the century: conventionalism and utopianism. The majority of writers such as Dinah Mulock Craik (*The Fairy Book*, 1863), Annie and E. Keary (*Little Wanderlin*, 1865), Tom Hood (*Fairy Realm*, 1865, verse renditions of Perrault's prose tales), Harriet Parr (*Holme Lee's Fairy Tales*, 1868), Edward Knatchbull-Hugessen (*Moonshine*, 1871, and *Friends and Foes from Fairy Land*, 1886), Jean Ingelow (*The Little Wonder-Horn*, 1872), Mrs. Molesworth (*The Tapestry Room*, 1879, and *Christmas-Tree Land*, 1884), Anne Isabella Ritchie (*Five Old Friends and a Young Prince*, 1868, and *Bluebeard's Keys*, 1874), Christina Rossetti (*Speaking Likenesses*, 1874), Lucy Lane Clifford (*Anyhow Stories*, 1882), Harriet Childe-Pemberton (*The Fairy Tales of Every Day*, 1882), Andrew Lang (*The Princess Nobody*, 1884, and *The Gold of Fairnilee*, 1888), Herbert Inman (*The One-Eyed Griffin and Other Fairy Tales*, 1897), and Edith Nesbit (*The Book of Dragons*, 1900) conceived plots conventionally to reconcile themselves and their readers to the status quo of Victorian society. Their imaginative worlds could be called exercises in complicity with the traditional opponents of fairy tales, for there is rarely a hint of social criticism and subversion in their works. It is almost as if the wings of the fairies had been clipped, for the "little people" do not represent a real threat to the established Victorian norms. Magic and nonsense are not liberating forces. After a brief period of disturbance, the fairies, brownies, elves, or other extraordinary creatures generally enable the protagonists to integrate themselves into a prescribed social order. If the fairies create mischief that makes the protagonists and readers think critically about their situation, they ultimately do this in the name of sobriety. Perseverance, good sense, and diligence are championed as virtues that must be acquired through trials in magical realms to prove they will become mature "solid citizens."

Yet, even in the works of the conventional writers, there seems to be a longing to maintain a connection to the fairy realm. Some of them, like Ingelow, Molesworth, and Nesbit, broke with convention at times. Respect was paid to those spirits of the imagination — the fairies, who reinvigorated British cultural life in the nineteenth century after years of banishment. Indeed, the return of the fairies became permanent, for writers of all kinds of persuasions discovered that they could be used to maintain a discourse about subjects germane to their heart. Unfortunately, by the end of the century such publishers as Raphael Tuck and George Routledge could make standard commodities out of the fairy tales, mainly the classical European tales, and published thousands of toy books and picture books to earn grand profits from what used to be considered pernicious items for sons and daughters of the middle classes.

Fairy tales for profit and fairy tales of conventionality were disregarded by English writers of the utopian direction. Their tales reveal a profound belief in the power of the imagination as a potent force that can be used to determine gender relations and sexual identity, and to question the value of existing social relations. There is also a moral impulse in this second direction. However, it does not lead to reconciliation with the status quo — rather, rebellion against convention and conformity. Fairy-tale protagonists are sent on quests, which change them as the world around them also changes. The fairies and other magical creatures inspire and compel the protagonists to alter their lives and pursue utopian dreams. In the works of MacDonald, Carroll, Mary De Morgan,

Juliana Horaria Ewing, Oscar Wilde, Rudyard Kipling, Kenneth Grahame, Evelyn Sharp, and Laurence Housman the creation of fairy-tale worlds allows the writers to deal symbolically with social taboos and to suggest alternatives to common English practice, particularly in the spheres of child rearing and role playing. In many instances the alternatives do not lead to a "happy end," or, if happiness is achieved, it is in stark contrast to the "happy" way of life in late Victorian and Edwardian England. In Humphrey Carpenter's critical study of the golden age of children's literature, *Secret Gardens* (1985), he makes the point that fantasy literature and fairy tales of the late nineteenth century stem from a deep dissatisfaction with the sociopolitical realities of England. "While it was not overtly 'realistic' and purported to have nothing to say about the 'real' world, in this fantastic strain of writing may be found some profound observations about human character and contemporary society, and (strikingly often) about religion. It dealt largely with utopias, and posited the existence of Arcadian societies remote from the nature and concerns of the everyday world; yet in doing this it was commentary, often satirically and critically, on real life."

The use of the fairy tale as commentary was pervasive in high and low culture. In her important forthcoming book *Victorian Periodicals and the Reinvention of the Fairy Tale*, Caroline Sumpter reveals that numerous fairy tales were published separately in monthlies, children's periodicals, little magazines, and socialist newspapers from the 1860s to the beginning of the twentieth century. Many well-known authors such as Kingsley, Kipling, MacDonald, Thackeray, Housman, and others published their fairy tales in magazines such as the *Cornhill Magazine* and *Macmillan's Magazine*. Sumpter shows that readers became engaged with these tales and helped shape the form and content of the tales. By the 1890s the utopian tendency of fairy tales came to the fore in three socialist newspapers, Keir Hardie's *Labour Leader*, John Trevor's *Labour Prophet*, and Robert Batehord's *Clarion*, in which young readers, adults, and editors participated in ideological discussions about the nature of socialism and a critique of industrial capitalism vis-à-vis the fairy tale.

Clearly, this development can be regarded as the culmination of the earlier tales by Dickens, Carroll, MacDonald, Wilde, Ewing, De Morgan, Molesworth, and other writers who defended the imagination and identified with the "enemies of the Enlightenment." In a period when first Christian socialism and later the Fabian movement had a widespread effect, these writers instilled a utopian spirit into the fairy-tale discourse that endowed the genre with a vigorous and unique quality of social criticism, which was to be developed even further by later writers of faerie works such as A. A. Milne, J. R. R. Tolkien, C. S. Lewis, and T. H. White. This endowment in itself was the major accomplishment of the utopian fairy-tale writers. But there were other qualities and features that they contributed to the development of the literary fairy tale as genre that deserve our attention.

To begin with, there is a strong feminine, if not feminist, influence in the writing of both male and female writers. In contrast to the *Kunstmärchen* tradition in Germany and folklore in general, which were stamped by patriarchal concerns, British writers created strong women characters and placed great emphasis on the fusion of female and male qualities and equality between men and women. For instance, in most of MacDonald's tales, particularly "The Day Boy and the Night Girl," "Cross Purposes," and "Little Daylight," the male and female protagonists come to realize their mutual dependency. Their so-called masculine and feminine qualities are not genetically determined but are relative and assume their own particular value in given circumstances. What is often understood as masculine is feminine in MacDonald's tales. Gender has no specificity — rather, both male and female can develop courage, honesty, intelligence, compassion, and so forth. The most important goal in MacDonald's fairy tales lies beyond the limits set by society. The worth of an individual is indicated by his or her willingness to explore nature and to change according to the divine insights they gain. Magic is nothing else but the realization of the divine creative powers one possesses within oneself. Here MacDonald differed from many of the traditional Victorian writers by insisting on self-determination for women.

MacDonald was not alone in this conviction. Mary De Morgan, Juliana Horatia Ewing, Mary Louisa Molesworth, Evelyn Sharp, and Edith Nesbit all depicted female protagonists coming into their own and playing unusually strong roles in determining their own destinies. Princess Ursula's refusal to conform to the wishes of her ministers in De Morgan's "A Toy Princess" (1877) celebrates the indomitable will of a young woman who is determined to run her life according to her needs rather than serve the royal court like a puppet. In Ewing's "The Ogre Courting" (1871), Managing Molly, a clever peasant's daughter, maintains her independence while making a fool out of a brutal male oppressor. Mrs. Molesworth's Princess Aureole in "Story of a King's Daughter" (1884) uses another technique to tame the brute in man: She sets an example of compassion that eventually induces Prince Halbert to learn to feel for the sufferings of his fellow creatures. Princess Aureole uses her courage and imagination to get her way and her man in the end, just as Firefly in Sharp's "The Spell of the Magician's Daughter" (1902) shows remarkable fortitude and creativity in disenchanting a country and captivating a young prince. Similarly, the Princess in Nesbit's "The Last of the Dragons" (1900) acts in a very "unladylike" way by taking the initiative and defeating the last of the dragons with love.

In all of these tales — as well as in other works, such as Christina Rossetti's fascinating poem *The Goblin Market* — there is an intense quest for the female self. In contrast to such fairy tales as "Cinderella" (1868) by Anne Isabella Ritchie and "All My Doing" (1882) by Harriet Childe-Pemberton, which are interesting examples of female self-deprecation, the narratives by De Morgan, Ewing, Molesworth, Sharp, and Nesbit allow for women's voices and needs to be heard. The narrative strategies of these tales strongly suggest that utopia will not be just another men's world. What is significant about the "feminist" utopian tales is not so much the strength shown by the female protagonists, but the manner in which they expose oppression and hypocrisy and challenge fixed categories of gender. Here, the social critique is both implicit and explicit as it pertains to Victorian society. The new "feminine quality" in these tales is part of the general reutilization of the traditional fairy-tale motifs and topoi by utopian writers to make up for gaps in their psychological development, and to express the need for a new type of government and society. All the formal aesthetic changes made in the tales are connected to an insistence that the substance of life be transformed, otherwise there will be alienation, petrification, and death. This is certainly the danger in De Morgan's "Toy Princess," and it is the reason why she also questioned and rejected arbitrary authority in such other tales as "The Necklace of Princess Fiormonde," "The Heart of Princess Joan," and "Three Clever Kings."

Male writers expressed their utopian inclinations in fairy tales by depicting English society as one that stifled and confined the creative energies of compassionate young protagonists. Both in his tales and his illustrations, Laurence Housman portrayed Victorian society symbolically as a rigid enclosure. In such tales as "The Rooted Lover," "The Bound Princess," "The White Doe," and "A Chinese Fairy-Tale," Housman's protagonists reject material gains to pursue love and beauty. The aesthetic composition of the fairy tale and the noble actions of his characters are contrasted to the vulgar materialism of late-Victorian society. Such a view of British society was shared by Oscar Wilde, who developed his critique of greed and hypocrisy in his two collections of fairy tales, *The Happy Prince and Other Tales* (1888) and *A House of Pomegranates* (1891). In particular, "The Happy Prince" is a sad commentary on how isolated the ruling class had become from the majority of English people by the end of the century. Like many utopian writers of this period, Wilde felt that social relations had become reified, and he disparaged the philanthropic movement of the upper classes as mere ornamental patchwork. If British society was to reform itself substantially, then it not only had to undergo a spiritual reformation but also class domination and the destructive effects of industrialization had to be brought to an end.

To oppose class domination and the crass exploitation of the "little people" became the underlying bond of many utopian fairy-tale writers toward the end of the nineteenth century. The unique quality of the individual tales often depended on the nonconformist message and the "nonsensical" play with words, plots, and motifs. These made sense once the reader realized that the writers were endeavoring to subvert those so-called sensible standards that appeared to fulfill the needs of the people but actually deceived them. For example, a fairy tale such as Kenneth Grahame's "The Reluctant Dragon" (1898) plays with the expectations of the readers and refuses to meet them because Grahame was more interested in fostering human compassion than in human deception. His tale reveals how the aggressive instincts of people can be manipulated and can lead to a false sense of chauvinism because of stereotyping — in this case, of knights and dragons. Kipling, too, in "The Potted Princess" (1893) composed an interesting tale that experimented with audience expectations and deception. In the process it allows for the rise of a lowly prince and the transformation of a young boy into a tale-teller. The theme of coming into one's own is closely tied to the rejection of the materialistic and artificial standards set by society.

The German romantic writer Novalis, who had a great influence on MacDonald, once remarked, "Mensch werden ist eine Kunst" — to become a human being is an art. This remark could have been Kipling's motto for his tale, and it certainly could have been the unwritten slogan of the utopian fairy-tale writers by the end of the nineteenth century. The fairy tale itself exhibited possibilities for the young to transform themselves and society into those Arcadian dreams conceived in childhood that the writers did not want to leave behind them. The artwork of the fairy tale assumed a religious quality in its apparent denial of the material world.

It is not by chance that many of the late-Victorian fairy-tale writers took a resolute stand against materialism. The Industrial Revolution had transformed an agrarian population into an urban one. Compelled to work and live according to a profit motive and competitive market conditions, people became accustomed to thinking instrumentally about gain and exploitation. Both in the middle and lower classes it became necessary to compete with and exploit others to achieve success and a modicum of comfort. Here, the Christian Church relied on philanthropy as a means to rationalize the material values of a society that had abandoned the essence of Christian humanism. This is why the Christian minister George MacDonald — and the same might be said of Lewis Carroll — distanced himself from the practices of the Anglican and Congregational churches. Most of his works, particularly his two fairy-tale novels *The Princess and the Goblin* and *The Princess and Curdie*, decry the lust for money in all social classes and the abandonment of Christian values based on human compassion.

Toward the end of the nineteenth century there was a growing tendency among writers to support the ideas of Christian and Fabian socialism, and this tendency was also very apparent in many socialist periodicals for young and old. It also marked the rise of utopian literature, which was connected to the fairy tale and indicated the writers' deep dissatisfaction with the way Great Britain had been drastically changed by the Industrial Revolution. William Morris's *News from Nowhere* (1891) and H. G. Wells's *The Time Machine* (1895) illustrate the criticism of those Victorian writers who feared that the machine age would destroy human creativity and integrity. Although Great Britain was at its height as an empire, there was also a strong sentiment among utopian writers that the empire had sold its soul to attain power and was using its power to maintain a system of domination and exploitation.

It is interesting to note that many of the late-Victorian fairy-tale writers held similar political views and worked in the same milieux in an effort to create a different English society. As is well known, MacDonald was a good friend of Ruskin and Carroll, and he shared many of the social convictions of Dickens and Morris, whom he also knew. Morris was very much influenced by Ruskin, and in turn his ideas attracted the author Mary De Morgan, as well as Laurence Housman and Walter Crane, who both illustrated and wrote numerous fairy-tale books. Kipling heard the tales of De Morgan as a child and was a great admirer of Juliana Horatia Ewing. Wilde studied with both Ruskin and Walter Pater and developed his own anarchical brand of socialism, which he expressed in his essay "The Soul of Man Under Socialism" (1889), written at the same time as his fairy tales. Crane illustrated *The Happy Prince and Other Tales* as well as *Christmas-Tree Land* by Mary Louisa Molesworth. Evelyn Sharp, Laurence Housman, and Kenneth Grahame belonged to the coterie of writers around *The Yellow Book*, founded by John Lane, who wanted to establish a new aesthetic while at the same time sought to retain respect for traditional craftsmanship. Grahame was greatly influenced by Frederick James Furnivall, an active member of the Christian Socialist movement, and the latter introduced Grahame to the works of Ruskin and Morris. Sharp went on to become one of the leading members of the women's suffragette movement as well as a socialist. At times she had contact with Laurence Housman, who also declared himself a socialist pacifist and became active in the political and cultural struggles of the early twentieth century. Nesbit was one of the founders of the Fabian Society with her husband, Hubert Bland, and she became close to George Bernard Shaw, H. G. Wells, and numerous other members of the Fabian movement.

The social and political views of the fairy-tale writers and the cultural climate of late-Victorian society make it evident that they felt the future of Britain and the young was at stake in their literary production. Such investment in their work enables us to understand why the literary fairy tale finally became a viable genre in Britain. The revolt of the fairies in the early part of the nineteenth century and their reintegration into English literature occurred at a time when British society was undergoing momentous social and political changes. The Puritan ban on fairy-tale literature that had existed since the late seventeenth century was gradually lifted because the rational discourse of the Enlightenment did not allow sufficient means to voice doubts and protest about conditions in England during the Industrial Revolution. Although many of the new fairy tales were contradictory, they opened up possibilities for children and adults to formulate innovative views about socialization, religious training, authority, sex roles, and art. For many late-Victorian authors, the writing of a fairy tale meant a process of creating an *other world*, from which vantage point they could survey conditions in the real world and compare them to their ideal projections. The personal impetus for writing fairy tales was simultaneously a social one for the Victorians. This social impetus has kept their tales alive and stimulating for us today, for the aesthetics of these fairy tales stems from an experimental spirit and social conscience that raises questions that twentieth-century reality has yet to answer. The "enemies of the Enlightenment" are still very much with us, and though they are often packaged as commodities and made to appear harmless, they will continue to touch a utopian chord in every reader who remains open to their call for change.

eight

Oscar Wilde's Tales
of Illumination

ntil 1887 Oscar Wilde had primarily published poems and essays about art and literature with a fair amount of success, but it was only after he started writing fairy tales that he developed confidence in his unusual talents as a prose writer. In fact, the fairy-tale form enabled him to employ his elegant style and keen wit to give full expression both to his philosophy of art and his critique of English high society. Therefore, it is not by chance that all his fairy tales, published between 1888 and 1891, coincided with the publication of his remarkable novel *The Picture of Dorian Gray* (1891), perhaps his finest achievement in prose. However, his stories were not just decorative stepping stones to this novel but more like finely chiseled gems that have been recognized as among the best of the fairy-tale genre. Moreover, they are almost prophetic in the manner that they depict the suffering that Wilde himself was to endure in the years to come because of his refusal to moderate his homosexual behavior or to abandon his role as an avant-garde writer.

Born in Dublin on October 16, 1854, Wilde was steeped in Irish folklore and was apparently well acquainted with the tales of the Brothers Grimm and Hans Christian Andersen. Both his mother, Speranza, a passionate nationalist and poetess, and his father, William, a famous ear and eye physician, were known to be great raconteurs. As a young boy, Wilde himself learned a great deal about narrative style simply by listening to them tell stories. Even before Wilde was born, his father, who was also a remarkable folklorist, had published an important work titled *Irish Popular Superstitions* (1852), while his mother wrote patriotic poems using Irish folk motifs. Throughout his youth at the Portora Royal School and Trinity College, Wilde was concerned with developing his own skills as a storyteller and poet. By the time he reached Oxford in 1874, he had become as talented as his mother and father as a raconteur and had begun publishing his poems in the *Dublin University Magazine* and the *Month and Catholic Review.*

While at Oxford, from 1874 to 1879, he continued to write poetry and studied classical Greek and Roman literature. Under the influence of Walter Pater and John Ruskin, he also began writing essays about art and literature. After graduation from Oxford, he earned his living largely from lecture tours about the new aestheticism in England, traveling widely in America and Britain, and he tried his hand at writing dramas. After his marriage to Constance Lloyd in 1884, Wilde settled in London, assumed the editorship of the magazine *The Woman's World*, and took an interest in writing prose fiction.

Although there is no evidence as to why he suddenly started writing fairy tales in the mid-1880s, the fact that Constance gave birth to their sons, Cyril (1885) and Vyvyan (1886), may have played a role since he enjoyed telling them tales. Yet, Wilde did not write them explicitly for children. In fact, he composed *The Happy Prince* as early as 1885 after entertaining some students in Cambridge, and later in 1888, in a letter to the poet George Herbert Kersley, he remarked, "I am very pleased you like my stories. They are studies in prose, put for Romance's sake into fanciful form: meant partly for children, and partly for those who have kept the childlike faculties of wonder and joy, and who find simplicity in a subtle strangeness" (fig. 10).

In general, there are several factors that led Wilde to turn his attention to the writing of fairy tales. For instance, there was a great renascence of fairy tales in England from 1865 to 1900, with writers such as John Ruskin, William Makepeace Thackeray, Lewis Carroll, Andrew Lang, and others making important contributions to the development of the genre, as I outlined in the previous chapter. Wilde's wife herself

Figure 10. "The Happy Prince." From Oscar Wilde's The Happy Prince and Other Tales. *Illustr. Walter Crane. London: David Nutt, 1888.*

was interested in fantasy literature and published two volumes of children's stories in 1889 and 1892, while his mother edited two important books on Irish folklore, *Ancient Cures, Mystic Charms, and Superstitions* (1888) and *Ancient Cures, Charms, and Usages of Ireland* (1890). Moreover, Wilde reviewed William Yeats's *Fairy and Folk Tales of the Irish Peasantry* in 1889 and showed a great awareness of the fairy-tale tradition. In short, it was almost natural for Wilde at one time in his life to turn to the fairy tale as if it were his proper mode. And certainly his familiarity with traditional folklore and the literary fairy tale explains why he was able to be so innovative in his own tales, for each one of them plays with standard audience expectations and subverts the customary happy ending with questions that make the reader think about social problems and the role of the artist as innovator.

What makes the tales even more striking is the manner in which Wilde weaves personal problems into his narratives, for it was during the mid-1880s that he became consciously aware of his homosexual inclinations and began having affairs with young men. To a certain extent, the symbolic nature of the fairy tale allowed him to write about his homoeroticism and link it to his aesthetic and social concerns in a veiled manner. In this light, both volumes of Wilde's stories, *The Happy Prince and Other Tales* (1888) and *A House of Pomegranates* (1891), can be regarded as artistic endeavors on the part of Wilde to confront what he already foresaw as the impending tragedy of his life — self-sacrifice due to unrequited or unfulfilled love and avant-garde notions about art and society. Since he disliked the personal and first-person narrative, the fairy-tale form allowed him to depersonalize his own problems and expand them to include his unique ideas about Fabian socialism that were clearly articulated in his essay "The Soul of Man Under Socialism" (1891). In many respects, the fairy tales prepared the way for his social philosophy about the artist espoused in this essay — the artist as a Christlike figure representing true individualism, and true individualism as being only possible if there were equal distribution of the wealth in society along with natural love, tolerance, and humility. Like Freud, Wilde was interested in "civilization and its discontents," and his fairy tales assume the form of an artistic companion piece to Freud's psychological diagnosis about the causes of unhappiness brought about through the civilizing process.

Just what were Wilde's artistic diagnoses?

The Happy Prince and Other Tales, an anthology about British civilization and its discontents, contained "The Happy Prince," "The Nightingale and the Rose," "The Selfish Giant," "The Devoted Friend," and "The Remarkable Rocket." "The Happy Prince" is perhaps the best known of all his tales, and the title already indicates the hallmark of Wilde's style as fairy-tale author — irony. The prince is anything but happy. It is only after his death, when he stands high above the city and realizes how irresponsible he has been, that he chooses to compensate for his past carefree life. Ironically, the more he sacrifices himself, the more he becomes happy and fulfilled. As a Christlike figure, the prince represents the artist whose task is to enrich other people's lives without expecting acknowledgment or rewards. On another level, the prince and the swallow are clearly male lovers, whose spiritual bond transcends the materialism and petty values of the town councillors. Implicit in this tale is that society is not yet ready to appreciate the noble role of the artist, who seeks to transform crass living conditions and beautify people's souls through his gifts. This theme is continued in "The Nightingale and the Rose," which is an ironic comment on Andersen's "The Nightingale." Whereas Andersen in his fairy tale portrays the nightingale as an artist and has him heal a king's sickness through his singing, Wilde is intent on revealing the shallow values of the student and his sweetheart and the vain efforts of the nightingale as artist to change them. However, not all Wilde's tales end on a note of fruitless sacrifice. For instance, "The Selfish Giant" illustrates how a landowner becomes happy and grows spiritually by sharing his property with children, who gain a deep sense of pleasure when they experience his change of heart. These are indeed the "ideal" childlike readers Wilde had in mind when he wrote his tales, and the giant, like the happy prince, is the artist par excellence who learns to give freely of his wealth. The opposites of the prince and giant can be found in "The Devoted Friend" and "The Remarkable Rocket." Based on Andersen's tale "Little Claus and Big Claus," "The Devoted Friend" is a sardonic depiction of a ruthless miller who drives Hans, a poor farmer, to death. What is frightening about the tale is that the miller is not touched by Hans's death or even aware of how destructive he is. This same unawareness is the central theme in "The Remarkable Rocket" with a slight variation. Here the rocket is a type of pompous artist, whose belief in his great talents and importance is deflated by the end of the tale.

Throughout the stories in *The Happy Prince and Other Tales* there is a sense of impending doom. All the protagonists — the prince, the nightingale, the giant, Hans, and the rocket — die through a sacrifice either out of love for humanity or love for art. The tales in *A House of Pomegranates* continue to explore the connections between love, art, and sacrifice, but Wilde abandoned the naive quality of the earlier tales as though he had become more painfully aware of the difficulties a "deviate" artist would encounter in British society, and his tales became more grave and less childlike than his earlier ones.

Wilde's depiction of the sixteen-year-old lad in "The Young King" is undoubtedly a homoerotic portrayal of an idealized lover, and the plot reveals Wilde's contempt for a society that wants a king designated by artificial apparel such as the robe, scepter, and crown. The derobing that the young king undertakes is an act of purification that lays bare the contradictions of his society. Although the derobing succeeds in this tale, it is entirely the opposite in "The Birthday of the Infanta," in which the spoiled and insensitive princess drives the dwarf to his death. If there is a derobing, it is an unmasking of the brutal if not sadistic treatment of the dwarf as artist and lover. Whereas Wilde was concerned in depicting the crass indifference of people of the upper classes, whose commands cause suffering for those beneath them, he also showed that there were possibilities for redemption. Thus, the prince in "The Star-Child" pays for his pride, cruelty, and selfishness by undergoing a transformation and sacrificing himself to help others. Yet, even here, Wilde sounds an ominous note at the conclusion of the tale by stating that the beneficent reign of the star-child lasted but a short time and was followed by that of an evil ruler. Wilde was convinced that, as long as society was intolerant, materialistic, and hypocritical, it would be impossible for love to develop. This conviction led him to reverse the theme of Andersen's "The Little Mermaid" and Chamisso's "Peter Schlemihl" in "The Fisherman and His Soul." Instead of the usual sea nymph seeking a human soul, Wilde has the fisherman give up his soul to join the mermaid and to enjoy sensual pleasures and her natural love. Ironically, his soul and the institution of the Church, represented by the priest, endeavor to destroy his wholesome love. Nevertheless, the fisherman recognizes that his "hedonistic" love is more holy than what society ordains as good, and he is reunited with the mermaid by the end of the tale in an act of rebellion against traditional morality.

As in *The Happy Prince and Other Tales*, the stories in *A House of Pomegranates* end on an unresolved or tragic note. The star-child, the dwarf, and the fisherman all die because their love and sacrifices go against the grain of their societies. Only the young king survives, but it is evident that his future reign, based on humility and material equality, will encounter great obstacles. There will obviously be no paradise on earth until it is unnecessary to have martyrs who lead Christlike lives and die for the sake of humanity.

Although Wilde did identify with the protagonists of his tales — the spurned artist and lover, the iconoclast, the innocent victim — he did not wallow in self-pity. Rather, he transcended his own problems in these tales and created symbolical analogues to the real contradictions between the avant-garde artist and British society of his time. Despite the fact that Wilde was often attacked by the upholders of civility as a decadent or degenerate during his lifetime, he revealed most poignantly in his tales how moral decadence was more often to be found among those who support law and order and are insensitive to the needs of the oppressed. For Wilde, the artist's role was to find the proper means to let the beautiful be illuminated against the harsh background of society's dark hues of regimentation. The lights in his fairy tales are thus glistening illuminations of sad conditions, and they beckon readers to contemplate the plight of his protagonists in reverence. In this respect, Oscar Wilde's fairy tales have a religious fervor to them that urges us to reconsider what has happened to the nature of humanity at the dawn of modern civilization.

nine

Carlo Collodi's *Pinocchio* as Tragic-Comic Fairy Tale

I f one were to believe Walt Disney's *American* film version of *Pinocchio* (1940), the wooden puppet turned human is a very happy boy at the end of his adventures. After numerous adventures, Pinocchio learns that honesty is the best policy, a message repeatedly driven home by the film. Yet, the *Italian* novel of 1882 by Carlo Collodi is a much different affair. Pinocchio is indeed content to turn human at the end of this narrative, but there is a tragic-comic element to the episodes that make one wonder why the puppet must endure so much suffering to become a proper and honest boy. Did Collodi intend to make an example out of Pinocchio, the good bad boy, who must learn to assume responsibility for his actions? Or, did he intend to show the harsh realities of peasant childhood in nineteenth-century Italy? Is *Pinocchio* perhaps a critical reflection of his own boyhood? After all, Carlo Collodi was not born to become a writer and journalist, nor was he born with the name Collodi. There was a fairy-tale element to his own education and development, and before we can fully understand why his Pinocchio, in contrast to Walt Disney's, is a tragic-comic figure, we might do well to look at Collodi's life and times.

I

Born Carlo Lorenzini in Florence on November 24, 1826, Collodi was
raised in a lower-class family with nine brothers and sisters, of which
only two of his siblings managed to survive childhood. His father and
mother, Domenico and Angela Lorenzini, worked as servants for the
Marquis Lorenzo Ginori, who paid for Collodi's education. In fact, if it
had not been for the Marquis Ginori's help, Collodi would never have
gone to school. Collodi's parents were very poor and had so many children that Collodi, as the oldest, was sent to live with his grandparents
in the little town of Collodi outside of Florence, where his mother was
born. When he was ten, the Marquis Ginori offered financial aid to
send young Collodi to the seminary at Colle Val d'Elsa to study for the
priesthood, but given his mischievous nature and dislike of monastic
discipline, Collodi discovered that he was not cut out to be a priest.
Therefore, by the time he was sixteen, Collodi began studying philosophy and rhetoric at the College of the Scolopi Fathers in Florence, and
two years later, found a position at the Librera Piatti, a leading bookstore, where he helped prepare catalogues for Giuseppe Aiazzi, one of the
leading specialists for manuscripts in Italy. It was during this time that
Collodi began meeting numerous intellectuals and literary critics and
developing an interest in literature. By 1848, however, Collodi was carried away by revolutionary zeal to fight for Italian independence against
the Austrians. After the defeat of Italian forces that very same year, he
was fortunate to obtain a position as a civil servant in the municipal
government while also working as a journalist, editor, and dramatist.
In 1853 he founded the satirical political magazine *Il Lampione* (The
Street Lamp), intended to enlighten the Italians about political oppression. This publication was soon banned because its polemical writings
were considered subversive by the Grand Duchy, loyal to the Austrian
authorities. Not easily defeated, Collodi started a second journal, *Lo
Scaramuccia* (The Controversy, 1854), which dealt more with theater
and the arts than politics and lasted until 1858. Aside from publishing
numerous articles, he also tried his hand at writing comedies, which did
not have much success. Indeed, he was more successful at politics and
became known as an activist in liberal circles.

When the Second War of Independence erupted in 1859, Collodi volunteered for the cavalry, and this time, the Italians were victorious. Not only were the Austrians defeated in northern Italy, but the entire country was also united under Giuseppe Garibaldi in 1861. It was during the period from 1859 to 1861 that Collodi, still primarily known as Lorenzini, became involved in a dispute about the new Italian unification with Professor Eugenio Alberi of Pisa, a reputable political writer, and he signed his defense of a unified Italy, a booklet titled *Il signor Alberi ha ragione! Dialogo apologetico* (1860), with the pseudonym Collodi in honor of his mother's native village, where he had spent his childhood. It was the first time that he used this name, not realizing that it would become world famous mainly through the later publication of a children's book.

Although convinced that unification was positive for Italy, Collodi soon discovered that the social changes he had expected for all Italians were not about to take place. Instead, the nobility profited most from the defeat of the Austrians, and corruption continued in the government that supported the development of industry and the wealthy classes. He himself was fortunate since he was able to keep his position as a civil servant from 1860 to 1881 in the Commission of Theatrical Censorship and in the Prefecture of Florence. These appointments enabled him to serve as the stage director of the Teatro della Pergola in Florence and on the editorial committee that began research for an encyclopedia of Florentine dialect. However, Collodi, who still wrote mainly under the name of Lorenzini, did not give up his career as journalist and freelance writer. In fact, he published a number of stories in *Io Fanfulla, Almanacco per il 1876* (1876) and in *Il Novelliere* (1876), which were reworked into sardonic sketches of Florentine life in *Macchiette* (Sketches, 1879), the first book to be published under the pseudonym Collodi. In addition, he translated eighteenth-century French fairy tales by Charles Perrault, Mme d'Aulnoy, and Mme Leprince de Beaumont under the title *I raconti delle fate* in 1876, and began reworking the didactic tales of the eighteenth-century Italian writer Parravinci in his book *Giannettino* (*Little Johnnie*) in 1879, which led to a series: *Il viaggio per l'Italia* (*Little Johnnie's Travels through Italy*, 1880), *La Grammatica di Giannettino* (The Grammar of Little Johnnie, 1882), *L'abbaco di Giannettino* (Little Johnnie's Book of Arithmetic, 1885), *La geografía di Giannettino* (Little Johnnie's Geography, 1886), and others, all published as textbooks for elementary-school children.

Collodi's fairy-tale translations and textbooks prepared the way for his writing of *Pinocchio*, which was never really conceived as a book. Collodi was asked in the summer of 1881 by the editors of a weekly magazine for children, *Giornale per i bambini* (Newspaper for Children), to write a series of stories, and he began the first installment in July of that year under the title of *Storia di un burattino* (Story of a Puppet). During the next two years Collodi continued to submit stories about Pinocchio to the magazine, and in 1883 they were gathered together in book form and published by Felice Paggi as *The Adventures of Pinocchio*. Although the book was an immense success and went through four editions by the time Collodi died in 1890, Collodi himself did not profit much from the publication due to the lack of good copyright laws to protect authors. The book was first translated into English in 1892 by Mary Alice Murray, and by the mid-twentieth century it had been printed in a hundred different languages, abridged, bowdlerized, parodied, and adapted for stage, film, and television. Such widespread popularity may be due to the fact that *Pinocchio* appears to be a symbolic narrative of boyhood that transcends its Italian origins and speaks to young and old about the successful rise of a ne'er-do-well. It is the consummate Horatio Alger story of the nineteenth century, a pull-yourself-up-by-the-bootstraps fairy tale, which demonstrates that even a log of wood has the potential to be good, human, and socially useful. Yet, it is also a story of punishment and conformity, a tale in which a puppet without strings has strings of social constraint attached so that he will not go his own way but respond to the pulls of superior forces, symbolized by the blue fairy and Geppetto. It is from the tension of the tragic-comic that Pinocchio as a character lives and appeals to all audiences. Most important it is the fairy-tale structure that provides the episodes with the form and optimistic veneer that makes us forget how grueling and traumatic boyhood can be, especially boyhood in late-nineteenth-century Italy.

II

Here it is important to remember the unique manner in which Collodi began *Pinocchio*:

> Once upon a time there was …
>   "A king!" my young readers will instantly exclaim.
>   No, children, that's where you're wrong. Once upon a time there was
> a piece of wood!

This beginning indicates that Collodi, just like William Makepeace Thackeray (*The Rose and the Ring*, 1855), Lewis Caroll (*Alice's Adventures in Wonderland*, 1865), and George MacDonald (*The Princess and the Goblin*, 1872), who had been experimenting in England, was about to expand upon the fairy-tale tradition in a most innovative manner. Collodi fused genres based on the oral folk tale and the literary fairy tale to create his own magical land inhabited by bizarre creatures. By turning genres and the real world upside down, he sought to question the social norms of his times and to interrogate the notion of boyhood.

In his use of folklore, Collodi consciously played with the tradition of "Jack tales," which generally deal with a naive well-intentioned lad, who, despite the fact that he is not too bright, manages to lead a charmed life and survives all sorts of dangerous encounters. Sometimes he becomes rich and successful at the end of the story. For the most part he is just content to return home safe and sound. In Italy there are numerous oral tales about bungling peasants, whose naïveté is a blessing and enables them to overcome difficulties in adventure after adventure. And, in Tuscany, the region in which Collodi grew up, there were many tales about Florentines, such as the one told by Italo Calvino in *Italian Folktales* titled "The Florentine," in which a young Florentine feels like a blockhead because he had never been away from Florence and never had any adventures to recount. After he leaves and travels about, however, he almost loses his life when he encounters a ruthless giant. Fortunately he escapes but loses a finger in the process. When he returns to Florence, he is cured of his urge to travel. What is significant in all the Jack tales, no matter what their country or region of origin, is that the essential "goodness" of the protagonist, that is, his good nature, protects him from evil forces, and in many cases, he learns to use his wits to trick his enemies who want to deceive or exploit him.

In the literary fairy-tale tradition of Europe, the Jack tales are not very prevalent because literary fairy tales were generally first written for upper-class audiences and mainly for adults; bungling peasant heroes were not of particular interest to the educated classes. However, noses were, and Collodi knew about the noses from French fairy tales, some of which he had translated. For instance, in Charles Perrault's "The Foolish Wishes," a woodcutter's wife is cursed when her husband makes a bad wish and a sausage is attached to her nose. In Madame Leprince de Beaumont's "Prince Désir," a prince is born with a very long nose and compels everyone in his kingdom to think that long noses are the best in the world until an old fairy punishes him for his arrogance and vanity. The motif of the unusual nose was obviously appealing to Collodi, but it was not just the nose alone that made his narrative about Pinocchio so unique. Rather it was his combination of the folklore and literary fairy-tale traditions to reflect upon the situation of illiterate playful *poor* boys during the latter half of the nineteenth century in Italy that make his narrative so compelling. Moreover, Collodi never wrote simply for an audience of young readers. His work was intended to appeal to children and adults and to suggest a mode of educating young boys, especially when they did not seem fit to be educated.

Read as a type of *Bildungsroman*, or fairy-tale novel of development, *Pinocchio* can be interpreted positively as a representation of how peasant boys, when given a chance, can assume responsibility for themselves and their families and become industrious members of society. After all, Pinocchio is literally carved out of wood, out of an inanimate substance, and turns miraculously into a human boy who becomes responsible for the welfare of his poor father. This theme of education or development, however, is very complex, for Collodi had not initially planned to allow Pinocchio to develop. In fact, he intended to end the series printed in *Il giornale per i bambini* at chapter 15, in which Pinocchio is left hanging on an oak tree, ostensibly dead. Yet, when this episode appeared in the November 10, 1881, issue of the newspaper with the "finale" printed at the end, there was such a storm of protest from the readers, young and old, that Collodi was forced to resume Pinocchio's adventures in the February 16, 1882, issue of the newspaper. In other words, Collodi was forced to "develop" or "educate" his wooden protagonist despite his initial pessimistic perspective. Therefore, if the development of a piece of wood as a young boy is the central theme of *Pinocchio*, it is a theme that the author ironically questioned from the very beginning of the adventures, just as he questioned the optimistic structure of the fairy tale. This questioning accounts for the tension of skepticism and optimism in the novel. Moreover, the very structure of all the episodes also contributes to the tension because the stories were never intended to culminate in a novel, just as Pinocchio was never intended to become human.

Collodi conceived each chapter for the newspaper to keep his readers interested in the strange fate of a "live" piece of wood that is turned into a puppet. He did this with irony and suspense. Although not predictable, each episode begins with a strange situation that leads to a near tragedy and borders on the ridiculous. However, since Collodi created a topsy-turvy fairy-tale world that faintly resembled Tuscany but constantly changed shape, anything was possible, and Collodi mischievously plays with the readers by leaving them hanging in suspense by the end of each chapter. Each episode is a predicament. And one predicament leads to the next. No chapter is ever finished. Even the end of the book can be considered "unfinished," for it is uncertain what lies ahead of Pinocchio even after he turns human. He is still a boy. He has very little money. He is not educated. There is no indication that he will prosper as in a traditional fairy tale, even though he has developed a sense of responsibility and compassion. Pinocchio has survived boyhood and has been civilized to take the next step into manhood — and it is uncertain where this step may lead.

Given the unfinished business of Pinocchio's development, Collodi's major and constant question throughout this fairy-tale novel of education is whether it is indeed worthwhile becoming "civilized." It is a question that Mark Twain was asking about the same time when he wrote *The Adventures of Huckleberry Finn*, and in some ways Huck Finn is the American version of Pinocchio, for both boys are brutally exposed to the hypocrisy of society and yet compelled to adapt to the values and standards that will allegedly enable them to succeed. Huck refuses civilization in the end, while Pinocchio appears to have made peace with law and order.

Yet, ultimately, Collodi asks us to consider how this socialization has come about, and if we consider how the "innocent" piece of wood, whose vices consist in his playfulness and naïveté, is treated by the people and social forces around him, then there is something "tragic" to the way he is beaten and lulled into submission. From the beginning, Pinocchio's origins are stamped by the fact that Geppetto carves him into a boy puppet because he wants to earn a living through the puppet. Simply put, his father "gives birth" to him because he wants to earn money through him. Geppetto has no interest in learning who his son is and what his desires are. His son is an investment in his own future. This is not to imply that Geppetto is an uncaring father, but his relationship to Pinocchio is ambivalent because of his initial "desire" to create a puppet that will know how to dance, fence, and turn somersaults so that he can earn a crust of bread and a glass of wine. In other words, Pinocchio is supposed to please him, and Geppetto literally holds the strings to the puppet's fate in his hands. In chapter 7, after Pinocchio has lost his feet, Geppetto at first refuses to make new feet for him until Pinocchio says, "I promise you, papa, that I will learn a trade, and that I will be the comfort and staff of your old age." Geppetto complies with Pinocchio's wish, and the puppet shows his gratitude by expressing his desire to go to school. In addition, he is extremely moved when Geppetto sells his own coat to purchase a spelling book required for school. Collodi comments: "And Pinocchio, although he was very merry by nature, became sad also; because poverty, when it is real poverty, is understood by everybody — even by boys" (fig. 11).

On the one hand, Pinocchio wants to be and is socialized to please his father; on the other, he cannot control his natural instincts to explore the world and to seek pleasure. Caught in a predicament — to please his father means to deny his own pleasures — Pinocchio as a *poor illiterate peasant boy* must learn the "ups and downs of the world," as Geppetto puts it; that is, he must be physically subdued and put in his place so that he functions properly as an industrious worker, curbed of his rebellious instincts. Collodi clearly demonstrates in a very specific class analysis that poor Italian boys of this period had very little

Figure 11. From Cario Collodi's Pinocchio: The Tale of a Puppet. *Illustr. Charles Folkard. London: J. M. Dent, 1911.*

choice if they wanted to advance in life. Using Pinocchio as a symbolic figure, Collodi torments and punishes the puppet each time Pinocchio veers from the norm of acceptable behavior. Among his punishments are the loss of legs through burning; the expansion of his nose due to lying; being hanged from an oak tree; imprisonment for four months; caught in a trap and used by a farmer as a watchdog; caught in a net and almost fried as a fish by the Green Fisherman; transformed into a donkey; compelled to work in a circus; drowned to escape skinning; and swallowed by a gigantic shark.

These forms of punishment in the novel are, of course, so preposterous that readers can take delight and laugh at the events. At the same time, the laughter is mixed with relief because the readers do not have to undergo such tortures. Moreover, the laughter is instructive, for readers learn what to avoid through Pinocchio's mistakes and how to attain dignity. It is this attainment of self-dignity as a human being that is most crucial at the end of Pinocchio's adventures. As in most fairy-tale narratives, Pinocchio is obliged to fulfill specific tasks to gain his reward: Pinocchio must first rescue his father, Geppetto; and second he must keep his promises to the blue fairy by showing that he can be obedient, honest, and industrious. No matter how much he suffers, he perseveres and earns the recognition of the blue fairy. He is also able to distinguish between good and bad, between ridiculous puppet and responsible boy behavior. In this regard, Collodi's narrative is a fairy-tale novel of development that makes a sober statement, despite its humor and grotesque scenes.

For readers of Collodi's time, who were largely from the middle and educated classes, *Pinocchio* represented a warning for mischievous scamps and set a model of proper behavior. For Collodi himself, one can speculate that he viewed *Pinocchio* in part as representing the difficulties he himself experienced and had to overcome if he wanted to be accepted in the Florentine society of his time, and this is a perspective that other readers from the lower classes may have had. For today's readers, Collodi's *Pinocchio* may come as a surprise, for most will probably be shocked to find that the novel is not the same as the Disney film, which they have probably seen before reading Collodi's original work. They will realize that Collodi let his imagination run more wild than Disney did, and that he developed his puppet in more extraordinary ways. Indeed, thanks to Collodi's wild imagination, we have a rich commentary on what it meant to develop as a peasant boy in the Italian society of the nineteenth century. But more important, perhaps, his fairy-tale novel transcends history and continues to raise questions about how we "civilize" children in uncivilized times.

ten

Frank Stockton, American Pioneer of Fairy Tales

lthough he wrote some of the most innovative fairy tales of the nineteenth century and was the first significant American writer of this genre, Frank Stockton is hardly known today. This is not to say that he has fallen into total oblivion. During the 1960s an anthology of his stories, *A Story-Teller's Pack* (1968), was published, and three of his best fairy tales, *The Griffin and the Minor Canon* (1963), *The Bee-Man of Orn* (1964), and *Old Pipes and the Dryad* (1968), were illustrated by such gifted artists as Maurice Sendak and Catherine Hanley. Yet, these publications represent only a small part of the achievement of Stockton as a writer of fairy tales. In fact, during his lifetime he was regarded as one of America's most popular novelists and held in high esteem due to his unusual works of fantasy.

Born on April 5, 1834, in Philadelphia, Stockton was the oldest of three sons in his father's second marriage to Emily Drean. His father, William, was one of the leading Methodists of his time and superintendent of the Alms House in Philadelphia when Frank was born. A severe and ascetic man, William, old enough to be his son's grandfather, was too busy conducting the affairs of the Alms House and writing religious tracts to supervise Frank's education. Consequently, his much younger wife, who was more open-minded, took charge of Frank's upbringing and gave him a good deal of freedom during his youth. Although partially lame from birth, Stockton enjoyed playing pranks, formed secret societies with his brothers, and read all kinds of fiction that his father condemned as scurrilous and decadent.

In 1844, Stockton and his brothers had to curtail their customary play at home when their father was dismissed as superintendent of the Alms House due to a minor financial scandal. The home was then turned into a sanctuary, where his father demanded a quiet atmosphere in order to write various religious books and speeches. Furthermore, his mother had less time to devote to him and his brothers since she had founded a school for young ladies in West Philadelphia to help supplement the family income. By 1848, Stockton enrolled at Central High School, which had an outstanding curriculum in the sciences and arts, equivalent to some small colleges today, and he developed a strong interest in writing and the arts, often inventing and memorizing stories on his way to and from school. In a recollection written later in life he commented: "I was very young when I determined to write some fairy tales because my mind was full of them. I set to work, and in course of time, produced several which were printed. These were constructed according to my own ideas. I caused the fanciful creatures who inhabited the world of fairy-land to act, as far as possible for them to do so, as if they were inhabitants of the real world. I did not dispense with monsters and enchanters, or talking beasts and birds, but I obliged these creatures to infuse into their extraordinary actions a certain leaven of common sense."

Despite his apparent literary proclivities, after graduation from high school in 1852 Stockton had to reach a compromise with his father, who was against his choosing a career as a writer. He decided to learn the trade of wood engraving, which would keep him in close contact with the arts and literature. From 1852 to 1860 Stockton had moderate success as a wood engraver, and he participated actively in the cultural affairs of the city. Aside from joining the Forensic and Literary Circle, a club in which various social issues were debated, he began submitting stories to publishers. After numerous rejections, his first short story "The Slight Mistake" was printed in the *American Courier*, but it was not until his next story, "Kate," published by the prestigious *Southern Literary Messenger* in December 1859, that Stockton gained the confidence he needed to pursue his writing career in an active way.

In more ways than one, 1860 was the turning point in his life. In April of that year he married Mary Ann (Marian) Tuttle, who had been teaching at the West Philadelphia School for Young Ladies established by Stockton's mother. Soon thereafter the couple moved to Knightly, New Jersey, to be in commuting distance from New York, where Stockton opened an engraving office. Later that year, as if to signal the completion of Stockton's independence as a young man, his father died at the age of seventy-five. From this point on, with the support of his wife, Stockton was bent on establishing himself as a writer. He continued in the engraving business just until he had the money to support himself and his wife as a writer.

In 1867 he returned to Philadelphia to help the Stockton family out of a financial dilemma and to assist his brother, John, who had helped found the newspaper *The Philadelphia Morning Post*. Interestingly, it was just at this time that Stockton wrote and published his first fairy tale, "Ting-a-ling," in *The Riverside Magazine*. From a biographical viewpoint, there is a connection between the tiny fairy, Ting-a-ling, who graciously helps friends and people in need with enterprising acts, and Stockton himself, who willingly came to the aid of his family and energetically embarked on a career of writing both for his brother's newspaper and for other journals. Two more "Ting-a-ling" tales soon appeared in *Riverside*, and all three stories were collected and published as Stockton's first book in 1870. Years later he was to comment:

> My first book was a long time in growing. It came up like a plant by the wayside of ordinary avocation, putting forth a few leaves at a time; and when at last it budded, there was good reason to doubt whether or not it really would blossom. At length, though, it did blossom, in red, brown, green, and blue. It was a book for young people and was called *Ting-a-ling*. It was made up of fairy stories, and when these first went out, each by itself, to seek a place in the field of current literature, it was not at all certain that they would ever find such a place. The fairies who figured in these tales were not like ordinary fairies. They went, as it were, like strangers or foreigners, seeking admission in a realm where they were unknown and where their rights as residents were some time in being recognized.

From the very beginning, Stockton's fairy tales eschewed the heavy didactic and Christian messages prevalent in children's literature at that time. The hallmark of his tales was formed by their droll humor and inquisitive spirit that led to a questioning of the norms of American society. Encouraged by the success of his early fairy tales, Stockton joined the staff of a new magazine, *Hearth and Home*, in December 1868. He was the assistant to the editor, Mary Mapes Dodge, author of *Hans Brinker, or the Silver Skates*, and contributed numerous fairy tales to this publication. Moreover, since the journal was not primarily for children, Stockton could write articles and stories for adults that led to the publication of his second book, *Roundabout Rambles* (1872), a collection of sixty-nine articles dealing with natural phenomena, geography, geology, insect life, and magical illusions. By 1874 his superb editorial work on *Hearth and Home* prompted Scribner's to offer him the position of assistant editor, again to Mrs. Dodge, of the new periodical for young people, *St. Nicholas Magazine*. Stockton accepted, and since Mrs. Dodge was only required to appear in the New York office once a week, he became the virtual editor of the magazine, which quickly became the most significant journal for young readers in America. However, due to the pressure of the editorial work (Stockton contributed more than forty-four pieces to *St. Nicholas*) and the impairment of his eyesight, he was compelled to resign his post in 1878.

Since it was extremely painful for Stockton to read or write, his wife, Marian, became his amanuensis, and he managed to continue publishing stories and novels for young and old on a prolific scale during the 1880s when his reputation began to soar. Indeed, aside from the successful appearance of his first novel for adults, *Rudder Grange*, in 1879, he published a fine collection of fairy tales: *The Floating Prince and Other Fairy Tales* (1881) (fig. 12); his most famous short story "The Lady, or the Tiger?" (1882); three volumes of short stories, *The Transferred Ghost* (1884), *The Lady, or the Tiger?* (1884), and *The Story of Viteau* (1884); the popular novels *The Casting Away of Mrs. Lecks and Mrs. Aleshine* (1886) and *The Hundredth Man* (1887); and his best collections of fairy tales, *The Bee-Man of Orn and Other Fanciful Tales* (1887) and *The Queen's Museum* (1887).

The Stocktons traveled a great deal during the 1880s and 1890s to Europe, the Bahamas, and throughout America. One purpose was to give Stockton's eyes a rest; another was to gather material for stories and

Figure 12. From Frank Stockton's The Floating Prince and Other Fairy Tales. *New York: Scribner's, 1881.*

novels. Their home during this time was near Morristown, New Jersey, and it was there that Stockton dictated most of his works to his wife or a professional secretary. From 1889 until his death in 1902, he ventured forth into the field of science fiction, utopian fantasy, and travel literature by publishing such works as *The Great War Syndicate* (1889), *The Adventures of Captain Horn* (1895), *The Associate Hermits* (1899), and *A Bicycle of Cathay* (1900), all of which were best sellers during his time but have been forgotten today. Toward the end of his life Stockton himself felt that he was becoming too quaint for the American public. Yet, he was not dismayed by the loss of attention. Like many of his fairy-tale protagonists, he learned to keep a level head in the face of adversity and believed that his works would not lose their value. In fact, he was supervising the Shenandoah collected edition of his writings and finishing a new novel when he died of a cerebral hemorrhage on April 20, 1902, while attending a banquet at the National Academy of Sciences in Washington, D.C.

Most of his fairy tales were written between 1868 and 1890 when few American authors were developing this genre. Though the majority of the tales were published in magazines for young people, Stockton did not write them expressly for children. In fact, aside from the "Ting-a-ling" series, he claimed that his tales were also for mature audiences, and he had published them in periodicals for young people because they were the only magazines that would print them at the time.

Clearly, Stockton's tales appeal to young and old audiences. They are gracefully written and possess a gentle humor that often conceals a deep concern with disturbing social issues. For instance, a good many of Stockton's tales were conceived at the close of the Civil War and reflect his abhorrence of war. His wife was a Southerner, and he objected to the way that the North was imposing its views on the South. Stockton was for a peaceful resolution of the conflict and thought it best to allow the South to secede from the Union. Consequently, in such tales as "Derido; or, The Giant's Quilt," "The Magical Music," and "The Accommodating Circumstance," Stockton draws allusions to social upheaval and portrays protagonists who refuse to engage in war. Moreover, Stockton's protagonists do not use violence to achieve their goals, unlike the heroes of traditional folk tales in which "might makes right" is a common theme. In fact, Stockton's tales all deal with the abuse of power, but instead of punishing the evil oppressors by executing them, his narratives expose their foibles and make them look ridiculous.

If there are lessons to be learned in Stockton's tales, they have little to do with dogma, nor are they imposed on the reader's sensibility. Like Mark Twain, a writer whom he greatly admired, Stockton criticized the materialism and greed of the Gilded Age, and the themes of his tales propose alternatives to what were becoming the American standards for measuring success based on competition and achievement. Rarely does a Stockton protagonist want to compete, and there are just as many unfulfilled quests as there are accomplished tasks. The Bee-Man of Orn sets out to become transformed only to change back into himself again. Loris and the Ninkum never reach the idyllic castle of Bim. The banished king resigns his post after learning that he was a bumbler. Gudra's daughter is educated by failing to obtain what her father wanted to obtain. The competition in "The Great Show in Kobol-Land" is undermined, and war and revolution are avoided because Millice and Chamian refuse to compete as the evil Gromiline had hoped. "Failure" for Stockton meant coming to one's senses, as one can readily see in a tale like "The Sisters Three and the Kilmaree," in which a fairy teaches the prince, the expectant heir, and clever Terzan how to make *sober* use of their gifts and appreciate what they have before they can visit the three sisters.

Stockton's technique as a writer was to describe all conditions and scenes, no matter how fabulous, as realistically as possible and to turn the world upside down by introducing extraordinary events and characters in a matter-of-fact way. By blending the normal with the abnormal, Stockton could create probable situations in which questions about arbitrary actions could be raised. Perhaps it was due to his rebellion against the strictures of his father and the Methodist Church, or simply his dislike of crude force and the violation of human rights. Whatever the case may be, Stockton's major concern in his fairy tales was to reveal the ridiculous nature of commands, impositions, and laws that are not developed by the people themselves and do not make common sense. Thus, in "The Queen's Museum," a stranger enables the queen to realize how foolish she had been to force her people to revere the objects in her museum. The prince in "The Floating Prince," who is thrown out of his kingdom, is able to establish a new one with the cooperation of an unusual assortment of people. The answer to the evil forces in Stockton's fairy tales is generally the exercise of kindness and compassion. In "Old Pipes and the Dryad" the shepherd is rewarded for his kindness to the dryad. The count in "The Poor Count's Christmas" is helped by the fairy and the giant because of his charitable ways. Selma in "The Emergency Princess" is given a gift of gold by the gnomes because she graciously agrees to raise the gnome prince. Of course, Stockton also depicted what would happen if people were ungrateful and, in his most "pessimistic" fairy tale, "The Griffin and the Minor Canon," which is similar to some of Twain's tales, he condemned the townspeople for their cowardice and selfishness and left his readers with a bleak picture of the future.

For the most part, however, Stockton's tales are optimistic and prepared the way for the next great writer of fairy tales and fantasy in America, L. Frank Baum, who began his Oz books about the time of Stockton's death. Indeed, Baum's creation of the Land of Oz, in which violence is deplored and compassion for others highly regarded, reflects a continuity with the major themes of Stockton's fairy tales. Both writers used fantasy to demonstrate how oppressed characters could resist force and form worlds in which they could determine a measure of their happiness. In particular, Stockton delighted in revealing how humans could transform their weaknesses and limitations into strengths, and the magical revelations of his fairy tales form the essence of their unusual appeal today.

eleven

L. Frank Baum and the Utopian Spirit of Oz

ome sweet home. When Dorothy Gale returns to Kansas at the end of her adventures in the Land of Oz, she declares that there is no place like home and appears content to be back on the farm with her Aunt Em and Uncle Henry. The MGM film based on *The Wonderful Wizard of Oz*, with which most people are nowadays more familiar than the novel, reiterates this message about home sweet home. But it is all a lie. Dorothy does not yet know what home is, and only those readers familiar with L. Frank Baum's fourteen fairy-tale novels about Oz know that home cannot be found in America. Home is Oz, a transcendent utopian paradise, which must be protected from America.

Of course, Baum himself was not certain what he wanted to do with Dorothy and Oz when he began writing *The Wonderful Wizard of Oz* in 1899. He wrote intuitively, and his novels began writing themselves after the first. When his readers demanded more sequels, and when he needed money and respite from financial pressures, he turned to Oz, constantly elaborating what he thought might be the ideal socialist society. Not that Baum was a conscious political thinker, but he was highly aware of what was missing in his life and in American society, and Oz came to embody Baum's vision of a utopian world. In order to understand this vision and why Baum was compelled to return time and again to Oz, it is important to trace the contours of his life that lead from the East Coast to the West, from Broadway to Hollywood, with important stopovers in Aberdeen, South Dakota, and Chicago.

I

Born in Chittenango, New York, with a heart defect, on May 15, 1856, Baum was very much like the cowardly lion — all heart. He was the seventh of nine children, and his parents, Benjamin Ward Baum and Cynthia Ann Stanton, were from respectable, well-to-do families. His mother, a devout Methodist, ran the household as a stern disciplinarian. His father owned a barrel factory, which he sold in 1860 to begin a prosperous oil business in western Pennsylvania and upstate New York. This was the same year that the Baum family moved to Syracuse. In 1861, Baum's father bought a fifteen-acre country home called Rose Lawn outside Syracuse, and it was here that Baum spent idyllic days exploring the country and developing a great interest in horticulture and chicken breeding. Because of his heart disease, Baum was at first educated at home and was fond of reading fairy tales and Victorian literature. However, in 1868 his parents decided that he needed more structure and discipline. So they sent him to Peekskill Military Academy, which he detested. In fact, due to the cruelty and corporal punishment that he experienced there, Baum lasted only two years, and in 1870, he returned to Syracuse, where he continued his education with private tutors, never obtaining a high school diploma.

When he turned fifteen, Baum received a printing press as a present and decided to produce a monthly magazine with his younger brother Harry. They called it *The Rose Lawn Journal*, and for the next three years they published stories, poems, riddles, articles, and advertisements. Already the young Baum, greatly influenced by Charles Dickens, showed a propensity for all kinds of writing and experiments. Never an idle dreamer, he always grabbed the initiative and sought to put his dreams into action. His dreams came to form his reality.

By 1873, Baum became editor of a local paper, *The Empire*, and also worked as a cub reporter for the *New York World*. After *The Empire* was forced to close due to loss of funds, Baum established his own print shop in Bradford, Pennsylvania, and wrote for the newspaper *The New Era* for several years. This work, however, was not entirely fulfilling for the imaginative and energetic Baum, who also worked as a salesman, bred chickens, and, as secretary of the Empire State Poultry Association, published a magazine called *The Poultry Journal*. In 1880, since his father owned some opera houses and theaters in New York and Pennsylvania, he began to manage them and became involved as a writer and actor, despite having no theatrical training. It took him little time to produce his first success, a sentimental musical play called *The Maid of Arran*, written in 1881 and based on William Black's novel, *A Princess of Thule* (1874). Baum even starred in the production, which was mounted in Pennsylvania, Syracuse, and New York City in 1882, and he now became confident that he could have a career in the theater, which would be his lifelong love.

In the meantime, he had fallen in love with Maud Gage, a student at Cornell, during a 1881 Christmas party at the home of Baum's sister. She was the daughter of Matilda Joslyn Gage, who collaborated with Susan B. Anthony and Elizabeth Cady Stanton to write the four-volume *History of Woman Suffrage* (1881–86), and who was famous for her own work, *Woman, Church and State* (1893). Highly educated and independent, Maud came from a different social environment than Baum, and yet they appeared to complement each other, she with her sober political ideas and practicality, and he with his boundless idealism and imagination. They were going to need both sobriety and idealism after their marriage on November 8, 1882, since a series of mishaps would send them on a course of downward social mobility and financial need.

In 1883, after settling in Syracuse, Baum continued writing plays, but with little success. At the same time he worked as a traveling salesman for Baum's Castorine Company, the family oil business. Maud gave birth to Frank Joslyn Baum, the first of four sons, on December 4, and it appeared that now the family had a secure future. However, in 1884, Baum lost his shares in an opera-house chain because of bad management and a fire. He then opened up a small company to sell crude oil products in conjunction with his father's business. But his father's firm was failing because an accountant was falsifying the financial statements, cheating the company, and causing great losses. In 1885, Baum's father had a serious accident that left him semiparalyzed. By the time Benjamin Baum died in 1887, the business had collapsed, and the oil fortune had all but vanished. With a second son to feed — Robert Stanton Baum who was born on February 1, 1886 — and his prospects for a theater career rather dim, Baum decided to move west as many Americans were doing at this time because of the land boom. Maud had two sisters and a brother living in Aberdeen, and Baum went to visit them in June 1888 to determine what he might be able to do in South Dakota territory. By September, he moved with his family and opened a general store called Baum's Bazar. For the next three years, he tried to establish himself in Aberdeen but could not have picked a worse time, for the crops were failing and the farmers were about to plunge into several years of economic depression.

Though enterprising, Baum was a poor businessman and did not know how to manage the stocks in his store properly to make ends meet. Moreover, he was generous to a fault and could not bear to force customers who were poverty stricken or had come upon hard times to pay their debts. He also preferred spinning stories to children outside the shop or supporting the local baseball team to running an efficient business. By January 1, 1890, he was obliged to close the store, and he soon found a job more suitable to his talents and proclivities. He took over a weekly, *The Aberdeen Saturday Pioneer*, as publisher and editor. For the next year and a half, Baum wrote all kinds of articles on social events, politics, sports, gossip, weather, and economics. Some of his editorials dealt with women's suffrage, theosophy, electoral campaigns, the church, horticulture, and husbandry. Baum had always supported the suffragette movement and came out strongly for women's equal rights. He was against organized religion and supported the Farmers' Alliance, criticizing the government and banking system for not lending greater support to the farmers. His most popular column was called "Our Landlady," which reported on conditions and people in a fictitious boardinghouse run by Sairy Ann Bilkins. Here Baum invented delightful stories that poked fun at well-known citizens in Aberdeen and included fantastic things such as electric blankets and flying machines. Yet, despite Baum's remarkable journalistic talents, the circulation of the weekly dwindled because people could not afford the luxury of a newspaper. Baum had to set his own type, lay out advertising, and do printing for other concerns. In March 1891 he returned the paper to its original owner and resigned as editor.

When son number three, Kenneth Gage Baum, was born on March 24, Baum was desperate for a job and fortunately found one in Chicago as a reporter for the *Chicago Evening Post*. Within months, however, he left this job because his salary had been reduced and began working for the chinaware firm of Pitkin and Brooks as a traveling salesman. At this time the Baums (which included his mother-in-law, Matilda Gage) lived in a Chicago home that had no bathroom or running water, and Maud gave embroidery lessons at ten cents an hour to help support the family. Gradually Baum became the best salesman at Pitkin and Brooks and also helped customers design show windows. At the same time, he continued writing stories and poems, which were published in local newspapers, joined the Theosophical Society, avidly attended baseball games, and supported populist causes, even taking part in a demonstration. In 1897, fatigue and nasal hemorrhages, signs of a stressed heart, caused him to retire as a salesman, and he assumed the editorship of *The Show Window*, the first magazine in America to be published for window decorators. As in everything else he did, Baum threw himself into this job with enthusiasm and became the secretary of the National Association of Window Trimmers. Imaginative and inventive, he wrote about and designed fascinating displays that would entice customers into stores. His experience in the theater played a major role here, for he envisioned the windows as scenes from fantastic plays and offered spectators a chance to change their lives through consuming the goods in the windows. But Baum was not interested so much in consumption as he was in writing and theater. Encouraged by his mother-in-law, who thought highly of his bedtime stories for his sons, he began producing children's books: *Mother Goose in Prose* (1897), illustrated by the famous Maxfield Parrish; *My Candelabra's Glare* (1898); and *Father Goose* (1899), his initial collaboration with W. W. Denslow, who had already established a reputation as a gifted illustrator in Chicago. All these books were relatively successful, but it was the publication of *The Wonderful Wizard of Oz*, with the marvelous illustrations by Denslow (fig. 13), in 1900 that enabled Baum to resign from his position as editor of *The Show Window* and dedicate himself totally to writing and the theater. Actually Baum never intended to write a series of Oz books. He followed *The Wonderful Wizard of Oz* with *Dot and Tot of Merryland* and *American Fairy Tales* in 1901, *The Life and Adventures of Santa Claus* in 1902, and *The Enchanted Island of Yew* in 1903. It was not until 1904 that he published a sequel, *The Marvelous Land of Oz*, and the reasons he continued the Oz story reveal a great deal about American culture and Baum's personal relationship to a utopian fantasy that literally took over his life. First, there had been a great demand for a sequel to *The Wonderful Wizard of Oz* by readers of all ages, and the huge success of the musical adaptation in 1902 stimulated even more interest in Oz. The play, which was a sentimental farce for adults that introduced new characters and creatures such as Imogene the Cow instead of Toto the dog, had a long run on Broadway and inspired Baum to try his hand at other Oz plays. Second, Baum kept writing short stories and tales with characters similar to those in Oz, but his readers kept urging him to place them in Oz. Finally, when Baum ran into financial difficulty because his theatrical ventures floundered, and because he liked to live extremely well when he had the money, he knew that sequels with dramatic possibilities would provide him with the funds he needed. Thus, he developed a curious relationship to Oz: it was his pot of luck to which he could turn when he needed money, and it was the means through which he formed a bond with hundreds if not thousands of readers who wrote and gave him suggestions for characters, incidents, and plots. To his credit, Baum, who called himself the Royal Historian of Oz, gradually realized that, after its creation, Oz did not belong to him. True, he had conceived this marvelous land and its inhabitants, but Baum had tapped a deeply rooted desire in himself and his readers to live in a peaceful country, one that maintained tolerance for the weirdest creatures and strange behavior in communities such as Crystal City, China Country, Time Town, Regalia, Blankenburg, and many others that were generally autonomous. That country was not America, and the more Baum cultivated the socialist-utopian relations and principles of Oz, the more he and his readers shared this knowledge.

Figure 13. From L. Frank Baum's The Wonderful Wizard of Oz. Illustr.
W. W. Denslow. Chicago: George M. Hill, 1900.

The 1902 play *The Wizard of Oz*, which was greatly rewritten by Julian Mitchell, the director, led to a dispute about the "property rights" to Oz with W. W. Denslow. For some time, Baum and Denslow had engaged in a kind of rivalry as to who should receive more credit for the creation of their books, especially *The Wonderful Wizard of Oz*. Since Denslow felt that he had been given a minor role in the production of the play and wanted a large share of the royalties, he split with Baum and went on to write and illustrate his own Oz books, which were not very successful. Since Baum had never truly appreciated Denslow's illustrations, he was, therefore, satisfied with this separation, and he now focused on the play and his theater career. Just as the profits from the earlier *Father Goose* had helped the Baum family buy a summer cottage in Macatawa, Michigan, the success of the musical helped the Baums to move into a more comfortable house in Chicago. In the meantime, Baum threw himself into theater projects. He finished *Search for Montague*, based on *Madre d'Oro an Aztec Play* (1889) by Emerson Hough, in 1903, but it was never produced. He wrote the playscript and lyrics for *Father Goose* and the prospectus for a new play, *The Maid of Athens*, which was printed but not performed. Finally, in 1904, he published *The Marvelous Land of Oz*, illustrated by John R. Neill, who would do the drawings for all the subsequent Oz books until his death in 1943. In this first sequel to *The Wonderful Wizard of Oz*, Baum introduced such memorable characters as Ozma, the rightful ruler of Oz, Jack Pumpkinhead, the Saw-Horse, and Professor H. M. Woggle-Bug. This book is notable because it obliged Baum to provide more historical information about Oz, its laws, and characters, and to sharpen his vision of a socialist-utopian society. In addition, Baum began publishing a series of twenty-seven stories under the title "Queer Visitors from the Marvelous Land of Oz" that appeared with illustrations by Walt McDougall in the comic pages of the *Philadelphia North American*, *Chicago Record Herald*, and other newspapers until February 1905. Soon there were all kinds of Oz novelties (sheet music, postcards, pins, and recordings) that furthered the distribution and sales of Baum's Oz books. In fact, the Woggle-Bug became something of a national fad and icon, leading Baum to publish *The Woggle-Bug Book*, illustrated by Ike Morgan, and to produce a largely unsuccessful play, *The Woggle-Bug* in 1905.

During the next two years Baum continued to publish works that were not related to Oz. For instance, in 1905 he completed a musical, *The King of Gee Whiz* with Emerson Hough, a traditional fairy-tale novel, *Queen Zixi of Ix*, which Baum thought was one of his best works, and a novel for adults, *The Fate of a Crown*, under the pseudonym Schuyler Staunton. The following year, after a trip with his wife to see Egypt and parts of Europe, he started a series for older girls with *Aunt Jane's Nieces* and *Aunt Jane's Nieces Abroad* under the pseudonym Edith Van Dyne, and a series for older boys, *Sam Steele's Adventures on Land and Seas* under the pseudonym Captain Hugh Fitzgerald. Yet, he could not abandon Oz, and over the coming years, he wrote *Ozma of Oz* (1907), *Dorothy and the Wizard in Oz* (1908), and *The Road to Oz* (1909). Nor could he abandon the theater, and he conceived a traveling stage production called *Fairylogue and Radio Plays*, in which he used slides, film, live actors, and music to tell Oz stories and other tales that he had written. He took this show on tour, opening on September 24, 1908, in Grand Rapids, Michigan, and closing on December 16 in New York City. Though the performances were well attended, Baum had underestimated the costs of staging such a large traveling show, and he consequently had financial troubles. Despite these problems, he invested in a film company and put all his energy into writing scripts for plays and in making films, which were reasons why he decided to end the Oz series with *The Emerald City of Oz* in 1910. Of course, Baum did not want to abandon Oz entirely, nor could he. Rather he wanted to use the medium of film to realize his Oz fantasies, and it was important then to move to Hollywood where the film industry was making great strides.

In December 1910, the Baums migrated to Hollywood and bought a house that they dubbed "Ozcot" with money that Maud had inherited from her mother. This was the house that Baum would occupy until his death in 1919, and it was here that he devoted himself to raising flowers and winning awards as an amateur horticulturist. Moreover, he returned to breeding chickens and kept Rhode Island Reds in his yard. But Baum was far from retiring as a country gentleman when he arrived in Hollywood and continued writing plays, filmscripts, and poems. Despite his productivity he had to declare bankruptcy in June 1911 because of the debts he had accumulated from *Fairylogue and Radio Plays*. When his plight was made public, Baum received well over one thousand letters, mainly from young readers, who offered to send him money or help him in any way they could. But Baum would not accept charity, and the only way that he knew to recover from financial debt was to continue writing at a furious pace.

Not only did he publish two new fantasies for children, *The Sea Fairies* (1911) and *Sky Island* (1912), but he also produced numerous books for his boy and girl series and was involved in the stage play *The Tik-Tok Man of Oz*, which opened at the Majestic Theater in Los Angeles on March 31. The favorable reviews of this play and the demands of his readers influenced Baum to resume the Oz series, and on July 1, 1913, *The Patchwork Girl of Oz* was published, followed by *Tik-Tok of Oz* (1914), *The Scarecrow of Oz* (1915), *Rinkitink in Oz* (1916), *The Lost Princess of Oz* (1917), *The Tin Woodman of Oz* (1918), *The Magic of Oz* (1919), and *Glinda of Oz* (1920) — the last two appearing posthumously. These works were all conceived by Baum while he was engaged in writing other Oz works either for the cinema or theater. Never one to give up, Baum had formed the Oz Film Manufacturing Company and used characters and motifs from *The Patchwork Girl of Oz*, which had also been made into a musical in 1913, for a film. Three other films based on Oz themes were produced in the coming years, and Baum wrote various short stories based on Oz themes and characters. Even after he had a gall bladder operation in February 1918 and his heart condition worsened, causing painful tics to his face, Baum kept working on his Oz books. Finally, he suffered a stroke and died at his home in Hollywood on May 6, 1919.

II

It is tempting to read the trajectory of Baum's life as that of a late-nineteenth-century pioneer who heads west into open territory when his opportunities run dry on the East Coast. In fact, Baum's social and economic decline led to his decision to seek new and brighter opportunities in the Dakota territory. When he suffered another setback during the depression years of the 1890s, he moved temporarily to Chicago, where he made and lost a fortune. Then, following his proclivity for experimenting with the latest technological inventions related to his art, he headed for California, always with rose-tinted glasses, optimistic until the end of his days. He was an incredibly talented man with an indomitable spirit and drive, despite the fact that he was born with a defective heart. He was a journalist, printer, chicken breeder, actor, theater manager, playwright, oil salesman, owner of a general store, editor of a newspaper, window dresser, editor of a professional journal for window display, carpenter, inventor, cinematist, theosophist, supporter of the suffragette movement, baseball fan, owner of a film company, horticulturist, father of four sons, and devoted husband. Throughout the journey of his life, Baum developed qualities by trying to fill all these roles, and many of the roles and qualities were incorporated into the Oz books. Like Dorothy, he traveled to discover his talents, and he gathered friends around him whom he helped and who helped him.

It is difficult not to idealize Baum, and certainly, when the first critical biography about his life is written, we may learn that he had an ugly and mean side. For instance, we already know that he wrote unkind remarks about Native Americans while living in Aberdeen. Certainly he was not without his contradictions. But no matter what is discovered about Baum, it is important to note and perhaps to emphasize that his conception of Oz stemmed from a tragicomic vision of America, and that Oz never stopped existing for him after the publication of *The Wonderful Wizard of Oz* in 1900. If we want to know his full vision and to realize the profundity of Oz, it is necessary to read the fourteen Oz novels so that we can begin to grasp the cultural process that produced this peculiar *American* utopian fantasy.

Until recently, most critics read the Oz books as some kind of homage to populism and to socialist utopianism. However, during the past twenty years several academicians have taken Baum to task for his contribution to the cult of consumerism in America, his antifeminism, and his retrogressive political ideas. Since these writers raise some important and serious issues about Baum as an artist and the "ultimate" meaning of Oz, if there can be an ultimate meaning, they serve as a good starting point for reconsidering the Oz series that, along with the numerous cinematic versions and literary offshoots, constitute an American myth.

In 1988, Stuart Culver began a shift in "Oz Scholarship" with his essay "What Manikins Want: *The Wonderful Wizard of Oz* and *The Art of Decorating Dry Goods Windows*." He declared that "Dorothy's search for the home imagined by Populist theory takes place in a gaudy, artificial fantasy world that is given over entirely to the values of consumerism. Oz's green capital city, lying midway between the yellow wastes ruled by the Wicked Witch of the West and the blue land of the Munchkins, is a place of mixing and exchange." Through a tour-de-force reading of Baum's *The Art of Decorating Dry Goods Windows* and his involvement in the window-display industry, Culver sought to prove that all relations in *The Wonderful Wizard of Oz* are commodity relations and reflect capitalist exchange values that cater to the needs of commerce. In his interpretation, the characters are similar to mannequins and are used to stimulate consumer desire. However, since this desire can never be entirely fulfilled, Baum's fantasy projects an ambivalent image in which the characters as customers (readers) are encouraged to buy commodities as false images and yet can never achieve the "genuine" identities they desire through consumption. Though Dorothy ultimately refuses to become trapped by commodity fetishism, she does want to "appease a decadent taste for spectacle in the purest sense of the word." In *Land of Desire: Merchants, Power and the Rise of a New American Culture* (1993) William Leach was much more severe in his critique of Baum and accused him of endorsing some of the worst aspects of consumer culture at the turn of the century. "Baum introduced into his fairy tale a mind-cure vision of America quite at home with commercial development of the country. Baum could have criticized American society. He could have used his fairy tale as a means of drawing attention to economic suffering and racial injustice, to the alienating new forms of industrial labor, to the extravagance and greed of many Americans, and to the pooling of wealth and power that was becoming a distinguishing, abiding feature of American capitalist society. ... More to the point, there is no trace of a critique of capitalism in *The Wizard of Oz*. The book is a totally upbeat American fairy tale that, far from challenging the new industrial society, endorsed its values and direction" (250–51). Both Leach and Culver maintain that America had undergone a major socioeconomic transformation at the end of the nineteenth century, making the home into a site of consumption rather than production. As a result, advertising through show windows and the mass media would turn women into "artistic" homemakers who could aesthetically arrange articles of accumulation acquired through the power of the male breadwinner. In this regard, all of Dorothy's contacts with the figures and places in the Oz books could be compared to the relations that "every girl" should cultivate as the perfect consumer. In 1992, Culver followed Leach's lead in another article, "Growing Up in Oz," which focused this time on *The Land of Oz*, interpreted as an antifeminist tract. Here Culver maintained that the plot serves to condition readers to establish their identities through shopping. This intriguing and complex novel reveals how the boy Tip is actually the Princess Ozma, and both Ozma and Dorothy join together to put down a revolt led by a female general. According to Culver, Ozma is developed into a type of figurine or image in the course of the novel that encourages readers to buy into commodity fetishism and accept the domestication of women. More recently, M. David Westbrook endeavored to rectify the political-economist approach to the Oz books in his 1996 essay "Readers of Oz: Young and Old, Old and New Historicist." Although agreeing with Leach and Culver that commodity fetishism and exchange value determine the relations between the various characters within Oz, he finds that their critique is inadequate because "Ozian commerce, like textual commerce in general, operates according to its own laws, laws distinct from those that govern the circulation of merely physical commodities." Westbrook focuses more on the relations between readers and the Oz texts, and demonstrates that the meaning of Oz is conditioned by the consumption of the texts. "While Culver sees the act of reading fantasy as an act of consumption that alienates the child reader from authentic experience and from production," he concludes, "Baum asks whether readers are consumers or whether the reproduction of Oz in the reader's imagination should be considered a productive process in its own right. In the case of Oz, the answers to the questions raised both by Culver and by Baum's own texts can be found more easily in the local particulars of Oz's circulation as a textual commodity than in a generalized discourse of political economy."

Although Westbrook does not sufficiently deal with the misreadings of the Oz books by Leach and Culver, his approach to the Oz books, with his reliance on reception aesthetics and readers' response theory, is an excellent starting point for understanding the significance of Oz as a cultural icon. Therefore, I should like to reflect upon his notions about "readerly cultural production" and "conceptions of cultural property" and how they have contributed to the formation of the meaning of Oz. Then I would like to return to the texts themselves to reconsider the social and economic relations that Baum established in the fictitious land of Oz to show that its compelling feature rests in the cultivation of gift exchange and a principle of hope.

III

Westbrook maintains that without grasping how readers received and appropriated the Oz books we cannot establish the value of Oz as cultural artifact and as commodity. His point is well taken. When Baum first produced *The Wonderful Wizard of Oz* with Denslow's drawings in 1900, he had no idea how successful this fantasy would be and how it would capture the imagination of young and old readers. Indeed, it was an immediate best seller, and he and Denslow sought to capitalize on the success in all sorts of ways that turned Oz and related characters into commodities. Not only did they enhance Oz's exchange value as commodity with the production of the musical *The Wizard of Oz* in 1902, but they expanded the audience, for the play was directed mainly at adults. From this point on, the market for Oz consisted of children and adults, and Baum and Denslow created all sorts of novelties (posters, postcards, pins, music sheets, boxes, and so on) that would continue to pique the interest and curiosity of loyal followers and potential customers. But what were Baum, Denslow, and the publishers of the Oz materials piquing? Clearly, the fascination with Oz on the part of the children and adults cannot be solely explained by consumer desire. In fact, as Westbrook shows, the reader input that compelled Baum (and Denslow, and later Neill, who seem to be forgotten by Leach, Culver, and Westbrook in their critiques) to continue producing Oz books is highly significant in determining what Oz meant and means. Oz was and still is more than just a commodity. In particular, Baum gave Oz as a kind of gift to the public and cultivated Oz in a singular rapport with his readers, who saw in Oz an embodiment of social relations that were not possible in America. Many readers maintained a personal relationship with the author through letters that influenced Baum in his attitude toward Oz, which, as we know, he protected from encroachment by hostile forces.

Oz did not die after Baum's death. Ruth Plumly Thompson was appointed Baum's successor by Maud Baum and the publishers, and Neill continued illustrating the "official" Oz books until his death in 1943. In the meantime, numerous other writers and artists wrote Oz parodies, sequels, stories, and novels, and Oz films were produced, the most significant being the MGM production in 1939 with Judy Garland as Dorothy, Bert Lahr as the Cowardly Lion, Ray Bolger as the Scarecrow, and Jack Haley as the Tin Woodman. This film was not initially a great success, and the reception of the Oz books had undergone somewhat of a change in the 1940s, with many librarians censoring the series either because of the positive images of witches or because of its alleged communist politics. But, in 1956, Oz returned to American consciousness with a vengeance when the MGM film was telecast to millions of viewers. Since then, it has been retelecast annually around Christmastime; new film adaptations have been made; and a classic video of the original MGM film has been reproduced. In addition, the International Wizard of Oz Club, formed by Justin Schiller in 1957, has flourished and sponsors Oz conventions and meetings, aside from publishing the important journal, *The Baum Bugle*, and other Oz-related works. Finally, talented writers such as Philip José Farmer (*A Barnstormer in Oz*, 1982), Geoff Ryman (*Was*, 1992), and Gregory Maguire (*Wicked: The Life and Times of the Wicked Witch of the West*, 1995 and *Son of a Witch*, 2005) have commemorated Oz in novels that reflect different readerly and artistic appropriations of Baum's original utopian fantasy.

Although Oz as book and icon has been commodified throughout the twentieth century, it has also been exchanged as a gift to readers by its author/begetter, and by readers to friends and other readers that transcends and subverts the commodity system. This creative act of gift exchange has endowed Oz with manifold meanings. Most of all, Oz has come to represent through readerly exchange and gift giving a world other than what America is, no matter how different readers' responses have been. This otherness also depicts another form of relationship: The Oz novels display how people can relate to things and nature in a manner that was not and is not typical of how relationships have been formed and forged in America.

IV

If we now focus on the texts, we can see how the Oz books themselves (as intended by Baum) have fostered a certain understanding of utopian otherness that may have a bearing on the way Oz has been received as a gift and interpreted by readers. Since Oz is generally associated with the first novel, *The Wonderful Wizard of Oz*, or with the MGM film, it is important to remember that all of Baum's Oz books are connected and somewhat dependent on one another: They represent a creative process in which the characters share gifts and talents with one another and with readers to express the hope that base materialist and gendered interests need not determine the way people relate to one another. Oz as a utopian home is constructed from these relationships, and its gradual development in the early twentieth century serves as a counter model to the rise of capitalist commodity exchange.

The mistake that critics like Culver, Leach, and Westbrook make in their analyses of the Oz books is that they identify Oz with America and imagine that there is some sort of commodity exchange that determines how the characters and creatures in Oz will behave. Yet, Oz is clearly another world with its own peculiar social economy. It may be a lost continent or territory; it may even be an island surrounded by deserts. Whatever or wherever it is, it is not part of the United States. Nor does it have a unified monetary system and commodity exchange. In the very first novel, Baum makes clear that Oz is *not* controlled by the Wizard, who only exerts power in the Emerald City. Nor does the Emerald City determine how people relate to each other outside its limits. If anything, the Wizard as an *American* con man has colonized the city, duped its gentle and naive inhabitants, and introduced American standards and norms based on salesmanship and deception that ultimately will not work in the land of Oz as a whole. The qualities that distinguish most of the "native" inhabitants of Oz from the beginning are their gentleness, generosity, and tolerance. The Munchkins and Witch of the North are grateful to Dorothy for accidentally killing the Wicked Witch of the East, and their first act is to give Dorothy the silver slippers as a gift. They expect nothing in return, and they all want to help her find her way back to Kansas. The second thing that Dorothy receives is a kiss from the Witch of the North that will protect her. Soon she will discover that the Munchkins, who are all good farmers and raise large crops (in contrast to the situation in Kansas), do not use money. They share their food and provide lodging for Dorothy without thinking of charging her anything. Everything is free in Oz, and the value of life (the government, morality, ethics) depends on the economy of gift giving that brings with it the obligation to give, accept, and reciprocate. Gifts are not only material objects but also spiritual qualities and talents. As Lewis Hyde has made clear in his superb book *The Gift: Imagination and the Erotic Life of Property*, "when gifts circulate within a group, their commerce leaves a series of interconnected relationships in its wake, and a kind of decentralized cohesiveness emerges. ... A circulation of gifts nourishes those parts of our spirit that are not entirely personal, parts that derive from nature, the group, the race, or the gods. Furthermore, although these wider gifts are a part of us, they are not 'ours'; they are endowments bestowed upon us. To feed them by giving away the increase they have brought with us is to accept that our participation in them brings with it an obligation to preserve their vitality" (xiv, 38). In contrast to the gift economy, Hyde argues, the capitalist commodity system is based on the exploitation of a gift and work for profit. It involves a negative reciprocity that brings about fragmentation, individualism, and clannishness.

Baum's first novel, *The Wonderful Wizard of Oz*, associates good with the vital progression of gift giving and evil with hoarding and oppression. What is spectacular in this novel is not the spectacle of the show window, but the extraordinarily gracious acts of the people and creatures who uncover false spectacle on their way to defining what Oz is as potential home. The three characters Dorothy meets and seeks to help on her way to Emerald City — the Scarecrow, the Tin Woodman, and the Cowardly Lion — already possess the talents they think they lack. During their journey Baum shows that, by sharing their talents with one another, they can easily overcome adversity. The irony of the first part of their trip is that they already are in full possession of their gifts when they meet the American con man who wants to manipulate and exploit them for his own selfish interests.

Culver and Leach exaggerate the significance of the commercialism of the Emerald City and argue that the commodity system is in full operation in Oz. Certainly, Baum describes Dorothy's first encounter with the city like this: "Many shops stood in the street, and Dorothy saw that everything in them was green. Green candy and green popcorn were offered for sale, as well as green shoes, green hats and green clothes of all sorts. At one place a man was selling green lemonade, and when the children bought it Dorothy could see that they paid for it with green pennies." This particular scene led Culver and Leach to generalize about Oz and some of the sequels as exemplifying consumer capitalism where the spectacle and illusion function to bind people to capitalist fetishism. However, the Emerald City is unlike most of Oz. It has been taken over by the American wizard, who is responsible for deluding the people and instituting a market system. When he vanishes by the end of the novel, his system disappears with him: It is almost as if he were tied to the wicked witches, who use magic for their own benefit. All the Oz books pose one major question as their theme: How can the gift of magic be used to benefit the majority of people so they can live in harmony and foster respect for differences?

For Baum, magic was a powerful art form, and his own writing brought about miraculous transformations as he sought to imagine a world that did not have to rely on deceit and transformation. In this respect, the Oz novels deal with the issue of how to honor the gift of magic so that it is used properly. With each Oz book, Baum gains a greater sense of how he wants to use his own "magic" to provide historical background for his utopian world and to illustrate how the gift of magic can foster communal cohesiveness and provide a true home for people. In his second work, *The Marvelous Land of Oz* (1904), Baum establishes two key principles that will be significant for his future elaboration of what Oz is: magic can only be used by Glinda and Ozma for the good of the people; the art of magic as a nurturing force will be in the hands of women. Interestingly, Dorothy does not appear in this novel because Baum is more concerned with recording how Oz came to be and how it will be shaped in the future. The work joins two plots that concern the machinations of the evil witch Mombi, who has transformed Ozma, the rightful ruler of Oz, into the boy Tip, and the rebellious forces of the female general Jinjur, who dethrones the Scarecrow. In the end, it is Glinda the Good who compels Mombi to restore Ozma to her real self and who helps bring about the defeat of Jinjur. As Glinda tells Tip/Ozma, she refuses to deal in transformations, "for they are not honest, and no respectable sorceress likes to make things appear to be what they are not. Only unscrupulous witches use the art, and therefore I must ask Mombi to effect your release from her charm, and restore you to your proper form. It will be the last opportunity she will have to practice magic."

From this point on in the Oz sequels, the government of Oz will be determined by the soft and gentle magic of Ozma, assisted by Glinda and at times by the reformed wizard, who returns in a later adventure. Although Baum clearly wrote *The Marvelous Land of Oz* as a spoof of some of the worst aspects of the suffragette movement, he did not belittle women, nor did he reify them as mannequins as Culver suggests. His own writing style and the governing style of Ozma/Glinda are strikingly similar: They are soothing and attentive to the peculiar desires and needs of characters. In all his works, the writing and magic appear to formulate psychological principles of object relations that are to guide parents in their nurturing of children. Baum sets up a space, a unique environment, in which his young characters can play creatively and explore their potential for development in relation to a mother figure. As D. W. Winnicott has pointed out, "the potential space between baby and mother, between child and family, between individual and society or the world, depends on experience that leads to trust. It can be looked upon as sacred to the individual in that it is here that the individual experiences creative living" (11). Each novel creates its own space called Oz, which is filled with the most eccentric and peculiar creatures and things, and Baum weaves their relations in such a way that their needs are respected and fulfilled without infringing upon the instinctual drives and needs of the others. If there is conflict — and there are always conflicts and adventures — the nurturing voices and wise responses of Ozma and Glinda the Good move the involved characters toward peaceful reconciliation. Creative exploration and artistic transformation of space into a home in which all the characters feel comfortable with themselves — this is the teleological force that guides all the Oz books and perhaps has influenced the response to Oz of readers and viewers during the past century.

In the next sequel, *Ozma of Oz* (1907), we have a perfect example of how Baum structured most of the novels in the series to emphasize magic as art and art as a manner of gift giving that can induce positive reciprocity in the object relations of the characters. Here Dorothy is on her way to Australia with her sick Uncle Henry when a storm strikes and causes a shipwreck. Saved by a chicken coop on the ocean, she encounters the talking hen Billina on the ocean. When they reach land, they find themselves in the Kingdom of Ev, and there she meets Tik-Tok the Machine Man, who tells them about the evil King of Ev, who has sold his wife and children to the Nome King. When Dorothy, Tik-Tok, and Billina enter the kingdom of Ev, they are incarcerated by the vain and treacherous Princess Langwidere, the temporary ruler, who has more than thirty heads that she can change to improve her looks, and she wants Dorothy's head. At this point, Ozma arrives to liberate Dorothy, Billina, and Tik-Tok. Eventually, they proceed to the Nome King's domain, where, with the help of the Tin Woodman and the Scarecrow, they capture the magic belt that gives the Nome King power. Once they free the Queen of Ev and her family through the use of Billina's eggs, which are like poison for the nomes, they return to Oz. Dorothy gives the magic belt to Ozma, and Ozma wishes Dorothy back to Kansas, where her sick Uncle Henry still needs her.

Throughout the novel Dorothy, Billina, Tik-Tok, and Ozma give of themselves. They lend their talents to oppressed characters who are being exploited out of vanity, greed, and lust for power. Once again, magic is being abused to transform people into ornaments and artificial things. It is through the use of their gifts — Billina's eggs, the Scarecrow's intelligence, Dorothy's bravery — that the relations are changed and the individuals inside and outside Oz can pursue their goals without harm or hindrance.

As Baum responded to the events he depicted in the first three novels and the network of relations he created in Oz, he was compelled to explain more to himself and to his readers how and why Oz came into being, and how relations were determined. By the time he came to write *The Emerald City of Oz* (1910), he was ready to finalize all its features and to define this utopian world as a socialist projection because he had decided this would be his last Oz novel. Therefore, this book is perhaps the most significant of the series and the most innovative. It lays out the principles of Oz as a type of socialist paradise, an alternative to the United States, which, by the end of the book, must be made invisible because of encroaching technology and capitalist expansion. Kansas is depicted now as a *place of exploitation*, where Uncle Henry and Aunt Em are at the mercy of bankers. The narrative structure assumes a dialectical and thus a dramatic quality with a twofold plot: (1) Dorothy seeks to find a refuge for Aunt Em and Uncle Henry. With the help of Ozma, she brings them to Oz for good and takes them on a tour to show them this splendid place and to explain the "object relations" of the different characters. This trip allows Baum to reintroduce most of the key charmingly eccentric creatures again — the Wizard of Oz, the Shaggy Man, the Cowardly Lion, the Tin Woodman, the Scarecrow, Jack Pumpkinhead, Billina, Tik-Tok, and Professor Woggle-Bug — as though in a grand finale in a musical show. (2) The Nome King amasses a large army with the Whimsies, Growleywogs, and the Phanfasms and attempts to avenge his previous defeat in *Ozma of Oz* by destroying Oz. His evil attitude can be likened to that of the bankers in America. He acts out of pure greed and wants to destroy a land that is not based on commodity exchange. Baum describes Oz very thoroughly in this volume to make sure that his readers understand what is at stake in the conflict:

> No disease of any sort was ever known among the Ozites, and so no one ever died unless he met with an accident that prevented him from living. This happened very seldom, indeed. There were no poor people in the Land of Oz, because there was no such thing as money, and all property of every sort belonged to the Ruler. The people were her children, and

she cared for them. Each person was given freely by his neighbors whatever he required for his use, which is as much as any one may reasonably desire. Some tilled the lands and raised great crops of grain, which was divided equally among the entire population, so that all had enough. There were many tailors and dressmakers and shoemakers and the like, who made things that any who desired them might wear. Likewise there were jewelers who made ornaments for the person, which pleased and beautified the people, and these ornaments also were free to those who asked for them. Each man and woman, no matter what he or she produced for the good of the community, was supplied by the neighbors with food and clothing and a house and furniture and ornaments and games. If by chance the supply ever ran short, more was taken from the great storehouses of the Ruler, which were afterward filled up again when there was more of any article than the people needed.

Every one worked half the time and played half the time, and the people enjoyed the work as much as they did the play, because it is good to be occupied and to have something to do. There were no cruel overseers set to watch them, and no one to rebuke them or to find fault with them. So each one was proud to do all he could for his friends and neighbors, and was glad when they would accept the things he produced.

Though there are evident contradictions in some of the Baum Oz novels that preceded *The Emerald City of Oz* — money is occasionally used, and there appear to be hunger and want, especially among the animals — all the sequels that followed this book tended to maintain the socialist principles outlined here. The assumption is that the Land of Oz must be protected at all costs. Oz is a wonder to behold, and the nurturing female rulers demonstrate that the art of magic or the magic of art can effectively be used to rearrange social relations for harmonious living.

What is perhaps most significant about the Oz books written in California from 1912 until Baum's death in 1919 is that Baum was literally compelled to write these novels because of the readers' demands for more Oz stories, Baum's own fascination with Oz, and his financial need. They were also written against a background of increasing industrial growth and expansion in the United States, floods of immigration to America, fierce struggles over workers' rights, and World War I. Although Baum made no direct allusions to these developments — after all he was writing mainly for children — it is clear that Oz as socialist paradise represents certain "good" values that are opposed by the "evil" machinations of characters that represent "American norms," such as genetic experimentation in *The Patchwork Girl of Oz* (1913); cruel oppression by the Nome King in *Tik-Tok of Oz* (1914); and the abuse of magic in *The Scarecrow of Oz* (1915), *Rinkitink in Oz* (1916), *The Lost Princess of Oz* (1917), *The Tin Woodman of Oz* (1918), and *The Magic of Oz* (1919). Toward the end of his life, Baum appeared to be somewhat obsessed by the expropriation of magic and its misuse. Perhaps he was worried about losing his own "magic" as his health declined during these years and he was unable to bring some of his projects to fruition. Within his texts, however, the meaning is more social and political.

If magic is a "powerful gift" of transformation, it could be very dangerous if it were to fall into the wrong hands. In Oz, this power resides with Ozma, a mother figure, who, as the head of a large family, nurtures the talents of her subjects and animates them through her art to share their talents for the welfare of all. Thus, the final highly significant novel, *Glinda of Oz*, provides different societal models and different ways in which magic is used to resolve conflict. Here Baum did in fact allude directly to World War I in the first chapter, "The Call to Duty," when Ozma discovers that there is a war in her realm about which she had known nothing: "Being the Princess of this fairyland it is my duty to make all my people — wherever they may be — happy and content and to settle their disputes and keep them from quarreling. So, while the Skeezers and Flatheads may not know me or that I am their lawful Ruler, I now know that they inhabit my kingdom and are my subjects, so I would not be doing my duty if I kept them away from them and allowed them to fight."

Whether the Flatheads are the Allies and the Skeezers the Germans and Austrians or vice versa does not matter, for Baum was more concerned in mocking war in general and ridiculing the perpetrators of the absurd war started by Queen Coo-ee-oh and Su-Dic (the Supreme Dictator), who are disempowered thanks to the collective action of Ozma and her friends. It is important that Ozma by herself cannot bring about a resolution to the conflict. She needs the aid of Glinda, Dorothy, the Patchwork Girl, and Reera the Red. In other words, these characters all lend their talents so that peace can return to Oz. As Ozma tells Dorothy at the beginning of their adventure, "no one is powerful enough to do everything."

With a fairy-tale structure similar to that of The Wonderful Wizard of Oz, this narrative depends on the reciprocal action of gift giving. Ozma helps everyone by giving of herself and is in turn helped by her friends and strangers who partake of the generous and gracious spirit in which she operates. This is also the spirit that inspires so much fascination in the readers.

Although Glinda of Oz was Baum's last Oz novel, it was not really the last word on Oz. There is no closure to the Oz stories. Baum had tried to close down Oz with The Emerald City of Oz, but he failed wonderfully. To this day no one can prevent Oz from continuing because it stems from deep social and personal desires that many Americans feel are not being met in this rich and powerful country that is also known for its pauperization of children. In this respect, the fairy tale of Oz is truly a very American fairy tale in its projection of an oppositional space that holds out the possibility for the enrichment of children, and its reception during the past one hundred years is also an American cultural phenomenon. Dorothy's pursuit of home, unlike Judy Garland's personal pursuit of home in America, is a successful one because she does not stay in Kansas. She did not allow herself or her Aunt Em and Uncle Henry to be ground to death by humiliating and inequitable conditions of labor on the great plains. She — and Baum — became magically touched by Oz in the first novel, and they experienced a resonating presentiment: home was not a nostalgic search for one's roots, but a move forward into the unknown where one might design and designate home with others. Home could be defined in an active process of transforming social relations that would bring about personal fulfillment and a utopian societal model. As an icon of utopian home, Oz reveals how differences might shine and be truly appreciated and how a communal spirit might flourish. Together Baum's novels serve as utopian markers about our potential to realize home concretely in reality. In giving us Oz, Baum not only celebrated and enjoyed his own imaginative gifts but also invited us to join his quest and to reciprocate by keeping alive our hope for a land in which poverty and greed are banished.

twelve

Revisiting J. M. Barrie's *Peter and Wendy* and Neverland

I t is difficult to write about a novel as unique as *Peter and Wendy*, made famous by its major protagonist but rarely read by children today, if it ever was widely read by youngsters. Certainly, millions of children (and adults) born in the latter part of the twentieth century and the beginning of the twenty-first know about Peter Pan, but mainly because they have experienced him flying across a stage, often impersonated by a woman like the wonderful actresses Jean Arthur and Mary Martin, or they have watched the Disney animated version. In fact, most young people and adults have probably been introduced to Peter and his friends through a Disney book, a television adaptation, Peter Pan artifacts, a local production of the play, or Steven Spielberg's film *Hook*. Very few have ever read J. M. Barrie's stories in *Peter Pan in Kensington Gardens* (1906) or the novel *Peter and Wendy* (1911), or seen the play *Peter Pan, or The Boy Who Wouldn't Grow Up* (final text in 1928) in the original. Even fewer are familiar with the name J. M. Barrie, nor may they really care who he is. Yet, there is a fascinating history behind James Matthew Barrie, the imaginative creator of Peter Pan, and how Peter Pan came into being, and it can help us understand why Peter Pan, the boy who refuses to grow up, continues to capture the imagination of people throughout the world.

I

Barrie and his Peter Pan works were held in high esteem in literary circles up through the 1970s, but the more recent critics of the play, produced in 1904, and the novel, published in 1911, can barely restrain themselves from charging Barrie with escapism and infantilism, and with taking some kind of perverse delight in the manipulation of children. Almost all the scholars identify Barrie with Peter Pan and introduce telltale biographical aspects into their interpretations of his works. After all, Barrie was a very short person, whimsical, moody, often generous and cruel, and unpredictable. He had great difficulty loving and being loved. Essentially he lived for his writing and died a loner. So it is not unfair to ask whether the figure of Peter Pan, whose play Barrie kept revising until its official publication in 1928, was a projection of his inner life. And, if so, did he subconsciously incorporate many of his secret longings in his writings about Peter Pan, Wendy, the Darling Brothers, and the lost boys that need more exposure? For instance, some critics have taken him to task for playing with and using the five young Llewelyn Davies boys he met in Kensington Gardens in both real life and in his works. They have suggested that Barrie might have been a pedophile or closet homosexual. One critic, Jacqueline Rose, has even elaborated on the Peter Pan works as a case study to argue that children's literature as a whole involves an exploitative, if not sadistic, treatment of the characters of children in narratives, and these narratives engender representations of childhood that basically satisfy the desires, urges, and drives of the author, rationalizing his or her behavior. Children's literature is thus not for the benefit or delight of children. Rather, the narrative manipulation can be somehow connected to the manner in which children are always used, if not exploited, by adults in the socialization process.

Viewed from biographical and psychoanalytical perspectives, the Peter Pan writings may indeed be loaded with controversial issues. Barrie was filled with all sorts of complexes and was clearly concerned about winning and holding his mother's love, developing his sexual prowess, and proving himself as a brilliant man and writer. But it would be a great mistake to read and interpret his works mainly from the viewpoint of his personal struggles. Most readers of the novel and viewers of the play are probably attracted to the boy who never grows up and who refuses to integrate himself in normal English society for many other reasons than those related to the struggles of Barrie's life. There is something compelling on a broad cultural level about the rebellious character of Peter Pan that demands greater attention than Barrie's problems, for Peter Pan is a cultural icon not afraid to kill to defend his lifestyle, and one who refuses to be civilized. In this regard he resembles other major figures of children's literature produced at about the same time he came into being: Huckleberry Finn of *The Adventures of Huckleberry Finn* (1884), and Dorothy of *The Wizard of Oz* (1900). Huck declares at the end of Mark Twain's novel that he would rather go to hell than to be civilized, while Dorothy refuses to return to Kansas in L. Frank Baum's sixth novel of the Oz series, and she remains in Oz for the rest of her life. What are we to make of these protagonists who reject their societies to live in other realms? What was in the air in America and England at the turn of the century that produced three of the great works of children's literature? Were these works of defiance? Why have they continued to play such a powerful role in American and British culture up through the beginning of the twenty-first century? More than Huck and Dorothy, Peter Pan keeps returning to insist that he can't stay. He is always in our presence, and yet, he denies us his presence even when we are induced by him during the performance of the play to cry out that we believe in fairies.

Admittedly we can never discover the "essential" meaning of the Peter Pan icon. The story behind the writer of the Peter Pan works and the story about the signification of the Peter Pan works have flown together, just as the stories, play, and novel about Peter Pan have merged and cannot really be separated. Ironically, however, it is important to try to separate the life from the works, to endeavor to see how they are connected and distinct at the same time.

II

James Matthew Barrie was born in the Scottish village of Kirriemuir on May 9, 1860. He was the third son and ninth child of David Barrie, a handloom weaver, and his wife Margaret Olgilvy. (In the Scottish tradition, a wife retained her family name.) One more daughter, Maggie, was born three years later. Although the family was large and money was scarce, the Barries were fiercely independent and believed deeply in the power of religion and education to improve their lot on this earth. David Barrie and Margaret Olgilvy were also very ambitious for their children. Whatever money was made through weaving was to be used to further the education of the boys and to provide good Christian training for the girls. Moreover, everyone was expected to demonstrate loyalty to the family, and they did indeed support one another throughout their lives. For instance, Alexander (Alec), the eldest brother, born in 1842, was already at Aberdeen University when Barrie was born. Soon after he became a master at Glasgow Academy, he helped finance his other brothers' educations and could always be called upon to provide counsel.

There were, however, a few problems in the Barrie household, which was somewhat typical for their time. The father was barely visible because he worked so many hours, while Margaret Ogilvy kept a tight control over the children to make sure they were clean and industrious, went to church every Sunday, read the Bible, and did well at school. Although each child was looked after with great care, it was clear that the second son, David, born in 1853, was her favorite and that she had high hopes he would become a famous protestant minister in Scotland. In 1866, David was sent to Bothwell in Lanarkshire, where Alexander was principal of a small school, to be prepared for entrance examinations at either Glasgow or Aberdeen University. However, right before David's fourteenth birthday in 1867, he had an accident while ice skating and died from a badly fractured skull. His death was particularly traumatic for his mother. According to Barrie's later account, *Margaret Ogilvy*, published in 1896, she went into a deep depression and remained melancholy for the rest of her life. Although he was only six at the time and barely remembered David, Barrie did recall how he himself made up his mind to restore her to good health and happiness by becoming a success in life. Although not as studious as his older brothers, Barrie was an avid reader, often reading books with his mother, and he took a great interest in theater, using toy theaters to dramatize scenes from the Old Testament. He was also a prankster and developed a great love for cricket. His parents' expectations were never great for him, but his mother did take comfort in sharing stories with him, and as he wrote, "I sat a great deal on her bed trying to make her forget him, which was my crafty way of playing physician."

To a certain degree, the young Barrie, who did not totally abandon his carefree ways, assumed the role of doctor in the family from this point on — a role that he would play throughout the rest of his life. Barrie came to love doctoring not just his mother. As he grew older, he doctored people in all his relations, prescribing how they should feel, what they should do, what medicine they should take in certain instances, and basically, ordering their lives for them. But first he had to learn and decide what he wanted to do himself.

From the age of eight until eighteen, his education was supervised by his brother Alec at Glasgow Academy and at Dumfries Academy. He was a better than average student, an avid reader of English and American literature, and founded an Amateur Dramatic Club. Yet his overall grades were not strong enough to win a scholarship to the university, and he hoped his family would support his decision to become a freelance writer upon graduation from Dumfries. Despite the fact that he had not won a scholarship, however, his parents insisted that he study for a degree at the university. Once again Alec intervened and told him that he would pay for his education at Edinburgh University, where David Masson, a great scholar of literature, might take him under his wing. Because Barrie could never bear to hurt his family, he agreed to study four years for a Master of Arts with a specialization in literature.

At eighteen Barrie had not grown much more than five feet one or two, and he felt awkward and shy in public. Nor had he ever had a romantic relationship with a girl. Socially his adaptation to university life was difficult at first. Moreover, he dreaded the required courses in the sciences and had to lead an ascetic life in Edinburgh due to meager finances. But Barrie was always enterprising and determined to make his mark as a writer. Within the first year of his studies, he managed to become a freelance drama critic for the Edinburgh *Courant* and reviewed plays in Edinburgh, Glasgow, and other cities. In addition, he joined a debating society and gradually learned to overcome his shyness. During his four years at the university he studied hard, attended the theater as much as possible, formed friendships only with other male students, and finally received his MA in April 1882.

Despite the degree, Barrie found himself in the same position in which he had been when he had graduated from Dumfries Academy four years earlier — a great desire to become a writer, but no job and no great prospects. That is, until the winter of 1882, when one of his sisters, Jane Ann, happened to see an advertisement for a leader-writer for an English newspaper, the *Nottingham Journal*. Barrie applied on a lark, and to his great surprise, he received the post and an opportunity to write not only the feature articles for the newspaper, but also reviews, stories, and a play. Some of these writings were also published in London magazines. Unfortunately, by October 1884, he was dismissed because the owners of the newspaper were losing money and decided to print syndicated articles instead of paying their own journalists.

No sooner did Barrie return to Kirriemuir than he began to make plans to move to London, where he had some success in selling articles to various magazines and newspapers. In March 1885 he finally took up residence in London near the British Museum, threw himself into his work, and within five years was regarded as one of the most promising young writers in England. He published numerous articles and stories in the *St. James's Gazette, Spectator, Chambers Journal*, and other newspapers and magazines, and wrote skits and small plays. His first major book publication, *Auld Licht Idylls* (1888), was a collection of sketches of rural Scotland during the early nineteenth century, based in part on his mother's reminiscences, and it was a relative success. It was followed by a similar book, *A Window in Thrums* (1889), which did not do well, but his first novel, *The Little Minister* (1891), had a huge popular reception. Set in Scotland during the Weavers' Riots in 1840, it concerns a "little" minister who falls in love with a gypsy and must contend with the people of his town, who object to his nonconformist behavior. The novel was adapted for the stage in 1897 and made a name for him in England and America. He was not only highly respected as a novelist, but also as a dramatist. However, he honed his skills first as a novelist and prose fiction writer before turning mainly to the theater.

In 1896, after publishing collections of his stories and sketches, he produced two important works, *Margaret Ogilvy*, the biography of his mother, which in part created the legend of young Jamie, who could never replace his dead brother in his mother's eyes, and *Sentimental Tommy*, which dealt with a young dreamer and had strong autobiographical elements that were incorporated into the sequel, *Tommy and Grizel* (1900). The second novel was a harbinger of Peter Pan, with such notable passages by the fictitious narrator as:

> Poor Tommy! he was still a boy, he was ever a boy, trying sometimes, as now, to be a man, and always when he looked round he ran back to his boyhood as if he saw it holding out its arms to him and inviting him to come back and play. He was so fond of being a boy that he could not grow up. … But here, five and twenty years later, is the biography, with the title changed. You may wonder that I had the heart to write it. I do it, I have sometimes pretended to myself, that we may all laugh at the stripping of a rogue, but that was never my main reason. Have I been too cunning, or have you seen through me all the time? Have you discovered that I was really pitying the boy who was so fond of boyhood that he could not with years become a man, telling nothing about him that was not true, but doing it with unnecessary scorn in the hope that I might goad you into crying, "Come, come, you are too hard on him."

These passages are significant because they reveal how early in his writings Barrie tried to objectivize himself as the boy who wouldn't grow up and to develop a manipulative narrative style through the use of a fictional author who plays on the sympathies of his readers with charm and wit. All the time Barrie was doctoring his life story, almost as if he were writing the "fairy tale of my life," as Hans Christian Andersen had done in his autobiography. Like Andersen, Barrie doctored his "exposure" to conceal terrifying insights into his own psyche and behavior and how and why he related to the world around him as he did.

And relate he did on a grand scale. The more famous he became in the 1890s, the more he began taking an interest in grand society and in young women. Barrie's financial situation had improved immensely, allowing him to move to grander living quarters and to dine and mix with people of the upper classes. At the same time, he began taking out young actresses, whom he had always admired but felt too shy to meet. By the time his play, *Walker, London* (1892), was produced in London, he had fallen in love with Mary Ansell, a talented, beautiful actress, and during a long courtship with her, he knew that she wanted to marry him, but hesitated for months to ask her. In one of the more telling accounts of his life, *J. M. Barrie: The Man Behind the Image*, Janet Dunbar comments:

> Heaven knows what dark night of the soul James Matthew Barrie went through at the idea of a union with a flesh and blood woman. He would never again be able to escape into romantic images when life brought his high-powered imagination into conflict with the realities of marriage. How much did Barrie know about himself? Did he know, or did he suspect, that he lacked virility and should not marry at all? It is difficult to believe that he never thought about sex, with that imagination; but, equally, it is not difficult to understand why he still flinched away from any full-blooded approach to women. Margaret Ogilvy had put her thumbmark on him in his most impressionable years, and subconsciously he still accepted her appalling puritanical attitude that a man's relations with his wife were "regrettable but necessary." It is probable that the only way he could resolve the complexes which this attitude set up was by sublimating his natural desires — turning them into a kind of romantic worship which he knew in his inner heart was false, but which he was not able to help. His pathological shyness must also have been a factor. (10)

Yet he overcame this shyness and doubts and married Mary Ansell on July 4, 1894. Then they traveled to Switzerland for their honeymoon, where, according to his wife, their marriage was never sexually consummated. Ironically, the unproductive years of their marriage that ended in divorce in 1909 coincided with one of Barrie's most productive periods. Not only did he write the novel *The Little White Bird* (1902), with key chapters introducing Peter Pan to the world, later published separately in *Peter Pan in Kensington Gardens* (1906), but he also produced some of his great plays such as *The Little Minister* (1897), *Quality Street* (1902), *The Admirable Crichton* (1902), *Little Mary* (1903), *Peter Pan* (1904), *What Every Woman Knows* (1908), and *A Slice of Life* (1910). Moreover, he corresponded with most of the great writers of this time, Arthur Conan Doyle, Robert Louis Stevenson, Thomas Hardy, H. G. Wells, and others, and was personally acquainted with many other leading figures in theatrical and literary circles. Thanks in large part to the gracious help of Mary Ansell, he held parties in his home or attended dinners at homes of the social elite in London, despite major difficulties within the marriage.

The most memorable and notable social event of this period was not, however, with adults, but with three small boys in Kensington Gardens. Barrie and his wife had moved to a spacious dwelling at Leinster Corner, very near Kensington Gardens, and Barrie customarily took walks there with his St. Bernard dog Porthos. In the summer of 1897, he happened to encounter Mary Hodgson, a nurse, who was taking a stroll with the Llewelyn Davies boys, four-year-old George, and his younger brothers Jack and Peter, ages three and one, respectively. Attracted to the boys, Barrie began performing magic feats and playing with them throughout the summer and into the fall, often inventing stories about fairies, pirates, magical islands, and strange characters. It was not until a dinner party later in the year that Barrie met their mother, Sylvia Llewelyn Davies, daughter of the novelist George du Maurier, and sister of the actor Gerald du Maurier, who would later make the role of Captain Hook famous. Sylvia Davies, a beautiful and gracious young woman, thirty-one at the time, was married to a young struggling lawyer named Arthur, who was thirty-four. Once Barrie realized that Sylvia was the mother of the Davies boys he had met in Kensington Gardens, he felt a strong rapport. Whether he fell in love with Sylvia as an ideal woman or mother is insignificant. What is significant is that Barrie literally embraced and consumed her and her family for the rest of their lives.

Whether one calls Barrie's relations with Sylvia and Arthur and their five sons — they added two more, Michael (born in 1900) and Nicholas (Nico, born in 1903) — invasive, infiltrating, manipulative, or obsessive, the fact is that he took over and "doctored" their lives the way he doctored his fictional works, endeavoring to alter and change the narratives of their lives according to his imagination and whimsy. This is not to say that Barrie was a monster and dictator, or that he was fully conscious of how intrusive he could be. Barrie was very loyal, generous, and kind. But he was also a driven man and apparently did not reflect much about the drives that possessed him in his relations with close friends, especially women. Thus there was always a price to be paid for the interest he took in people and his generosity. Arthur Davies for one

— and later one of his sons, Peter — did not appreciate Barrie's involvement in the family.

Yet, once attached, Barrie would not be shaken off. By 1898, after he had met Sylvia, he was not satisfied just meeting the boys in Kensington Gardens, he followed them home and often invited himself for tea or dinner. His stories about fairies expanded, and he named Peter Pan after the third Davies son and the mythic god of herds, known for his riotous behavior and revelry. Of course, Barrie's Pan was not as virile and licentious as the Arcadian god. Rather, he was a little boy locked out of his mother's home. He could fly and had to learn to fend for himself in the fairy realm of Kensington Gardens, but outside this realm he was powerless.

In the meantime, Mary Barrie, who had very early realized she was in a dilemma of a marriage, had bought a country cottage in Surrey outside London, which she redecorated and made into a country home to which friends and relatives were invited. The Davies were among the guests, and it was there that Barrie took photographs of the boys and Porthos that he made into a book titled *The Boy Castaways of Blacklake Island Being a Record of the Terrible Adventures of the Brothers Davies in the Summer of 1901*. He kept one copy for himself, and he gave the other to the boys' father, Arthur, who significantly left the book in a train. However, despite this "literary" loss, Barrie was not done yet with the Davies boys and Peter Pan.

Their next appearance was to take place in several chapters that he had already begun writing for *The Little White Bird* (1902), a novel published for adults, in which the narrator muses about his encounters in Kensington Gardens with a little boy named David. It was also during this time, at Christmas to be exact, that Barrie took Jack, George, and Peter Davies to see a musical play for children in London — *Bluebell in Fairyland*. One of the first commercial plays explicitly performed for children, it concerned a little flower girl who wanders off to fairyland where she has exciting adventures only to learn at the end of the play that she had been dreaming. The charming plot influenced Barrie's own imagination. More important, it prompted him to consider writing a fairy-tale play for children and adults in which he could incorporate the many notes that he had been writing about Peter Pan.

Due to other projects, Barrie could not fully turn his attention to the figure of Peter Pan, who haunted his imagination, until October 1903. Then, as his private notebooks reveal, he worked feverishly on the play and completed a first draft on March 1, 1904. He intended to offer the play to his American friend and producer Charles Frohman, who was due to arrive in London at Easter. In the meantime, he tried to interest the great English actor Beerbohm Tree in the role of Mr. Darling and gave him a private reading. Surprised by this spectacular fairy-tale play, something Barrie had not produced up to that time, Tree wrote to Frohman to alert him that "Barrie has gone out of his mind. ... I'm sorry to say it, but you ought to know it. He's just read me his new play. He is going to read it to you. I know I have not gone woozy in my mind, because I have tested myself since hearing the play; but Barrie must be mad."

The play had just the opposite effect on Frohman, who became so enthusiastic about it, that he scheduled it for production at the Duke of York's Theatre in time for Christmas on December 27, 1904. With such encouragement, Barrie began an intense period of preparing *Peter Pan* for performance and rewrote the script six times. Afraid that the audience — largely adults — would not respond all that well to the fantastic story, he instructed the members of the orchestra to put down their instruments and clap when Peter appealed for help to save Tinker Bell's life and cried out, "If you believe in fairies, clap your hands." However, there had been no need for these instructions, for the audience clapped thunderously, causing Nina Boucicault, the actress playing Peter, to burst into tears. The play was such a success that the first run lasted until April 1905, went on tour, and was successfully produced in New York. Indeed, *Peter Pan* continued to be performed in London every Christmas during Barrie's lifetime and beyond. However, he did not publish the final revised script until 1928, the year he bequeathed all royalties to the Hospital for Sick Children, Great Ormond Street.

Even if *Peter Pan* had not been such a success, Barrie had already achieved fame as a playwright. The play only made him extraordinary famous and wealthy. Yet, fame and money never went to his head; he lived for his projects. Barrie carried a notebook with him at all times and was constantly jotting down ideas for stories or plays. He was the consummate workaholic who neglected his wife and felt more at home in his study than anywhere else. Perhaps, one could argue, he felt more at home in another realm of his imagination. If Barrie had spare time, it was spent mainly with the Llewelyn Davies family, but a series of tragedies was soon to disrupt the "idyllic" relations he thought he had formed.

In 1906, Barrie, who had already lost his mother and father and other members of his family, was saddened to learn that Arthur Davies had cancer. Although Barrie had always been distrusted and disliked by Davies, the famous little man became more devoted to him and his family, often providing financial assistance. After a courageous struggle, Davies died on April 19, 1907. Meanwhile, unknown to Barrie, who had now assumed the role of father/husband in the Davies family, his own wife was having an affair. Although he had just written one of his best social satires about human relations, *What Every Woman Knows* (1908), he was not very perceptive about his most intimate relationship, and his own marriage ended in a divorce in 1909, when he finally learned about Mary's affair. Shaken by this break, he could barely write major plays after this, for not only had Mary left him, but Sylvia Davies had become seriously ill in the summer of 1909 and died the following year on August 27, 1910.

Distraught and depressed, Barrie took solace in the thought that Sylvia had supposedly promised to marry him. What probably saved him more was his new role as surrogate father to the five Davies boys. Later in his life Peter Davies commented on some of Barrie's letters: "Though it is nowhere explicitly stated, there is a clear enough underlying assumption that the principal part in the direction of her sons' destinies would be taken by J.M.B. He is named more often and more prominently than any of the other 'trustees and guardians.' On the other hand there is no suggestion that he was able to have sole control, either financially — but perhaps the financial vagueness of the will suggests that this was taken for granted — or as guide counsellor and friend" (*J.M. Barrie: The Man Behind the Image*, 241). Actually, it did not matter what the will stated, Barrie now took control of the boys. Significantly, it was exactly at this time that Barrie adapted the play *Peter Pan* and wrote the novel *Peter and Wendy*, which he published in 1911 (fig. 14).

Even as he sought to take control of "my boys," as he called them, and even though he was anointed a baron and became Sir James Barrie in

Figure 14. From J.M. Barrie's Peter and Wendy. *Illustr. Francis Donkin Bedford. London: Hodder and Stoughton, 1911.*

1913, he could not determine their destinies nor his own role as surrogate father. The tragedies continued. Barrie's brother Alec, who had played such a great role in his youth, died in 1913. George, the eldest Davies son, was killed in 1915, while fighting the Germans during World War I. That same year, his close friend Charles Frohman, who had produced *Peter Pan*, lost his life when the luxury liner *Lusitania* was torpedoed and sunk on May 7. Among other things, Frohman was traveling to London to see Barrie. Peter, the third-eldest Davies son, went off to France in 1917, only to return from the war somewhat shattered. Even after the war ended in 1918 and Barrie visited France as a guest of the American army, there was more tragedy in store for him when his favorite Davies son, Michael, died in a swimming accident on May 27, 1921.

This last death was particularly devastating for Barrie, because he had been very close to Michael and had had great expectations for him. Fortunately for Barrie, in 1917, he had met Lady Cynthia Asquith, who had become his private secretary and emotional support in his later years. Lady Cynthia was thirty years old at that time and the mother of two sons. A beautiful and gifted woman, who eventually published some books for children and her memoirs, Lady Cynthia was also a replacement for the dead Sylvia Davies. Yet, she played a different role than Sylvia Davies. As much as Barrie proceeded to invade and take over her life and family, she took over his and became responsible for the organization of his life, especially during the 1930s.

Although Barrie had one last successful play, *Mary Rose*, produced in 1920, he had lost joy in writing for the stage, for he never reconciled himself to Michael's death. On the other hand, with the help of Lady Asquith, he began writing and giving speeches, as well as publishing short stories, attending social gatherings, and monitoring the activities of the last three Davies sons, Peter, Jack, and Nico. He made one final surprising effort to write a play, *The Boy David* (1936), a philosophical drama based on David's days before he became king of Israel. But it was produced in Edinburgh and London without much success. Barrie's creative powers had reached an end. During the last couple years of his life his health was deteriorating, and he had many bouts of depression. Lady Asquith was called upon to nurse him, even though she herself was ill at that time. Barrie went in and out of depression and, at times, appeared morose and crazed. By June 1937 he rarely left his apartment in London, even though he might occasionally enjoy an evening out. On June 13, he became seriously ill, and the Asquiths and Peter and Nicholas Davies took turns attending to him until he died on June 19th and was buried in his hometown of Kirriemuir next to his mother, father, and siblings.

III

Very few critics have taken note that the novel *Peter and Wendy* was published in 1911, one year after Sylvia Llewelyn Davies's death, and that Barrie had not yet published a final version of the play. It was as though Barrie were prompted by her death to fix the script of all the Peter Pan writings to memorialize her and his encounters with her children. Up to that point he had produced numerous works that directly involved Peter Pan and friends: *The Boy Castaways of Blacklake Island* (privately printed, 1901), *The Little White Bird* (1902), scripts for the production of *Peter Pan, or The Boy Who Wouldn't Grow Up* (1904), and *Peter Pan in Kensington Gardens* (1906). There were also other publications not authored by him — Daniel S. O'Connor, *Peter Pan Keepsake* (1907), Daniel S. O'Connor and Alice Woodward, *The Peter Pan Picture Book* (1907), O. Herford, *The Peter Pan Alphabet Book* (1909), and G. D. Drennan, *Peter Pan, His Book, His Pictures, His Career, His Friends* (1909). Interestingly, the novel is the only Peter Pan writing that mentions a character other than Peter in its title, and significantly it is Wendy, that is, the mother/wife figure related to Sylvia, the love of Barrie's life, the dead woman who supposedly wanted to marry him.

Although Barrie wrote a scenario for a silent film of *Peter Pan* and a short story, "The Blot on Peter Pan" in 1926 and was to continue to doctor and revise the play *Peter Pan*, until he published the full text in 1928, there is a sense that he wanted to provide definitive closure of the story with the publication of the prose novel in 1911: Peter goes on living in this work while Wendy dies. And even though Wendy dies, her daughter and their daughters return to the immortal Peter. He will never be without her and her offspring, just as we are never without some version of *Peter Pan*.

The "definitive" novel is the most complicated and sophisticated of all the versions of *Peter Pan*. Although it may have been directed in part at young readers, it is clearly a testament to Sylvia and written primarily for adults. It is *not* fiction for children. There are just too many in-jokes, asides, allusions, and intrusions made with the wink of an eye for children to grasp what is fully occurring throughout the novel. Not that adult readers can entirely comprehend the meaning of Peter and Neverland, but it is apparent that the narrator of the novel is sharing his story with adults and, given his intimate knowledge of children and their world — something he tends to lord over his readers — he has made it his mission to explain children to adults:

> I don't know whether you have ever seen a map of a person's mind. Doctors sometimes draw maps of other parts of you, and your own map can become intensely interesting, but catch them trying to draw a map of a child's mind, which is not only confused, but keeps going round all the time. There are zigzag lines on it, just like your temperature on a card, and these are probably roads in the island; for the Neverland is always more or less an island with astonishing splashes of colour here and there, and coral reefs and rakish-looking craft in the offing, and savages and lonely lairs, and gnomes who are mostly tailors, and caves through which a river runs, and princes with six elder brothers, and a hut fast going to decay, and one very small old lady with a hooked nose.

After commenting that each child has a Neverland that has its own unique qualities, the narrator continues: "On the whole the Neverlands have a family resemblance, and if they stood still in a row you could say of them that they have each other's nose, and so forth. On these magic shores children at play are for ever breaching their coracles. We too have been there; we can still hear the sound of the surf, though we shall land no more."

Paradoxically, it is the impossibility of conveying the fantastic experiences that Barrie himself has sought to capture or recapture through the invention of an omniscient narrator, who takes delight in playing with his readers and imparting his vast knowledge about children. This reading experience that Barrie offers to adults is in direct contrast to the experience that he had already provided them in his drama. Whereas the play, which can be equally enjoyed by children and adults, is demonstrative and filled with action that needs no real explanation, the novel, which is difficult for young readers to enjoy and at times ponderous, is explanatory and serves as a commentary to the play, with which, Barrie had to assume, most readers were familiar and still are.

Peter and Wendy is thus an anti-fairy tale that seeks to explicate mystery where fairy tales simply display magic and mystery. It is a self-help book written by a doctoring author for those adults who have lost touch with their imagination and need to regain it through a reintroduction to children's imaginative play. It is a prosaic novel intended to rekindle the light of a possible childhood experience that the narrator wants to preserve for eternity, or at least, as long as he lives, otherwise he would not tell it and explain to us so many details about the figment of his conceived notion of children's imaginations.

In her brilliant analysis of the Peter Pan writings and cultural phenomenon, Jacqueline Rose maintains that "what Barrie's *Peter and Wendy* demonstrates too clearly for comfort is that language is not innocence (word and thing), but rather a taking of sides (one word against the other). In *Peter and Wendy*, the line between the narrator and his characters is not neat and/or invisible; it is marked out as a division, not to say opposition, or even war" (72–73). Rose argues that the narrator is never sure and assumes different roles as servant, author, and child. Moreover, Barrie himself as author was trying to bring together two different strands of children's fiction that collided with each other in his novel: the adventure story for boys and the domestic and fairy story for girls. Barrie was unable to weave these strands satisfactorily. Rather he revealed more about the impossibility of defining children and childhood than he realized. "*Peter and Wendy* was ... the response to a demand for a 'classic,' the definitive written text for children. Something definitive is, however, exactly what Barrie's text failed to provide — either inside the book (the sliding of the narrator) or outside the book (all the other, more simple, versions which were to follow)" (85).

Although there is a great deal of validity to Rose's arguments and many other interpretative comments in her book, she makes a major mistake in considering *Peter and Wendy* a novel for children, that is, fiction for children. Though Barrie uses multiple narrative devices and shifts the perspective, the "doctoring" narrator is *always* addressing other adults as implicit readers of this novel, just as he does in *Peter Pan in Kensington Gardens*. And, although there is what Rose calls "slippage," that is, though the narrator is slippery, Barrie, the author, is not. He is clearly in command of the characters, plot, and setting. He knows what he wants to present and did not hesitate to present an image of imaginative play by children.

Or course there are multiple ways to interpret *Peter and Wendy*, and Rose's interpretation is one of the most productive. However, some critics have astutely pointed out that the novel and the play reflect male anxiety at the end of the nineteenth century when modernization was bringing about great changes in the family and workplace. Others have examined the nostalgic longing for an idyllic past of carefree boyhood, or the obvious unresolved oedipal relationship represented by the mother role played by Wendy. None have viewed the novel, however, as a metacommentary on the proper roles of fathers and mothers, or as a handbook for adults on how imaginative play must be safeguarded for children so that they can evolve into responsible adults.

Peter Pan in Kensington Gardens and *Peter Pan*, which predated *Peter and Wendy*, were incomplete works because they did not explain to adults what was missing in the stories and what the adults were missing in raising children. Therefore, Barrie wrote the "definitive" book to fix the text and our view of Peter and friends, especially Peter and a special friend. Instead of viewing Peter Pan merely as an escapist figure, the eternal adolescent, the unfulfilled son, I would argue that Peter in Barrie's narrator's version is mainly a rebel who consciously rejects the role of adulthood in conventional society because it has failed him. Adults have failed Peter. In some respects, Barrie's work reflects his own struggle to conceive a different type of parent and familial relations that he missed during his youth. Therefore, parents and potential parents must be reeducated so that they will grant their children the freedom to fly off into their own realms and receive the nurturing that they want and need. It is through Peter's help, for instance, that Wendy learns to become a mother, and Peter a father. In Neverland, Peter does indeed become the consummate father, while Wendy gains a strong sense of her maternal instincts. The entrance and passage through Neverland is a training ground for all children who have the good fortune to be allowed to release their imagination. This construct enabled Barrie to postulate a theory of mothering and fathering in which he strongly believed, even though he never had his "own" children. In *Peter and Wendy* he did take complete ownership to show how a proper father/mother should treat his/her offspring. Viewed from this vantage point, Barrie's sublimated neurosis has broader sociopsychological ramifications in his work, for Peter continually returns to children in the conventional world to guide them through experiences that enable them to love, understand, trust, and be loved in a conflicted but nurturing environment. Neverland thus retains a utopian value as part of what Herbert Marcuse in *Eros and Civilization* designated the romantic "great refusal" to participate in a society bent on "instrumentalizing the imagination."

There is a price to be paid for the position of a rebel. The narrator tells us that Peter "had ecstasies innumerable that other children can never know; but he was looking through the window at the one joy from which he must be for ever barred." This is in the next to last chapter, and the play, too, echoes his seemingly lonely position. But the novel does not end this way. In the final chapter, Peter is not alone, and the narrator explains the importance of flights into fantasy and mothering. In fact, Wendy is the one who looks out the window in envy as her daughter Jane flies off with Peter to Neverland. The narrator tells us that Margaret, Jane's daughter, will do the same, "and thus it will go on, so long as children are gay and innocent and heartless."

As we know, children are not gay, innocent, and heartless. As we know, we cannot generalize about children and childhood. But Barrie is not afraid to generalize, and he does this by creating a confident and wise narrator whom Sigmund Freud might envy. The narrator speaks almost as if he were a professional child and family psychologist and knew all there was to know about children and their imaginative realms and the necessity to keep fantasy alive.

Once he created Peter Pan, Barrie wanted his readers and viewers to keep returning to him and all the writings about Peter Pan. He did not mind the various spectacles made out of his symbolic figure, and probably would not have minded the Disney film and all the other films and artifacts that have followed, because he had fixed the story as his-tory and commentary in *Peter and Wendy*. Ironically, Peter, who declares

thirteen

Hermann Hesse's Fairy Tales and the Pursuit of Home

ermann Hesse's fairy tales are not really fairy tales in the traditional sense of the term; yet they are deeply embedded in both the Western and Oriental traditions of fairy tales. Written between 1900 and 1933, Hesse's unusual narratives record his endeavors to experiment with the fairy-tale genre and to make his own life as an artist into a fairy tale. He failed as far as his life was concerned because he could never really achieve the ideal state he desired, but his tales were successful exactly because of this failure: They are filled with the inner turmoil of a writer desperately and seriously playing with aspects of a literary genre to find some semblance of peace and perfect harmony. To know Hermann Hesse's fairy tales is to know the trauma, doubts, and dreams of the artist as a young man in Germany at the beginning of a tumultuous century. Like many other European writers, Hesse perceived the events around him — the rapid advance of technology, the rise of materialism, the world wars, the revolutions, and the economic inflations and depressions — as indicative of the decline of Western civilization. It was through art, especially the fairy tale, that Hesse sought to contend with what he perceived to be the sinister threat of science and commercialism.

I

Born in Calw, a small town in Swabia, on July 2, 1877, Hesse was raised in a religious household. His father, Johannes, who had been a Pietist missionary in India, continued to work in the ministry when he returned to Germany, and his mother, Marie, was an assistant to her father, Hermann Gundert, director of the Calw Publishing House, one of the leading Pietist book companies in Europe. Both parents were highly educated and totally dedicated to their religious beliefs, but they were not overly sectarian. Hesse found his Pietistic home with its bourgeois routines to be oppressive, and early in his childhood he rebelled against the traditional ways of his parents and resisted authority of any kind. At one point, in 1883, after his parents had moved to Basel, Switzerland, they gave serious thought to institutionalizing their son because he was so contrary. Fortunately for him, Hesse became more compliant and adjusted to the Swiss elementary school system. Three years later, in 1886, his parents returned to Germany to assume charge of the Calw Publishing House, and Hesse once again underwent rebellious phases. For the most part, however, he adhered to the Pietistic principles that his parents upheld and seemed prepared to pursue the highly regimented course of studies in Germany.

In 1890, he was sent away to a private school in Göppingen, another small Swabian city, so that he could prepare for the entrance examinations that would enable him to be admitted to one of the Protestant schools in this region. Yet, once he began his studies at an exclusive academy in Maulbronn in 1892, he suffered from headaches and insomnia and ran away from the school. His parents then sent him to an institution for mentally disturbed children, but Hesse continued to resist help from doctors and teachers as well as his parents, whom he thought had deserted him, and contemplated suicide. For over a year, Hesse went in and out of different schools, homes, and sanitariums, until his parents brought him back to Calw in October 1893.

During the next two years, he appeared to gain control over his moods. He helped his father at the Calw Publishing House, worked in the garden, and had brief apprenticeships in a bookstore and a clock factory. By this time, Hesse, who was an inveterate reader, was already writing poems and stories and wanted to dedicate himself to a literary career. However, his father refused to give him permission to leave home to try his luck as a writer. Then, in October 1895, he was finally allowed to begin an apprenticeship as a bookseller at the Heckenbauer Bookshop in Tübingen, a university city with a famous cultural tradition.

It was in Tübingen that Hesse began to feel at ease with himself and had his first success as a poet. He stayed there until 1899, formed important friendships with other young writers, immersed himself in reading, and began publishing his poems in various literary magazines. Most important of all, Hesse began to replace the Pieticism of his parents with his own personal religion — aestheticism. If there ever was a creed that he devoutly followed, it was the German romantic Novalis's notion of "*Mensch werden ist eine Kunst*" — to become a human being is art. For Hesse, art — the ultimate self-fulfillment — meant connecting with a profound, essential feeling that was always associated with "home." But this home was not the home of his parents. Home was something intangible that was linked to aesthetic intuition and nurturing maternalism, but was unique in each individual. It was both a return and a moving forward at the same time, and it could only be attained through art — through artful formation of the self.

In Tübingen, free of family constraints and the pressure of formal schooling, Hesse began to sense the direction that he wanted his life to take as a writer. Not only did he associate with like-minded friends, but he also published his first book of poems, *Romantic Songs* (*Romantische Lieder*, 1898), and his first book of short prose pieces, *An Hour after Midnight* (*Eine Stunde hinter Mitternacht*, 1899), and underwent his own literary apprenticeship by reading medieval literature, the German romantics, and Oriental works.

In 1899, Hesse accepted a position as an assistant bookseller in Reich's Bookshop in Basel, where he spent the next five years. Here, too, he resumed his literary activities and made many new acquaintances, although he regarded himself more as an outsider and loner. In December 1900, he published *The Posthumous Writings and Poems of Hermann Lauscher* (*Hinterlassene Schriften und Gedichte von Hermann Lauscher*), which showed the strong influence of E. T. A. Hoffmann and other romantic writers. In addition, he continued writing poems and book reviews and, in 1903, had his first major success with the publication of *Peter Camenzind*, a novel that depicts the development of a young romantic protagonist, who eventually turns his back on the cosmopolitan world to dedicate himself to art. It was somewhat the opposite with Hesse, who was learning more and more how to enjoy the company of literary circles at this point in his life. In 1904, he married Maria Bernoulli, a gifted photographer, and since he was now able to support himself through his writing, they moved to a farmhouse in a village called Gaienhofen near Lake Constance on the Swiss-German border, where he and Maria hoped to be closer to nature and dedicate themselves to writing, painting, music, and photography. However, the period that Hesse spent in Gaienhofen, from 1904 to 1912, was anything but idyllic.

To be sure, Hesse continued his prolific writing. He published *Under the Wheel* (*Unterm Rad*, 1904), an autobiographical novel about the brutality of educational institutions and authoritarianism in Germany; *This Side* (*Diesseits*, 1907) and *Neighbors* (*Nachbarn*, 1908), two collections of stories; *Gertrud* (1910), a novel; and *Underway* (*Unterwegs*, 1911), a volume of poems. He became an editor for an important cultural and political magazine, *März*, founded in 1908, and wrote numerous reviews for different German newspapers and journals. He also became the father of three boys — Bruno in 1905, Heiner in 1909, and Martin in 1911 — won literary prizes, and formed friendships with well-known musicians, artists, and writers. He was not happy in his marriage with Maria, however, who was nine years older than he was and too self-sufficient and independent for him. Within a short period after their move to Gaienhofen, each began going his/her own way, and they had very little in common except for the children. Hesse began feeling more and more lonely and isolated in the country and often took trips by himself or traveled to give lectures. But leaving home only exacerbated his discontent, anguish, and ennui. He tried vegetarianism, painting, theosophy, and the religions of India. In 1911, he took a trip to Ceylon, Sumatra, and Malaya, hoping that he would find spiritual peace on the subcontinent. However, he never reached India because of dysentery and was upset by the poverty in the Orient and the commercial manner in which Buddhism was treated. He returned to Gaienhofen sick, exhausted, and still unhappy in his marriage. In another endeavor to change these conditions, he and his wife decided to move to Bern in 1912.

Unfortunately, the change of environment did not help Hesse, nor did certain events that led to increasing psychological stress in his life. His son Martin was stricken by an unusual disease and had to be placed in a foster home in 1914. He and his wife barely communicated. His father's death in 1916 led to great feelings of guilt. And after the outbreak of World War I, he gradually found himself at odds with most of his German compatriots. Though he sympathized with Germany, he began taking a public position against war, for which the German press constantly attacked him. Since his eyesight had prevented him from serving in the army, he cared for German prisoners of war in Bern for more than two years, but in 1917, he suffered a nervous breakdown and went to Sonnmatt, a private sanitarium near Lucerne, where he underwent electrotherapy and had numerous analytic sessions with a Jungian psychologist. Finally, in spring 1919, he separated completely from his wife and moved to the village of Montagnola in the Italian part of Switzerland and appeared to be coming out of his depression.

It is astounding to see that, despite or perhaps because of all his psychological troubles, Hesse wrote some of his best works during this time. In 1913, he published his diary, *Out of India (Aus Indien)*, about his journey to the Far East, and followed this with the novel *Rosshalde* in 1914. It was also during this year that he published his provocative essay, "Oh, Friends Not These Tones!" ("O Freunde nicht diese Töne!"), a pacifist tract that enraged the German public. Until this time, Hesse had been the "classic aesthete" and had rarely participated in politics. Now, however, the war awakened him, and though he never became a political activist, his writings began to assume a political dimension that they had never revealed before and can be traced in his essays and fairy tales of that period, especially "A Dream about the Gods" (1914), "Strange News from Another Planet" (1915), "If the War Continues" (1917), and "The European" (1918). Time and again, Hesse courageously stood up for his pacifist convictions, and he often exploded with frustration as one of his letters to his friend Hans Sturzenegger in 1917 clearly demonstrates:

> They laugh about the conscientious objectors! In my opinion these individuals constitute the most valuable symptom of our times, even if a per-

son here and there gives some strange reasons for his actions. ... I have
not been wounded nor has my house been destroyed but I have spent the
last two and a half years taking care of the victims of the war, the prisoners, and just in this sector, in this small part of the war, I have learned
all about its senselessness and cruel horror. I could care less that the
people are seemingly enthused by the war. The people have always been
dumb. Even when they had the choice between Jesus and the murderer,
they decided for Barabbas with great zeal. Perhaps they will continue
to decide for Barabbas. But that is not a reason at all for me to go along
with their decision.

Of course, the dominant theme in his works continued to concern
art and the artist, but as his collected fairy tales Märchen (1919) revealed,
Hesse had moved from a solipsistic position to consider the responsibility of the artist in society. At the same time, he also wanted to provide
counsel for young readers in Germany, and such other works as Demian
(1919), published under the pseudonym Emil Sinclair, who appears in "If
the War Continues," and Zarathustra's Return (Zarathustras Wiederkehr,
1919) dealt with chaos and nihilism and were clear gestures of reconciliation with his German readers after the destruction and turmoil of
World War I.

It was from his retreat in Montagnola that Hesse felt paradoxically
that he had enough distance to become more open and engaged with
social and political problems. He never had the inclination to align
himself with a particular ideology; he was still the searcher, the artist on
a quest to find himself. But by now he had found some tentative answers
that he was willing to impart in his writings. Hesse had completely
broken from his Christian and bourgeois upbringing, had been strongly
influenced by Nietzsche, the German Romantics, and Oriental religions,
and sought to combine these strands of thought in his own existentialist
philosophy concerned with finding the path home and discovering the
divine within the essential nature of each individual. The book that
perhaps best expressed his thinking at this time was Siddhartha (1922),
which is a fairy-tale journey of rebellion and self-discovery, exuding the
peace of mind that Hesse contemplated for himself.

The 1920s were not entirely peaceful for Hesse, however. In 1923,
due in part to the continual harsh criticism of his works in Germany,

Hesse became a Swiss citizen. This was also the year that he ended his marriage with Maria Bernoulli. Then, in 1924, Hesse married Ruth Wenger, who was twenty-five years younger than he was. A sensitive young woman, she was a talented singer who was dedicated to a career of her own, but her health was very fragile, and she suffered from tuberculosis. Given the differences in their ages and temperaments, this marriage was bound to fail, and within eleven weeks they parted ways. Again Hesse went through a major psychological crisis and contemplated suicide. But then he made a conscious decision to overcome his despair and introverted nature by frequenting taverns, dance halls, and places in Zurich and Bern where he had never before spent much time. To a certain extent, Hesse recorded these experiences in his famous novel *Steppenwolf* (1927), and with the publication of this work, it was as if he had cathartically released the wildness within him and could settle down again in Montagnola to focus on his writing. At the same time he met Ninon Dolbin, an art historian, who began living with him in 1928 and married him in 1929. A remarkably independent and wise person, Dolbin was to have a steadying influence on Hesse throughout the rest of his life, and although his difficulties with women and his own sexuality were not put to rest with this marriage, Hesse was able to establish a rapport with Dolbin that he had not been able to do in his other relationships.

It was also clear that, with this marriage, Hesse entered the mature period of his writing. He had begun numerous stories and novels during the 1920s and continued to publish literary essays and reviews in Germany and Switzerland. By the beginning of the 1930s he finished two important works, *Narcissus and Goldmund* (*Narziss and Goldmund*, 1930) and *Journey to the East* (*Die Morgenlandfahrt*, 1932), both begun earlier, and rounded out many of the existentialist, romantic, and Oriental ideas with which he had been experimenting during the 1920s. Now, in 1932, he was ready to begin his magnum opus, *The Glass Bead Game* (*Das Glasperlenspiel*), which would take him ten years to complete.

Although Hesse had always enjoyed traveling and giving lectures and visiting such Swiss cities as Basel and Bern, he felt great pleasure in his large home in Montagnola. During the next twelve years, he rarely left his Swiss retreat where he had cultivated a set routine with Dolbin. Mornings and afternoons were devoted to painting, gardening, and correspondence, while evenings he read and wrote. Hesse had become a respected watercolor painter and had also illustrated some of his own books; he continued to develop his talents as a painter during the 1930s and 1940s. There was also another talent that he cultivated during this time: "host."

During the Nazi period numerous political refugees and friends fled Germany, and Hesse spent a great deal of his time helping them and providing them with a place to stay. However, he never published an official or public condemnation of Hitler and nazism during the 1930s and 1940s. The reason for this was that Hesse had been burned during World War I and the Weimar period because of the public stand he had taken in behalf of peace. He firmly believed that the artist could not change society, but that politics could ruin an artist's perspective, perhaps even destroy it. The artist's role was to remain true to his art and not be influenced by ideologies either on the Right or the Left. Of course, in his private correspondence and in the reviews that he wrote for various journals in Sweden and Switzerland, he made his position against nazism quite clear, and yet he would not issue a public declaration stating his opposition to German fascism. This refusal is clearly explained in a 1936 letter to his editor at Fischer Verlag:

> If I ask myself what more do you expect from me, then I find the following: you expect that I, as writer, should finally show a minimum of heroism once and for all and reveal my colors. But my dear colleague, I have done this continually since 1914, when my first essay against the war led to my friendship with (Romain) Rolland. Ever since 1914 I have had those forces against me that seek to prohibit religious and ethical behavior (and permit the political). I have had to swallow hundreds of attacks in newspapers and thousands of hate letters since my awakening during wartime, and I swallowed them, and my life was made bitter because of this, my work was made more difficult and complicated, and my private life went down the drain. And I was not always attacked just by one side and then protected by another, but since I did not belong to any party, both sides liked to choose me as a target for their barrages. So, once again I am now being vilified simultaneously by the emigrants and the Third Reich. And I firmly believe that my place is that of the outsider and that of the man without a party, a place where I have my little bit of humanity and Christianity to show.

These views and many other reflections about art and education were incorporated into *The Glass Bead Game*, which was first published in Zurich in 1943 and subsequently in Germany in 1946. It was also his last novel, and fittingly it encompassed a wide range of topics and issues that had been central to his writing since the turn of the century. *The Glass Bead Game* reads like an autobiographical novel of development. The young protagonist, Josef Knecht, is chosen to attend an elite school in Castalia, a province dedicated to intellectual and aesthetic pursuits. Like many of Hesse's other young "heroes," he must undergo an apprenticeship under the guidance of a wise man, in this case the Magister Musicae of Monteport, who teaches him to comprehend dreams and embrace the opposites in life, play with them and become one with them. Once Knecht has achieved everything he possibly can as the grand Magister Ludi in this spiritual realm, he decides that he wants to leave Castalia and make a more practical contribution in the outside world. He had been bothered by the esotericism and elitism of Castalia and felt that a Magister of his stature should assume more social responsibility. Yet, his tragic death at the end of the novel reflects Hesse's own ambivalent attitude toward the social commitment of the artist, as well as his self-questioning position in regard to aestheticism. However, Hesse never questioned the value of art as a means of maintaining social values and imparting wisdom against the barbarism of his times.

After World War II, Hesse's own artistic productivity declined out of choice, and his time was consumed by responding to demands from the outside world and trying to lead a "normal" private life. All of a sudden, after 1945, Hesse had become famous and was sought out by critics, the media, and literary societies, not to mention numerous friends who could now travel freely in Europe. Nor could he avoid controversy. At first, there was a difficult period when it seemed that Hesse's works might be banned by the American occupying forces simply because they had not been banned by the Nazis. This censorship never occurred, and Hesse began writing numerous political essays about the necessity for moral regeneration in Germany and for overcoming a militarist mentality. Four of his most important essays of the immediate postwar period were later published in *War and Peace* (*Krieg und Frieden*) in 1949.

Hesse always suspected that his admonishments would never be taken seriously in Germany. In fact, immediately following the war, he was so disappointed and embittered by the continuation of certain forms of fascist and materialist thought in Germany and his conflicts with the Allied authorities that his nerves became frayed. Even though he received the Goethe Prize in 1946 followed by the prestigious Nobel Prize, also in 1946, he became so depressed that he withdrew to a sanitarium for treatment. Only in March 1947 did he feel sufficiently healthy to return to Montagnola, where he spent the last fifteen years of his life following his artistic pursuits and nursing his frail health.

Although many writers, politicians, and friends who took an active role in politics in the name of peace called upon Hesse, Hesse continued to refuse to commit himself to any one party, country, or ideology. In reviews, essays, and letters, he wrote about both the dangers of American capitalism for Europe — what he called the Americanizing of Europe — and the totalitarian threat of the Soviet Union. It was clear that his noninvolvement had a great deal to do with his "politics" of nonviolence. Hesse refused to compromise his integrity and support causes that might be manipulated for nefarious ends. Humanity came first for him, not a political party or movement, and peace could only be achieved if people were given freedom to realize their humanitarian impulses. Such was Hesse's stance in almost all his writings that were connected with politics, and the more the Cold War escalated in the 1950s, the more Hesse felt inclined to withdraw from the world's stage and to keep his opinions to himself.

With the exception of some short stories, he spent most of his time painting, maintaining a vigorous correspondence, and fighting various debilitating illnesses. He had always had periodic spells of depression and physical exhaustion and after 1950 his eyes began to weaken. In 1955, a heart condition prevented him from leaving the area around Montagnola. It was also about this time that the doctors discovered he was suffering from leukemia, which became virulent at the end of 1961. Thanks to blood transfusions, he was able to live fairly comfortably until his death on August 8, 1962.

II

In many respects, Hesse's great achievement as a writer was in the domain of fairy tales and fantasy literature. He wrote his very first fairy tale called "The Two Brothers" ("Die beiden Brüder") when he was only ten years old, and his first significant period as a writer, from 1895 to 1900, was a time when he immersed himself in reading and emulating European and Oriental fairy-tale writers. Like no other writer of the twentieth century, all of Hesse's works drew in some way on the great fairy-tale tradition of Europe and the Orient. He was most successful as a writer when he combined the different traditions with his own personal experiences and endowed them with an unusual lyrical, sometimes sentimental, but strong note of refusal.

Hesse was the fairy-tale writer of the "modern romantic" refusal par excellence, a notion conceived by the philosopher Herbert Marcuse to indicate the resolute unwillingness of individuals to yield to social and political forces that tend to instrumentalize them and make them into objects of manipulation. This is why Hesse's heroes refuse to comply with the norms of bourgeois life and reject the hypocrisy and superficiality of European society corrupted by materialism. They are loners, rebels, poets, intellectuals, painters, and eccentrics, who represent the soul of a humanitarian tradition under siege. In order to tell the stories of their lives amid the growing alienation caused by technology and capitalism, Hesse experimented with the fairy-tale genre to commemorate the struggles of marginal types who survive on the fringes of society. Like his characters, he was tormented by the arbitrary social codes, the rigid Manichean principles of the Judeo-Christian tradition, and the onslaught of technology.

It would be too simplistic, however, to take each of Hesse's tales in chronological order and demonstrate how it reflected a phase of his own life, and how each of his protagonists was merely a variation of his own personality. Such an approach to his fairy tales, though defensible and valid, would do these works an injustice, for Hesse was a remarkably conscious artist who used the fairy-tale conventions to gain distance from his personal problems, and he found the symbolic forms, motifs, and topoi useful for generalizing his experiences and endowing them with multiple meanings through plots reminiscent of ancient Oriental and German Romantic tales.

One of the first fairy tales he ever published is a good example of the technique he would try to refine over and over again to realize his own peculiar form of the modern fairy tale. The story is actually a novella titled *Lulu*, and it appeared as part of *The Posthumous Writings and Poems of Hermann Lauscher* (1900). On the one hand, it is possible to relate the incidents in this fairy tale to a summer vacation that Hesse spent with friends in August 1899. On the other hand, the work is more an aesthetic experiment that reveals his great debt to E. T. A. Hoffmann and the German Romantics. The tale concerns the poet Lauscher and two friends who meet in a village during the summer and fall in love with a waitress named Lulu, who works in the village inn. They also have strange encounters with an eccentric philosopher, who seems to be strangely involved with Lulu. At the same time, one of the friends has had a fairy-tale dream about a princess named Lilia, who is threatened by a witch named Zischelgift: Lauscher and his friends soon conflate the identities of Lulu and Lilia, and the boundaries between reality, dream, and fairy tale dissolve. Their pursuit of Lulu/Lilia is transformed into a pursuit of the blue flower, a well-known romantic symbol of ideal love and utopia. Lauscher and his friends are brought back to reality, however, when a fire breaks out in the inn and Lulu and the philosopher mysteriously disappear.

This fairy-tale novella contains poems by Lauscher and his friends and is written in a hyperbolic sentimental manner that makes the story and characters at times appear too contrived. Yet, despite this artificiality, the novella is the key to understanding the narrative technique that Hesse was to develop more artistically in the fairy tales that were to follow. Like the German Romantic writers Wilhelm Heinrich Wackenroder, Ludwig Tieck, Novalis, Joseph von Eichendorff, and Hoffmann, major influences on his work, Hesse sought to blend the worlds of reality and imagination. All kinds of experience assume startling symbolical meanings that demand interpretation if the Hesse protagonist is to know himself. Only by seeking to go beyond the veil of symbols can the essence of life be grasped. But first the ordinary has to be appreciated as extraordinary through the artful transformation of all experience, and this is the task of all of Hesse's heroes. The obstacles confronting them are not the traditional witches, ogres, tyrants, and magicians, but rather science, materialism, war, alienation, and philistinism. Like the German Romantics before him, Hesse chose the fairy-tale form paradoxically to demonstrate how difficult it was to make life into a fairy tale, and he preferred tragic and open endings to the uplifting harmonious endings of the classical fairy tales. Yet, he did not abandon the utopian "mission" of the traditional fairy tale, for even though many of his narratives are tragic, they leave us with a sense of longing, intended to arouse us so that we might contemplate changing those conditions that bring about the degradation of humanity.

In his early tales, such as "The Dwarf" (1903), "Shadow Play" (1906), and "Doctor Knoelge's End" (1910), Hesse describes the process by which harmless individuals with poetic sensibilities are crushed by narrow-minded people. The central question in all of his writings concerns whether the individual with a poetic nature, who represents more than Hesse himself or artists in general, will be able to come into his own when social conditions are adverse to the arts and humanity. In only a few of his tales, such as "The Beautiful Dream" (1912), "Flute Dream" (1913), "The Poet" (1913), "The Forest Dweller" (1914), and "The Painter" (1918), does Hesse portray young men who rebel, seek, and realize their full potential as artistic human beings. Yet, even here, after hard experiences and apprenticeships, they are alone at the end: never married, never wealthy. The poet appears to be totally isolated and can find fulfillment only in his art. There are also characters, similar to these poet types, like Martin in "Shadow Play" (1906), Augustus in "Augustus" (1913), the climber in "The Difficult Path" (1917), and Anselm in "Iris" (1918), who lead terribly painful lives and must come to terms with their alienation and find solace in death by returning to what appears to be home or the eternal mother.

To a certain extent it is embarrassing to read how Hesse portrayed women and their roles in his tales. Like many German writers of his generation, Hesse depicted women either as gentle muses who had a mysterious wisdom that men did not possess, or as strong and sensitive martyrs, who are in contact with the source of knowledge. If female characters are included in his tales — very few of any substance appear — they are generally there to save the men from themselves. Whether young or old, they are associated with eternal harmony, Isis, Maya, truth, and home. All are artificial constructs that appear to smack of an infantile fixation on the mother; yet they represent more than Hesse's Oedipal attachment to his mother or the Oedipal complex itself. For Hesse, the mother figure and home represented lost innocence, a feeling of oneness with nature and one's own body, that is destroyed by the alienating process of civilization, often represented by norms of material success and science. Given the cruel nature of the institutions of socialization and civilization, governed mainly by men, Hesse believed that conformity to their rules and regulations would lead to the perversion of humanity. Adjustment to a sick reality was in itself a sick thing to do. Therefore, his protagonists break away from society and often are helped by sagacious elderly men, who can only be found on the margins of society. But these men, who are nonconformists themselves, are not sufficient enough to help the young man achieve harmony because there must be a harmony of the opposites. They can only point out the direction that the protagonist must take himself, and it is often toward a "mystical mother." To return to the mother at the end of some of his tales is thus recognition of what has been lost in the process of "civilization" and a refusal to go along with this process anymore. The mother figure is consequently a symbol of rejection and refusal to accept a "male" or "logical" way of regarding the world that leads to war and destruction.

As we know, Hesse was a staunch opponent of the military, masculine aggressiveness, and war. Some of his very best fairy tales, such as "A Dream about the Gods" (1914), "Strange News from Another Planet" (1915), "If the War Continues" (1917), "The European" (1918), and "The Empire" (1918), contain devastating critiques of the barbaric mentality and the conditions that engender conflicts and devastation. Hesse believed, as one can glean from both "The European" and "The Empire," that nationalism was the most dangerous force because it could inspire people to become obsessed by lust for power and caught up in war for war's sake. He never pointed his finger at any particular nation as the major perpetuator of wars. Rather, Hesse believed that there were certain cycles in the world, portrayed in "The City" (1910) and "Faldum" (1916), that reflected the general conditions, which either enhanced the potential for developing humane societies or led to barbarism. As his stories reveal, he was convinced that the divisive forces of technology, nationalism, totalitarianism, and capitalism were most detrimental to the causes of individual freedom and peaceful coexistence. Therefore, his fairy tales repeatedly pointed to the possibilities of individual refusal and the goal of inner peace.

Altogether, Hesse's fairy tales, written between 1900 and 1933, are a record of his own personal journey and the social and political conflicts in Europe of that period. Although he often followed the traditional form of the folk tale in works like "The Three Linden Trees" (1912), or used some of Hans Christian Andersen's techniques, as in "Conversation with an Oven" (1920) and "Inside and Outside" (1920), he generally preferred to break with the traditional plots and conventions of the classical fairy tale to experiment with science fiction, the grotesque and macabre, romantic realism, and dreams in order to generate his own unique form and style. Here, too, Hesse followed in the tradition of romantic refusal. To be sure, some of his aesthetic experiments lapse into narcissistic musings as in "A Dream Sequence" (1916), but when Hesse is at his best, his tales are filled with a keen sense of longing for a home that is the utopian counterpart to everything we are witnessing in our present day and age.

Bibliography

Primary Literature

Andersen, Hans Christian. 1846. *Wonderful Stories for Children.* Trans. Mary Botham Howitt. 1st English ed. London: Chapman and Hall.

———. 1852. *Danish Fairy Legends and Tales.* Trans. Caroline Peachey. 2d ed., with a memoir of the author. London: Addey.

———. 1961. *Das Märchen meines Lebens. Briefe. Tagebücher.* Ed. Erling Nielsen. Munich: Winkler.

———. 1974. *The Complete Fairy Tales and Stories.* Trans. Erik Christian Haugaard. New York: Doubleday.

———. 1979. *Märchen meines Lebens ohne Dichtung.* Trans. Michael Birkenbijl. Frankfurt am Main: Insel.

———. 2002. *Schräge Märchen.* Trans. Heinrich Detering. Munich: Deutscher Taschenbuch Verlag.

———. 2003. *The Stories of Hans Christian Andersen.* Trans. Diane Crone Frank and Jeffrey Frank. Boston: Houghton Mifflin.

———. 2004. *Fairy Tales.* Trans. Tiina Nunnally. New York: Viking.

Anstey, F. (pseudonym of Thomas Anstey Guthrie). 1892. *The Talking Horse and Other Tales.* London: Smith, Elder.

———. 1894. *The Giant's Robe.* London: Smith, Elder.

———. 1898. *Paleface and Redskin.* London: Grant, Richards.

Apuleius. 1951. *The Golden Ass.* Trans. Robert Graves. New York: Farrar, Straus & Giroux.

The Arabian Nights. 1990. Trans. Husain Haddawy. New York: W. W. Norton.

The Arabian Nights II: Sindbad and Other Popular Stories. 1995. Trans. Husain Haddawy. New York: W. W. Norton.

Attic Press. 1985. *Rapunzel's Revenge.* Dublin: Attic Press.

———. 1986. *Ms. Muffet and Others.* Dublin: Attic Press.

———. 1987. *Mad and Bad Fairies.* Dublin: Attic Press.

———. 1989. *Sweeping Beauties.* Dublin: Attic Press.

Auerbach, Nina, and U. C. Knoepflmacher, eds. 1992. *Forbidden Journeys: Fairy Tales and Fantasies by Victorian Women Writers.* Chicago: University of Chicago Press.

Aulnoy, Marie-Catherine Le Jumel de Barneville, Comtesse d'. 1690. *Histoire d'Hyppolyte, comte de Duglas.* 2 vols. Paris: L. Sylvestre.

———. 1697–98. *Les Contes des fées.* 4 vols. Paris.

————. 1698. *Contes nouveaux ou les Fées à la mode*. 4 vols. Paris: Veuve de Théodore Girard.

————. 1895. *The Fairy Tales of Madame D'Aulnoy*. Trans. Annie Macdonell. Intro. Anne Thackeray Ritchie. London: Lawrence & Bullen.

Auneuil, Louise de Bossigny, Comtesse d'. 1702. *La Tyrannie des fées détruite*. Paris: Barbin.

————. 1702. *Nouvelles diverses du temps, La Princesse de Pretinailles*. Paris: Ribou.

Barlow, Jane. 1894. *The End of Elfn-Town*. London: Macmillan.

Barrie, J. M. 1896. *Margaret Ogilvy*. London: Hodder and Stoughton.

————. 1896. *Sentimental Tommy*. London: Cassell.

————. 1900. *Tommy and Grizzel*. London: Cassell.

————. 1902. *The Little White Bird*. London: Hodder and Stoughton.

————. 1906. *Peter Pan in Kensington Gardens*. Illustr. Arthur Rackham. London: Hodder and Stoughton.

————. 1911. *Peter and Wendy*. Illustr. F. D. Bedford. London: Hodder and Stoughton.

————. 1915. *Peter Pan and Wendy*, the story of *Peter Pan* extracted from *Peter Pan and Wendy*. Illustr. F. D. Bedford, authorized school edition. London: Henry Frowde, Hodder and Stoughton.

————. 1923. *Dear Brutus*. London: Hodder and Stoughton.

————. 1924. *Mary Rose*. London: Hodder and Stoughton.

————. 1926. "The Blot on Peter Pan." In *The Flying Carpet*, ed. Cynthia Asquith. London: Partridge.

————. 1928. *Peter Pan, or The Boy Who Would Not Grow Up* in *The Plays of J. M. Barrie*. London: Hodder and Stoughton.

Barthelme, Donald. 1967. *Snow White*. New York: Atheneum.

Basile, Giambattista. 1932. *The Pentamerone of Giambattista Basile*. Trans. and ed. N. M. Penzer. 2 vols. London: John Lane, The Bodley Head.

————. 1986. *Lo Cunto de li Cunti*. Ed. Michele Rak. Milan: Garazanti.

————. 1994. *Il racconto dei racconti*. Ed. Alessandra Burani and Ruggero Guarini. Trans. Ruggero Guarini. Milan: Adelphi Edizioni.

Baum, L. Frank. 1900. *The Wonderful Wizard of Oz*. Illustr. W. W. Denslow. Chicago: George M. Hill.

————. 1901. *American Fairy Tales*. Illustr. Harry Kenny, Ike Morgan, and N. P. Hall. Chicago: George M. Hill.

————. 1901. *Dot and Tot of Merryland*. Illustr. W. W. Denslow. Chicago: George M. Hill.

————. 1901. *The Master Key: An Electrical Fairy Tale*. Illustr. Fanny Y. Cory. Indianapolis: Bobbs-Merrill.

————. 1903. *The Enchanted Island of Yew*. Illustr. Fanny Y. Cory. Indianapolis: Bobbs-Merrill.

————. 1903. *Prince Silverwings*. Chicago: A. C. McClurg.

———. 1903. *The Surprising Adventures of the Magical Monarch of Mo and His People.* Illustr. Frank Ver Beck. Indianapolis: Bobbs-Merrill.

———. 1904. *The Marvelous Land of Oz.* Illustr. John R. Neill. Chicago: Reilly & Britton.

———. 1905. *Queen Zixi of Ix; or the Story of the Magic Cloak.* Illustr. Frederick Richardson. New York: Century.

———. 1907. *Ozma of Oz.* Illustr. John R. Neill. Chicago: Reilly & Britton.

———. 1908. *Dorothy and the Wizard in Oz.* Illustr. John R. Neill. Chicago: Reilly & Britton.

———. 1909. *The Road to Oz.* Illustr. John R. Neill. Chicago: Reilly & Britton.

———. 1910. *The Emerald City of Oz.* Illustr. John R. Neill. Chicago: Reilly & Britton.

———. 1912. *Sky Island.* Illustr. John R. Neill. Chicago: Reilly & Britton.

———. 1913. *The Patchwork Girl of Oz.* Illustr. John R. Neill. Chicago: Reilly & Britton.

———. 1914. *Tik-Tok of Oz.* Illustr. John R. Neill. Chicago: Reilly & Britton.

———. 1915. *The Scarecrow of Oz.* Illustr. John R. Neill. Chicago: Reilly & Britton.

———. 1916. *Rinkitink in Oz.* Illustr. John R. Neill. Chicago: Reilly & Britton.

———. 1917. *The Lost Princess of Oz.* Illustr. John R. Neill. Chicago: Reilly & Britton.

———. 1918. *The Tin Woodman of Oz.* Illustr. John R. Neill. Chicago: Reilly & Britton.

———. 1919. *The Magic of Oz.* Illustr. John R. Neill. Chicago: Reilly & Lee.

———. 1920. *Glinda of Oz.* Illustr. John R. Neill. Chicago: Reilly & Lee.

Bayley, F. W. N. 1844. *Comic Nursery Tales.* London: W. S. Orr.

Bernard, Catherine. 1696. *Inès de Cardoue, nouvelle espagnole.* Paris: Jouvenel.

———. 1967. "Riquet à la houppe." In *Contes de Perrault*, ed. Gilbert Rouger, 271–78. Paris: Garnier.

Bethell, Augusta. 1865. *Echoes of an Old Bell and Other Tales of Fairy Lore.* London: Griffith & Farran.

———. 1874. *Feathers and Fairies, or Stories from the Realms of Fancy.* London: Griffith & Farran.

———. 1883. *Among the Fairies.* London: Sonnerschein.

Bignon, Jean-Paul. 1712–14. *Les Aventures d'Abdalla, fils d'Hanif.* Paris: Pierre Witte.

Bleiler, Everett Franklin, ed. 1967. *The Best Tales of Hoffmann.* New York: Dover.

Bly, Robert. 1990. *Iron John: A Book about Men.* Reading, Mass.: Addison-Wesley.

Broumas, Olga. 1977. *Beginning with O.* New Haven, Conn.: Yale University Press.

Browne, Frances. 1856. *Granny's Wonderful Chair, and the Tales It Told.* London: Griffith, Farran, Okeden, & Welsh.

Browne, Maggie (pseudonym of Margaret Hammer). 1890. *Wanted — A King*. London: Cassell.

Bullock, Michael, ed. and trans. 1963. *The Tales of Hoffmann*. New York: Ungar.

Burkhardt, C. B. 1849. *Fairy Tales and Legends of Many Nations*. New York: Scribner's.

Burnett, Frances Hodgson. 1892. *Children I Have Known and Giovanni and the Other*. London: Osgood, McIlvaine.

Burton, Richard F. 1885–86. *The Book of the Thousand Nights and a Night. A Plain and Literal Translation of the Arabian Nights Entertainment*. 10 vols. Stoke Newington: Kamashastra Society.

———. 1886. *Supplemental Nights to the Book of the Thousand Nights and a Night, with Notes Anthropological and Explanatory*. 6 vols. Stoke Newington: Kamashastra Society.

Byron, May. 1925. *The Little Ones' Peter Pan and Wendy*. Retold for the nursery. Illustr. Mabel Lucie Attwell. London: Hodder and Stoughton.

———. 1925. *Peter Pan and Wendy*. Retold for boys and girls. Illustr. Mabel Lucie Attwell. London: Hodder and Stoughton.

Calvino, Italo, ed. 1956. *Fiabe Italiene*. Torino: Einaudi.

———. 1980. *Italian Folktales*. Trans. George Martin. New York: Harcourt Brace Jovanovich.

Carroll, Lewis (pseudonym of Charles Lutwidge Dodgson). 1865. *Alice's Adventures in Wonderland*. London: Macmillan.

———. 1867. "Bruno's Revenge." *Aunt Judy's Magazine* (December).

———. 1871. *Through the Looking Glass, and What Alice Found There*. London: Macmillan.

———. 1889. *Sylvie and Bruno*. London: Macmillan.

———. 1893. *Sylvie and Bruno Concluded*. London: Macmillan.

Carter, Angela. 1979. *Bloody Chamber and Other Tales*. London: Gollancz.

Caylus, Anne-Claude-Philippe de Tubières Grimoard de Pestels de Lévis, comte de. 1741. *Féeries nouvelles*. La Haye.

Cazotte, Jacques. 1742. *Milles et Une Fadaises. Contes à dormir debout*. A Baillons, chez Endormy.

Chase, Pauline. 1913. *Peter Pan in the Real Never Never Land*. London: Horace Cox.

Chatelain, Clara de Pontigny. 1847. *The Silver Swan*. London: Grant & Griffith.

———. 1850. *Child's Own Book of Fairy Tales*. New York: Hurst.

———. 1851. *Merry Tales for Little Folk*. London: Addey.

———. 1857. *Little Folks' Books*. New York: Leavitt & Allen.

———. 1866. *The Sedan-Chair: Sir Wilfred's Seven Flights*. London: Routledge.

Childe-Pemberton, Harriet. 1882. *The Fairy Tales of Every Day*. London: Christian Knowledge Society.

———. 1883. *Olive Smith; or, an Ugly Duckling.* London: Christian Knowledge Society.

———. 1884. *No Beauty.* London: Christian Knowledge Society.

Clifford, Lucy Lane. 1882. *Anyhow Stories.* London: Macmillan.

———. 1886. *Very Short Stories and Verses for Children.* London: Walter Scott.

———. 1892. *The Last Touches and Other Stories.* London: Adam & Charles Black.

Cohen, J. M., ed. and trans. 1951. *Tales from Hoffmann.* London: The Bodley Head.

Collodi, Carlo. 1883. *Le Avventure di Pinocchio.* Florence: Felice Paggi.

———. 1986. *The Adventures of Pinocchio: Story of a Puppet.* Trans. Nicolas J. Perella. Berkeley: University of California Press.

———. 1996. *The Adventures of Pinocchio.* Trans. Ann Lawson Lucas. Oxford: Oxford University Press.

Comfort, Lucy Randall. 1868. *Folks and Fairies.* New York: Harper.

Coover, Robert. 1970. *Pricksongs & Descants.* New York: Dutton.

———. 1991. *Pinocchio in Venice.* New York: Simon & Schuster.

———. 1996. *Briar Rose.* New York: Grove.

Corkran, Alice. 1883. *The Adventures of Mrs. Wishing-to-be; and Other Stories.* London: Blackie & Son.

———. 1887. *Down the Snow Stairs.* London: Blackie & Son.

Craik, Dinah Mulock. 1852. *Alice Learnmont. A Fairy Tale.* London: Macmillan.

———. 1859. *Romantic Tales.* London: Smith, Elder.

———. 1863. *The Fairy Book.* London: Macmillan.

———. 1874. *The Little Lame Prince.* London: Daldy, Isbister.

Crane, Walter. 1874. *Walter Crane's New Toybook.* London: Routledge.

Crowquill, Alfred (pseudonym of Alfred Henry Forrester). 1840. *Crowquill's Fairy Book.* New York: Hurst.

———. 1856. *The Giant Hands.* London: Routledge.

———. 1856. *Tales of Magic and Meaning.* London: Griffith & Farran.

———. 1857. *Fairy Tales.* London: Routledge.

———. 1860. *Fairy Footsteps; or Lessons from Legends.* London: H. Lea.

Cruikshank, George. 1853–54. *George Cruikshank's Fairy Library.* London: David Bogne.

———. 1885. *The Cruikshank Fairy-Book.* London: G. Bell.

Dahl, Roald. 1982. *Revolting Rhymes.* London: Jonathan Cape.

Datlow, Ellen, and Terri Windling, eds. 1993. *Black Thorn, White Rose.* New York: William Morrow.

———, eds. 1994. *Snow White, Blood Red.* New York: William Morrow.

———, eds. 1995. *Ruby Slippers, Golden Tears.* New York: William Morrow.

———, eds. 1997. *Black Swan, White Raven.* New York: Avon.

Davenport, Tom, and Gary Carden. 1992. *From the Brothers Grimm. A Contemporary Retelling of American Folktales and Classic Stories.* Fort Atkinson, Wis.: Highsmith.

De Morgan, Mary. 1877. *On a Pincushion.* London: Seeley, Jackson & Halliday.

———. 1880. *The Necklace of Princess Fiorimonde.* London: Macmillan.

———. 1900. *The Windfairies.* London: Seeley, Jackson & Halliday.

Deulin, Charles. 1879. *Les Contes de ma Mère l'Oye avant Perrault.* Paris.

Dickens, Charles. 1843. *A Christmas Carol.* London: Routledge.

———. 1868. *Holiday Romance.* Published in four parts in *Our Young Folks: An Illustrated Magazine for Boys and Girls* IV (January–May).

Donoghue, Emma. 1997. *Kissing the Witch: Old Tales in New Skins.* London: Hamish Hamilton.

Doyle, Richard. 1842. *Jack the Giant Killer.* London: Eyre & Spottiswoode.

Drennan, G. D. 1909. *Peter Pan, His Book, His Pictures, His Career, His Friends.* London: Mills and Boon.

Dumas, Alexandre. 1845. *Histoire d'un casse-noisette.* Paris: J. Hetzel.

———. 1962–67. *Oeuvres d'Alexandre Dumas père.* Ed. Gilbert Sigaux. 38 vols. Lausanne: Éditions Rencontre.

Durand, Catherine Bédacier. 1699. *La Comtesse de Mortane.* Paris: Barbin.

———. 1702. *Les Petits Soupers de l'été de l'année 1699, ou Avantures galantes avec l'Origine des fées.* Paris: Musier and Rolin.

Edmonstron, Maysie. 1914. *The Duke of Christmas Daisies and Other Fairy Plays.* Adapted from *The Little White Bird* of Sir J. M. Barrie. London: Wells, Gardner, Darton.

Ende, Michael. 1973. *Momo.* Stuttgart: Thienemann.

———. 1979. *Unendliche Geschichte.* Stuttgart: Thienemann.

———. 1984. *Neverending Story.* New York: Penguin.

Estés, Clarissa Pinkola. 1993. *Women Who Run with the Wolves: Myths and Stories of the Wild Woman Archetype.* New York: Ballantine.

Ewing, Juliana Horatia. 1882. *Old-Fashioned Fairy Tales.* London: Society for Promoting Christian Knowledge.

Farmer, Philip José. 1982. *A Barnstormer in Oz.* New York: Berkeley.

Fénelon, François de Salignac de la Mothe-. 1983. *Oeuvres.* Ed. Jacques Le Brun, Paris: Gallimard.

Fleutiaux, Pierrette. 1984. *Métamorphoses de la reine.* Paris: Gallimard.

France, Anatole. 1909. *Les sept femmes de la Barbe-Bleue et autres contes merveilleux.* Paris: s.n.

———. 1920. *The Seven Wives of Bluebeard and Other Marvelous Tales.* Trans. D. B. Stewart. London: The Bodley Head.

Francis, Beata. 1897. *The Gentlemanly Giant and Other Denizens of the Never, Never Forest.* London: Hodder & Stoughton.

Galland, Antoine. 1704–17. *Les Milles et une nuit.* 12 vols. Vols. 1–4, Paris: La Veueve Claude Barbin, 1704; vols. 5–7, ibid., 1706; vol. 8, ibid., 1709; vols. 9–10, Florentin Delaulne, 1912; vols. 11–12. Lyon: Briasson.

Garner, James Finn. 1994. *Politically Correct Bedtime Stories.* New York: Macmillan.

———. 1995. *Once Upon a More Enlightened Time: More Politically Correct Fairy Tales.* New York: Macmillan.

Gatty, Mrs. Alfred. 1851. *The Fairy Godmothers and Other Tales.* London: George Bell.

Goethe, Johann Wolfgang von. 1962. *The Sorrows of Young Werther and Selected Writings.* Trans. Catherine Hunter. New York: New American Library.

Grahame, Kenneth. 1898. *Dream Days.* London: John Lane.

Grimm, Brüder. 1980. *Kinder- und Hausmärchen.* Ed. Heinz Rölleke. 3 vols. Stuttgart: Reclam.

Grimm, Jacob, and Wilhelm Grimm. N.d. *Kinder- und Hausmärchen der Brüder Grimm. Vollständige Ausgabe in der Urfassung.* Ed. Friedrich Panzer. Wiesbaden: Emil Vollmer.

———. 1823. *German Popular Stories, Translated from the Kinder- und Hausmärchen.* Trans. Edgar Taylor. London: C. Baldwin.

———. 1882. *Household Stories from the Collection of the Brothers Grimm.* Trans. Lucy Crane. London: Macmillan.

———. 1887. *Grimm's Fairy Tales.* Trans. Mrs. H. B. Paull. London: Frederick Warne.

———. 1894. *Fairy Tales from Grimm.* Intro. S. Baring-Gould. London: Wells Gardner, Darnton.

———. 1962. *Kinder- und Hausmärchen. In der ersten Gestalt.* Ed. Walter Killy. 1st ed. Frankfurt am Main: Fischer.

———. 1975. *Die älteste Märchensammlung der Brüder Grimm. Synopse der handschriftlichen Urfassung von 1810 und der Erstdrucke von 1812.* Ed. Heinz Rölleke. Cologny-Geneva: Foundation Martin Bodmer.

———. 1976. *Kinder- und Hausmärchen gesammelt durch die Brüder Grimm.* Intro. Ingeborg Weber-Kellermann. 3 vols. Frankfurt am Main: Insel.

———. 1980. *Kinder- und Hausmärchen. Ausgabe Letzter Hand mit den Originalanmerkungen der Brüder Grimm.* Ed. Heinz Rölleke. 3 vols. Stuttgart: Philipp Reclam.

———. 1982. *Kinder- und Hausmärchen. Nach der zweiten vermehrten und verbesserten Auflage von 1819.* Ed. Heinz Rölleke. 2 vols. Cologne: Diederichs.

———. 1985. *Im Himmel steht ein Baum, Dran häng ich meinen Traum. Volkslieder, Kinderlieder, Kinderzeichnungen.* Ed. Gabriele Seitz. Munich: Winkler.

———. 1985. *Kinder- und Hausmärchen. Kleine Ausgabe von 1858.* Ed. Heinz Rölleke. Frankfurt am Main: Insel.

————. 1986. *Kinder- und Hausmärchen. Vergrößerter Nachdruck von 1812 und 1815 nach dem Handexemplar des Brüder Grimm-Museums Kassel mit sämtlichen handschriftlichen Korrekturen und Nachträgen der Brüder Grimm.* Ed. Heinz Rölleke and Ulrike Marquardt. 2 vols. with Ergänzungsheft. Göttingen: Vandenhoeck & Ruprecht.

————. 1987. *The Complete Fairy Tales of the Brothers Grimm.* Trans. and ed. Jack Zipes. New York: Bantam.

Gripari, Pierre. 1967. *La sorcère de la rue Mouffetard et autres contes de la rue Broca.* Paris: La Table Ronde.

————. 1967. *Le gentil petit diable et autres contes de la rue Broca.* Paris: La Table Ronde.

Hamilton, Comte Antoine. 1730. *Histoire de Fleur-d'Epine.* Paris: Josse.

Harrison, Mrs. Burton. 1885. *Folk and Fairy Tales.* London: Ward & Downey.

Hassall, J. 1915. *The Peter Pan Painting Book.* London: Lawrence and Jellicoe.

Hauff, Wilhelm. 1826. *Märchen-Almanach auf das Jahr 1826 für Söhne und Töchter gebildeter Stände.* Stuttgart: Verlag der J. B. Metzler'schen Buchhandlung.

————. 1827. *Märchenalmanach für Söhne und Töchter gebildeter Stände auf das Jahr 1827.* Stuttgart: Franckh.

————. 1986. *Sämtliche Märchen.* Ed. Hans-Heino Ewers. Stuttgart: Reclam.

Hay, Sara Henderson. 1982. *Story Hour.* Fayetteville: University of Arkansas Press.

Hearn, Michael, ed. 1988. *The Victorian Fairy Tale Book.* New York: Pantheon.

Herford, O. 1907. *The Peter Pan Alphabet.* London: Hodder and Stoughton.

Hesse, Hermann. 1919. *Märchen.* Berlin: S. Fischer.

————. 1995. *The Fairy Tales of Hermann Hesse.* Trans. Jack Zipes. New York: Bantam.

Hoffmann, E. T. A. 1960. "Der Nußknacker und der Mausekönig." In *Kinder-Märchen.* 1816. Berlin: Realschulbuchhandlung.

————. *Fantasie- und Nachtstücke.* 1960. Ed. Walter Müller-Seidel. Munich: Winkler.

————. 1963. *Die Serapions-Brüder.* Ed. Walter Müller-Seidel. Munich: Winkler.

————. 1965. *Späte Werke.* Ed. Walter Müller-Seidel. Munich: Winkler.

————. 1969. *Tales of E. T. A. Hoffmann.* Trans. and ed. Leonard Kent and Elizabeth Knight. Chicago: University of Chicago Press.

————. 1982. *Tales.* Ed. Victor Lange. New York: Continuum.

Hollingdale, R. J., ed. 1982. *Tales of Hoffmann.* Harmondsworth, Middlesex, England: Penguin.

Hood, Thomas. 1865. *Fairy Realm.* London: Cassell, Peter, & Galpin.

————. 1870. *Harlequin, Little Red Riding Hood, or The Wicked Wolf and the Virtuous Woodcutter.* London: Scott.

————. 1870. *Petsetilla's Posy. A Fairy Tale for the Nineteenth Century.* London: Routledge.

Hood, Thomas, and Jane Hood. 1882. *Fairy Land, or Recreation for the Rising Generation*. London: Griffith & Farran.

Housman, Laurence. 1894. *A Farm in Fairyland*. London: Kegan Paul.

———. 1895. *The House of Joy*. London: K. Paul, Trench, Trubner.

———. 1898. *The Field of Clover*. London: John Lane.

———. 1904. *The Blue Moon*. London: John Murray.

Ingelow, Jean. 1869. *Mopsa the Fairy*. London: Longmans, Green.

———. 1872. *The Little Wonder-Hom. A New Series of Stories Told to a Child*. London: Henry S. King.

———. 1887. *The Fairy Who Judged Her Neighbours and How the Crow Flies*. London: Griffith, Farran, Okeden, & Welsh.

Inman, Herbert E. 1893. *Up the Spider's Web*. London: J. Clarke.

———. 1897. *The One-Eyed Griffin and Other Fairy Tales*. London: Frederick Warne.

———. 1898. *The Owl King and Other Fairy Stories*. London: Frederick Warne.

———. 1900. The *Two-Eyed Griffin*. London: Frederick Warne.

———. 1902. *The Admiral and I: A Fairy Story*. London: Ward, Lock.

———. 1913. *The Did of Didn't Think*. London: Frederick Warne.

Irwin, Robert. 1994. *The Arabian Nights: A Companion*. London: Penguin Press.

Janosch (Horst Eckert). 1972. *Janosch erzählt Grimm's Märchen*. Weinheim: Beltz.

Jones, Harry. 1896. *Prince Booboo and Little Smuts*. London: Gardner Darton.

Kabbani, Rana. 1986. *Europe's Myths of the Orient*. New York: Macmillan.

Keary, Annie, and E. Keary. 1865. *Little Wanderlin and Other Fairy Tales*. London: Macmillan.

Kelen, Jacqueline. 1986. *Les nuits de Schéhérazade*. Paris: Albin Michel.

Kent, Leonard, and Elizabeth Knights, eds. & trans. 1972. *Tales of Hoffmann*. Chicago: University of Chicago Press.

Kingsley, Charles. 1863. *The Water Babies. A Fairy Tale for a Land-Baby*. London: Macmillan.

———. 1870. *Madame How and Lady Why*. London: Macmillan.

Kipling, Rudyard. 1893. The Potted Princess. In *St. Nicholas Magazine* (January).

———. 1902. *Just So Stories*. London: Macmillan.

———. 1906. *Puck of Pook's Hill*. London: Macmillan.

———. 1910. *Rewards and Fairies*. London: Macmillan.

Kirby, Mary, and Elizabeth Kirby. 1856. *The Talking Bird*. London: Grant and Griffith.

Kirkup, James, trans. 1966. *Tales of Hoffmann*. London: Blackie.

Knatchbull-Hugessen, Edward H. (Lord Brabourne). 1869. *Stories for My Children*. London: Macmillan.

———. 1870. *Crackers for Christmas*. London: Macmillan.

———. 1871. *Moonshine*. London: Macmillan.

———. 1872. *Tales at Tea Time*. London: Macmillan.

———. 1874. *Queer Folk*. London: Macmillan.

———. 1875. *Higgedly-Piggedly*. London: Longmans, Green.

———. 1875. *River Legends*. London: Dalby, Isbister.

———. 1875. *Whispers from Fairyland*. London: Longmans, Green.

———. 1879. *Uncle Joe's Stories*. London: George Routledge.

———. 1880. *Other Stories*. London: Routledge.

———. 1881. *The Mountain Sprite's Kingdom*. London: Routledge.

———. 1882. *Ferdinand's Adventure and Other Stories*. London: Routledge.

———. 1886. *Friends and Foes from Fairy Land*. London: Longmans, Green.

———. 1894. *The Magic Oak Tree and Prince Filderkin*. London: T. Fisher Unwin.

Kunert, Günter. 1976. *Jeder Wunsch ein Treffer*. Velber: Middelhauve.

La Force, Charlotte-Rose Caumont de. 1698. *Les Contes des contes par* Mlle de ***. Paris: S. Bernard.

Lane, Edward William. 1838–40. *A New Translation of the Tales of a Thousand and One Nights; Known in England as the Arabian Nights' Entertainments*. London: Charles Knight & Co.

Lang, Andrew. 1884. *The Princess Nobody*. London: Longmans.

———. 1888. *The Gold of Fairnilee*. Bristol: Arrowsmith.

———. 1889. *The Blue Fairy Book*. London: Longmans.

———. 1889. *Prince Prigio*. Bristol: Arrowsmith.

———. 1890. *The Red Fairy Book*. London: Longmans.

———. 1892. *The Green Fairy Book*. London: Longmans.

———. 1893. *Prince Ricardo of Pantouflia: Being the Adventures of Prince Priglio's Son*. Bristol: Arrowsmith.

———. 1894. *The Yellow Fairy Book*. London: Longmans.

———. 1897. *The Pink Fairy Book*. London: Longmans.

———. 1898. *The Arabian Nights Entertainment*. London: Longmans.

———. 1900. *The Grey Fairy Book*. London: Longmans.

———. 1901. *The Violet Fairy Book*. London: Longmans.

———. 1903. *The Crimson Fairy Book*. London: Longmans.

———. 1904. *The Brown Fairy Book*. London: Longmans.

———. 1906. *The Orange Fairy Book*. London: Longmans.

———. 1907. *The Olive Fairy Book*. London: Longmans.

———. 1908. *The Book of Princes and Princesses*. London: Longmans.

———. 1910. *The Lilac Fairy Book*. London: Longmans.

Lazare, Christopher, ed. and trans. 1946. *Tales of Hoffmann*. New York: Wyn.

Lee, Tanith. 1972. *Princess Hynchatti and Some Other Surprises*. London: Macmillan.

———. 1983. *Red as Blood or Tales from the Sisters Grimmer*. New York: DAW.

Lem, Stanislaw. 1974. *The Cyberiad: Fables for the Cybernetic Age*. Trans. Michael Kandel. New York: Seabury.

Lemon, Mark. 1849. *The Enchanted Doll. A Fairy Tale for Little People.* London: Bradbury & Evans.

———. 1869. *Tinykin's Transformations.* London: Bradbury & Evans.

Le Noble, Eustache, Baron de Saint-Georges et de Tennelière. 1700. *Le Gage touché. Histoires galantes.* Amsterdam: n.p.

Leprince de Beaumont, Marie. 1756. *Magasin des enfans, ou Dialogue d'une sage gouvernante avec ses élèves de la première distinction.* Lyon: Reguilliat.

Lhéritier de Villandon, Marie-Jeanne. 1696. *Ouevres meslées.* Paris: J. Guignard.

———. 1705. *La Tour Ténebreuse et Les Jours lumineux.* Paris: Barbin.

Lubert, Mile de. 1743. *La Princesse Camion.* La Haye.

———. 1743. *La Princesse Couleur-de-rose et le prince Céladon.* La Haye.

Lucas, E. V. 1905. *Old Fashioned Tales.* London: Wells Gardner.

Lucas, F. Lancaster. 1901. *The Fish Crown in Dispute. A Submarine Fairy Tale.* London: Skeffington.

Lucas, J. Templeton. 1871. *Prince Ubbely Bubble's Fairy Tales.* London: Frederick Warne.

Lurie, Alison, ed. 1993. *The Oxford Book of Modern Fairy Tales.* Oxford: Oxford University Press.

Lushington, Henrietta. 1865. *Hacco the Dwarf, or The Tower on the Mountain, and Other Tales.* London: Griffith & Farran.

MacDonald, George. 1867. *Dealings with the Fairies.* London: Alexander Strahan.

———. 1872. *The Princess and the Goblin.* London: Blackie & Son.

———. 1874. *The Light Princess and Other Stories.* London: Dalby, Isbister.

———. 1875. *The Wise Woman.* London: Alexander Strahan.

———. 1882. *The Gifts of the Christ Child and Other Tales.* 2 vols. London: Sampson Low.

———. 1883. *The Princess and Curdie.* London: Chatto & Windus.

Macleod, Norman. 1861. *The Gold Thread.* Edinburgh.

Maguire, Gregory. 1995. *Wicked: The Life and Times of the Wicked Witch of the West.* Thorndike, Maine: Thorndike Press.

———. 2005. *Son of a Witch: A Novel.* New York. Regan Books.

Mailly, Jean de. 1698. *Les Illustres fées, contes galans.* Paris: Brunet.

Mayer, Charles-Joseph, ed. 1785–89. *Le cabinet des fées; ou Collection choisie des contes des fées, et autres contes merveilleux.* 41 vols. Amsterdam: s.n.

McKinley, Robin. 1981. *The Door in the Hedge.* New York: Greenwillow.

———. 1995. *A Knot in the Grain and Other Stories.* New York: HarperCollins.

Mieder, Wolfgang, ed. 1979. *Grimms Märchen — modern.* Stuttgart: Reclam.

———, ed. 1983. *Mädchen pfeif auf den Prinzen! Märchengedichte von Günter Grass bis Sarah Kirsch.* Cologne: Diederichs.

———, ed. 1985. *Disenchantments: An Anthology of Modern Fairy Tale Poetry.* Hanover: University Press of New England.

Mitchison, Naomi. 1936. *The Fourth Pig.* London: Constable.

———. 1957. *Five Men and a Swan*. London: Allen and Unwin.

Molesworth, Mary. 1875. *Tell Me a Story*. London: Macmillan.

———. 1879. *The Tapestry Room*. London: Macmillan.

———. 1884. *Christmas-Tree Land*. London: Macmillan.

———. 1890. *The Children of the Castle*. London: Macmillan.

———. 1892. *An Enchanted Garden*. New York: Cassell.

———. 1911. *Fairies Afield*. London: Macmillan.

Montalba, Anthony (pseudonym of W. R. Whitehill). 1849. *Fairy Tales of All Nations*. London: Chapman and Hall.

Morley, Henry. 1859. *Fables and Fairy Tales*. London: Cassell.

———. 1860. *Oberon's Horn: A Book of Fairy Tales*. London: Cassell.

Murat, Henriette-Julie de Castelnau, Comtesse de. 1698. *Contes de Fées*. Paris: Barbin.

———. 1698. *Les Nouveaux Contes de fées*. Paris: Barbin.

Napoli, Donna Jo. 1993. *The Prince of the Pond: Otherwise Known as De Fawg Pin*. New York: Dutton.

———. 1993. *The Magic Circle*. New York: Dutton.

———. 1996. *Zel*. New York: Dutton.

Nesbit, Edith. 1900. *The Book of Dragons*. London: Harper.

———. 1901. *Nine Unlikely Tales for Children*. London: T. Fisher Unwin.

———. 1912. *The Magic World*. London: Macmillan.

———. 1925. *Five of Us — and Madeleine*. London: T. Fisher Unwin.

Nöstlinger, Christine. 1972. *Wir pfeifen auf den Gurkenkönig*. Weinheim: Beltz.

O'Connor, Daniel S. 1907. *The Peter Pan Picture Book*. Illustr. Alice B. Woodward. London: Bell.

———. 1912. *The Story of Peter Pan*. A reading book for use in schools. Illustr. Alice B. Woodward. London: Bell.

———. 1919. *The Story of Peter Pan for Little People*. Simplified from Daniel O'Connor's story of Sir J. M. Barrie's fairy play. Illustr. Alice B. Woodward. London: Bell.

———, ed. 1907. *Peter Pan Keepsake*. The story of *Peter Pan* retold from Mr. Barrie's fantasy, foreword by W. T. Stead. London: Chatto & Windus.

Opie, Iona, and Peter Opie, eds. 1974. *The Classic Fairy Tales*. London: Oxford University Press.

Paget, Francis Edward. 1844. *The Hope of the Katzekopfs*. London: The Juvenile Englishman's Library.

Parr, Harriet, 1860. *Legends from Fairyland*. London: Frederick Warne.

———. 1861. *The Wonderful Adventures of Tuflongbo*. London: Frederick Warne.

———. 1862. *Tuflongbo's Journey in Search of Ogres*. London: Frederick Warne.

———. 1868. *Holme Lee's Fairy Tales*. London: Frederick Warne.

Payne, John. 1882–84. *The Book of the Thousand Nights and One Night*. 9 vols. London: Villon Society.

————. 1884. *Tales from the Arabic of the Breslau and Calcutta Editions of the Book of the Thousand and One Nights.* 3 vols. London: Villon Society.

————. 1889. *Alaeddin and the Enchanted Lamp; Zein ul Asnam and the King of the Jinn.* London: Villon Society.

Pennell, Cholmondeley, ed. 1863. *The Family Fairy Tales; or Glimpses of Elfand at Heatherston Hall.* London: John Camden Hotten.

Perrault, Charles. 1697. *Histoires ou contes du temps passé.* Paris: Claude Barbin.

————. 1964. *Parallèlle des anciens et des modernes.* 1688–97. Munich: Eidos.

————. 1989. *Contes,* ed. Marc Soriano. Paris: Flammarion.

Phillip, Neil. 1989. *The Cinderella Story: The Origins and Variations of the Story Known as "Cinderella."* London: Penguin.

————. 1996. *American Fairy Tales.* New York: Hyperion.

Planché, J. R. 1865. *An Old Fairy Tale Told Anew.* London: Routledge.

————, ed. and trans. 1860. *Fairy Tales by Perrault, De Villeneuve, De Caylus, De Lubert, De Beaumont and Others.* Illustr. Eduard Courbould and Harvey Godwin. London: Routledge.

————, ed. and trans. 1865. *D'Aulnoy's Fairy Tales.* Illustr. Gordon Browne and Lydia F. Emmet. London: Routledge.

Pollock, Lady Juliet, W. K. Clifford, and W. W. Pollock. 1874. *The Little People.* London.

Pourrat, Henri. 1948–62. *Le Trésor des Contes.* 16 vols. Paris: Gallimard.

Préchac, Jean de. 1698. *Contes moins contes que les autres.* Paris: Barbin.

Quiller-Couch, Sir Arthur. 1910. *The Sleeping Beauty and Other Fairy Tales.* London: Hodder & Stoughton.

Ragan, Kathleen. 1998. *Fearless Girls, Wise Women, and Beloved Sisters.* New York: W. W. Norton.

Redgrove, Peter. 1989. *The One Who Set Out to Study Fear.* London: Bloomsbury.

Rilke, Rainer Maria. 1963. *Stories of God.* Trans. M. D. Herter Norton. New York: W. W. Norton.

Ritchie, Anne Isabella. 1868. *Five Old Friends and a Young Prince.* London: Smith, Elder.

————. 1874. *Bluebeard's Keys and Other Stories.* London: Smith, Elder.

Ritson, Joseph. 1831. *Fairy Tales.* London: Payne & Foss.

Robert, Raymonde. 1984. *Il était une fois: Contes des XVIIe et XVIIIe siècles.* Nancy: Presse Universitaire de Nancy.

Rossetti, Christina. 1862. *The Goblin Market.* London: Blackie & Son.

————. 1874. *Speaking Likenesses.* London: Macmillan.

Rousseau, Jean Jacques. 1758. *La Reine Fantasque, conte cacouac.* Geneva.

Rushdie, Salman. 1990. *Haroun and the Sea of Stories.* New York: Viking.

Ruskin, John. 1841. *The King of the Golden River.* London: J. Wiley.

Ryder, Frank G., and Robert M. Browning, eds. 1983. *German Literary Fairy Tales.* New York: Continuum.

Ryman, Geoff. 1992. *Was*. New York: Knopf.

Schwitters, Kurt. 1974. *Das literarische Werk*. Ed. F. Lach. 2 vols. Cologne: DuMont.

Ségur, Sophie, Comtesse de. 1856. *Nouveaux contes de fées pour les petits enfants*. Paris: Hachette.

———. 1869. *Fairy Tales*. Philadelphia: Porter & Coates.

Selous, Henry Courtney. 1874. *Granny's Story-Box*. London: Griffith & Farran.

Sexton, Anne. 1971. *Transformations*. Boston: Houghton Mifflin.

Sewell, Elizabeth M. 1869. *Uncle Peter's Fairy Tale for the Nineteenth Century*. London: Longmans, Green.

Sewell, William. 1871. *The Giant*. London: Longmans, Green.

Sharp, Evelyn. 1898. *All the Way to Fairyland*. London: John Lane.

———. 1900. *The Other Side of the Sun*. London: John Lane.

———. 1902. *Round the World to Wympland*. London: John Lane.

———. 1916. *The Story of the Weathercock*. London: Blackie & Son.

Sherwood, Mrs. (Mary Martha). 1820. *The Governess, or, The Little Female Academy*. London: F. Houlston.

Sigler, Carolyn, ed. 1997. *Alternative Alices: Visions and Revisions of Lewis Carroll's Alice Books*. Lexington: University Press of Kentucky.

Sinclair, Catherine. 1839. *Holiday House: A Book for the Young*. London: Ward, Lock.

Sondheim, Stephen, and James Lapine. 1988. *Into the Woods*. Adapt. and illustr. Hudson Talbott. New York: Crown.

Stockton, Frank. 1870. *Ting-a-ling*. Boston: Hurd and Houghton.

———. 1881. *The Floating Prince and Other Fairy Tales*. New York: Scribner's.

———. 1887. *The Queen's Museum*. Illustr. Frederick Richardson. New York: Scribner's.

———. 1892. *Clocks of Rondaine and Other Stories*. Illustr. E. H. Blashfield, W. A. Rogers, D. C. Beard, and others. New York: Scribner's.

———. 1901. *Ting-a-ling Tales*. Illustr. E. B. Bensell. New York: Scribner's.

Straparola, Giovan Francesco. 1894. *The Facetious Nights*. Trans. William G. Waters. Illustr. E. R. Hughes. London: Lawrence and Bullen.

———. 1975. *Le Piacevoli Notti*. Ed. Pastore Stocchi. Rome-Bari: Laterza.

Strauss, Gwen. 1990. *Trail of Stones*. London: Julia MacRae Books.

Summerly, Felix (pseudonym of Sir Henry Cole). 1843. *Beauty and the Beast*. London: Joseph Cundall.

———. 1843. *The Chronicle of the Valiant Feats, Wonderful Victories and Bold Adventures of Jack the Giant-Killer*. London: Joseph Cundall.

———. 1845. *The Traditional Fairy Tales of Little Red Riding Hood, Beauty and the Beast, and Jack and the Bean Stalk*. London: Joseph Cundall.

Tabart, Benjamin. 1818. *Popular Fairy Tales; or, A Lilliputian Library*. London: Phillips.

Thackeray, William Makepeace. 1855. *The Rose and the Ring, or The History of Prince Giglio and Prince Bulbo*. London: Smith, Elder.

Thurber, James. 1940. *Fables for Our Time and Famous Poems*. New York: Harper & Row.

Tournier, Michel. 1983. *The Fetishist*. Trans. Barbara Wright. New York: Doubleday.

Turin, Adela, Francesca Cantarelli, and Wella Bosnia. 1977. *The Five Wives of Silver-beard*. London: Writers and Readers Publishing Cooperative.

Turin, Adela, and Sylvie Selig. 1977. *Of Cannons and Caterpillars*. London: Writers and Readers Publishing Cooperative.

Villeneuve, Gabrielle-Suzanne Barbot d'. 1740. *La jeune Ameriquaine et Les Contes marins*. La Haye aux dépens de la Compagnie.

Voltaire (François-Marie Arouet). 1926. *Zadig and Other Romances*. Trans. H. I. Woolf and Wilfrid S. Jackson. Illustr. Henry Keen. London: The Bodley Head.

———. 1929. *The White Bull*. Trans. C. E. Vulliamy. London: Scholartis.

———. 1979. *Romans et contes*. Ed. Jacques van den Heuvel. Paris: Gallimard.

Walker, Wendy. 1988. *The Sea-Rabbit Or, The Artist of Life*. Los Angeles: Sun & Moon Press.

Warner, Sylvia Townsend. 1960. *The Cat's Cradle Book*. London: Chatto & Windus.

West, Mark, ed. 1989. *Before Oz: Juvenile Fantasy Stories from Nineteenth-Century America*. Hamden, Conn.: Archon Books.

Wilde, Oscar. 1888. *The Happy Prince and Other Tales*. London: David Nutt.

———. 1891. *The House of Pomegranates*. London: Osgood, McIlvaine.

Williams, Jay. 1979. *The Practical Princess and Other Liberating Tales*. New York: Parents' Magazine Press.

Windling, Terri, ed. 1995. *The Armless Maiden and Other Tales for Childhood's Survivors*. New York: Tor Books.

Yolen, Jane. 1983. *Tales of Wonder*. New York: Schocken.

———. 1985. *Dragonfield and Other Stories*. New York: Ace Books.

———. 1992. *Briar Rose*. New York: Tor Books.

Yonge, Charlotte. 1855. *The History of Thomas Thumb*. London: Hamilton, Adams.

Zipes, Jack, ed. 1986. *Don't Bet on the Prince: Contemporary Feminist Fairy Tales in North America and England*. New York: Methuen.

———, ed. 1989. *Beauties, Beasts, and Enchantment: French Classical Fairy Tales*. New York: New American Library.

———, ed. 1991. *Spells of Enchantment: The Wondrous Fairy Tales of Western Culture*. New York: Viking.

———, ed. 1993. *The Trials and Tribulations of Little Red Riding Hood*. 2d ed. New York: Routledge.

―――, ed. 1994. *The Outspoken Princess and the Gentle Knight.* New York: Bantam.

Secondary Literature

Ali, Muhsin Jassim. 1981. *Scheherazade in England: A Study of Nineteenth-Century English Criticism of the Arabian Nights.* Washington, D.C.: Three Continents Press.

Andersen, Jens. 2005. *Hans Christian Andersen: A New Life.* Trans. Tiina Nunnally. New York: Overlook Duckworth.

Anderson, Graham. 2000. *Fairytale in the Ancient World.* London: Routledge.

―――. 2003. "Old Tales for New: Finding the First Fairy Tales." In *A Companion to the Fairy Tale.* Ed. Hilda Ellis Davidson and Anna Chaudrhi, 85–98. Cambridge: D. S. Brewer.

Atterbery, Brian. 1980. *The Fantasy Tradition in American Literature: From Irving to Le Guin.* Bloomington: Indiana University Press.

Avery, Gillian. 1970. *Victorian People: In Life and Literature.* New York: Holt, Rinehart & Winston.

―――. 1975. *Childhood's Pattern: A Study of the Heroes and Heroines of Children's Fiction.* London: Hodder & Stoughton.

Avery, Gillian, and Angela Bull. 1965. *Nineteenth-Century Children: Heroes and Heroines in English Children's Stories 1780–1900.* London: Hodder & Stoughton.

―――. 1986. "The Cult of Peter Pan." *Word & Image* 2(2):173–85.

―――. 1992. "Introduction." In J. M. Barrie, *Peter Pan or The Boy Who Would Not Grow Up.* Illustr. Paula Rego. London: The Folio Society.

Baader, Renate. 1986. *Dames de Lettres: Autorinnen des preziösen, hocharistokratischen und "modernen" Salons (1649–1698): Mlle de Scudéry — Mlle de Montpensier — Mme d'Aulnoy.* Stuttgart: Metzler.

Bacchilega, Cristina. 1997. *Postmodern Fairy Tales: Gender and Narrative Strategies.* Philadelphia: University of Pennsylvania Press.

Bacon, Martha. 1973. "Puppet's Progress: Pinocchio." In *Children and Literature: Views and Reviews.* Ed. Virginia Havilland, 71–77. Glenview, Ill.: Scott, Foresman.

Barchilon, Jacques. 1975. *Le Conte merveillieux français de 1690 à 1790.* Paris: Champion.

Barchilon, Jacques, and Peter Flinders. 1981. *Charles Perrault.* Boston: Twayne.

Baum, Frank Joslyn, and Russell P. MacFall. 1961. *To Please a Child.* Chicago: Reilly & Lee.

Baum, Rob K. 1998. "Travesty, Peterhood, and the Flight of a Lost Girl." *New England Theatre Journal* 9:71–97.

Beckson, Karl E. 1970. *Oscar Wilde: The Critical Heritage*. London: Routledge & Kegan Paul.

Bell, A. Craig. 1950. *Alexandre Dumas: A Biography and a Study*. London: Cassell.

Bell, Elizabeth. 1996. "Do You Believe in Fairies? Peter Pan, Walt Disney and Me." *Women's Studies in Communication* 19(2):103–26.

Belz, Josephine. 1919. *Das Märchen und die Phantasie des Kindes*. Berlin; reprinted by Springer Press in Berlin, 1977.

Bencheikh, Jamel Eddine. 1988. *Les Mille et une Nuits ou La parole prisonnière*. Paris: Gallimard.

Bettelheim, Bruno. 1976. *The Uses of Enchantment: The Meaning and Importance of Fairy Tales*. New York: Alfred A. Knopf.

Bewley, Marius. 1970. "The Land of Oz: America's Good Place." In *Masks and Mirrors*, 255–67. New York: Atheneum.

Billman, Carol. 1983. "'I've Seen the Movie': Oz Revisited." In *Children's Novels and the Movies*, ed. Douglas Street, 92–100, New York: Ungar.

Birkin, Andrew. 1979. *J. M. Barrie and the Lost Boys*. London: Constable.

Bisseret, Noelle. 1979. *Education, Class Language and Ideology*. London: Routledge & Kegan Paul.

Blackburn, William. 1983. "Peter Pan and the Contemporary Adolescent Novel." In *The Child and the Story: An Explorative of Narrative Forms*, ed. Priscilla Ord, 47–53. Boston: Children's Literature Association.

Blount, Margaret. 1974. *Animal Land: The Creatures of Children's Fiction*. New York: Avon.

Borges, Jorge Luis. 1981. "The Translators of the 1001 Nights." In *Borges: A Reader*, ed. Emir Rodriguez and Alastair Reid, 73–86. New York: E. P. Dutton.

Bottigheimer, Ruth B., ed. 1986. *Fairy Tales and Society: Illusion, Allusion, and Paradigm*. Philadelphia: University of Pennsylvania Press.

Boulby, Mark. 1967. *Hermann Hesse: His Mind and His Art*. Ithaca, N.Y.: Cornell University Press.

Bratton, Jacqueline S. 1981. *The Impact of Victorian Children's Fiction*. London: Croom Helm.

Bredsdorff, Elias. 1975. *Hans Christian Andersen: The Story of His Life and Work, 1805–75*. London: Phaidon.

Briggs, K. M. 1967. *The Fairies in Tradition and Literature*. London: Routledge & Kegan Paul.

———. 1970. "The Folklore of Charles Dickens." *Journal of the Folklore Institute* 8:3–20.

———. 1976. *Dictionary of Fairies*. London: Allen Lane.

Brottnan, Jordan. 1969. "A Late Wanderer in Oz." In *Only Connect: Readings in Children's Literature*, ed. Sheila Egoff, G. T. Stubbs, and L. F. Ashley, 156–69. New York: Oxford University Press.

Burton, Richard F. 1934. Terminal Essay in *The Book of the Thousand Nights and a Night. A Plain and Literal Translation of the Arabian Nights Entertainment*, 3653–3870. Vol. 5/6. New York: Heritage Press.

Cambi, Franco. 1985. *Collodi, De Amicis, Rodari: Tre immagini d'infanzia.* Bari: Edizioni Dedalo.

Cambon, Glauco. 1973. "Pinocchio and the Problem of Children's Literature." *Children's Literature* 2:50–60.

Canepa, Nancy, ed. 1997. *Out of the Woods: The Origins of the Literary Fairy Tale in Italy and France.* Detroit: Wayne State University Press.

Caracciolo, Peter L., ed. 1988. *The Arabian Nights in English Literature: Studies in the Reception of the Thousand and One Nights into British Culture.* New York: St. Martin's Press.

Carlo Collodi. 1983. *Children's Literature Review*, ed. Gerald J. Senick, 69–87. Detroit: Gale Research.

Carpenter, Humphrey. 1985. *Secret Gardens: The Golden Age of Children's Literature.* London: George Allen & Unwin.

Carpenter, Humphrey, and Mari Prichard. 1984. *The Oxford Companion to Children's Literature.* Oxford: Oxford University Press.

Chaston, Joel D. 1994. "If I Ever Go Looking for My Heart's Desire: 'Home' in Baum's 'Oz' Books." *The Lion and the Unicorn* 18:209–19.

———. 1997. "The 'Ozification' of American Children's Fantasy Films: *The Blue Bird, Alice in Wonderland,* and *Jumanji.*" *Children's Literature Association Quarterly* 22 (Spring):13–20.

Clinton, Jerome W. 1985. "Madness and Cure in the 1001 Nights." *Studia Islamica* 61:107–25.

Clouard. Henri. 1954. *Alexandre Dumas.* Paris: Albin Michel.

Conant, Martha Pike. 1908. *The Oriental Tale in England in the Eighteenth Century.* New York: Columbia University Press.

Cott, Jonathan, ed. 1973. *Beyond the Looking Glass: Extraordinary Works of Fairy Tale and Fantasy.* New York: Stonehill.

Crafton, Donald. 1989. "The Last Night in the Nursery: Walt Disney's Peter Pan." *The Velvet Light Trap* 24:33–52.

Cro, Stelio. 1993. "When Children's Literature Becomes Adult." *Merveilles et Contes* 7:87–112.

Crouch, Marcus. 1962. *Treasure Seekers and Borrowers.* London: The Library Association.

Culver, Stuart. 1988. "What Manikins Want: *The Wonderful Wizard of Oz* and *The Art of Decorating Dry Goods Windows.*" *Representations* 21 (Winter):97–116.

————. 1992. "Growing Up in Oz." *American Literary History* 4 (Winter):607–28.

Daemmrich, Horst. 1974. *The Shattered Self: E. T. A. Hoffmann's Tragic Vision*. Detroit: Wayne State University Press.

Dahlerip, Pil. 1991. "Splash! Six Views of 'The Little Mermaid.'" *Scandinavian Studies* 63(2):141–63.

Darton, F. J. Harvey. 1929. *J. M. Barrie*. London: Nisbet.

————. 1982. *Children's Books in England*. 3d rev. ed. by Brian Alderson. Cambridge: Cambridge University Press.

Dégh, Linda. 1969. *Folktales and Society*. Bloomington: Indiana University Press.

Detering, Heinrich. 2002. "Nachbemerkung." In Hans Christian Andersen. *Schräge Märchen*, 280–83. Munich: Deutscher Taschenbuchverlag.

Dorson, Richard. 1976. *Folklore and Fakelore*. Cambridge: Harvard University Press.

Duffy, Maureen. 1972. *The Erotic World of Faery*. London: Hodder & Stoughton.

Dunbar, Janet. 1970. *J. M. Barrie: The Man Behind the Image*. London: Collins.

Dundes, Alan, ed. 1965. *The Study of Folklore*. Englewood Cliffs, N.J.: Prentice-Hall.

————, ed. 1982. *Cinderella: A Folklore Casebook*. New York: Garland.

————, ed. 1989. *Little Red Riding Hood: A Casebook*. Madison: University of Wisconsin Press.

Easterlin, Nancy. 2001. "Hans Christian Andersen's Fish Out of Water." *Philosophy and Literature* 25(2):251–77.

Egan, Michael. 1982. "The Neverland of Id: Barrie, Peter Pan and Freud." *Children's Literature* 10:37–55.

Elardo, Ronald J. 1980. "E. T. A. Hoffmann's 'Nussknacker und Mausekönig': The Mouse-Queen in the Tragedy of the Hero." *The Germanic Review* 55:1–8.

Elias, Norbert. 1977. *Über den Prozeß der Zivilisation*. 2 vols. Frankfurt am Main: Suhrkamp.

Ellman, Richard. 1987. *Oscar Wilde*. New York: Random House.

Engen, Rodney K. 1975. *Walter Crane as a Book Illustrator*. London: Academy Editions.

————. 1983. *Laurence Housman*. Stroud, England: Catalpa.

Erickson, Donald H. 1977. *Oscar Wilde*. Boston: Twayne.

Erisman, Fred. 1968. "L. Frank Baum and the Progressive Dilemma." *American Quarterly* 20 (Fall):616–23.

Evans, R. J. 1950. *The Victorian Age 1815–1914*. London: Edward Arnold.

Ewers, Hans-Heino. 1987. "Nachwort." In C. W. Contessa, Friedrich Baron de la Motte Fouqué, and E. T. A. Hoffmann, *Kinder-Märchen*, ed. Hans-Heino Ewers, 327–50. Stuttgart: Reclam.

Field, G. W. 1970. *Hermann Hesse*. New York: Twayne.

Filstrup, Jane Merrill. 1980. "Thirst for Enchanted Views in Ruskin's 'The King of the Golden River.'" *Children's Literature* 8:68–79.

Fisher, Jennifer. 2003. *"Nutcracker" Nation: How an Old World Ballet Became a Christmas Tradition in the New World*. New Haven, Conn.: Yale University Press.

Foucault, Michel. 1978. *Discipline and Punish: The Birth of the Prison*. New York: Pantheon.

Frank, Diane Crone, and Jeffrey Frank. 2001. "A Melancholy Dane." *The New Yorker* January 8:78–84.

———. 2003. "The Real Hans Christian Andersen." In *The Stories of Hans Christian Andersen*, trans. Diane Crone Frank and Jeffrey Frank, 1–36. Boston: Houghton Mifflin.

Freud, Sigmund. 1985. *The 'Uncanny'*. Trans. James Strachey. London: Penguin.

Gallagher, Catherine. 1985. *The Industrial Reformation of English Fiction: Social Discourse and Narrative Form*. Chicago: University of Chicago Press.

Galton, Fancis. 1869. *Hereditary Genius*. London: Macmillan.

Gannon, Susan R. 1980. "A Note on Collodi and Lucian." *Children's Literature* 8:98–192.

———. 1981–82. "Pinocchio: The First Hundred Years." *Children's Literature Association Quarterly* 6 (Winter):I, 5–7.

Gardner, Martin. 1996. "The Tin Woodman of Oz: An Appreciation." *The Baum Bugle* (Fall):14–19.

Gardner, Martin, and Russell B. Nye. 1957. *The Wizard of Oz and Who He Was*. East Lansing, Mich.: Michigan State University Press.

Geduld, Harry M. 1971. *Sir James Barrie*. New York: Twayne.

Gerhardt, Mia A. 1963. *The Art of Story-Telling: A Literary Study of the Thousand and One Nights*. Leiden: Brill.

Gérin, Winifred. 1981. *Anne Thackeray Ritchie*. Oxford: Oxford University Press.

Ghazoul, Ferial J. 1980. *The Arabian Nights: A Structural Analysis*. Cairo: Cairo Associated Institution for the Study and Presentation of Arab Values.

Gilbert, Sandra M., and Susan Gubar. 1979. *The Mad Woman in the Attic: The Woman Writer and the Nineteenth-Century Imagination*. New Haven, Conn.: Yale University Press.

Gilead, Sarah. 1991. "Magic Abjured: Closure in Children's Fantasy Fiction." *PMLA* 106 (March):277–93.

Gilman, Todd. 1995–96. "'Aunt Em: Hate You! Hate Kansas! Taking the Dog. Dorothy': Conscious and Unconscious Desire in *The Wizard of Oz*." *Children's Literature Association Quarterly* 20 (Winter):161–67.

Gobineau, Arthur de. 1852. *Essai sur l'inégalité des races humaines*. 4 vols. Paris: Didot.

Golemba, Henry L. 1981. *Frank Stockton*. Boston: Twayne.

Gougy-François, Marie. 1965. *Les grands salons féminins*. Paris: Nouvelles Editions Debresse.

Green, Roger Lancelyn. 1946. *Andrew Lang. A Critical Biography*. Leicester: Ward.

———. 1946. *Tellers of Tales*. Rev. ed. New York: Franklin Watts.

———. 1954. *Fifty Years of 'Peter Pan.'* London: Peter Davies.

———. 1960. *J. M. Barrie*. London: The Bodley Head.

———. 1960. *Lewis Carroll*. London: The Bodley Head.

———. 1962. *Andrew Lang*. London: The Bodley Head.

Greene, David L., and Dick Martin. 1977. *The Oz Scrapbook*. New York: Random House.

Griffin, Martin I. J. 1965 (1939). *Frank Stockton: A Critical Biography*. Port Washington, N.Y.: Kennikat Press.

Griffith, John. 1979. "Making Wishes Innocent: Peter Pan." *The Lion and the Unicorn* 3(1):28–37.

Griswold, Jerry. 1974. "Sacrifice and Mercy in Wilde's 'The Happy Prince.'" *Children's Literature* 3:103–6.

———. 1992. *Audacious Kids: Coming of Age in America's Classic Children's Books*. Oxford: Oxford University Press.

———. 1987. "There's No Place but Home: *The Wizard of Oz*." *The Antioch Review* 45 (Fall):462–75.

Gronbech, Bo. 1980. *Hans Christian Andersen*. Boston: Twayne.

Grossman, Judith. 1980. "Infidelity and Fiction: The Discovery of Women's Subjectivity in the *Arabian Nights*." *The Georgia Review* 34:113–26.

Harmetz, Haljean. 1978. *The Making of the Wizard of Oz*. New York: Alfred A. Knopf.

Hearn, Michael Patrick, ed. 1973. *The Annotated Wizard of Oz*. New York: Clarkson N. Potter.

———. 1979. "L. Frank Baum and the 'Modernized Fairy Tale.'" *Children's Literature in Education* (Spring):57–66.

———. 1983. Preface. In *The Wizard of Oz*, ed. Michael Hearn, ix–xiv. New York: Schocken.

Heins, Paul. 1982. "A Second Look: *The Adventures of Pinocchio*." *Horn Book Magazine* 58:200–204.

Heintz, Günter. "Mechanik und Phantasie. Zu E. T. A. Hoffmanns Märchen 'Nußknacker und Mausekönig.'" *Literatur in Wissenschaft und Unterricht* 7 (1974):1–15.

Heisig, James W. 1974. "Pinocchio: Archetype of the Motherless Child." *Children's Literature* 3:23–35.

Hemmings, Frederick W. J. 1979. *Alexandre Dumas: The King of Romance*. New York: Scribner's.

Hewett-Thayer, Harvey W. *Hoffmann: Author of the Tales*. Princeton, N.J.: Princeton University Press, 1948.

Heyden-Rynsch, Verena von der. 1992. *Europäische Salons: Höhepunkte einer versunkenen weiblichen Kultur*. Munich: Artemis & Winkler.

Hollindale, Peter. 1991. Introduction. In *Peter Pan in Kensington Gardens and Peter and Wendy*, vii–xxviii. Oxford: Oxford University Press.

Houe, Poul. 2006. "Hans Christian Andersen's Andersen and the Andersen of Others: On Recent Andersen Literature." *Orbis Litterarum* 61(1):53–80.

Hovannisian, Richard G., and Georges Sabagh, eds. 1997. *The Thousand and One Nights in Arabic Literature and Society*. Cambridge: Cambridge University Press.

Howells, William Dean. 1887. "Stockton's Stories." *Atlantic Monthly* 59 (January):130–32.

———. 1897. "A Story-Teller's Pack." *Harper's Weekly* 41 (May 29):538.

———. 1900. "Stockton and His Works." *Book Buyer* 20 (February):19.

———. 1901. "Stockton's Novels and Stories." *Atlantic Monthly* 87 (January):136–38.

Hyde, H. Montgomery. 1976. *Oscar Wilde*. London: Methuen.

Hyde, Lewis. 1983. *The Gift: Imagination and the Erotic Life of Property*. New York: Random House.

Inglis, Fred. 1981. *The Promise of Happiness. Value and Meaning in Children's Fiction*. Cambridge: Cambridge University Press.

Irwin, Robert. 2004. "Political Thought in *The Thousand and One Nights*. *Marvels & Tales* 18(2):246–57.

Jack, Ronald D. S. 1990. "The Manuscript of Peter Pan." *Children's Literature* 18:101–13.

———. 1991. *The Road to the Never Land: An Assessment of J. M. Barrie's Dramatic Art*. Aberdeen: University of Aberdeen Press.

Jan, Isabelle. 1974. *On Children's Literature*. New York: Schocken.

Jones, Glyn W. 1970. *Denmark*. New York: Praeger.

Jones, Michael Wynn. 1978. *George Cruikshank: His Life and London*. London: Macmillan.

Julian, Philippe. 1969. *Oscar Wilde*. London: Constable.

Jung, Carl G. 1968. "The Phenomenology of the Spirit in Fairytales." In *The Archetypes and the Collective Unconscious*, vol. 9 of *The Collected Works of C. G. Jung*. Princeton, N.J.: Princeton University Press.

Kleßmann, Eckart. 1988. *E. T. A. Hoffmann oder die Tiefe zwischen Stern und Erde*. Stuttgart: Deutsche Verlags-Anstalt.

Knoepflmacher, U. C. 1983. "The Balancing of Child and Adult: An Approach to Victorian Fantasies for Children." *Nineteenth-Century Fiction* 37 (March):497–530.

———. 1983. "Little Girls without Their Curls: Female Aggression in Victorian Children's Literature." *Children's Literature* 11:14–31.

———. 1985. "Resisting Growth through Fairy Tale in Ruskin's King of the Golden River." *Children's Literature* 13:3–30.

———. 1998. *Ventures into Childland: Victorians, Fairy Tales, and Femininity.* Chicago: University of Chicago Press.

Koelb, Clayton. 1988. *Inventions of Reading: Rhetoric and the Literary Imagination.* Ithaca, N.Y.: Cornell University Press.

Kolbenschlag, Madonna. 1979. *Kiss Sleeping Beauty Good-bye: Breaking the Spell of Feminine Myths and Models.* New York: Doubleday.

Kotzin, Michael C. 1970. "The Fairy Tale in England, 1800–1870." *Journal of Popular Culture* 4 (Summer):130–54.

———. 1972. *Dickens and the Fairy Tale.* Bowling Green, Ohio: Bowling Green University Popular Press.

Lahy-Hollebecque, Marie. 1927. *Le féminisme de Schéhérazade.* Paris: Radot.

Langstaff, Eleanor De Selms. 1978. *Andrew Lang.* Boston: Twayne.

Laski, Marghanita. 1951. *Mrs. Ewing, Mrs. Molesworth and Mrs. Hodgson Burnett.* New York: Oxford University Press.

Leach, William. 1993. *Land of Desire, Merchants, Power and the Rise of the New American Culture.* New York: Pantheon.

Lerner, Laurence, ed. 1978. *The Victorians.* New York: Holmes & Meier.

Lewis, Naomi. 1978. "J. M. Barrie." In *Twentieth Century Children's Writers,* ed. Daniel Kirkpatrick, 18–35. New York: Macmillan.

Lewis, Philip. 1996. *Seeing Through the Mother Goose Tales: Visual Turnings in the Writings of Charles Perrault.* Stanford, Calif.: Stanford University Press.

Littlefield, Henry M. 1964. "The *Wizard of Oz*: Parable of Populism." *American Quarterly* 16 (Spring):47–58.

Lochhead, Marion. 1956. *Their First Ten Years: Victorian Childhood.* London: John Murray.

———. 1959. *Young Victorians.* London: John Murray.

———. 1977. *The Renaissance of Wonder in Children's Literature.* Edinburgh: Canongate.

Lucas, Ann Lawson. 1996. Introduction. In *The Adventures of Pinocchio.* Trans. Ann Lawson Lucas, vii–li. Oxford: Oxford University Press.

Lüthi, Max. 1970. *Once Upon a Time. On the Nature of Fairy Tales.* Trans. Lee Chadeayne and Paul Gottwald. New York: Ungar.

———. 1975. *Das Volksmärchen als Dichtung.* Cologne: Diederichs.

———. 1982. *The European Folktale: Form and Nature.* Trans. John D. Niles. Philadelphia: Institute for the Study of Human Issues.

———. 1985. *The Fairy Tale as Art Form and Portrait of Man.* Trans. Jon Erickson. Bloomington: Indiana University Press.

Lurie, Alison. 1990. *Don't Tell the Grown-ups: Subversive Children's Literature*. Boston: Little Brown.

Macdonald, D. B. 1932. "A Bibliographical and Literary Study of the First Appearance of the Arabian Nights in Europe." *The Literary Quarterly* 2:387–420.

Mahdi, Muhsin. 1973. "Remarks on the 1001 Nights." *Interpretation* 3 (Winter):157–68.

Manlove, C. N. 1975. *Modern Fantasy*. London: Cambridge University Press.

Marcus, Stephen. 1964. *The Other Victorians: A Study of Sexuality and Pornography in Mid-Nineteenth-Century England*. New York: Basic Books.

Martin, Robert K. 1979. "Oscar Wilde and the Fairy Tale: 'The Happy Prince' as Self-Dramatization." *Studies in Short Fiction* 16:74–77.

Marzolph, Ulrich, ed. 2004. *The Arabian Nights: Past and Present*. Special Issue. *Marvels & Tales* 18:2.

Maurois, André. 1957. *Les Trois Dumas*. Paris: Hachette.

Mauss, Marcel. 1990. *The Gift: The Form and Reason for Exchange in Archaic Societies*. Trans. W. D. Halls. New York: W. W. Norton.

McCord, David. 1978. "L. Frank Baum." In *Twentieth Century Children's Writers*, ed. D. L. Kirkpatrick, 91–93. New York: St. Martin's Press.

Mikhail, E. H. 1978. *Oscar Wilde. An Annotated Bibliography of Criticism*. Totowa, N.J.: Rowman & Littlefield.

Milek, Joseph. 1978. *Hermann Hesse: Life and Art*. Berkeley: University of California Press.

Miller, Patricia. 1982. "The Importance of Being Earnest: The Fairy Tale in Nineteenth-century England." *Children's Literature Quarterly* 7 (Summer):11–14.

Miner, Harold E. 1976. "America in Oz: Conclusion." *The Baum Bugle* 20:7–12.

Moore, Raylyn. 1974. *Wonderful Wizard, Marvelous Land*. Bowling Green, Ohio: Bowling Green University Popular Press.

Morrisey, Thomas J. 1982. "Alive and Well but Not Unscathed: A Response to Susan T. Gannon's *Pinocchio: The First Hundred Years*." *Children's Literature Association Quarterly* 7 (Summer):37–39.

Morrissey, Thomas J., and Richard Wunderlich. 1983. "Death and Rebirth in *Pinocchio*." *Children's Literature* 11:64–75.

Muir, Percy. 1954. *English Children's Books 1600–1900*. New York: Praeger.

Naithani, Sadhana. 2004. "The Teacher and the Taught: Structures and Meaning in the *Arabian Nights* and the *Panchatantra*." *Marvels & Tales* 18(2):272–85.

Nassaar, Christopher S. 1974. *Into the Demon Universe: A Literary Exploration of Oscar Wilde*. New Haven, Conn.: Yale University Press.

Nathanson, Paul. 1991. *Over the Rainbow: The Wizard of Oz as a Secular Myth.* Albany: State University of New York Press.

Orr, H. Allen. 2005. "Devolution: Why Intelligent Design Isn't." *The New Yorker* May 30:40–52.

Perella, Nicolas J. 1986. "An Essay on *Pinocchio.*" In *The Adventures of Pinocchio: Story of a Puppet,* trans. Nicolas J. Perella, 1–69. Berkeley: University of California Press.

Petzold, Dieter. 1918. *Das englische Kunstmärchen im neunzehnten Jahrhundert.* Tübingen: Niemeyer.

Phillips, Robert, ed. 1971. *Aspects of Alice.* New York: Vanguard.

Picard, Roger. 1946. *Les Salons littéraires et la société française 1610–1789.* New York: Brentano's.

Prickett, Stephen. 1979. *Victorian Fantasy.* London: Harvester.

Propp, Vladimir. 1968. *Morphology of the Folktale.* Ed. Louis Wagner and Alan Dundes. 2d rev. ed. Austin: University of Texas Press.

———. 1984. *Theory and History of Folklore.* Trans. Adriana Y. Martin and Richard P. Martin. Ed. Anatoly Liberman. Minneapolis: University of Minnesota Press.

Raby, Peter. 1988. *Oscar Wilde.* Cambridge: Cambridge University Press.

Rahn, Suzanne. 1988. "Life at the Squirrel Inn: Rediscovering Frank Stockton." *The Lion and the Unicorn* 12 (December):224–39.

Reckford, Kenneth. 1988. "Allegiance to Utopia." *The Baum Bugle* 32 (Winter):11–13.

Reis, Richard H. 1972. *George MacDonald.* Boston: Twayne.

Rockoff, Hugh. 1990. "The 'Wizard of Oz' as a Monetary Allegory." *Journal of Political Economy* 98:739–60.

Rodari, Gianni. 1976. "Pinocchio nella letteratura per l'infanzia." In *Studi Collodiani,* 37–57. Pescia: Fondazione Nazionale Carlo Collodi.

Rose, Jacqueline. 1984. *The Case of Peter Pan, or the Impossibility of Children's Fiction.* London: Macmillan; 2d ed. Philadelphia: University of Pennsylvania Press, 1993.

Routh, Chris. 2000. "Peter Pan: Flawed or Fledgling 'Hero'?" In *A Necessary Fantasy? The Heroic Figure in Children's Popular Culture,* 291–307. New York: Routledge.

Rowe, Karen E. 1979. "Feminism and Fairy Tales." *Women's Studies* 6:237–57.

———. 1983. "'Fairy-born and human-bred': Jane Eyre's Education in Romance." In *The Voyage in: Fictions of Female Development,* ed. Elizabeth Abel, Marianne Hirsch, and Elizabeth Langland, 69–89. Hanover: University Press of New England.

Rustin, Michael. 1985. "A Defense of Children's Fiction: Another Reading of Peter Pan." *Free Dissociations* 2:128–48.

Saadawi, Nawal El. 1980. *The Hidden Face of Eve.* London: Zed Press.

Sackett, S. J. 1960. "The Utopia of Oz." *Georgia Review* (Fall):275–90.

Safranski, Rüdiger. 1984. *E. T. A. Hoffmann: Das Leben eines skeptischen Phantasten.* Munich: Hanser.

Sale, Roger. 1978. *Fairy Tales and After: From Snow White to E. B. White.* Cambridge: Harvard University Press.

Sandner, David. 1996. *The Fantastic Sublime: Romanticism and Transcendence in Nineteenth-Century Children's Fantasy Literature.* Westport, Conn.: Greenwood.

Schuman, Samuel. 1973. "Out of the Frying Pan into the Pyre: Comedy, Myth and *The Wizard of Oz.*" *Journal of Popular Culture* (Fall):302–4.

Seifert, Lewis C. 1996. *Fairy Tales, Sexuality, and Gender in France, 1690–1715: Nostalgic Utopias.* Cambridge: Cambridge University Press.

Shewan, Rodney. 1977. *Oscar Wilde.* New York: Barnes and Noble.

Soriano, Marc. 1968. *Les Contes de Perrault. Culture savante et traditions populaires.* Paris: Gallimard.

———. 1972. *Le Dossier Charles Perrault.* Paris: Hachette.

———. 1975. *Guide de littérature pour la jeunesse.* Paris: Flammarion.

St. John, Tom. 1982. "Lyman Frank Baum: Looking Back to the Promised Land." *Western Humanities Review* (Winter):349–60.

Steinecke, Hartmut. 2004. *Die Kunst der Fantasie: E. T. A. Hoffmann's Leben und Werke.* Frankfurt am Main: Insel.

Stockton, Marian. 1899–1904. "A Memorial Sketch of Mr. Stockton." In *The Novels and Stories of Frank Stockton,* vol. 23, 189–206. New York: Scribner's.

Stone, Harry. 1979. *Dickens and the Invisible World: Fairy Tales, Fantasy, and Novel-Making.* Bloomington: University of Indiana Press.

Storer, Mary Elizabeth. 1925. *La Mode des contes de fées 1685–1700.* Paris: Champion.

Stowe, Richard. *Alexandre Dumas.* Boston: Twayne, 1976.

Sullivan, Kevin. 1972. *Oscar Wilde.* New York: Columbia University Press.

Sullivan, Paula. 1978. "Fairy Tale Elements in *Jane Eyre.*" *Journal of Popular Culture* 12:61–74.

Summerfield, Geoffrey. 1984. *Fantasy and Reason. Children's Literature in the Eighteenth Century.* London: Methuen.

Sumpter, Caroline. *Victorian Fairy Tales and the Reinvention of the Fairy Tale.* London: Palgrave. (Forthcoming)

Supple, Barry. 1978. "The Governing Framework: Social Class and Institutional Reform in Victorian Britain." In *The Victorians,* ed. Laurence Lerner, 90–119. New York: Holmes & Meier.

———. 1978. "Material Development: The Condition of England 1830–1860." In *The Victorians,* ed. Laurence Lerner, 49–69. New York: Holmes & Meier.

Sutcliff, Rosemary. 1960. *Rudyard Kipling.* London: The Bodley Head.

Tarr, Carol Anita. 1993. "Shifting Images of Adulthood: From Barrie's Peter Pan to Spielberg's Hook." In *The Antic Art: Enhancing Children's Literary Experiences through Film and Video*, 63–72. Fort Atkinson, Wis.: Highsmith.

Tatar, Maria M. 1987. *The Hard Facts of the Grimms' Fairy Tales*. Princeton, N.J.: Princeton University Press.

———. 1992. *Off with Their Heads: Fairy Tales and the Culture of Childhood*. Princeton, N.J.: Princeton University Press.

Teahan, James. T. 1985. Introduction. In *The Pinocchio of C. Collodi*, trans. James T. Teahan, xv–xxx. New York: Schocken.

———. 1988. "C. Collodi 1826–1890." In *Writers for Children: Critical Studies of Major Authors Since the Seventeenth Century*, ed. Jane M. Bingham, 129–37. New York: Charles Scribner's Sons.

Teschner, Heinrich. 1914. "Hans Christian Andersen und Heinrich Heine: Ihre literarischen und persönlichen Beziehungen." Ph.D. diss. University of Münster: Westfällische Vereinsdruckerei.

Thompson, Stith. 1946. *The Folktale*. New York: Holt, Rinehart & Winston.

Thwaite, Mary F. 1972. *From Primer to Pleasure in Reading: An Introduction to the History of Children's Books in England from the Invention of Printing to 1914*. Boston: Horn.

Vidal, Gore. 1977. "The Wizard of the 'Wizard.'" *The New York Review of Books* 24 (September 29):10–15.

———. 1977. "On Rereading the Oz Books." *The New York Review of Books* 24 (October 13):38–42.

Wagenknecht, Edward. 1929. *Utopia Americana*. Seattle: University of Washington Book Store.

Warner, Marina. 1994. *From the Beast to the Blonde: On Fairytales and Their Tellers*. London: Chatto & Windus.

West, Mark I. 1922. "The Dorothys of Oz: A Heroine's Unmaking." In *Stories and Society: Children's Literature in Its Social Context*, ed. Dennis Butts, 125–31. New York: St. Martin's Press.

Westbrook, M. David. 1996. "Readers of Oz: Young and Old, Old and New Historicist." *Children's Literature Association Quarterly* 21 (Fall):111–19.

Wiley, Roland John. 1985. *Tchaikovsky's Ballets: Swan Lake, Sleeping Beauty, The Nutcracker*. Oxford: Clarendon.

Winnicott, D. W. 1993. "The Location of Cultural Experience." In *Transitional Objects and Potential Spaces: Literary Uses of D. W. Winnicott*, ed. Peter L. Rudnytsky, 3–12. New York: Columbia University Press.

Wittkop-Ménardeau, Gabrielle. 1992 (1966). *E. T. A. Hoffmann: Mit Selbstzeugnissen und Bilddokumenten*. 2nd ed. Reinbek: Rowohlt.

Woodcock, George. 1950. *The Paradox of Oscar Wilde*. London: Boardman.

Worth, Katharine. 1983. *Oscar Wilde*. London: Macmillan.

Wullschlager, Jackie. 1995. *Inventing Wonderland: The Lives and Fantasies of Lewis Carroll, Edward Lear, J. M. Barrie, Kenneth Grahame, and A. A. Milne.* London: Methuen.

———. 2000. *Hans Christian Andersen: The Life of a Storyteller.* London: Penguin.

Wunderlich, Richard. 1988. *The Pinocchio Catalogue.* New York: Greenwood.

———. 1995. "De-Radicalizing *Pinocchio.*" In *Functions of the Fantastic,* ed. Joe Sanders, 19–28. Westport, Conn.: Greenwood Press.

Wunderlich, Richard, and Thomas J. Morrisey. 1982. "The Desecration of *Pinocchio* in the United States." *The Horn Book Magazine* 58 (April):205–12.

———. 1982. "*Pinocchio* Before 1920: The Popular and the Pedagogical Traditions." *Italian Quarterly* 23 (Spring):61–72.

Yolen, Jane. 1981. *Touch Magic: Fantasy, Faerie and Folklore in the Literature of Childhood.* New York: Philomel.

Zago, Ester. 1988. "Carlo Collodi as Translator: From Fairy Tale to Folk Tale." *Lion and Unicorn* 12:61–73.

Ziolkowski, Jan. 2006. *Fairy Tales from Before Fairy Tales: The Medieval Latin Past of Wonderful Lies.* Ann Arbor: University of Michigan Press.

Zipes, Jack. 1979. *Breaking the Magic Spell: Radical Theories of Folk and Fairy Tales.* London: Heinemann.

———. 2006. *Fairy Tales and the Art of Subversion: The Classical Genre for Children and the Process of Civilization.* 2nd ed. New York: Routledge.

———. 1988. *The Brothers Grimm: From Enchanted Forests to the Modern World.* New York: Routledge.

———. 1990. "Negating History and Male Fantasies through Psychoanalytic Criticism." *Children's Literature* 18:141–43.

———. 1994. *Fairy Tale as Myth/Myth as Fairy Tale.* Lexington, Ky.: University Press of Kentucky.

———. 1997. *Happily Ever After: Fairy Tales, Children, and the Culture Industry.* New York: Routledge.

Sources For the Essays In This Book

Spells of Enchantment: An Overview of the History of Fairy Tales. Introduction. In *Spells of Enchantment: The Wondrous Fairy Tales of Western Culture.* New York: Viking, 1991.

The Rise of the French Fairy Tale and the Decline of France. In *Beauties, Beasts, and Enchantment: Classic French Fairy Tales.* New York: New American Library, 1989.

The Splendor of the Arabian Nights. Afterword. In *Arabian Nights: The Marvels and Wonders of the Thousand and One Nights*, adapted from Richard F. Burton's unexpurgated translation. New York: New American Library, 1991.

Once There Were Two Brothers Named Grimm. In *The Complete Fairy Tales of the Brothers Grimm*. New York: Bantam, 1987.

The "Merry" Dance of the Nutcracker: Discovering the World through Fairy Tales. In *The Nutcracker and the Mouse King*. Translated by Joachim Neugroschel. New York: Viking, 2007.

The Hans Christian Andersen We Never Knew. In *The Fairy Tales of Hans Christian Andersen*. Trans. Marte Hult. New York: Barnes and Noble, 2007.

Critical Reflections about Hans Christian Andersen, the Failed Revolutionary. In *Marvels & Tales*. 2007.

The Flowering of the Fairy Tale in Victorian England. In *Victorian Fairy Tales*. New York and London: Methuen, 1987.

Oscar Wilde's Tales of Illumination. Afterword. In *The Complete Fairy Tales of Oscar Wilde*. New York: New American Library, 1990.

Carlo Collodi's *Pinocchio* as Tragic-Comic Fairy Tale. Afterword. In *Pinocchio*. New York: Signet Classic, 1996.

Frank Stockton, American Pioneer of Fairy Tales. Afterword. In *The Fairy Tales of Frank Stockton*. New York: New American Library, 1990.

L. Frank Baum and the Utopian Spirit of Oz. Introduction. In L. Frank Baum, *The Wonderful World of Oz*. New York: Viking, 1997.

Revisiting J. M. Barrie's *Peter and Wendy* and Neverland. In *Peter Pan: Peter Pan and Wendy and Peter Pan in Kensington Gardens*. New York: Penguin Classics, 2004.

Hermann Hesse's Fairy Tales and the Pursuit of Home. Introduction. In *The Fairy Tales of Hermann Hesse*. New York: Bantam Books, 1995.

Index

A

A Barnstormer in Oz, (Farmer), 209
A Bicycle of Cathay, (Stockton), 192
"A Chinese Fairy Tale," (Housman), 162
"A Christmas Tree," (Dickens), 155
Addison, Joseph, influence of *The Thousand and One Nights* on, 64
"A Dream about the Gods," (Hesse), 243, 252
"A Dream Sequence," (Hesse), 253
Adult fairy tales, modern, 26
Agnete and the Merman, (Andersen), 113
A House of Pomegranates, (Wilde), 162, 170
  themes of, 172–173
Aiazzi, Giuseppe, 176
"Aladdin," (Galland), 54
Aladdin motif, 112
Alberi, Eugenio, 177
Alf laylah wa-laylah (A Thousand and One Nights), 56
"Ali Baba," (Galland), 54
"Alice's Adventures in Wonderland," (Carroll), 22

Alice's Adventures in Wonderland, (Carroll), 155
Alienation, themes of in 19th century fairy tales, 21
"All My Doing," (Childe-Pemberton), 161
America
  fairy tale authors (*See* Baum, L. Frank; Stockton, Frank; specific authors)
  magic fairy tales in the nineteenth century, 79
  popularity of *The Nutcracker* ballet in, 86
American Fairy Tales, (Baum), 22, 200
Ancient Cures, Charms, and Usages of Ireland, (Wilde, S.), 169
Ancient Cures, Mystic Charms, and Superstitions, (Wilde, S.), 169
Ancient German Law, (Grimm, Jacob), 70
Andersdatter, Anne Marie, 110
Andersen, Hans, 110
Andersen, Hans Christian, 20, 28, 51, 225, 253
  adaptation of folklore by, 121–122

Agnete and the Merman, 113
anthropomorphization of animals
    and nature in tales of, 124
To Be or Not to Be, 118
biographical information, 110–112
"Clod Hans," 118, 133
critical analysis of tales, 126–142
E.T.A. Hoffmann's influence on,
    99
evangelical and religious tales of,
    123–124
"Everything in Its Proper Place,"
    125
The Fairy Tale of My Life, 127
Fairy Tales Told for Children, 115
"Father's Always Right," 118
"Holger the Dane," 125
humanization of toys and objects
    in tales of, 124–125
"Ib and Little Christine," 123, 133
ideological compromise, 135–137
imitation of German Romantics
    by, 128
interpretation of fairy tales of,
    119–120
legends of, 125–126
"Little Claus and Big Claus," 113,
    128, 141
    influence of on Wilde's "The
        Devoted Friend," 171
"Little Ida's Flowers," 113, 129
Love at St. Nicholas Tower, 112
Lucky Peter, 118
The Moorish Maiden, 115
The Mulatto, A Comedy in Green,
    113
Only a Fiddler, 113
original fairy tales of, 122–123
O.T. Life in Denmark, 113

revolutionary approach to fairy
    tales for children, 129–130
Schräge Märchen, 137
schräg quality of tales, 137–142
Shadow Pictures, 113
social Darwinism, 124
"The Bronze Pig," 123, 133
"The Dung Beetle," 124
"The Emperor's New Clothes,"
    113, 122, 128, 141
"The Gardener and the Gentry,"
    118, 120–121, 136
"The Girl Who Stepped on
    Bread," 124
"The Ice Maiden," 133
"The Little Match Girl," 124
"The Little Mermaid," 113, 119,
    122, 133
    influence of on Wilde's "The
        Fisherman and His Soul,"
        172
    influence of *Undine* on,
        128–129
themes in tales of
    intelligent design, 131–132
    patronage and society, 120–121
    religious, 121–122, 123–124,
        131–135
"The Naughty Boy," 113, 123, 129,
    141
"The Nightingale," 116, 119, 135
"The Princess on the Pea," 113,
    121, 128
"The Red Shoes," 20, 123, 134
"The Shadow," 21, 116, 122,
    140–141
"The Shepherdess and the
    Chimney Sweep," 125
"The Snow Queen," 116, 123, 133

"The Spruce Tree," 124
"The Steadfast Tin Soldier," 124
"The Swineherd," 122, 133, 141
"The Tinderbox," 121, 128, 135
    importance of, 113
"The Traveling Companion," 121,
    128, 132
"The Ugly Duckling," 20, 116, 119
"The Writer," 139
"Thumbelina," 113, 128
treatment of female characters by,
    134
The True Story of My Life, 116
The Two Baronesses, 116
A Walking Tour from the Holmen
    Canal to the Eastern Point of
    Amager, 112
Wonderful Stories for Children, 149
Andersen, Jens, 112
Anderson, Graham, *Fairytale in the*
    Ancient World, 2
"Anguillette," (de Murat), 45
An Hour after Midnight, (Hesse), 241
Ansell, Mary, 225–227
Anthony, Susan B., 197
Antifeminist themes, Oz critiques
    and, 207
Anyhow Stories, (Clifford), 157
Apollinaire, "Cinderella Continued,"
    23
"Apologie des femmes," (Perrault), 39
A Princess of Thule, (Black), 197
Apuleius, "Cupid and Psyche," 8
Arab culture, 54
Arabian Nights, 54
    (Lane), 149
Arabic fairy tales
    Alf laylah wa-laylah (A Thousand
        and One Nights), 56
    editions of *The Book of the*
        Thousand Nights and a
        Night, 56
    influence on 18th century
        Western writers, 15–16
Arendt, Hannah, 24
Arthur, Jean, 219
Art tales, 19
A Slice of Life, (Barrie), 226
Asquith, Lady Cynthia, 232
A Story-Teller's Pack, (Stockton), 187
"A Thousand and One Follies,"
    (Cazotte), 17
"A Toy Princess," (De Morgan),
    160–161
Attic Press, 25
Atwood, Margaret, 25, 51
"Augustus," (Hesse), 251
Auld Licht Idylls, (Barrie), 224
Aunt Jane's Nieces, (Baum), 203
Aunt Jane's Nieces Abroad, (Baum),
    203
A Walking Tour from the Holmen
    Canal to the Eastern Point of
    Amager, (Andersen), 112
A Window in Thrums, (Barrie), 224

B

Baader, Renate, *Dames de Lettres*, 34
Bachmann, Ingeborg, "The Smile of
    the Sphinx," 24
Balanchine, George, 86
"Barak and His Wives," (Jokai), 21
Barrie, Alec, 222, 232
Barrie, David, 221–223

Barrie, David (son of David and
  Margaret), 222
Barrie, James Matthew
  The Admirable Crichton, 226
  Auld Licht Idylls, 224
  biographical information, 221–223
  The Boy Castaways of Blacklake
    Island, 228, 233
  The Boy David, 232
  early writings, 224
  Little Mary, 226
  The Little Minister, 224
  The Little White Bird, 226, 228
  Margaret Olgilvy, 224
  Mary Rose, 232
  meanings ascribed to Peter Pan,
    220–221
  Peter and Wendy, 219, 230
    analysis of, 233–238
  Peter Pan in Kensington Gardens,
    219, 226, 233
  Peter Pan, or The Boy Who
    Wouldn't Grow Up, 219, 233
  Quality Street, 226
  Sentimental Tommy, 225
  A Slice of Life, 226
  "The Blot on Peter Pan," 233
  Tommy and Grizel, 225
  Walker, London, 225
  What Every Woman Knows, 226,
    230
  A Window in Thrums, 224
Barrie, Jane Ann, 223
Bartheleme, Donald, 25
Barth, John, influence of The
    Thousand and One Nights
    on, 64
Basile, Giambattista, 37
  Lo Cunto de li cunti, 9

The Pentameron, 9, 33
  Burton's translation of, 57
  "The Merchant's Two Sons," 11
Batehord, Robert, 159
Baum, Benjamin Ward, 196
Baum, Frank Joslyn, 197
Baum, Harry, 196
Baum, Kenneth Gage, 199
Baum, L. Frank, 194, 200, 221. See
    also Oz
  American Fairy Tales, 22, 200
  Aunt Jane's Nieces, 203
  Aunt Jane's Nieces Abroad, 203
  biographical information,
    196–204
  Dorothy and the Wizard of Oz, 203
  Dot and Tot of Merryland, 200
  The Emerald City of Oz, 203
  The Enchanted Island of Yew, 200
  Fairylogue and Radio Plays, 203
  The Fate of a Crown, 203
  Father Goose, 199
    theatrical adaptation of, 202
  financial misfortunes of, 198–199,
    203–204
  Glinda of Oz, 204
  The King of Gee Whiz, 203
  The Life and Adventures of Santa
    Claus, 200
  The Lost Princess of Oz, 204
  The Magic of Oz, 204
  The Maid of Arran, 197
  The Maid of Athens, 202
  The Marvelous Land of Oz, 200,
    202
  Mother Goose in Prose, 199
  motifs of Oz books (See specific
    titles)
  My Candelabra's Glaze, 199

newspaper work, 198–199
Ozma of Oz, 203
The Patchwork Girl of Oz, 204
Queen Zixi of Iz, 203
"Queer Visitors from the
    Marvelous Land of Oz," 202
Rinkitink in Oz, 204
The Road to Oz, 203
*Sam Steele's Adventures on Land
    and Seas*, 203
The Scarecrow of Oz, 204
The Sea Fairies, 204
Search for Montague, 202
The Show Window, 199
Sky Island, 204
socialist and utopian themes of
    Oz books, 215–217 (*See also*
    utopia)
theatrical writings of, 197, 200,
    202–204
"The Queen of Quok," 22
The Tik-Tok Man of Oz, 204
Tik-Tok of Oz, 204
The Tin Woodman of Oz, 204
The Woggle-Bug Book, 202
The Woggle-Bug (Play), 202
The Wonderful Wizard of Oz, 22,
    195, 199
Baum, Robert Stanton, 198
Beast, (Napoli), 30
"Beauty and the Beast," 15, 19, 45,
    149
    (de Villeneuve), 48
    Disney, 28
    (Leprince de Beaumont), 17, 50
    musical productions of, 27
    television series, 27
Bechstein, Ludwig, 21

*Deutsches Märchenbuch (German
    Book of Fairy Tales)*, 79
Beckford, William, influence of *The
    Thousand and One Nights*
    on, 64
Belz, Josephine, *Das Märchen und
    die Phantasie des Kindes
    (The Fairy Tale and the
    Imagination of the Child)*, 81
Bender, Aimee, 25
Bernard, Catherine, 44
    Inès de Cordoue, 41
    "Ricky with the Tuft," 41
    cruelty in, 45
Bernoulli, Maria, 242
Bettelheim, Bruno, 1
Bible, 2
Bibliothèque Bleue, 16, 50
Bibliothèque orientale, (d'Herbelot),
    54
Bignon, Abbé Jean-Paul, *Les
    Aventures d'Abdalla, fils
    d'Anif*, 47
Bignon, Jean-Paul, *The Adventures of
    Abdalah, Son of Anif*, 16
Bildungsroman, 180
Black Swan, White Raven, 26
Black Thorn, White Rose, 26
Black, William, *A Princess of Thule*,
    197
Blake, William, 146
Bland, Hubert, 164
Blaue Bibliothek, 18
Block, Francesca Lia, 25
"Blue Beard," 15
    (Perrault), 13, 39
"Bluebeard's Daughter," (Warner), 25
"Bluebeard's Ghost," (Thackeray), 21
Bluebeard's Keys, (Ritchie), 157

Bluebell in Fairyland, 228
Bly, Robert, *Iron John*, 26
Boccaccio, Giovanni, *The
    Decameron*, 9
Boileau, Nicolas, 39
    "Quarrel of the Ancients and
        Moderns," 37
Bolger, Ray, 209
Borges, Jorge Luis, influence of *The
    Thousand and One Nights*
    on, 64
Börne, Ludwig, 71
Boucicault, Nina, 229
Brecht, Bertolt, 23
Brentano, Clemens, 18, 95, 98
    *Des Knaben Wunderhorn (The
        Boy's Magic Horn)*, 73
Breslau edition of A Thousand and
    One Nights, 56
Briar Rose, (Coover), 25
Bright, Matthew, *Freeway*, 28
Broumas, Olga, 25
Browne, Frances, *Granny's Wonderful
    Chair*, 152
"Bruno's Revenge," (Carroll), 156
Brutality, 45
Büchner, Georg, 71
Bulak edition of A Thousand and
    One Nights, 56
Bürger, Christa, 82
Burton, Richard
    biographical history of, 56–57
    *The Book of the Thousand Nights
        and a Night*, 56
    The Kasidah, 57
    Kuma Sutra of Vatsyayana, 57
    *Pilgrimage to El-Medinah and
        Mecca*, 57

*Sindh, and the Races that Inhabit
    the Valley of the Indus*, 57
    travels of, 57
Byatt, A.S., 25, 51
Byron, Lord George Gordon, 146

C

Calcutta I edition of A Thousand
    and One Nights, 56
Calcutta II edition of A Thousand
    and One Nights, 56
Calvinism, effect of on literary fairy
    tales in England, 144
Calvino, Italo
    Fiabe Italiane, 24
    Italian Folktales, 179
    "The Florentine," 179
Campbell, Joseph, psychoanalytical
    interpretations of fairy tales
    by, 82
Canada, modern fairy tale authors,
    25
Canonized fairy tales, 21
Carlyle, Thomas
    Condition of England Debate, 147
    German Romances, 149
    Sartor Resartus, 149
Carpenter, Humphrey, *Secret
    Gardens*, 159
Carroll, Lewis, 153, 155–156, 164, 168
    Alice's Adventures in Wonderland,
        22, 155, 179
    "Bruno's Revenge," 156
    "Sylvie and Bruno," 156
    Through the Looking Glass, 155
    utopian writings of, 158

Carter, Angela, 25, 28, 51
Cazotte, Jacques, influence of *The
    Thousand and One Nights*
    on, 64
Cazotte, Jean-Jacques, "A Thousand
    and One Follies," 17
Chamisso, Adelbert von, 18, 95, 98,
    113, 149
    comparison of Andersen's tales
        with those of, 129
    Peter Schlemihl, 122, 140
        influence of on Wilde's "The
            Fisherman and His Soul,"
            172
Chapbooks, 16, 19, 50
Chaucer, Geoffrey, 143
    The Canterbury Tales, 12
Child and the Tale, (Favat), 82
Childe-Pemberton, Harriet
    "All My Doing," 161
    The Fairy Tales of Every Day, 157
Children
    comic and conventional fairy
        tales for, 47
    educational use of fairy tales for,
        50
    fairy tales for
        bourgeois attitudes toward, 20
        changes made to, 78
        17th and 18th century
            England, 145
        18th century, 16
        19th century, 19
    literary fairy tales for, 48
    parenting of by the bourgeoisie,
        100
    socialization of, 180–185
    19th century English fairy tales
        for, 149–150

Children's and Household Tales,
    (Grimm), 18, 69
Children's Fairy Tales, (Hoffmann),
    95
Christianity
    effect of on literary fairy tales in
        17th century England, 144
    effect of on literary fairy tales in
        19th century England, 152
    fairy tales and, 15
    materialism of, 163–164
    morality of, 83 (*See also* Protestant
        ethic)
    motifs of in Andersen's fairy tales,
        123–124
    oral folks tales and, 8
Christiansen, William, 86
Christian socialism, 160
Christmas Books, (Dickens), 154
Christmas-Tree Land, (Molesworth),
    157
"Cinderella," 15, 19
    Ever After, 28
    (Grimm), 18, 78
        moral lessons of, 81
    musical productions of, 27
    (Perrault), 13, 39
    (Ritchie), 161
"Cinderella Continued,"
    (Apollinaire), 23
Cinderella on the Ball, 25
Civilité, 13, 48
Civilizing process, 16, 21
Clarion, 159
Clifford, Lucy Lane, *Anyhow Stories*,
    157
"Clod Hans," (Andersen), 118
    religious motifs in, 133
Coleridge, Hartley, 146

Coleridge, Samuel, 146
    influence of *The Thousand and
        One Nights* on, 64
Collin, Edvard, 115, 119, 140
Collin, Jonas, 111, 115
Collodi, Carlo, 21
    biographical information, 176–178
    early political writings of, 176
    Giannettino, 177
    The Grammar of Little Johnnie, 178
    *Il signor Alberi ha ragione! Dialogo
        apologetico*, 177
    I raconti delle fate, 177
    Little Johnnie, 177
    Little Johnnie's Book of Arithmetic,
        178
    Little Johnnie's Geography, 178
    *Little Johnnie's Travels through
        Italy*, 177
    Pinocchio, 178
Colporteurs, 16
Comic fairy tales, 47–51
Commodity relations in Oz books,
    206
Condition of England Debate,
    146–147
Conte de fée, 13, 36. *See also* fairy
    tales
Conte merveilleux, 3
Contes de fées, (de Murat), 41
Contes moins contes que les autres,
    (de Prechac), 41
*Contes orientaux tirés des manuscrits
    de la bibliothèque du roi de
    France*, (de Caylus), 47
Contessa, Carl Wilhelm Salice, 95,
    99
Conventional fairy tales, 47–51
Conventionalism, 157–158

"Conversation with an Oven,"
    (Hesse), 253
Coover, Robert
    Briar Rose, 25
    "The Dead Queen," 25
Coppard, A.E., 24
Coppélia, (Delibes), 23
Corneille, *Psyché*, 37
Cornhill Magazine, 159
Craik, Dinah Mulock, *The Fairy
    Book*, 157
Crane, Walter, 164
Crébilon fils, influence of *The
    Thousand and One Nights*
    on, 64
Critics
    educators, 81
    literary, 82
    psychoanalytical, 81
"Cross Purposes," (MacDonald), 156,
    160
Crowley, John, 26
Crowquill, Alfred, 21
    Crowquill's Fairy Book, 150
    The Giant Hands, 152
Crowquill's Fairy Book, (Crowquill),
    150
Cruelty, 45
Cruikshank, George, 20, 21, 148, 154
Culver, Stuart, 210, 212
    "Growing Up in Oz," 207
    "What Manikins Want: The
        Wonderful Wizard of Oz and
        *The Art of Decorating Dry
        Goods Windows*," 206
"Cupid and Psyche," (Apuleius), 8, 13

D

Dames de Lettres, (Baader), 34
Das Märchen und die Phantasie des
    Kindes, (Belz), 81
Datlow, Ellen, 26
D'Aulnoy, Marie-Catherine, 16, 37,
    39, 41, 48, 145, 148, 177
"Green Serpent," 13
    violence in, 44
Histoire d'Hippolyte, comte de
    Duglas, 12, 41
Les Contes des fées, 41
"The Discreet Princess," cruelty
    in, 45
"The Island of Happiness," 12, 42
"The Ram," violence in, 44
    violence in tales of, 44
D'Auneuil, Louise, La Tyrannie des
    fées détruite, 41
Davenport, Tom, 28
Davies, Arthur, 227, 230
Dealings with the Fairies,
    (MacDonald), 156
De Caylus, Anne-Claude-Philippe
Contes orientaux tirés des
    manuscrits de la bibliothèque
    du roi de France, 47
Féerie novelles, 47
De Chatelain, Clara, The Silver
    Swan, 152
De La Croix, Pétis
L'Histoire de la Sultane de Perse et
    des Visirs. Contes turcs, 47
The Thousand and One Days, 47
De Lafayette, Mme., 35
De la Force, Charlotte-Rose, 43, 145

"Fairer than a Fairy," cruelty in,
    45
Les Contes des Contes, 41
"Parslinette," 13
"The Good Woman," cruelty in,
    45
De la Motte Fouqué, Friedrich, 18,
    95, 99
comparison of Andersen's tales
    with those of, 129
Undine, 94, 122, 148
Delibes, Léo, Coppélia, 23
De Mailly, Chevallier, 43
Les Illustres Fées, contes galans, 41
"The Queen of the Island of
    Flowers," 45
Demian, (Hesse), 244
De Montpensier, Mlle., 35
De Morgan, Mary, 164
"A Toy Princess," 160–161
depiction of female protagonists
    by, 160–161
"The Heart of Princess Joan," 161
"The Necklace of Princess
    Fiormonde," 161
"The Three Clever Kings," 22
"Three Clever Kings," 161
utopian writings of, 158
De Murat, Henriette-Julie, 37, 44
"Anguillette," cruelty in, 45
Contes de fées, 41
Histoires sublimes et allégoriques,
    41
"Perfect Love," cruelty in, 45
"The Palace of Revenge," cruelty
    in, 45
Denecke, Ludwig, 82
Denslow, W.W., 199, 208
Oz books by, 202

De Prechac, Sieur, *Contes moins contes que les autres*, 41

De Quincey, Thomas, influence of *The Thousand and One Nights* on, 64

"Der Doppeltgänger," (Hoffmann), 140

"Derido; or, the Giant's Quilt," (Stockton), 192

"Der Nußknacker und der Mausekönig," (Hoffmann), 85

De Scudéry, Madeleine, 35

De Ségur, Comtesse Sophie, 21

De Sévigné, Marie, 35

Des Knaben Wunderhorn, (Brentano), 73

Deutsches Märchenbuch, (Bechstein), 79

De Villeneuve, Gabrielle, "Beauty and the Beast," 48

Devrient, Ludwig, 95

D'Herbelot, Barthélemy, *Bibliothèque orientale*, 54

Diab, Youhenna, 16

Diab, Youhenna (Hanna), 53

Dickens, Charles, 118, 154–155, 159, 164

"A Christmas Tree," 155

Christmas Books, 154

The Christmas Carol, 86

Condition of England Debate, 147

Holiday Romance, "The Magic Fishbone," 155

Household Words, "Frauds on Fairies," 154

influence of on L. Frank Baum, 196

"Prince Bull," 154

"The Thousand and One Humbugs," 154

Dick, Philip K., "The King of the Elves," 24

Diderot, Denis, influence of *The Thousand and One Nights* on, 64

Disney

cinematic fairy tales, 28, 142, 175

commercialization of fairy tales by, 26

Divertissement, 17

Döblin, Alfred, 23

"Doctor Knoelge's End," (Hesse), 251

Dodge, Mary Mapes, *Hans Brinker, or the Silver Skates*, 190

Doerffer, Johann Ludwig, 92

Doerffer, Luisa Albertine, 91

Doerffer, Minna, 92

Dolbin, Ninon, 245

"Donkey Skin," (Perrault), 13, 38, 45

Donoghue, Emma, 25

Kissing the Witch: Old Tales in New Skins, 30

Doppelgänger motif, 21

Dorothy and the Wizard of Oz, (Baum), 203

Dot and Tot of Merryland, (Baum), 200

Doyle, Arthur Conan, 226

Dream sequences, 48

Dreamworks, *Shrek* films, 29

Drean, Emily, 187

Drennan, G.D., *Peter Pan, His Book, His Pictures, His Career, His Friends*, 233

Dschinnistan, (Wieland), 18

Dumas, Alexandre

The Count of Monte Cristo, 104

"L'histoire d'un casse-noisette," 85

The Man in the Iron Mask, 104

"The Story of a Nutcracker," 85, 103–106

"The Woman with the Velvet Necklace," 104

The Three Musketeers, 104

Du Maurier, George, 227

Du Maurier, Gerald, 227

Dunsany, Lord, 24

Durand, Catherine, *Les Petits Soupers de l'été de l'année*, 41

Duvall, Shelley, *Faerie Tale Theatre*, 26

E

Educational critics, 81

Educational uses of fairy tales

Collodi's reworking of Parravinci Little Johnnie tales, 178

Grimms' tales, 79, 81

Mme. Leprince de Beaumont, 50

Peter Pan, 238

Elitism, themes of in Disney cinematic fairy tales, 28

Ende, Michael, 25, 51

"Enemies of the Enlightenment," 145, 150, 159–160, 165

England

literary fairy tales in, 12

modern fairy tale authors, 25

role of women in 19th century fairy tales, 160–161

suppression of the literary fairy tale in the 17th century, 144

17th century, 144–145

19th century

conventional fairy tale writers, 157–158

utopian fairy tale writers, 158–160

Victorian, 146

Enlightenment, 146

Eros and Civilization, (Marcuse), 237

Estés, Clarissa Pinkola, *Women Who Run with the Wolves*, 26

E.T., similarities to Hoffmann's "The Strange Child," 103

Europäische Salons, (von der Heyden-Rynsch), 34

Europe

effect of Oriental literature on fairy tales of, 54

fairy-tale themes in 19th century musical world, 23

magic fairy tales in the nineteenth century, 79

European magic realism, 98

Ever After, 28

"Everything in Its Proper Place," (Andersen), 125

Ewing, Juliana Horatia, 153, 164

depiction of female protagonists by, 160–161

"The Ogre Courting," 161

utopian writings of, 159

Exchange value, 207

F

Fabian movement, 160, 163–164, 170

Faerie Tale Theatre, Duvall, Shelley, 26

"Fairer than a Fairy," (de la Force), 45

Fairies, role of in 19th century British fairy tales, 157–158

Fairy and Folk Tales of the Irish Peasantry, (Yeats), 169

Fairylogue and Radio Plays, (Baum), 203

Fairy Realm, (Hood), 157

Fairy-tale discourse, 18

Fairytale in the Ancient World, (Anderson), 3

Fairy tales. *See also* literary fairy tales; oral fairy tales

  acceptance of in 19th century England, 150

  adult, 26

  alienation, 21

  American, 22

  canonized, 21

  Christianity and, 15

  Cold War influence, 24

  comic and conventional, 47–51

  commercialization of, 26

  definition of, 7

  dream sequences in, 48

  early evidence of, 8

  educational use of, 50

    Grimms' tales, 79

  fascist, 24

  gender roles in, 25

  influence of wars on, 23

  institutionalization of, 13, 18, 37

    20th century, 22

  "Jack tales," 179–180

  magic, 79

  musical expression of themes, 23

  narrative structure of, 11

Oriental, 46–47

  burlesques of, 48

  effect of on literary fairy tales in Europe and North America, 54

  for profit, 158

  romantic, 19

  17th century, 12

  19th century, 20

  20th century, 22

  vernacular use, 9

  Victorian writers, 153

    social criticism used by, 159

Fairy Tales from Before Fairy Tales, (Ziolkowski), 3

Fairy Tales of All Nations, (Montalba), 149

Fairy Tales Told for Children, (Andersen), 115

Fantasy Pieces, (Hoffmann), 95

Farmer, Philip José, *A Barnstormer in Oz*, 209

Fascist fairy tales, 24

Father Goose, (Baum), 199

  theatrical adaptation of, 202

"Father's Always Right," (Andersen), 118

Favat, André, *Child and the Tale*, 82

Féerie novelles, (de Caylus), 47

Femininity

  conceptual differences of by British authors, 153

  19th century British fairy tales, 160–161

Fénelon, 16

Fiabe Italiane, (Calvino), 24

Fielding, Sarah, *The Governess, or Little Female Academy*, 17, 147

Film, fairy tales and, 28

Fisher, Jennifer, "Nutcracker" Nation, 85

Fitzgerald, Captain Hugh. *See* Baum, L. Frank

"Five Men and a Swan," (Mitchison), 25

Five Old Friends and a Young Prince, (Ritchie), 157

"Fleur d'Epine," (Hamilton), 48

Fleutiaux, Pierrette, 25

"Flute Dream," (Hesse), 251

Folklorists, categorization of Grimms' tales by, 79

Folk tales
history of, 2
Middle Ages, Great Britain, 143
nature and meaning of, 6
oral, transformation of, 37

Fouqué. *See* de la Motte Fouqué, Friedrich

Frame narrative, 9
literary fairy tales and, 8
use of by Mme. Leprince de Beaumont, 17

France
fairy tales
institutionalization of, 18
17th century writers, 13
themes of, 37
violent themes in, 44
folk tales through the 16th century, 34
function of literary fairy tale in, 17
modern fairy tale authors, 25
rise of fairy tales in, 12

"Frauds on Fairies," (Dickens), 154

Freeway, 28

French Revolution, 19

Freud, Sigmund, 170
"The Uncanny," 105

Friends and Foes from Fairy Land, (Knatchbull-Hugessen), 157

Frohman, Charles, 229, 232

Fromm, Erich, psychoanalytical interpretations of fairy tales by, 82

Furnivall, Frederick James, 164

G

Gage, Matilda Joslyn, 197

Gage, Maud, 197

Gallagher, Catherine, *The Industrial Reformation of English Fiction 1832–1867,* 147

Galland, Antoine, 15
"Aladdin," 54
"Ali Baba," 54
Paroles remarkables, bons mots et maximes des Orientaux, 53
"Prince Ahmed and His Two Sisters," 54
"Prince Ahmed and the Fairy Pari-Banou," 15, 54
"The Voyages of Sinbad," 54
The Thousand and One Nights, 13, 46, 53

Garibaldi, Giuseppe, 177

Garland, Judy, 209

Garner, James, *Politically Correct Bedtime Stories,* 26

Gatty, Mrs. Alfred, *The Fairy Godmothers and Other Tales,* 150

Gender roles in fairy tales, 25, 160–161

German Book of Fairy Tales, (Bechstein), 79

German Dictionary, (Grimm), 71

German Grammar, (Grimm, Jacob), 70

German Legends, (Grimm), 69

German Popular Stories, (Taylor), 20, 148

German Precedents, (Grimm, Jacob), 72

German Romances, (Carlyle), 149

German Romantics, 19
   imitation of by Andersen, 128
   influence of on Hermann Hesse, 250

Germany
   development of the literary fairy tale in, 18
   modern fairy tale authors, 25
   politicization of fairy tales in, 24

Gertrud, (Hesse), 242

Gesta Romanorum, 8

Gift economy, portrayal of in Oz books, 211

Ginori, Marquis Lorenzo, 176

Girls
   treatment of female figures in Andersen's tales, 134
   use of fairy tales to instruct, 50

Glinda of Oz, (Baum), 204
   use of magic in, 217

Goethe, Johann Wolfgang, 51, 89
   "Das Märchen," 149
   "The Fairy Tale," 19

Goldstein, Lisa, 26

Gougy-Francois, Marie, Les grands salons feménins, 34

Gracie, the Pixie of the Puddle, (Napoli), 30

Graf, Oskar Maria, 23

Grahame, Kenneth, 164
   "The Reluctant Dragon," 162
   utopian writings of, 159

Granny's Wonderful Chair, (Browne), 152

Grass, Günter, 25

Grateful dead motif, 121

Great Britain. See also England
   modern fairy tale authors, 25

Greece, classical literature of, 46

Greek myths, 2

"Green Serpent," (d'Aulnoy), 13, 44

Grétry, André-Ernest Modeste, Zémire et Azore, 23

Grimm, Carl Friedrich, 66

Grimm, Charlotte Amalie, 66

Grimm, Dorothea Zimmer, 66

Grimm, Ferdinand Philipp, 66

Grimm, Jacob
   Ancient German Law, 70
   German Grammar, 70
   German Precedents, 72
   The History of the German Language, 71
   Irish Elf Tales, 70
   On the Old German Meistergesang, 69

Grimm, Jacob and Wilhelm, 28, 51
   adaptation of tales of by Andersen, 121
   biographical information, 66–72
   categorization of tales of, 79
   changes in tales of over time, 76
   Children's and Household Tales, 69
   incorporation of childlike tone in second edition, 129

success of, 79

"Cinderella," 78

   moral lessons of, 81

comparison of Andersen's tales
   with those of, 129

critical interpretations of stories
   of, 79–84

editing styles of, 75

German Dictionary, 71

German Legends, 69

Grosse Ausgabe (Large Edition), 78

influence of French literary fairy
   tales on, 18

interpretation of tales of in early
   20th century, 81

Kinder- und Hausmärchen, 18, 69

"King Thrushbeard," influence
   of "Prince Behram and the
   Princess Al-Datma" on, 63

Kleine Ausgabe (Small Edition), 78

"Little Farmer," 128

"Little Red Riding Hood," 78

   moral lessons of, 81

magical themes in stories of,
   79–84

"Mother Trudy," 78

Ölenberg manuscripts, 74

origin of tales of, 73

political idealism of, 69

psychological impact of tales, 81

"Rapunzel," 77

"Sleeping Beauty," 78

"Snow White," 76, 78

   moral lessons of, 81

Song of Hildebrand, 69

targeting of fairy tales toward
   children by, 20

"The Blue Light," 121, 128

"The Frog King," 78

"The Little Farmer," 121

"The Stubborn Child," 78

"The Three Spinners," 77

"The Wolf and the Seven Young
   Kids," moral lessons of, 81

"Thumbling's Travels," 128

violence in tales of, 44

Wessobrunner Prayer, 69

Grimm, Ludwig Emil, 66

Grimm, Philipp Wilhelm, 66

Grimm, Wilhelm

   The German Heroic Legend, 70

   Old Danish Heroic Songs, 69

Gripari, Pierre, 25

"Griseldis," (Perrault), 39

"Growing Up in Oz," (Culver), 207

Guellette, Thomas Simon, influence
   of *The Thousand and One
   Nights* on, 64

Gundert, Hermann, 240

H

Haddawy, Hussain

   The Arabian Nights, 59

   The Arabian Nights II, 59

Haley, Jack, 209

Hamilton, Antoine

   "Fleur d'Epine," 48

   influence of *The Thousand and
   One Thousand Nights* on, 64

   "Les Quatre Facardins," 48

Hanley, Catherine, 187

Hans Brinker, or the Silver Skates,
   (Dodge), 190

*Hans Christian Andersen: A New
   Life*, (Andersen, J.), 112

Hänsel and Gretel, (Humperdinck),
   23
"Hans My Hedgehog," 9
Hardie, Keir, 159
Hardy, Thomas, 226
Haroun and the Sea of Stories,
   (Rushdie), 29
Harris, John
   The Court of Oberon; or, The
      Temple of Fairies, 148
   Mother Bunch's Fairy Tales, 148
Hassenpflug, 70
Hassenpflug family, 73
Hatt, Cora (Dora), 92
Hauff, Wilhelm, 149
   influence of *The Thousand and*
      One Nights on, 64
   Märchen Almanach, 20
   "The Story of Little Muck," 20
Hawthorne, Nathaniel, "Mosses
   from an Old Manse," 21
Heine, Heinrich, 71, 137
Henson, Jim, 28
Herford, O., *The Peter Pan Alphabet
   Book*, 233
Hesse, Bruno, 242
Hesse, Heiner, 242
Hesse, Hermann
   "A Dream about the Gods," 243,
      252
   "A Dream Sequence," 253
   An Hour after Midnight, 241
   "Augustus," 251
   biographical history, 240–248
   "Conversation with an Oven,"
      253
   Demian, 244
   "Doctor Knoelge's End," 251
   early literary work of, 241–242

"Flute Dream," 251
Gertrud, 242
The Glass Bead Game, 245
   art and education motifs in,
      247
"If the War Continues," 243, 252
"Inside and Outside," 253
"Iris," 251
Journey to the East, 245
Lulu, 250
Narcissus and Goldmund, 245
Neighbors, 242
"Oh, Friends Not These Tones!",
   243
Oriental influences, 249
Out of India, 243
pacifist writings of, 243–244, 252
Peter Camenzind, 242
portrayal of women by, 251
*The Posthumous Writings and
   Poems of Hermann Lauscher*,
   241, 250
postwar essays, 247–248
Romantic Songs, 241
Rosshalde, 243
"Shadow Play," 251
Steppenwolf, 245
"Strange News from Another
   Planet," 23, 243, 252
"The Beautiful Dream," 251
"The Difficult Path," 251
"The Dwarf," 251
"The European," 243, 252
"The Forest Dweller," 23, 251
theme of the artist in society, 244,
   246–248, 251
"The Painter," 251
"The Poet," 251
"The Three Linden Trees," 253

"The Two Brothers," 249
This Side, 242
Underway, 242
War and Peace, 247
Under the Wheel, 242
Zarathustra's Return, 244
Hesse, Johannes, 240
Hessel, Franz, 23
Hesse, Marie, 240
Hesse, Martin, 242
Hezâr afsân (A Thousand Stories), 56
"Hinzelmeier," (Storm), 21
Hippel, Theodor, 91–93, 97
Histoire de Mélusine, (Nodot), 41
Histoire d'Hippolyte, comte de Duglas,
  (d'Aulnoy), 12, 41
Histoires ou contes du temps passé
  original publication of, 40
  (Perrault), 13, 38, 41
Histoires sublimes et allégoriques, (de
  Murat), 41
History of Woman Suffrage, 197
Hitzig, Julius, 88, 93–95, 97, 98–99
Hoernle, Edwin, 23
Hoffmann, Cäcilia, 93–94
Hoffmann, Christoph Ludwig, 91
Hoffmann, E.T.A., 18, 48, 149
  biographical history of, 91–97
  Children's Fairy Tales, 95
  comparison of Andersen's tales
    with those of, 129
  "Der Doppelgänger," 140
  The Devil's Elixirs, 95
  doppelgänger motif of, 21
  Fantasy Pieces, 95
  importance of imagination in
    writings of, 97–103
  influence of on Hans Christian
    Andersen, 112, 122–123

influence of on Hermann Hesse,
  241, 250
influence of Roussseau on, 102
"Little Zaches Named Zinnober,"
  144
"Master Flea," 97
Night Pieces, 95
philosophies of, 88–90
political views of, 96–97
The Serapion Brothers, 95–96, 99
"The Golden Pot," 88, 95
"The Knight Gluck," 94
"The Merry Musicians," 93
"The New Year's Adventure," 122
"The Nutcracker and the Mouse
  King," 85, 95, 98, 124
  plot of vs. *The Nutcracker*
    ballet, 106–108
"The Sandman," 105
"The Strange Child," 99, 102–103
Tom Cat's Views on Life, 95
Undine, 23, 94–96
Hoffmann, Heinrich, 21
"Holger the Dane," (Andersen), 125
Holiday House, (Sinclair), 152
Holiday Romance, (Dickens), 155
Holme Lee's Fairy Tales, (Parr), 157
Home Treasury, (Summerly), 149
Hood, Thomas, 145
  Condition of England Debate, 147
  Fairy Realm, 157
Hook, (Spielberg), 219
Hough, Emerson
  The King of Gee Whiz, 203
  Madre d'Oro an Aztec Play, 202
Household Words, (Dickens), 154
Housman, Laurence, 164
  "A Chinese Fairy Tale," 162
  "The Bound Princess," 162

"The Rooted Lover," 162
"The White Doe," 162
utopian writings of, 159
Howitt, Mary, *Wonderful Stories for Children* (translation of Andersen's tales), 149
Howl's Moving Castle, 29
Humperdinck, Engelbert, *Hänsel and Gretel*, 23
Hyde, Lewis, *The Gift: Imagination and the Erotic Life of Property*, 211

I

"Ib and Little Christine," (Andersen), 123
religious motifs in, 133
Identity formation, 122
Ideological meaning, reconstructing, 6
"If the War Continues," (Hesse), 243, 252
Il Lampione (The Street Lamp), (Collodi), 176
Illustrators
Crane, Walter, 164
Cruikshank, George, 20, 148
Denslow, W.W., 199
Hanley, Catherine, 187
McDougall, Walt, 202
Morgan, Ike, 202
Neill, John R., 202
Parrish, Maxfield, 199
Pyle, Howard, 22
Sendak, Maurice, 187
Imagination

importance of in literary fairy tales of 19th century England, 147, 150
importance of in the writings of E.T.A. Hoffmann, 97–103
power of, 156
Indian culture, 54
Industrial Revolution, 146–147, 163–164
Inès de Cordoue, (Bernard), 41
Ingelow, Jean, 153, 157–158
The Little Wonder-Horn, 157
Ingemann, B.S., 112, 128
Inman, Herbert, *The One-Eyed Griffin and Other Fairy Tales*, 157
"Inside and Outside," (Hesse), 253
Intelligent design, themes of in Andersen's works, 131–132
International Wizard of Oz Club, 209
Into the West, 28
Into the Woods, 26
Ireland
Attic Press, 25
folklore of, films based on, 28
Irish Elf Tales, (Grimm), 70
"Iris," (Hesse), 251
Irish Popular Superstitions, (Wilde, W.), 168
Iron John, (Bly), 26
Irving, Washington, influence of *The Thousand and One Nights* on, 64
Irwin, Robert, *The Arabian Nights: A Companion*, 59
Italian Folktales, (Calvino), 179
Italy
literary fairy tales in, 11

literary tradition, as models for
    French fairy tales, 37
modern fairy tale authors, 25

J

"Jack and the Beanstalk," 149
Jack tales, 179–180
"Jack the Giant Killer," 19
Jaffé, Aniela, psychoanalytical
    interpretations of fairy tales
    by, 82
Jahn, Friedrich Ludwig, 96–97
Janosch, 25
Johnson, Samuel, influence of *The
    Thousand and One Nights*
    on, 64
Jokai, Mor, "Barak and His Wives,"
    21
Jordan, Neil, *The Company of
    Wolves*, 28
Journey to the East, (Hesse), 245
"Judar and His Brothers," 63
"Julnar the Mermaid," 63
Jung, C.G., 1
    psychoanalytical interpretations
        of fairy tales by, 82

K

Kaiser, Georg, "The Fairy Tale of the
    King," 24
Kästner, Erich, "The Fairy Tale
    about Reason," 24
"Kate," (Stockton), 188

Keary, Annie and E., *Little
    Wanderlin*, 157
Keats, John, 146
Keller, Gottfried, "Spiegel the Cat,"
    21
Kinder- und Hausmärchen, (Grimm),
    18, 69
King of the Golden River, (Ruskin),
    150
Kingsley, Charles, *The Water Babies*,
    152
Kipling, Rudyard, 162–163
    "The Potted Princess," 162
    utopian writings of, 159
Kirby, Mary and Elizabeth, *The
    Talking Bird*, 152
*Kissing the Witch: Old Tales in New
    Skins*, (Donoghue), 30
Knatchbull-Hugessen, Edward
    Friends and Foes from Fairy Land,
        157
    Moonshine, 157
Knoepflmacher, U.C., *Ventures into
    Childland: Victorians, Fairy
    Tales, and Femininity*, 153
Koreff, David Ferdinand, 95
Krause, Johann Friedrich
    (Wachtmeister), 74
Kreisleriana, (Schumann), 23
Kreisler, Johannes, 94
Kress, Nancy, 26
Kuma Sutra of Vatsyayana, (Burton),
    57
Kunert, Günter, 25
Kunstmärchen, 19, 160
Künzler, Rosemarie, 25

L

La Baionette, 23

Laboulaye, Edouard-René, "Zerbin
    the Wood-Cutter," 21

Labour Leader, 159

Labour Prophet, 159

La Cenerentola, (Rossini), 23

Lahr, Bert, 209

Lamb, Charles, 145

Land of Desire: Merchants, Power and
    the Rise of a New American
    Culture, (Leach), 206

Lane, Edwin, Arabian Nights, 149

Lane, John, The Yellow Book, 164

Lang, Andrew, 168
    The Gold of Fairnilee, 157
    The Princess Nobody, 157

Latin fairy tales, focus of, 8

La Tyrannie des fées détruite,
    (d'Auneuil), 41

Leach, William, 210, 212
    Land of Desire: Merchants, Power
    and the Rise of a New
    American Culture, 206

Leander, Richard, "The Princess
    with the Three Glass
    Hearts," 21

Le Cabinet des Fées, (Mayer), 18, 51

Lee, Tanith, 25

Le Gage touché, (Le Noble), 41

Lemon, Mark, The Enchanted Doll,
    152

Lem, Stanislaw, "Prince Ferix and
    the Princess Crystal," 25

Le Noble, Eustache, Le Gage touché,
    41

Le piacevoli notti (The Pleasant
    Nights), (Straparola), 9

Leprince de Beaumont, Jeanne-
    Marie, 145, 177
    "Beauty and the Beast," 17, 50
    establishment of literary fairy
    tales for children by, 48
    Magasin des Enfans, 17
    "Prince Chéri," 17
    "Prince Désir," 50
    "Princess Mignone," 50

Les Aventures d'Abdalla, fils d'Anif,
    (Bignon), 47

Les Contes des Contes, (de la Force),
    41

Les Contes des fées, (d'Aulnoy), 41

Lesesucht, 19

Les grands salons féménins, (Gougy-
    Francois), 34

Les Illustres Fées, contes galans, (de
    Mailly), 41

Les Petits Soupers de l'été de l'année,
    (Durand), 41

"Les Quatre Facardins," (Hamilton),
    48

Les Salons Littéraires et la société
    française 1610–1789,
    (Picard), 34

Le Trésor des Contes, (Pourrat), 24

Lewis, C.S., 160

Lewis, Philip, Seeing through the
    Mother Goose Tales: Visual
    Turns in the Writings of
    Charles Perrault, 40

Lhértier, Marie-Jeanne, 16, 37, 39,
    145
    Oeuvres Meslées, 41
    "Ricdin-Ricdon," 13

L'Histoire de la Sultane de Perse et des Visirs. Contes turcs, (de La Croix), 47

"Libussa," (Musäus), 18

Linklater, Eric, 24

Literary fairy tales
  Charles Perrault, 13
  for children, 48
  Condition of England Debate, 147
  creation of type by Grimm
      brothers, 75
  development of the genre, 7
    England, 12
    France, 12
    Germany, 18
    Italy, 11
  effect of Oriental literature on,
      46–47, 54
  expansion of in the 20th century,
      23
  France, 34
    17th century, 41
  functions of, 15
    18th century France, 17
  history of, 1
  institutionalization of, 13, 50
    20th century, 22
  interaction with oral tales, 50
  pedagogic, 50 (*See also*
      educational uses of fairy
      tales)
  politicization of in the 20th
      century, 23
  subversive themes in, 7
  19th century England, 143
  wonder in, 5

Literary salons, 12, 34, 39, 41–46

"Little Claus and Big Claus,"
      (Andersen), 113, 141

  as adaptation of folklore, 121
  revolutionary tone of, 129–130
  similiarity to Grimm Brothers'
      "Little Farmer," 128

"Little Daylight," (MacDonald), 160

"Little Farmer," (Grimm), 128

"Little Ida's Flowers," (Andersen),
      113, 129

Little Johnnie, (Collodi), 177

Little Mary, (Barrie), 226

"Little Red Cap," (Grimm). *See also*
      "Little Red Riding Hood"
  moral lessons of, 81

"Little Red Riding Hood," 15, 19, 149
  (Grimm), 18, 78 (*See also* "Little
      Red Cap")
  (Perrault), 13, 39
  rape motif of, 28

"Little Red Riding Hood as a
      Dictator Would Tell It,"
      (Phillips), 24

Little Wanderlin, (Keary), 157

"Little Zaches Named Zinnober,"
      (Hoffmann), 144

Llewelyn Davies, George, 227, 232

Llewelyn Davies, Jack, 227, 232

Llewelyn Davies, Michael, 227, 232

Llewelyn Davies, Nicholas, 227, 232

Llewelyn Davies, Peter, 227, 232

Llewelyn Davies, Sylvia, 227, 230
  publication of *Peter and Wendy*
      following death of, 233

Lloyd, Constance, 168

Lorenzini, Carlo. *See* Collodi, Carlo

Lorenzini, Domenico and Angela,
      176

Lo Scaramucci (The Controversy),
      (Collodi), 176

Louis XIV, 37

effect of reign of on literary fairy
  tales, 42
Oriental fairy tales and the
  decline of, 47
Love at St. Nicholas Tower,
  (Andersen), 112
Lubert, Mlle., "Princesse Camion,"
  48
Lucky Peter, (Andersen), 118
Lulu, (Hesse), 250
Lüthi, Max, *Once Upon a Time,* 82

M

MacDonald, George, 153, 156–157,
  163–164
"Cross Purposes," 156, 160
Dealings with the Fairies, 156
"Little Daylight," 160
The Princess and Curdie, 156, 163
The Princess and the Goblin, 156,
  163, 179
"The Day Boy and the Night
  Girl," 22, 157, 160
"The Giant's Heart," 156
"The Golden Key," 156
"The Light Princess," 156
"The Shadows," 156
utopian writings of, 158–160
Macmillan's Magazine, 159
Macnaghten, William Hay, Calcutta
  II edition of A Thousand
  and One Nights, 57
Madre d'Oro an Aztec Play, (Hough),
  202
Magasin des Enfans, 50
Magic

European realism, 98, 122–123
evolution of in Oz books, 212–214
Magic fairy tales, Grimm brothers'
  tales, 79–84
Maguire, Gregory, 25
  *Wicked: The Life and Times of the
  Wicked Witch of the West,*
  209
Male dominance, 7, 15, 21
Mann, Thomas, *The Magic
  Mountain,* 23
Märchen Almanach, (Hauff), 20
Marcuse, Herbert, 249
  Eros and Civilization, 237
Margaret Olgilvy, (Barrie), 224
Marlowe, Christopher, 143
Martin, Mary, 219
Mary Rose, (Barrie), 232
März, 242
Masson, David, 223
"Master Flea," (Hoffmann), 97
Mayer, Charles, *Le Cabinet des Fées,*
  18, 51
McDougall, Walt, 202
McKinley, Robin, 25
Meckel, Christoph, "The Crow," 25
Meisling, Simon, 111
Melville, Herman, influence of *The
  Thousand and One Nights*
  on, 64
Mendés, Catulle, "The Sleeping
  Beauty," 22
Meredith, George, influence of *The
  Thousand and One Nights*
  on, 64
Merton, Ambrose, *The Old Story
  Books of England,* 149

Millhauser, Steven, influence of *The Thousand and One Nights* on, 64
Milne, A.A., 160
Mitchison, Naomi, "Five Men and a Swan," 25
Miyasaki, Hayao, fairy tale films of, 29
Molesworth, Mary Louisa, 164
 Christmas-Tree Land, 157
 depiction of female protagonists by, 160–161
 "Story of a King's Daughter," 161
 The Tapestry Room, 157
 utopian writings of, 159
Molière, 37
Montalba, Anthony, *Fairy Tales of All Nations*, 149
Moonshine, (Knatchbull-Hugessen), 157
Morgan, Ike, 202
Morphology of the Folk Tale, (Propp), 3, 82
Morris, William, 164
 News from Nowhere, 164
Mortimer, Elizabeth, 147
"Mosses from an Old Manse," (Hawthorne), 21
Mother Bunch's Fairy Tales, (Harris), 148
Mother Goose, 148
Mother Goose in Prose, (Baum), 199
"Mother Trudy," (Grimm), 78
Mozart, Wolfgang Amadeus, *The Magic Flute*, 23
Mühlen, Hermynia zur, 23
Murray, Mary Alice, 178
Musäus, Johann Karl, 149
 "Libussa," 18

Volksmärchen der Deutschen, 18
Music, fairy tale themes and, 23, 26
Muslim culture, role of women in, 59
My Candelabra's Glaze, (Baum), 199
Mynona, 23

N

Napoleonic Wars, fairy tales in Germany during, 19
Napoli, Donna Jo, 25
 fairy tale novels for adolescents by, 30
Narcissus and Goldmund, (Hesse), 245
Nazi ideology, use of fairy tales to promote, 24
Neighbors, (Hesse), 242
Neill, John R., 202, 209
Nesbit, Edith, 157–158, 164
 The Book of Dragons, 157
 depiction of female protagonists by, 160–161
 "The Last of the Dragons," 161
Newell, Mike, *Into the West*, 28
News from Nowhere, (Morris), 164
Night Pieces, (Hoffmann), 95
Nodot, François, *Histoire de Mélusine*, 41
North America, effect of Oriental iterature on fairy tales of, 54
Novalis, 18, 48, 98, 149, 163, 250
 comparison of Andersen's tales with those of, 129
Nutcracker Suite, 23

O

Oates, Joyce Carol, 26
O'Connor, Daniel S.
  Peter Pan Keepsake, 233
  The Peter Pan Picture Book, 233
Oeuvres Meslées, (Lhértier), 41
"Of Feminine Subtlety," 8
Offenbach, Jacques, The Tales of
  Hoffmann, 23
"Oh, Friends Not These Tones!"
  (Hesse), 243
Old Danish Heroic Songs, (Grimm,
  Wilhelm), 69
Old Pipes and the Dryad, (Stockton),
  187, 194
Ölenberg manuscripts, 74
Olgilvy, Margaret, 221
Once Upon a Time, (Lüthi), 82
Only a Fiddler, (Andersen), 113
On the Old German Meistergesang,
  (Grimm, Jacob), 69
Oral fairy tales
  history of, 1
  interaction with literary fairy
    tales, 50
  literary tradition as a source for,
    16
Oral folk tales, transformation of, 37
Oriental fairy tales, 16, 46–47, 53–64
  burlesques of, 48
  influence of on the writings of
    Hermann Hesse, 249
Oriental motif
  use of in French fairy tales, 46
  use of in German literary fairy
    tales, 18
Ørsted, H.C., 112

The Spirit of Nature, 131
O.T. Life in Denmark, (Andersen),
  113
Otmar, 149
Out of India, (Hesse), 243
Oz. See also Baum, L. Frank
  analysis of, 200, 205–218
  commercialization of, 202
  as cultural icon, 208–210
  International Wizard of Oz Club,
    209
  portrayal of gift economy in, 211
  socialist themes of books, 215–217
  utopian nature of, 210
  as utopian paradise, 195
Ozma of Oz, (Baum), 203
  gift giving and art motifs in, 214

P

Pagan themes, 15
  as models for French fairy tales,
    37
Paget, Francis Edward, The Hope of
  the Katzekopfs, 152
Pamela, (Richardson), 145
Pardigmatic functions of wonder
  tales, 3
Paroles remarkables, bons mots et
  maximes des Orientaux,
  (Galland), 53
Parravinci, 177
Parr, Harriet, Holme Lee's Fairy
  Tales, 157
Parrish, Maxfield, 199
Pater, Walter, 164, 168
Patriarchalism, 37, 78, 83

in Arabic culture, 59

Dickens' treatment of, 155

Payne, John, *The Book of the Thousand Nights and One Night*, 58

Pedagogic fairy tales, 50. *See also* educational uses of fairy tales

"Perfect Love," (de Murat), 45

Perrault, Charles, 12, 16, 28, 43, 50, 145, 177

"Apologie des femmes," 39

biographical information, 38

"Blue Beard," 39

"Cinderella," 13, 39

"Donkey Skin," 13, 38, 45

"Griseldis," 39

Histoires ou contes du temps passé, 13, 38, 41

original publication of, 40

"La Siécle de Louis le Grand," 38

"Little Red Riding Hood," 13, 39

"Portrait de la voix d'Iris," 38

"Portrait d'Iris," 38

"Puss in Boots," 39

"Quarrel of the Ancients and the Moderns," 38, 40

"Rickey with the Tuft," 13, 39

"Sleeping Beauty," 13, 39

"The Fairies," 13, 39

"The Foolish Wishes," 13, 38

"Tom Thumb," 13, 39, 45

violence and brutality in stories of, 45

Persian culture, 54

Persian fairy tales

Hezâr afsân (A Thousand Stories), 56

influence on 18th century Western writers, 16

Peter and Wendy, (Barrie), 219, 230

analysis of, 233–238

Peter Camenzind, (Hesse), 242

Peter Pan, analysis of, 220–221

Peter Pan, His Book, His Pictures, His Career, His Friends, (Drennan), 233

Peter Pan in Kensington Gardens, (Barrie), 219, 226, 233

Peter Pan Keepsake, (O'Connor), 233

Peter Pan, or The Boy Who Wouldn't Grow Up, (Barrie), 219, 233

Peter Pan (Play), (Barrie), 226

revision and publication history, 233

Peter Schlemihl, (Chamisso), 122, 140

influence of on Wilde's "The Fisherman and His Soul," 172

Petipa, Marius, 85

Phillips, H.I., "Little Red Riding Hood as a Dictator Would Tell It," 24

Picard, Roger, *Les Salons Littéraires et la société française 1610–1789*, 34

Pilgrimage to El-Medinah and Mecca, (Burton), 57

Pinocchio

(Collodi), 178

socialization of, 180–185

(Disney), 175

Poe, Edgar Allan, influence of *The Thousand and One Nights* on, 64

Politically Correct Bedtime Stories, (Garner), 26

Popular Fairy Tales, (Tabart), 148
Populist theory in Oz books, 206
"Portrait de la voix d'Iris," (Perrault),
        38
"Portrait d'Iris," (Perrault), 38
Pourrat, Henri, *Le Trésor des Contes*,
        24
Précieuses, 34, 44
"Prince Ahmed and His Two
        Sisters," (Galland), 54
"Prince Ahmed and the Fairy Pari-
        Banou," (Galland), 15, 54
"Prince Behram and the Princess
        Al-Datma," 63
"Prince Bull," (Dickens), 154
"Prince Désir," (Leprince de
        Beaumont), 50
"Prince Ferix and the Princess
        Crystal," (Lem), 25
"Princesse Camion," (Lubert), 48
"Princess Mignone," (Leprince de
        Beaumont), 50
Propp, Vladimir, *Morphology of the
        Folk Tale*, 3, 82
Protestant ethic
    principles of in literary fairy tales
        of the nineteenth century,
        21
    Grimm brothers' tales, 78
    romantic movement and, 145
Psyché, (Corneille), 37
Psychoanalytical critics, 81
Puritanism, effect of on literary fairy
        tales in England, 144
"Puss in Boots," 9, 15
    (Perrault), 39
Pyle, Howard, 22
    "Where to Lay the Blame," 22

Q

Quality Street, (Barrie), 226
"Quarrel of the Ancients and
        Moderns"
    (Boileau), 37
    (Perrault), 38, 40
Queen Zixi of Iz, (Baum), 203
"Queer Visitors from the Marvelous
        Land of Oz," (Baum), 202

R

Racine, Jean, 39
"Rapunzel," 13, 15
    (Grimm), changes to story over
        time, 77
Rapunzel's Revenge, 25
"Readers of Oz: Young and Old,
        Old and New Historicist,"
        (Westbrook), 207
Reconciliation, themes of in Disney
        cinematic fairy tales, 28
Redgrove, Peter, 25
*Remarkable Words, Sayings and
        Maxims of the Orientals*,
        (Galland), 53
Richardson, Samuel, *Pamela*, 145
Richter, Dieter, 82
"Ricky with the Tuft"
    (Bernard), 41, 44
    (Perrault), 13, 39
Ride on Rapunzel, 25
Rinkitink in Oz, (Baum), 204
Ritchie, Anne Isabella
    Bluebeard's Keys, 157
    "Cinderella," 161

Five Old Friends and a Young
    Prince, 157
Robin Hood, 148
Rodari, Gianni, 25
Roheim, Gerza, psychoanalytical
    interpretations of fairy tales
    by, 82
Rohrer, Maria Thekla Michaelina,
    93
Rölleke, Heinz, 82
Roman myths, 2
Romantic fairy tales, 145
    German, 19
Romantic Songs, (Hesse), 241
Rome, classical literature of, 46
Rose, Jacqueline, 235
Rossetti, Christina, 153
    The Goblin Market, 161
    Speaking Likenesses, 157
Rosshalde, (Hesse), 243
Rossini, Gioacchino, *La Cenerentola,*
    23
Roundabout Rambles, (Stockton), 190
Rousseau, Jean-Jacques
    influence of on E.T.A. Hoffmann's
        work, 102
    "The Queen Fantasque," 17
Routledge, 158
Ruby Slippers, Golden Tears, 26
Rudder Grange, (Stockton), 190
"Rumpelstiltskin," 13, 15
Runge, Philipp Otto
    "The Fisherman and His Wife,"
        75
    "The Juniper Tree," 75
Rushdie, Salman
    Haroun and the Sea of Stories, 30
    influence of *The Thousand and*
        One Nights on, 64

Ruskin, John, 164, 168
    Condition of England Debate, 147
    King of the Golden River, 150
Ryman, Geoff, *Was,* 209

S

Sadomasochism, 45
Salon fairy tales, 12, 36, 41–46
    conventionalization of, 48
Sam Steele's Adventures on Land and
    Seas, (Baum), 203
Sand, George, 51
Sartor Resartus, (Carlyle), 149
Sayles, John, *The Secret of Roan*
    Innish, 28
Schiller, Friedrich, influence of *The*
    Thousand and One Nights
    on, 64
Schiller, Justin, 209
Schräge Märchen, (Andersen), 137
Schumann, Robert, *Kreisleriana,* 23
Schwitters, Kurt, 23
Scott, Sir Walter, "On the
    Supernatural in Fictitious
    Composition," 88
Search for Montague, (Baum), 202
Secret Gardens, (Carpenter), 159
Self-abnegation, 134
Self-help books, adult fairy tales in,
    26
Sendak, Maurice, 187
Sentimental Tommy, (Barrie), 225
Sex roles in fairy tales, 25
Sexton, Anne, 25
Shadow Pictures, (Andersen), 113
"Shadow Play," (Hesse), 251

Shakespeare, William, 143
Sharp, Evelyn, 164
  depiction of female protagonists
      by, 160–161
  "The Spell of the Magician's
      Daughter," 161
Shaw, George Bernard, 164
Sheherezade/Shahriyâr
  narratives, 56
  role of in *Nights* narratives, 59–61
Shelley, Percy Bysshe, 146
Sherwood, Mary Martha, 147
Shirwanee Edition of A Thousand
      and One Nights, 56
Shrek films, 29
Simpson, Helen, 24
Sinbad stories, 54
"Sinbad the Seaman and Sinbad the
      Landsman," 63
Sinclair, Catherine, 21
  Holiday House, 152
  "Uncle David's Nonsensical Story
      about Giants and Fairies,"
      152
Sinclair, Emil. *See* Hesse, Hermann
*Sindh, and the Races that Inhabit the
      Valley of the Indus,* (Burton),
      57
Sky Island, (Baum), 204
"Sleeping Beauty," 15, 19
  (Grimm), 18, 78
  (Mendés), 22
  (Perrault), 13, 39
  (Tschaikovsky), 23
"Snow White and the Seven
      Dwarfs," Disney, 28
Snow White, Blood Red, 26
"Snow White," (Grimm), 78
  changes to story over time, 76

  moral lessons of, 81
Social criticism, Victorian fairy tales,
      159
Social Darwinism, 124
Social discourse, 19th century
      English fairy tales, 149–150
Socialist newspapers, 163
  fairy tales in, 159
Socialization, fairy tales as the agent
      of, 21
Somerville, Edith Anna, 24
Song of Hildebrand, (Grimm), 69
Southey, Robert, 145
  influence of *The Thousand and
      One Nights* on, 64
Speaking Likenesses, (Rossetti), 157
Spenser, Edmund, 143
  The Faerie Queen, 12
"Spiegel the Cat," (Keller), 21
Spinners, (Napoli), 30
Spirited Away, 29
Stanton, Cynthia Ann, 196
Stanton, Elizabeth Cady, 197
Staunton, Schuyler. *See* Baum, L.
      Frank
Stead, Christina, 24
Steppenwolf, (Hesse), 245
Stern, G.B., 24
Stevenson, Robert Louis, 226
  influence of *The Thousand and
      One Nights* on, 64
  "The Bottle Imp," 22
St. Nicholas Magazine, 190
Stockton, Frank, 22
  The Adventures of Captain Horn,
      192
  analysis of tales, 192–194
  The Associate Hermits, 192
  The Bee-Man of Orn, 187

The Bee-Man of Orn and Other Fanciful Tales, 190
A Bicycle of Cathay, 192
biographical information, 187–192
The Casting Away of Mrs. Lecks and Mrs. Aleshine, 190
"Derido; or, the Giant's Quilt," 192
The Floating Prince and Other Fairy Tales, 190
The Great War Syndicate, 192
The Griffin and the Minor Canon, 22, 187, 194
The Hundredth Man, 190
"Kate," 188
Old Pipes and the Dryad, 187, 194
The Queen's Museum, 190, 193
Roundabout Rambles, 190
Rudder Grange, 190
The Story of Viteau, 190
A Story-Teller's Pack, 187
"The Accommodating Circumstance," 192
"The Emergency Princess," 194
"The Great Show in Kobol-Land," 193
"The Lady, or the Tiger!" 190
"The Magical Music," 192
"The Poor Count's Christmas," 194
"The Sisters Three and the Kilmaree," 193
"The Slight Mistake," 188
Ting-a-ling, 189
The Transferred Ghost, 190
Stockton, John, 189
Stockton, William, 187
Storm, Theodor, "Hinzelmeier," 21

"Story of a King's Daughter," (Molesworth), 161
Story of a Puppet, (Collodi). *See Pinocchio*
"Strange News from Another Planet," (Hesse), 23, 243, 252
Straparola, Giovan Francesco, 37
"Constantino," 9
Le piacevoli notti (The Pleasant Nights), 9
The Pleasant Nights, 33
"The Pig Prince," 9
Sturzenegger, Hans, 243
Subversion, role of fairy tales in the nineteenth century, 22
Summerly, Felix, *Home Treasury*, 149
Sumpter, Caroline, *Victorian Periodicals and the Reinvention of the Fairy Tale*, 159
Supple, Barry, *The Victorians*, 146
Swift, Jonathan, 143
"Sylvie and Bruno," (Carroll), 156

T

Tabart, Benjamin, *Popular Fairy Tales*, 148
Taylor, Edgar, 129
German Popular Stories, 20, 148
Tchaikovsky, Pyotr Ilyich, 85
Nutcracker Suite, 23
Sleeping Beauty, 23
Tendresse, 12
Tennant, Andy, *Ever After*, 28

Thackeray, William Makepeace, 153, 168
  "Bluebeard's Ghost," 21
  Condition of England Debate, 147
  The Rose and the Ring, 152, 179
"The Accommodating Circumstance," (Stockton), 192
The Admirable Crichton, (Barrie), 226
The Adventures of Abdalah, Son of Anif, (Bignon), 16
The Adventures of Captain Horn, (Stockton), 192
The Adventures of Huckleberry Finn, (Twain), 181, 221
The Arabian Nights, 15, 148. *See also The Thousand and One Nights*
  (Haddawy), 59
  philosophical disposition of, 62
The Arabian Nights: A Companion, (Irwin), 59
The Arabian Nights II, (Haddawy), 59
The Associate Hermits, (Stockton), 192
The Baum Bugle, 209
"The Beautiful Dream," (Hesse), 251
The Bee-Man of Orn and Other Fanciful Tales, (Stockton), 190
The Bee-Man of Orn, (Stockton), 187
"The Birthday of the Infanta," (Wilde), 172
"The Blot on Peter Pan," (Barrie), 233
"The Blue Bird," 15
"The Blue Light," (Grimm), 121, 128
The Book of Dragons, (Nesbit), 157

The Book of the Thousand Nights and a Night, (Burton), 56
The Book of the Thousand Nights and One Night, (Payne), 58
"The Bottle Imp," (Stevenson), 22
"The Bound Princess," (Housman), 162
The Boy Castaways of Blacklake Island Being a Record of the Terrible Adventures of the Brothers Davies, (Barrie), 228, 233
The Boy David, (Barrie), 232
The Boy's Magic Horn, (Brentano), 73
"The Bronze Pig," (Andersen), 123
  religious motifs in, 133
The Canterbury Tales, (Chaucer), 12
The Casting Away of Mrs. Lecks and Mrs. Aleshine, (Stockton), 190
The Company of Wolves, 28
The Count of Monte Cristo, (Dumas), 104
The Court of Oberon; or, The Temple of Fairies, (Harris), 148
"The Crow," (Meckel), 25
"The Day Boy and the Night Girl," (MacDonald), 22, 157, 160
"The Dead Queen," (Coover), 25
The Decameron, (Boccaccio), 9
The Devil's Elixirs, (Hoffmann), 95
"The Devoted Friend," (Wilde), 170–171
"The Difficult Path," (Hesse), 251
"The Discreet Princess," (d'Aulnoy), 45

"The Dung Beetle," (Andersen),
  anthropomorphization of
  animals, 124
"The Dwarf," (Hesse), 251
"The Ebony Horse," 63
The Emerald City of Oz, (Baum), 203
  utopian portrayal of Oz in, 215
"The Emergency Princess,"
  (Stockton), 194
"The Emperor's New Clothes,"
  (Andersen), 113, 141
  as adaptation of folklore, 122
  derivation of from oral tradition,
  128
  revolutionary tone of, 129–130
The Enchanted Doll, (Lemon), 152
The Enchanted Island of Yew, (Baum),
  200
"The European," (Hesse), 243, 252
The Faerie Queen, (Spenser), 12
The Fairies, Or, New Tales for Old,
  24
"The Fairies," (Perrault), 13, 39
The Fairy Book, (Craik), 157
*The Fairy Godmothers and Other
  Tales*, (Gatty), 150
"The Fairy Tale about Reason,"
  (Kästner), 24
*The Fairy Tale and the Imagination of
  the Child*, (Belz), 81
"The Fairy Tale," (Goethe), 19
The Fairy Tale of My Life,
  (Andersen), 127
"The Fairy Tale of the King,"
  (Kaiser), 24
"The Fairy Tale of the 672nd Night,"
  (von Hofmannsthal), 22
The Fairy Tales of Every Day,
  (Childe-Pemberton), 157

The Fate of a Crown, (Baum), 203
"The Fisherman and His Soul,"
  (Wilde), 22
  influence of Andersen and
  Chamisso on, 172
"The Fisherman and His Wife,"
  (Runge), 75
"The Fisherman and the Jinnee," 62
*The Floating Prince and Other Fairy
  Tales*, (Stockton), 190
"The Florentine," (Calvino), 179
"The Foolish Wishes," (Perrault),
  13, 38
"The Forest Dweller," (Hesse), 23,
  251
"The Frog King," (Grimm), 78
"The Gardener and the Gentry,"
  (Andersen), 118
  ideological compromise, 136
  patronage theme of, 120–121
The German Heroic Legend, (Grimm,
  Wilhelm), 70
The Giant Hands, (Crowquill), 152
"The Giant's Heart," (MacDonald),
  156
"The Girl and the Wolf," (Thurber),
  24
"The Girl Who Stepped on Bread,"
  (Andersen), 124
The Glass Bead Game, (Hesse), 245
The Goblin Market, (Rossetti), 161
The Golden Ass, 8
"The Golden Key," (MacDonald),
  156
"The Golden Pot," (Hoffmann), 88,
  95, 98
The Gold of Fairnilee, (Lang), 157
"The Good Woman," (de la Force),
  45

"The Great Show in Kobol-Land,"
    (Stockton), 193
The Great War Syndicate, (Stockton),
    192
The Griffin and the Minor Canon,
    (Stockton), 22, 187, 194
The Happy Prince and Other Tales,
    (Wilde), 162, 170
    themes of, 170–171
"The Happy Prince," (Wilde),
    170–171. See also The Happy
    Prince and Other Tales
"The Heart of Princess Joan," (De
    Morgan), 161
"The Hedgehog and the Pigeons," 63
The History of the German Language,
    (Grimm, Jacob), 71
The Hobbit, (Tolkien), 24
The Hope of the Katzekopfs, (Paget),
    152
"The Hunchback," 62
The Hundredth Man, (Stockton), 190
"The Ice Maiden," (Andersen),
    religious motifs in, 133
The Iliad, 2
The Invisible Man, (Wells), 164
"The Island of Happiness,"
    (d'Aulnoy), 12, 42
"The Juniper Tree," (Runge), 75
The Kasidah, (Burton), 57
The King of Gee Whiz, (Baum &
    Hough), 203
"The King of the Elves," (Dick), 24
"The Knight Gluck," (Hoffmann), 94
"The Lady, or the Tiger!" (Stockton),
    190
"The Last of the Dragons," (Nesbit),
    161

The Life and Adventures of Santa
    Claus, (Baum), 200
"The Light Princess," (MacDonald),
    156
"The Little Match Girl,"
    (Andersen), 124
    (Disney), 142
"The Little Mermaid,"
    (Andersen), 113, 119
    influence of on Wilde's "The
        Fisherman and His Soul,"
        172
    influence of Undine on,
        128–129
    religious motifs in, 133
    (Disney), 142
The Little Minister, (Barrie), 224
The Little Minister (Play), (Barrie),
    226
The Little White Bird, (Barrie), 226,
    228, 233
The Little Wonder-Horn, (Ingelow),
    157
The Lost Princess of Oz, (Baum), 204
    abuse of magic in, 217
"The Magical Music," (Stockton),
    192
The Magic Circle, (Napoli), 30
"The Magic Fishbone," (Dickens),
    155
The Magic Flute, (Mozart), 23
The Magic Mountain, (Mann), 23
The Magic of Oz, (Baum), 204
    abuse of magic in, 217
The Maid of Arran, (Baum), 197
The Maid of Athens, (Baum), 202
The Man in the Iron Mask, (Dumas),
    104

The Marvelous Land of Oz, (Baum), 200, 202

"The Merchant and the Jinnee," 62

"The Merry Musicians," (Hoffmann), 93

The Moorish Maiden, (Andersen), 115

The Mulatto, A Comedy in Green, (Andersen), 113

"The Naughty Boy," (Andersen), 113, 123, 129, 141

"The Necklace of Princess Fiormonde," (De Morgan), 161

"The New Year's Adventure," (Hoffmann), 122

"The Nightingale," (Andersen), 116, 119

    art and the artist in, 120

    ideological compromise in, 135

"The Nightingale and the Rose," (Wilde), 170–171

"The Nutcracker and the Mouse King," (Hoffmann), 85, 95, 98

    symbolic roles of Drosselmeier and Marie in, 100–102

The Nutcracker ballet

    plot of vs. Hoffmann's original tale, 106–108

    popularity of over the 19th and 20th centuries, 86

The Odyssey, 2

"The Ogre Courting," (Ewing), 161

The Old Story Books of England, (Merton), 149

The One-Eyed Griffin and Other Fairy Tales, (Inman), 157

"The Painter," (Hesse), 251

"The Palace of Revenge," (de Murat), 45

The Patchwork Girl of Oz, (Baum), 204

    genetic experimentation in, 217

The Pentameron, (Basile), 9, 33

The Peter Pan Alphabet Book, (Herford), 233

The Peter Pan Picture Book, (O'Connor & Woodward), 233

"The Philosopher's Stone," (Wieland), 18

The Picture of Dorian Gray, (Wilde), 167

The Pleasant Nights, (Straparola), 33

"The Poet," (Hesse), 251

"The Poor Count's Christmas," (Stockton), 194

The Posthumous Writings and Poems of Hermann Lauscher, (Hesse), 241, 250

"The Potted Princess," (Kipling), 162

The Prince of the Pond: Otherwise Known as De Fawg Pin, (Napoli), 30

The Princess and Curdie, (MacDonald), 156, 163

The Princess and the Goblin, (MacDonald), 156, 163

The Princess Nobody, (Lang), 157

"The Princess on the Pea," (Andersen), 113

    as adaptation of folklore, 121

    derivation of from oral tradition, 128

"The Princess with the Three Glass Hearts," (Leander), 21

"The Queen Fantasque," (Rousseau), 17
"The Queen of Quok," (Baum), 22
"The Queen of the Island of Flowers," (de Mailly), 45
The Queen's Museum, (Stockton), 190, 193
"The Ram," (d'Aulnoy), 44
"The Red Shoes," (Andersen), 20
  as evangelical literature, 123
  treatment of female figures in, 134
"The Reluctant Dragon," (Grahame), 162
"The Remarkable Rocket," (Wilde), 170–171
The Road to Oz, (Baum), 203
"The Rooted Lover," (Housman), 162
The Rose and the Ring, (Thackeray), 152
The Rose Lawn Journal, 196
"The Sandman," (Hoffmann), 105
The Scarecrow of Oz, (Baum), 204
  abuse of magic in, 217
The Sea Fairies, (Baum), 204
The Secret of Roan Innish, 28
"The Selfish Giant," (Wilde), 170–171
The Serapion Brothers, (Hoffmann), 95–96, 99
"The Shadow," (Andersen), 21, 116
  autobiographical and allegorical nature of, 140–141
"The Shadows," (MacDonald), 156
"The Shepherdess and the Chimney Sweep," (Andersen), 125
The Show Window, 199
The Silver Swan, (de Chatelain), 152
"The Sisters Three and the Kilmaree," (Stockton), 193

"The Slight Mistake," (Stockton), 188
"The Smile of the Sphinx," (Bachmann), 24
"The Snow Queen," (Andersen), 116
  as evangelical literature, 123
  religious motifs in, 133–134
  (Disney), 142
"The Soul of Man Under Socialism," (Wilde), 164
"The Spell of the Magician's Daughter," (Sharp), 161
"The Spruce Tree," (Andersen), anthropomorphization of nature, 124
"The Star-Child," (Wilde), 172
"The Steadfast Tin Soldier," (Andersen), 124
"The Story of Little Muck," (Hauff), 20
The Story of the Sultan of the Persians and the Visirs. Turkish Tales, (de La Croix), 47
The Story of Viteau, (Stockton), 190
"The Strange Child," (Hoffmann), 99, 102–103
"The Stubborn Child," (Grimm), 78
"The Swineherd," (Andersen), 141
  as adaptation of folklore, 122
  religious motifs in, 133
"The Tale about the Thief of Alexandria and the Chief of Police," 63
"The Tale of the Three Apples," 62
The Tales of Hoffmann, (Offenbach), 23
The Talking Bird, (Kirby), 152

The Taming of the Shrew, influence of "Prince Behram and the Princess Al-Datma" on, 63

The Tapestry Room, (Molesworth), 157

The Thousand and One Days, (de La Croix), 47

"The Thousand and One Humbugs," (Dickens), 154

The Thousand and One Nights. See also The Arabian Nights (Galland), 13, 46, 53
influence of on subsequent authors, 64
layers of, 56

"The Three Clever Kings," (De Morgan), 22

"The Three Linden Trees," (Hesse), 253

The Three Musketeers, (Dumas), 104

"The Three Spinners," (Grimm), changes to story over time, 77

The Tik-Tok Man of Oz, (Baum), 204

"The Tinderbox," (Andersen)
as adaptation of folklore, 121
ideological compromise in, 135
importance of, 113
revolutionary tone of, 129–130
similiarity to Grimm Brothers' "The Blue Light," 128

The Tin Woodman of Oz, (Baum), 204
abuse of magic in, 217

The Transferred Ghost, (Stockton), 190

"The Traveling Companion," (Andersen)
as adaptation of folklore, 121

derivation of from oral tradition, 128
intelligent design motif in, 132
religious motifs in, 133

The True Story of My Life, (Andersen), 116

The Two Baronesses, (Andersen), 116

"The Two Brothers," (Hesse), 249

"The Ugly Duckling," (Andersen), 20, 116, 119
anthropomorphization of animals, 124
religious motifs in, 133

"The Uncanny," (Freud), 105

"The Voyages of Sinbad," (Galland), 54

The Water Babies, (Kingsley), 152

"The White Bull," (Voltaire), 17

"The White Cat," 15

"The White Doe," (Housman), 162

"The Wily Dalilah," 63

The Wizard of Oz. See also The Wonderful Wizard of Oz (MGM film), 209

The Woggle-Bug Book, (Baum), 202

The Woggle-Bug (Play), (Baum), 202

"The Wolf and the Seven Young Kids," (Grimm), moral lessons of, 81

The Wonderful Wizard of Oz, (Baum), 22, 195, 199
commodity value of, 208
gift giving in, 211
musical/theatrical adaptation of, 200–202

The Yellow Book, (Lane, J.), 164

"The Yellow Dwarf," 15

"The Young King," (Wilde), 172

This Side, (Hesse), 242

Thompson, Ruth Plumly, 209
"Three Clever Kings," (De Morgan),
    161
Through the Looking Glass, (Carroll),
    155
"Thumbelina," (Andersen), 113
"Thumbelina," (Andersen),
    similiarity to Grimm
    Brothers' "Thumbling's
    Travels," 128
"Thumbling's Travels," (Grimm), 128
Thurber, James, "The Girl and the
    Wolf," 24
Tieck, Ludwig, 18, 95, 98, 113, 149,
    250
    comparison of Andersen's tales
        with those of, 129
Tik-Tok of Oz, (Baum), 204
    oppression in, 217
Ting-a-ling, (Stockton), 189
To Be or Not to Be, (Andersen), 118
Tolkien, J.R.R., 160
    The Hobbit, 24
Tom Cat's Views on Life, (Hoffmann),
    95
Tommy and Grizel, (Barrie), 225
"Tom Thumb," (Perrault), 13, 39, 45
Tournier, Michel, 25, 51
Transformation, 22
Trevor, John, 159
Trimmer, Sarah, 147
Tuck, Raphael, 158
Tuttle, Mary Ann (Marian), 189
Twain, Mark, 193
    The Adventures of Huckleberry
        Finn, 181, 221

U

"Uncle David's Nonsensical Story
    about Giants and Fairies,"
    (Sinclair), 152
Under the Wheel, (Hesse), 242
Underway, (Hesse), 242
Undine
    (de la Motte Fouqué), 94, 122, 148
    influence of on Andersen's
        "The Little Mermaid,"
        128–129
    (Hoffmann), 23, 94–96
United Kingdom. See England
United States, modern fairy tale
    authors, 25
Utilitarianism, 144
Utopia, 4
    Neverland, 237
    Oz, 195, 200, 210
    themes of in 17th century French
        fairy tales, 37
Utopianism, 158–160

V

Van Dyne, Edith. See Baum, L.
    Frank
Ventures into Childland: Victorians,
    Fairy Tales, and Femininity,
    (Knoepflmacher), 153
Vernacular, use of in early fairy tales,
    9
Verse fairy tales, 38
Victorian England, 146
    authors, 163–164
    conventional, 157–158

utopian, 158–160
*Victorian Periodicals and the
Reinvention of the Fairy Tale,*
(Sumpter), 159
Viehmann, Dorothea, 74
Violence, 44
Völkisch, 24
Volksmärchen der Deutschen,
(Musäus), 18
Voltaire
influence of *The Thousand and
One Nights* on, 64
"The White Bull," 17
Von der Heyden-Rynsch, Verena,
Europäische Salons, 34
Von Droste-Hülshoff, Jenny and
Annette, 74
Von Eichendorff, Joseph, 18, 250
Von Franz, Maria, psychoanalytical
interpretations of fairy tales
by, 82
Von Haxthausen family, 74
Von Haxthausen, Werner, 74
Von Hofmannsthal, Hugo
"The Fairy Tale of the 672nd
Night," 22
influence of *The Thousand and
One Nights* on, 64
Von Kamptz, Karl Albert, 97
Von Savigny, Friedrich Karl, 67
Vsevolojsky, Ivan Alexandrovitch, 86

W

Wackenroder, Wilhelm Heinrich, 18,
98, 250

influence of *The Thousand and
One Nights* on, 64
Walker, London, (Barrie), 225
Walpole, Horace, influence of *The
Thousand and One Nights*
on, 64
War and Peace, (Hesse), 247
Warner, Sylvia Townsend,
"Bluebeard's Daughter," 25
Was, (Ryman), 209
Wells, H.G., 226
The Invisible Man, 164
Wenger, Ruth, 245
Wessobrunner Prayer, (Grimm), 69
Westbrook, M. David, 210
"Readers of Oz: Young and Old,
Old and New Historicist,"
207
What Every Woman Knows, (Barrie),
226
"What Manikins Want: *The
Wonderful Wizard of Oz* and
*The Art of Decorating Dry
Goods Windows,*" (Culver),
206
"Where to Lay the Blame," (Pyle), 22
White, T.H., 160
*Wicked: The Life and Times of the
Wicked Witch of the West,*
(Maguire), 209
Wieland, Christoph Martin
Dschinnistan, 18
"The Philosopher's Stone," 18
Wild, Dortchen, 70
Wilde, Cyril, 168
Wilde, Oscar, 164
analysis of fairy tales of, 170–173
biographical information,
167–168

The Happy Prince and Other Tales,
    162, 168, 170
A House of Pomegranates, 162, 170
    themes of, 172–173
influences on fairy tales of,
    168–170
The Picture of Dorian Gray, 167
"The Birthday of the Infanta,"
    172
"The Devoted Friend," 170–171
"The Fisherman and His Soul,"
    22, 172
"The Nightingale and the Rose,"
    170–171
"The Remarkable Rocket,"
    170–171
"The Selfish Giant," 170–171
"The Soul of Man Under
    Socialism," 164, 170
"The Star-Child," 172
"The Young King," 172
utopian writings of, 159
Wilde, Speranza, 167
    *Ancient Cures, Charms, and
        Usages of Ireland*, 169
    *Ancient Cures, Mystic Charms,
        and Superstitions*, 169
Wilde, Vyvyan, 168
Wilde, William, 167
    Irish Popular Superstitions, 168
Wild family, 73
Windling, Terri, 26
Wolfe, Gene, 26
Wollenweber, Bernd, 82
Woman, Church and State, (Stanton),
    197
Women, domestication of, themes of
    in Oz books, 207

Women Who Run with the Wolves,
    (Estés), 26
Wonder, definition of, 5
Wonderful Stories for Children,
    (Andersen, trans. Howitt),
    149
Wonder tales
    ideological intention of, 6
    pagan themes in, 15
    paradigmatic functions of, 3
Woodward, Alice, *The Peter Pan
    Picture Book*, 233
Wordsworth, William, 146
Wulff, Peter Frederick, 112

Y

Yeats, William, *Fairy and Folk Tales
    of the Irish Peasantry*, 169
Yolen, Jane, 25, 51
Young Germany movement, 71

Z

Zadah, Sheikh, 47
Zarathustra's Return, (Hesse), 244
Zaubermärchen, 3
Zel, (Napoli), 30
Zémire et Azore, (Grétry), 23
"Zerbin the Wood-Cutter,"
    (Laboulaye), 21
Zimmer, Henriette, 66
Ziolkowski, Jan, *Fairy Tales from
    Before Fairy Tales*, 2, 8

Printed in the United States
133667LV00003B/228/P

9 780415 980067